Soviet Communism from Reform to Collapse

PROBLEMS IN EUROPEAN CIVILIZATION SERIES

Soviet Communism from Reform to Collapse

Edited by
Robert V. Daniels
University of Vermont

D. C. HEATH AND COMPANY
Lexington, Massachusetts   Toronto

Address editorial correspondence to:

D. C. Heath and Company
125 Spring Street
Lexington, MA 02173

Acquisitions Editor: James Miller
Developmental Editor: David Light
Production Editor: Ron Hampton
Designer: Alwyn Velásquez
Photo Researcher: Billie Porter
Production Coordinator: Charles Dutton
Permissions Editor: Margaret Roll

Cover: Liu Heung Shing/M. Photo, Hong Kong
This and the other photo by Liu Heung Shing are part of
a body of work awarded the 1992 Pulitzer Prize for spot
news photography.

Published simultaneously in Canada.

Printed in the United States of America.

International Standard Book Number: 0-669-33144-9

Library of Congress Catalog Number: 94-71084

10 9 8 7 6 5 4 3 2 1

Preface

The Problems in European Civilization series encompasses works focusing on great critical episodes in the history of Europe, including Russia and the Soviet Union. Volume by volume, it brings together samplings of the best, most representative scholarship by presenting selections from a series of expert commentators as well as key statements by the makers of history in each case. It is not usual that very recent events should stand out as candidates for such concentrated study, but one remarkable exception is the crisis of reform and collapse in the Union of Soviet Socialist Republics from 1985 to 1991, the era of Mikhail Gorbachev and his ill-fated program of reconstruction, or *perestroika*.

The events leading to the breakdown of communism in the Soviet Union and in Eastern Europe are so interesting as well as complex that no anthology as conceived in the Problems in European Civilization series could do justice to the whole situation. This book concentrates on internal reform and crisis within the Soviet Union alone and deals only briefly with developments before 1985. It does not directly attempt to cover parallel events in Eastern Europe or in Soviet relations with the outside world, although these connections are often alluded to and naturally have to be kept in mind. However, the national minorities of the Soviet Union, as one of the principal forces in the demise of the Old Regime, are given constant emphasis.

In making selections for this book I have tried to reflect the international nature of scholarship on the former Soviet Union. Australian, British, Canadian, French, Italian, Polish, and Swedish contributions are all represented as well as American studies and statements by Russians freed by *glasnost* from a dictated party line. I am indebted to many friends and colleagues in the United States and abroad for their work in paving the way for the present collection. Thanks also to those who reviewed the contents and helped me to make final choices for the book: Audrey Altstadt of the University of Massachusetts—Amherst; Alan Ball of Marquette University; Robert Devlin of Adelphi University; George

Liber of the University of Alabama at Birmingham; Hugh Ragsdale of the University of Alabama at Tuscaloosa; Donald Raleigh of the University of North Carolina, Chapel Hill; Marshall Schatz of the University of Massachusetts—Boston; and Ted Uldricks of the University of North Carolina, Asheville. Finally, I am particularly grateful to my wife, Alice M. Daniels, without whose skillful editorial and word-processing assistance this project would never have come to fruition.

Robert V. Daniels

Contents

V Reflections 321

Chronology of Events

1917	February Revolution (in March, by the Western calendar); fall of Tsar Nicholas II; Provisional Government
	October (November) Revolution: Bolsheviks (Communists) led by Lenin establish Soviet Republic
1918–1921	Civil war and "war communism"
1921–1928	New Economic Policy (NEP)
1922 (Mar.)	Stalin made General Secretary of the Communist party
(Dec.)	USSR formed
1924 (Jan.)	Death of Lenin
1928–1929	Stalin becomes dictator; Stalin Revolution with five-year plans and collectivization begins
1931	Gorbachev and Yeltsin born
1936–1938	Purges
1941–1945	World War II
1953 (Mar.)	Death of Stalin
1956 (Feb.)	"De-Stalinization" under Khrushchev
1964 (Oct.)	Fall of Khrushchev; Brezhnev General Secretary
1982 (Nov.)	Death of Brezhnev; Andropov General Secretary

1984 (Feb.)	Death of Andropov; Chernenko General Secretary
1985 (Mar.)	Death of Chernenko; Gorbachev General Secretary, begins *perestroika*
(Nov.)	Geneva Summit (Gorbachev and Reagan)
1986 (Feb.)	Twenty-Seventh Party Congress
(Apr.)	Chernobyl disaster; Gorbachev begins *glasnost*
(Oct.)	Reykjavik Summit (Gorbachev and Reagan)
1987 (Jan.)	Central Committee plenum: Gorbachev begins democratization
(summer)	Gorbachev writes *Perestroika*
(Nov.)	Gorbachev's anniversary speech
(Dec.)	Washington Summit (Gorbachev and Reagan; INF treaty signed)
1988 (Jan.)	Law on State Enterprises
(Feb.)	Struggle over Nagorno-Karabakh begins
(Mar.)	"Andreyeva letter": conservative threat
(Apr.)	Geneva Agreement on Afghanistan
(June–July)	Nineteenth Party Conference
(Sept. 30)	"September Revolution"—defeat of conservatives
(Oct. 1)	Gorbachev chairman of Supreme Soviet; constitution democratized
1989 (Mar. 26)	Election of Congress of People's Deputies
(Apr.)	Tbilisi massacre
(May)	Congress convenes, elects new Supreme Soviet
(July)	Miners' strike Commission on Economic Reform
(Oct.–Dec.)	Anti-Communist revolutions in Eastern Europe
(Dec.)	Malta Summit (Gorbachev and Bush; Cold War ended)

1990 (Feb.)	Party gives up monopoly
(Mar.)	Gorbachev elected president by Supreme Soviet
	Election of republic parliaments; Popular Front victories
(Mar.–May)	Baltic republics declare independence
(May)	Yeltsin chairman of Supreme Soviet of Russia
(July)	Twenty-Eighth Party Congress; Yeltsin quits Communist party
(Aug.–Sept.)	500 Days economic reform plan
(Dec.)	Gorbachev appoints conservatives; Shevardnadze resigns; death of Sakharov
1991 (Jan.)	Vilnius massacre
(Mar.)	Democracy demonstration; Gorbachev rejects repression
(Apr.)	Novo-Ogarevo Agreements (9 + 1)
(June)	Yeltsin elected president of Russia
(July)	Last Central Committee plenum; new party program
	Moscow Summit (Gorbachev and Bush; START treaty signed)
(Aug. 19–21)	Attempted coup; Communist party leadership dissolved
(Nov.)	Yeltsin gets emergency powers, starts economic decontrol
(Dec. 8)	Minsk Agreements: Soviet Union dissolved, Commonwealth of Independent States proclaimed
(Dec. 25)	Gorbachev resigns
1992 (Jan.)	Yeltsin decontrols prices; inflation accelerates
1993 (Sept.–Oct.)	Yeltsin dissolves Russian parliament, suppresses resistance
(Dec.)	Election: new constitution adopted; Communist and nationalist comeback

Variety of
Opinion

*The development of the country outraced the governing abilities
of the networks in power. Discordances and imbalances spread
throughout the system.*

Moshe Lewin (1991)

*It will be possible to overcome the tragic conflicts and dangers of
our time only through the convergence of capitalism and the socialist regime. . . . I consider the democratization of society, the
development of openness in public affairs, the rule of law, and
the safeguarding of basic human rights to be of decisive importance.*

Andrei Sakharov (1972)

*The stability and longevity of the existing pattern . . . have been
conditional on . . . gradualism in major policy and gradualism,
to say the least, in personnel replacement. . . . We do not know
whether . . . the mood of the leadership and the elite will swing
toward revitalization and major reforms. . . . We do know . . .
that . . . gradualism in personnel replacement will most probably
not obtain.*

Seweryn Bialer (1980)

*The social mechanism of economic development as it functions
at present in the USSR does not ensure satisfactory results . . . .
This mechanism is "tuned" not to stimulate, but to thwart the
population's useful economic activity.*

Tatiana Zaslavskaya (1983)

Perestroika *is no whim. . . . Any delay in beginning* perestroika *could have led to an exacerbated internal situation . . . , fraught with serious social, economic, and political crises.*

Mikhail Gorbachev (1987)

Glasnost *is not irreversible. . . . What if the revelations and the debates do not lead to an improvement?* Glasnost *was based on hope. . . . But if the changes do not materialize, the hopes are bound to fade and the air will again get stale.*

Walter Laqueur (1989)

Today, the question of the role and place of socialist ideology has taken on a very acute form. . . . The authors of opportunistic constructs are eroding the boundaries of scientific ideology, manipulating openness, and propagating an extrasocialist pluralism which objectively impedes restructuring in social consciousness.

Nina Andreyeva (1988)

Gorbachev's *most dramatic departure . . . was not simply the scope of his program, but the change of venue for its proposed realization. As he gradually shifted the locus of his power from the party to the state, the Soviet Constitution became the principal framework for the articulation of the reform objectives.*

Robert Sharlet (1992)

Looking back on the Congress [of People's Deputies] after the demise of the Soviet Union itself . . . , we can see its importance in an essential transitional stage . . . in which the formal vestiges of a one-party system faced the realities of a de facto multiparty democracy. . . . Soviet society showed great democratic vitality and promise.

Giulietto Chiesa (1992)

Gorbachev . . . is the only man who can stop the ultimate collapse of the party. . . . Our huge country is balanced on a razor's edge, and nobody knows what will happen to it tomorrow.

Boris Yeltsin (1989)

It is perhaps most surprising how long it took before the Soviet leadership became aware of the economic crisis. . . . There is an abyss between a command economy and a market economy. . . . First the old system must be destroyed—what Gorbachev has largely accomplished in the USSR—then the foundations of the new market economy must be built on the other side of the abyss, presupposing that society as a whole has dared to leap across the chasm.

Anders Åslund (1991)

The crisis in society continues to deepen. . . . Work to extricate the country, continue the democratic transformations in society, and further radicalize the economic reform while simultaneously carrying out measures of social support for the population [is] to be placed above all else.

Novo-Ogaryovo Agreement (1991)

After all the years of his political balancing act . . . , he had finally summed up the two sides of the political choice he had long been unwilling to make, and—before the world's press—he had publicly made that choice. Unfortunately for Gorbachev, it had come too late.

Martin Sixsmith (1991)

In the autumn of 1991 . . . the economy of the former USSR and of the Russian Federation was in deep disintegration. . . . We have the typical syndrome of a non-planned, non-market economy, without sufficient microeconomic motivation or the means to achieve macroeconomic equilibrium. Moreover, the government [did] not have political support, and it [was] prepared to buy temporary social peace in exchange for inflationary money.

Marek Dabrowski (1993)

The Soviet Union evaporated. . . . The heirs of Marx, who so disputed the importance of the national problem, suddenly discovered, after rejecting Marxism, that this is the most serious problem they face.

Hélène Carrère D'Encausse (1993)

Mikhail Gorbachev . . . launched a thrilling project of human renewal; but the empire he destroyed was his own.

Charles H. Fairbanks (1993)

We are inclined to exaggerate greatly the socialist or even communist quality of our former social-economic set-up. . . . And just as our quasi-socialism would not last a day without its own sort of permanent reanimation by black markets and illegal freedoms, Western capitalism without strong socialist components would long ago have been blown up.

Alexander Rubtsov (1992)

For the first time in Russian history, a revolution has been carried out in defense of the law rather than against it.

A. Salmin (1991)

Could Russia in search of a post-Communist identity harmonize its strivings toward liberal, pluralistic democracy with its search to recover conservative, religious authority?

James H. Billington (1992)

Reference Map

SWEDEN FINLAND *Barents Sea*

GERMANY *Baltic Sea*

LITHUANIA Tallinn ESTONIA
RUSSIAN FEDERATION Riga
CZECH REP. Vilnius LATVIA
POLAND

SLOVAKIA Minsk
HUNGARY **BELARUS**

ROMANIA **MOLDOVA**
Chişinău
BULGARIA **UKRAINE**
Kiev

● Moscow

RUSSIAN
FEDERATION

BREAKUP OF THE USSR, 1991

——— Boundary of USSR prior to 1991
——— International boundaries
········· Boundaries of the Soviet republics
● Capitals of the Soviet republics

0 —————— 500 kilometers
0 —————— 500 Miles

Black Sea

KAZAKHSTAN

TURKEY
GEORGIA *Caspian Sea*
ARMENIA ●Tbilisi
Erevan ●**AZERBAIJAN**
SYRIA ●Baku
NAGORNO-KARABAKH

Aral Sea

Lake Balkhash

UZBEKISTAN
●Almaty
●Bishkek
Tashkent ● **KYRGYZSTAN**

JORDAN
TURKMENISTAN
IRAQ ●Ashgabad
Dushanbe ● **TADZHIKISTAN** CHINA
SAUDI ARABIA IRAN AFGHANISTAN PAKISTAN

xix

Introduction

During the years 1985 to 1991 the Union of Soviet Socialist Republics experienced one of the most cataclysmic episodes of political change in all history, equalling in its effects the Russian Revolution of 1917. Out of it emerged new countries, the former republics of the Soviet Union; new politics, as totalitarian rule by the Communist party was dismantled and repudiated; and new economic systems, as the socialist command economy was rejected in favor of the model of free-market capitalism. But the immediate consequences of change throughout the former Soviet Union were distressingly negative: from imposed order to ethnic hatred and strife, from modest but secure living standards to impoverishment and corruption, from the system of command and obedience to wild political infighting and rampant criminality. *Perestroika*—restructuring, as the whole era is now known— proved to be a time of intense and deepening crisis throughout the Soviet Union, the ultimate outcome of which still remains far from certain.

Such an extraordinary development demands explanation in and of itself. Further, *perestroika* and the gathering crisis accompanying it are keys to understanding the Russian and Soviet past, revealing the contradictions and weaknesses that contributed to the collapse of the Soviet system. At the same time, the transformation of the Soviet Union that took place in the Gorbachev era is the necessary basis for anticipating the future of the region and for interpreting new events and new crises as these unfold.

Understanding reform and crisis in the Soviet Union under Mikhail Gorbachev—and since—naturally requires some appreciation of the Communist background. What was reform proceeding from? What was the system that collapsed? The easy answer is misleading: that the Soviet period was simply a time of ideology in power, a 74-year utopian experiment that failed despite the attempts of reformers to salvage it. This common notion overstates both the role of ideology and the permanency of its meaning. It misses the vast transformations that the Soviet system underwent after the revolutions of 1917, from the era of "War Communism," through the New Economic Policy of the 1920s, the Stalin Revolution of the 1930s (with its radical and reactionary phases), the vast if uneven modernization of the country over the decades, and the struggles between reformers and conservatives from Khrushchev through Brezhnev to Andropov. By the 1980s the Soviet system was in no meaningful sense a revolutionary experiment, but more in the nature of a synthesis of old Russian bureaucracy and imperialism together with an overgrown statist industrialism, glossed over with a thin veneer of ideological pretense. Communism was not an immutable fantasy or curse, but only a set of verbal formulas twisted and bent to legitimate a deeply changing reality.

Why did this system, so firmly embedded for decades, fall apart so quickly in the late 1980s and early 1990s? This question, one way or another, is central for practically all the contributors to this volume. Convincing answers are still far from being agreed upon—was it too much reform? not enough reform? or the destiny of a system already suffering irremediable contradictions?

In retrospect it is easy to see the merit of the latter view. Why, then, was the collapse of Communism not more clearly foreseen by outside observers? This is a familiar question, raised by many who fault the premises and methods of "sovietology." In fact, as many of the selections in this work demonstrate, the imminence of change in the Soviet Union was noted by numerous specialists on the area who felt it impossible for Moscow to pursue business as usual either in the economy or in government. On the other hand, no one, either inside or outside the Soviet Union, foresaw how far or how deeply the forces of change would cut once they had been released. Nor could this have been foreseen, considering the role of key individuals and the unpredictability of people's reactions to unpredictable events.

One point of contention still is whether the Soviet Union was really capable of significant change, whether for ideological or institutional reasons. Was it perhaps unable to accommodate reform, yet vulnerable to revolutionary forces that brought about its collapse? This view makes too much of verbal polarities: where is the line between modifying a social system and replacing it? After all, the same people remain in the same place, whether they experience small or great changes in the institutions that shape their lives. Changes intended to save a system can add up to changes that can be said to have replaced it.

Perestroika certainly began as no more than a program of limited change aimed at improving the existing system, with no hint of the radical overturn that it led to. Indeed, the experience of 1985–1991 can readily be divided into sub-periods, reflecting changing relations between the political leadership and the society they were trying to reform. In the first phase, from 1985 through 1988, roughly, change came from the top down, as Gorbachev and his associates tried to deal with the immobilism or stagnation they had inherited from Brezhnev. These efforts began modestly, but they had to be stepped up as resistance to them stiffened. In the second phase, in 1989 and 1990, forces of reform, in Moscow politics and in relations between the center and the national minorities of the Soviet Union, ran ahead of the governmental leadership, while the impersonal forces of the economy turned in the negative direction. The third phase, 1991, was truly a time of collapse, accelerated by the abortive conservative coup of August of that year, and resulting in economic disaster, the breakup of the Soviet Union, and the repudiation of the Communist party and its ideology.

Why did reform (that is, moderate change) fail, yet lead to what could well be called revolution (that is, radical change)? Was this because of some inherent unreformability of the old system, capable of resisting serious change until overwhelmed by its ardent enemies? This assumption exaggerates the effectiveness both of the enemies of change and of the enemies of the system. As the selections in this work show, the course of *perestroika* can better be understood as a sequence of one thing leading to another, with implications surprising both the opponents of any change and the impatient advocates of faster change. All of this was complicated, besides, by the role of willful and powerful individuals whose actions, as so often in history, produced results that they never expected.

Among writers who have attempted to analyze the Gorbachev era or particular aspects of it, anticipation of the extent of these changes depended on one's proximity in time to the final collapse of the Communist regime. Looking back from 1988, as did Moshe Lewin in *The Gorbachev Phenomenon*, it was not hard to see how underlying social trends—the modernization, industrialization, and urbanization pushed by the Soviet regime itself—were making it impossible for the system to go on functioning in the old totalitarian way. My own article, "The Revolutionary Legacy," originally composed a year and a half into *perestroika*, predicted a deepening of reform as the final stage of the revolutionary experience in Russia, though it did not anticipate such a drastic disruption of the system as eventually occurred. Andrei Sakharov, the great liberal dissident, was a voice crying in the wilderness in the early 1970s, unaware of the victories for democracy that lay in store.

When Seweryn Bialer wrote *Stalin's Successors* at the end of the 1970s, it was already possible to discern a major impending political changeover, as the generation of Stalinists, installed in office after the purges of the 1930s, aged in office and began to die out. By the early 1980s, Soviet insiders like Tatiana Zaslavskaya in her "Novosibirsk Report" could warn confidentially of the country's social and economic impasse and the urgency of reform. By 1989, when Archie Brown published his essay on the post-Brezhnev succession, it was clear that the rapid demise of a series of Stalinist leaders had opened the way for reforms that might address the country's real problems and bring government into line with social and economic reality.

It did not take Gorbachev long after his installation as general secretary in March 1985 to come to grips with the problems he had inherited, and to set in motion his successive remedies of *perestroika* in the economy, *glasnost* (openness or publicity) in the media, and democratization in politics. So concerned was he to repair his government's image at home and abroad that he took leave of his duties in 1987 long enough to prepare a book, *Perestroika*, encompassing his critique of the past and his hopes for a future of peace with democratic socialism. This prospect was detailed at the same time by Gorbachev's aide Abel Aganbegyan in *The Economic Challenge of Perestroika*. From outside came a mid-course assessment of *glasnost* and its difficulties, *The Long Road to Freedom*, by Walter Laqueur, while Paul Goble in his article "Imperial Endgame" outlined the incipient strains among the Soviet national minorities that *glasnost* and democratization were opening up.

Meanwhile, conservative Communist resistance to the direction of Gorbachev's reforms was summed up in the "Andreyeva Letter" published in March 1988. Gorbachev successfully overcame this challenge, and capped the first, top-down phase of reform with major constitutional amendments in the fall of 1988 that turned the country decisively toward real democratization. Robert Sharlet assessed the background and impact of these developments in *Soviet Constitutional Crisis.*

Pursuant to Gorbachev's constitutional reforms a new Congress of People's Deputies was elected in March 1989 through a process described by Michael Urban in *More Power to the Soviets*, partially democratic but still significantly manipulated. The work of this Congress and the new Supreme Soviet that it chose from among its membership were analyzed in detail by Giulietto Chiesa in *Transition to Democracy.* One of the consequences of these steps toward democratization was the ability of one-time Gorbachev aide Boris Yeltsin to return from political oblivion as a rival to his former chief, a feat described both by Yeltsin's biographer John Morrison, and by Yeltsin himself in his autobiography. At the same time, as Anders Åslund recounted the story in *Gorbachev's Struggle for Economic Reform*, the reformers found that their efforts in that area were only making matters worse. A variety of remedies were proposed in 1989 and 1990, most notably the 500 Days plan of marketization and privatization prepared by a team under Stanislav Shatalin. To complicate matters further, the national minorities erupted in vigorous and sometimes violent independence movements, chronicled by Stephen White in *Gorbachev and After.*

By 1991 the forces of democratic defiance, economic disruption, and ethnic separatism were washing away the power base of Gorbachev's entire reform venture. Too little and too late, he offered major concessions to the minorities in the so-called Novo-Ogaryovo Agreements and a new Union Treaty. He managed to drag the Communist party to the point of surrendering its old monopoly of power and adopting a program that left both Marx and Lenin out in the cold. But he could not bridge the widening political chasm between reformers and resisters, and fell between the two when the latter attempted the unforgettable putsch of August 1991, reported on the spot by Martin Sixsmith in *August Coup*.

Following the failure of the coup, Gorbachev's government and the USSR as a country quickly came apart. As described by John Miller in *Mikhail Gorbachev and the End of Soviet Power*, and by J. L. Black in *Into the Dustbin of History*, the weakened and discredited Communist party succumbed helplessly to the bans imposed by Yeltsin in Russia and by the leaders of the minority republics (themselves mostly ex-Communists like Yeltsin). Similarly, the remains of the planned economy crumbled into chaos, as Peter Rutland in his article "Economic Crisis and Reform" and Marek Dabrowski in "The First Half-Year of Russian Transformation," describe it. And along with the political and economic wreck of the Soviet system, the national minorities—those organized in the Union Republics—successfully asserted full independence, a victory recounted by Hélène Carrère D'Encausse in *The End of the Soviet Empire*. The formal end of the USSR came with ridiculous ease in December 1991, as Yeltsin and the presidents of Ukraine and Belarus proclaimed the Union dissolved, leaving Gorbachev only the choice of a dignified exit by resigning his now empty presidency.

Overall, the transformation and breakdown suffered by the Soviet Union generated a wide array of comments and explanation. Charles Fairbanks in "The Nature of the Beast" sees it as a crisis within Communism's own terms. Thomas Remington in "Reform, Revolution, and Regime Transition" proposes a sociological explanation of the possibility of democratization. Alexander Rubtsov puts the question in a Russian context in "Between Capitalist Socialism and Socialist Capitalism." Elizabeth Teague in "Manual Workers and the Workplace" looks at reform as it affected ordinary people. A group of Russian scholars still sympathetic to Gorbachev weigh the prospects in their roundtable discussion, "Authoritarianism or Democracy?". James Billington in *Russia Transformed* considers the same question in the long perspective of Russia's history. All have hopes for the outcome; none are sure.

What can an in-depth understanding of the Gorbachev era tell us about the stressful events that have taken place since that time in the former Soviet Union, or about the direction of developments that are still to come? To begin with, such an inquiry shows that the downfall of the Communist regime was not a sudden event, brought about by the heroes on the barricades of 1991, nor even the result of a brief flurry of reform beginning in 1985. It was the outcome of rigidity and rot intensifying within the old regime for many years. Much of the history of the Gorbachev era can be seen as a losing battle to deal with this burdensome heritage. *Perestroika* validates Alexis de Tocqueville's maxim that revolutions come when attempts at reform have weakened the Old Regime's ability to resist change, but have not satisfied the forces demanding a new deal.

Thanks to *perestroika* and *glasnost*, the already fictitious governing ideology of communism was totally discredited, never to be seriously revived. What remains a force is the true—as opposed to verbal—emotional content of the Stalinist system, namely authoritarian and imperialistic nationalism, recrystallized in 1993 as the potent Liberal-Democratic Party of Vladimir Zhirinovsky. Self-styled Communists splintered hopelessly after the 1991 coup; the most moderate and most successful of them, led by Gennady Ziuganov, more or less follow the reformist party program of 1991.

Ethnicity proved to be the most intractable problem for the Gorbachev government. Some observers did in fact foresee that if the Soviet regime attempted to democratize, it would run the risk of disintegrating into its component nationalities, or else have to return to totalitarian force. Actually the Soviet Union did not entirely disintegrate; it is more accurate to think of the events of 1991 as decolonization within the Russian Empire, leaving its Russian core intact but resentful. An analogy is France of the late 1950s and early 1960s, when President Charles deGaulle, gaining power in a coup, suddenly let Algeria and the other African colonies go in spite of bitter opposition within France itself.

For the average Soviet citizen the most grievous effect of reform and regime collapse was economic—the breakup of trade relations, wild inflation, and the flourishing of a speculator class in the face of plummeting production—while successive governments loosened and then overthrew the controls of the old planned economy. Whatever future governments in any of the newly independent states may attempt by way of the free market ideal or some sort of "social market" economy, the consequences of economic disruption and impoverishment will be with those unfortunate lands for a long time to come.

After Gorbachev's resignation amid the ruin of his reform efforts, Russian politics revolved around the man who had come to personify radical repudiation of the Soviet past—Boris Yeltsin. Yeltsin's career as leader of the successor regime in Russia, checkered and controversial as it has become, could well be the subject of a future anthology. But the problems with which Russia had to contend—the economy, its relations with its former subjects, the working out of genuine democracy against old Russian habits of authoritarianism—were all rooted in the years of *perestroika* that are documented here. To one degree or another all the other former Soviet republics faced the same challenges—in most cases, as in Russia, under ex-Communist strongman leadership.

What will a future Russia look like, along with its neighbors of the "near abroad"? The answer depends on how these massive problems inherited from the Gorbachev era, and from the long Stalinist and neo-Stalinist experience before that, may be resolved. We cannot predict future choices. But with historical insight we can comprehend at least in part the circumstances in which they must be made.

Soviet Communism from Reform to Collapse

The Old Regime: General Secretary Leonid Brezhnev, ca. 1981. (Archive Photos)

PART

Backgrounds

Moshe Lewin

Modernization
and Social Change

Moshe Lewin, professor of history at the University of Pennsylvania, is an internationally recognized authority on the social history of the Soviet Union. Born in Poland and a veteran of the Red Army, he studied in Israel and in France to become a specialist on the Russian peasantry and Soviet economic development. His latest work, *The Gorbachev Phenomenon*, excerpted here, undertakes a many-sided explanation of how that reform movement arose. Focusing on the social pressures for reform, Lewin shows that the Brezhnev era preceding perestroika was not the "era of stagnation" as it was represented by the reformers but a time of dynamic social development, urbanization, and educational progress, all of which contributed to undermining the old regime.

Various factors trigger and sustain the creation of urban settlements and an urban system: industrialization, first and foremost, and such developments as educational and scientific achievements, the growth of administrations, and the momentum of urban society itself once it takes root and manifests its potentials. But for our purposes it is the outcome of these undertakings that is our key theme and focus. From the demographic data concerning the growth of Soviet urban society in the last half century much can be inferred about the series of deep transformations the USSR went through and about the latest, crucial stage in which it finds itself today.

The pace of Soviet urban development in the 1930s, its scope, intensity, and speed, was described by the American geographer Chauncy Harris as "record breaking." The urban population grew at an annual rate of 6.5 percent between 1926 and 1939, peaking at an annual rate of over 10 percent in the later thirties. Concurrently, the urban share of the USSR's population rose from 18 percent to over 32 percent. Such an increase, Harris notes, required three decades in the United States, from 1856 to 1887. He might have added that in the Soviet case these percentage shifts represented far greater numbers of people: in the 1930s the Soviet urban population grew from 26.3 million to 56.1 million. Many new cities were created, and many others saw their populations double or triple in twelve years. Further, these figures include only those people who permanently settled in the cities. Millions of others arrived in towns and cities only to soon wander away or run away, according to their circumstances.

Such a degree of social flux could not but trigger crises and mutations. But let us follow the story into the postwar period, when the USSR crossed the threshold of urbanization. In 1960 the urban population accounted for 49 percent of the total; by 1972 urban dwellers outnumbered rural dwellers, 58 percent to

42 percent. Between 1972 and 1985 the dominantly urban Soviet society became almost predominantly urban, accounting for 65 percent of the total population and 70 percent of the population of the RSFSR [Russian Soviet Federated Socialist Republic]. Today over 180 million Soviet citizens live in cities—compared to 56 million just before World War II. . . .

. . . In the past ten years it has been the migration from smaller to larger cities that has come to the fore in fashioning the character of the urban phenomenon. The overall size of the urban sector is remaining steady, giving the new complex urban system time to assimilate decades of momentous change. New cities are still being created, especially in Siberia, but everywhere the system and its institutions are, as it were, taking stock.

Thus it is evident that the postwar years, a period of Soviet history that many Western observers characterize as an era of stagnation, actually constitute a period of deep social change. Unfortunately, all too often, the Soviet urban phenomenon has escaped the attention of analysts. . . .

. . . By 1959 the peasantry had been slowly replaced by a working class. However, initially, one type of predominantly physical labor was merely replacing another, although the new jobs were located in different and crucially important sectors. The earlier stages of this development deserve the epithet "extensive," as quantity and speed were the slogans of those years.

But during the next twenty years, we see the making of a more variegated and professionally differentiated national and urban social structure. Urbanization, industrial and scientifico-technical development, mass schooling and quality schooling, communications and arts, state policies and myriad spontaneous events changed the nation's overall social, professional, and cultural profile, and the social structure underwent a significant qualitative transformation. Workers in the national economy soared from about 24 million before the war, to almost 81 million in 1983; of these, the number engaged in industry jumped from 11 million to over 31 million. Transportation, construction, and communications also grew at a rapid pace; much more modest growth of employment was registered in different services. The role of the working class in the economy is underscored by the fact that it is now the prevailing group in society and in the cities:

61.5 percent of the population, almost twice their share in 1939. In comparison, the kolkhoz peasants, once over half of the population, are now barely 12.5 percent of the nation.

A second group, presented in Soviet statistics as "employees," increased from 11 million in 1941 to about 35 million in 1983, a rate of growth surpassing that of workers. To understand the importance of this group, we must turn to another way of classifying them.

"Specialists"—otherwise also called in the Soviet literature "intelligentsia"—show an even faster rate of growth than the category of "officials." Most notably, in 1941 only about 2.4 million of the 11 million employees had higher or specialized technical education; in 1960 only half of the 16 million employees were "specialists"; today, an overwhelming majority of officials accede to this category, thanks to considerably improved standards of professional education. Recent figures show over 31.5 million specialists, among them 13.5 million with higher education and over 18 million with specialized secondary training.

Before we turn to those officials *qua* "intelligentsia," let us survey the educational standards of the whole population. In 1939 the overwhelming majority of the workers and peasants had only an elementary education (four years of primary school). By 1959, little had changed: 91.3 percent of workers and 98.2 percent of kolkhoz peasants still achieved only elementary standards. But by 1984 no more than 18.5 percent of manual laborers had only an elementary education—and, one would assume, a majority of the least educated were from the older generation.

In the population at large the massive educational efforts yielded significant results. Forty-six million people received a "secondary incomplete" education (seven years of schooling). Fifty-eight million enjoyed a full secondary education, which is now legally obligatory for all children. Alumni of the "secondary specialized" establishments that train technicians of all denominations numbered 28 million. A full higher education was received by 18.5 million people, and another 3.6 million received an incomplete higher education.

Among university and high school graduates, the numbers of men and women are substantially equal. Women constitute 54 percent of university students, 58 percent of the enrollment in secondary specialized schools, and 60 percent of all specialists with both higher and secondary education. Further, though women constitute 51 percent of the labor force as a whole, they account for about 56 percent of educated specialists, and 40 percent of scientists and scholars. This emancipation of women—for centuries the predominantly uneducated mass and the most neglected—is perhaps the most visible part of what can be called the Soviet "cultural revolution." (This term was improperly applied by official propaganda to the 1930s, when most citizens received barely three to four years of elementary education. Today, millions attend universities and high schools, and all children have access to at least a modicum of instruction. But by now, of course, "cultural revolution" acquires a new meaning again.)

Thus the development of professional and educational standards that began in the 1930s only to be interrupted by the ordeal of World War II, has come to fruition on a large scale during the last three decades. In particular, we must emphasize the making and remaking of the Soviet intelligentsia.

The history of the intelligentsia is tortuous, even tortured, but it has now become, in fact, a mass of people, composed of all the professionals the modern world requires and of numerous groups, subgroups, and categories: technical, managerial-administrative, scientific, artistic, educational, and political. Even if we restrict ourselves to those with a higher education, their number reaches now about 15 million, a vast pool of "grey matter" and the fastest-growing part of the new social structure. While the employed population grew by 155 per cent between 1960 and 1986, the number of specialists grew fourfold. Over 5 million students are attending institutions of higher education, taught by half a million professors.

An even slightly more rapid growth has occurred in the sector of scientific and technological research. Scientists and engineers working in research today number almost 1.5 million, flanked by a large cadre of auxiliary technicians—a serious and sizable "branch of the national economy," as a Soviet scholar termed it.

We will not at this point enter into the problems faced by these groups and classes—the imbalances, inefficiencies and general shortfalls that have resulted, notably, from their hectic formation. Whatever the problems, ailments, and even crises, they reflect a qualitatively different social structure [from] that of fifty years ago. In effect, in the past five decades the USSR has leaped into the twentieth century, although in the 1930s most of the nations of the territory still belonged to a far earlier age. The creation of the techno-scientific and intellectual class, accompanying the urbanization process, is thus a momentous development. The further advance of the economy and the survival of the political system are dependent on this layer, which has become a large, almost "popular" mass.

I will later explore the political sequels of these phenomena, but some implications are obvious already. The new intelligentsia, members of the different categories of this stratum, have moved beyond research institutes and universities. Numbers of them are government experts, medium- and top-level executives, participants and members of the highest administrative and political *apparaty*.[1] And it is a sign of the new times in Russia that this amalgam is deepening and expanding. Studying this stratum, which supplies "cadres"—we may also say "elites"—for the system, will help us to understand the future of Russia and how it will meet the next century. . . .

. . . We see a substantial increase in the numbers engaged in the service and information professions, and a corresponding decrease in unskilled manual laborers and agriculturists. From the very start of their careers, twice as many of this cohort are entering the intellectual labor force as the physical labor force. Herein we see the industrial era yielding to the scientific-industrial-information era. Already this youngest generation lives in a different environment and faces different pressures.

Gordon and Komarovskii [two Soviet sociologists] calculate that in contemporary society one-fourth of each generation moves up the socioprofessional ladder, and they predict that vocational mobility will probably accelerate. Unfortunately, these authors do not indicate whether this rate of intergenerational mobility is sufficient, nor do they cite the relevant Western figures for comparison. But, as they note, this rate is high enough to create tensions among the generations. The young quickly develop different styles of life, form new approaches to life and work, and

---

[1] *Apparat:* "apparatus," any bureaucratic organization.—Ed.

often reject, we can safely add, the methods and culture of their predecessors.

Such tensions are unavoidable and not unexpected, and they are likely to increase in the coming decade as intragenerational changes accelerate. In the 1990s, Gordon and Komarovskii project, the proportion of crude agricultural and industrial labor will drop to barely 10 percent among the third generation, as it approaches its career peak, and close to 40 percent of this cohort will be employed in intellectual professions. And the researchers predict that 30–40 percent of the workforce will be involved in sociocultural and other services and in professions related to the creation and processing of information. These projections lag behind current Western professional profiles: In the West more people are already engaged in information and services, fewer in industry, and very few in agriculture. But the authors do not seem unduly worried, for the lag, they observe, can be addressed by informed government policies. (The researchers are probably quite sincere. The best of contemporary social science in the Soviet Union is no longer content to issue soothing and reassuring prognoses, as was expected of them by the older-style leaders. Today, a growing number of scholars seeks to expose the sharper and more menacing aspects of social life; they issue warnings and demand action.)

Yet Gordon and Komarovskii caution that this inter- and intragenerational thrust forward into modern intellectual and professional life portends social trouble of great magnitude if it is not matched by reforms in the prevailing economic mechanism and in the "relations of production." The different spheres of the socioeconomic system suffer from discordances that threaten the nation's entire professional and educational endeavor. The state cannot allow "a socioprofessional structure adequate to the needs of a scientific-industrial system to be straitjacketed into a production system that is still stuck in an earlier technical and technological age." In the absence of reform, not only will professionalization not improve the performance of the system, it could also create widespread social crises and even pressures to return to the old patterns.

The stern warning sounded by these researchers may seem overly alarmist, but it reflects recent developments well known to readers of Soviet sociology. The list is long: widespread job dissatisfaction among educated youth and highly trained professionals; low morale—poor "sociopsychological climate" is the Soviet term—in many workplaces; underutilized engineers and scientists who waste their time on menial jobs because of a shortage of technicians and auxiliary personnel; hordes of poorly trained people parading, easily, as engineers or scientists. These images of a wasted generation and a potentially disastrous backsliding for the whole country certainly hang over the heads of the nation's political and economic leadership. . . .

In the late 1950s and early 1960s, Khrushchev's efforts to open up and reform the system met with some success. But his initiatives were often frustrated by the growing complexity of problems, by the immense scale of social change, and by the limitations of a political system that provided for the handling of basic needs but did not promote any broader strategies for more substantive change. Still, the sum of small improvements—and a few spectacular ones—was far from negligible. The battered and much maligned bureaucracy had become more stable and potent, and it succeeded in imposing on the system a more acceptable and, from the bureaucracy's point of view, a far more secure and more professional method of ruling. More attention to the laws, better control of the police, elimination of the Stalinist concentration camps, the implementation of group or "collective" leadership: the list of improvements is impressive. For the first time, a consolidated ruling apparatus exercised control over the whole of the state machinery, and the stabilization and security thereby offered to functionaries resulted in many of the improvements that the citizens of the USSR experienced up through the late sixties.

But in the following two decades, the elite and the medium and lower layers in government began to lose momentum and to lose touch. The development of the country outraced the governing abilities of the networks in power. . . . Discordances and imbalances spread throughout the system, widening the chasm between the mentality and professional abilities of top and medium-ranking cadres and the new realities of the day.

Was there during the 1970s and early 1980s enough renovation within the system to prepare a change of guard, whether the older generation wanted it or not? Was there some open or subterranean influx of new cadres in the bureaucracies and the networks close to them?

We know that changes were taking place on an intergenerational level in the working population at large. Something was going on in the party and state, too—though we have less material about them, except for data on the improved educational standards of most cadres. Too, it is unmistakably clear that the praktiki were disappearing.[2] At the end of 1956, 57.2 percent of all industrial specialists of the USSR were still praktiki. Unbelievable as it may sound for a country that was already a superpower, 68.4 percent of factory directors, even 32.9 percent of all chief engineers and technical directors, belonged to this category. By the mid-sixties the proportions of praktiki had fallen substantially, and today the phenomenon is largely vestigial. Parallel developments have taken place in the political *apparaty*, with those at the very top being more resilient to the call of changing times than the layers just below them.

Further evidence of a partial modernization in the top cadres and their outlook comes from a study of the efforts deployed by a group of leaders to reform the economy in the mid-sixties. An alliance of experts, managers, top government officials, and some party leaders fought tooth and nail for the preferred changes. Their main promoter was Prime Minister Kosygin, and with his support some battles were won. The reforms were launched, but were blocked by a coalition of conservatives and hard-line ideologues. The infighting and internal struggles of those years seem to prefigure the even broader alliances that are battling it out today.

[2] Persons trained on the job without formal higher education.—Ed.

Robert V. Daniels

The Revolutionary Process

Shortly after Gorbachev came to power in 1985, I was invited to comment on perestroika in the Italian communist journal *Rinascita*

From Robert V. Daniels, "The Revolutionary Legacy," Chapter 7 of *Is Russia Reformable? Change and Resistance from Stalin to Gorbachev*, pp. 127–133. Copyright © 1988. Reprinted by permission of Westview Press, Boulder, CO.

(by then very critical of the Soviet Union). The article was later published in English in my collection, *Is Russia Reformable?* It looked at Gorbachev in the perspective of revolution as a long process that had already been experienced in many other countries. In this view, Gorbachev represented the final stage of the revolutionary process and was turning the country back more or less to the ideals of 1917.

Zdeněk Mlynař, Ideological Secretary in the Prague Spring government [of Czechoslavakia] in 1968 and Gorbachev's university roommate in the early 1950s, recently remarked perceptively that it would be politically risky for the cause of reform in the Soviet Union to reopen questions of the past. Mikhail Gorbachev started his regime saying the same thing. Yet no genuine and durable reform of the present Soviet system can be accomplished without a fundamental reexamination of the relation of this system to the historical past that generated it, including its origins in the Revolution of 1917.

It is still not possible to judge the Soviet system without reference to the revolutionary process that began almost seventy years ago. The Soviet Union today represents a very late stage in the typical life history of a revolution. It is the outcome of a series of political convulsions, beginning with the liberal revolution of February 1917, and continuing with the radical revolution of Lenin in October, the violent and utopian adventure of War Communism, the Thermidorean consolidation of the New Economic Policy of the 1920s, and the Bonapartist postrevolutionary dictatorship of Stalin (including its phases of radical reconstruction, 1929–1934, and conservative consolidation, 1934–1939).

Stalin's postrevolutionary synthesis of revolutionary rhetoric, traditional values, and totalitarian methods, his amalgam of socialism, nationalism, and bureaucracy, remains the basis of the present Soviet political system. But this existing order may not be the final phase in the Russian revolutionary process. Certain historical parallels with the classic revolutions of European history suggest an as yet unrealized potential for profound reform in the Soviet system. Seventeenth-century England, after civil war, the

Puritan Commonwealth, and the Stuart Restoration, turned back to the first principles of the parliamentary revolution in the "Glorious Revolution" of 1688. Similarly, France, after the Great Revolution, the Terror, the Napoleonic era, and the Bourbon Restoration, returned in the Revolution of 1830 to the constitutional ideas of 1789. In general, no revolutionary society has rested indefinitely in the grip of its counterrevolutionary sequel. It appears that the revolutionary experience is not complete until the nation has an opportunity to overthrow the postrevolutionary dictatorship (or the restored monarchy) and accomplish what I term the "moderate revolutionary revival." This last phase recaptures the early principles of the revolution, but avoids the extremist fanaticism that carried it into subsequent violent and despotic behavior. Similar outcomes have manifested themselves where the postrevolutionary dictatorship took the form of right-wing totalitarianism, which in Germany gave way after the destruction of Hitlerism to a revival of the Weimar regime in the Federal Republic, and in Spain after the death of Franco in 1975 to a restoration of the democracy of 1931–1936.

The logic of the revolutionary process manifested in all these historical situations suggests that a similar final step is due to take place sooner or later in Soviet Russia. In this case historical parallelism would call for throwing off the legacy of Stalinism and returning to the original hopes and enthusiasm of 1917, based on a democratic, multi-party, decentralized, participatory socialism. This was the ultra-democratic Russia of the early soviets, hailed even by Lenin in his *State and Revolution*, but overwhelmed by one-party dictatorship after the hope of a government of all socialist parties was aborted by the Bolsheviks' violent seizure of power.

The possibility of a return to revolutionary beginnings in the Soviet Union is not just a matter of hypothetical historical reasoning. The real pressure for such a renovation, based on the rejection of the Stalinist system, has been demonstrated time and again by attempts at reform in Eastern Europe—in Poland and in Hungary in 1956, in Czechoslovakia in 1968, and again in Poland in 1980. In a more qualified way it has figured in Yugoslavia since the early 1950s and in China under Deng Xiao-ping.

For Russia itself the first opportunity for the moderate revolutionary revival was the death of Stalin. The cultural thaw and

Khrushchev's de-Stalinization compaign were important steps toward actualizing this possibility. But Khrushchev failed to attack the Stalinist system of rule, in distinction to its excesses, and did not develop an independent social base for reform, such as the English aristocracy provided in 1688 or the French bourgeoisie in 1830. The potential was there, in the form of the cultural and technical intelligentsia, but these elements had neither the independence nor the organization to influence the party or resist the police once their personal patron was unseated. Khrushchev left intact the postrevolutionary dictatorship, moderated and modernized to some extent, discredited in the outside world, but unchanged in its essentials at home. Now in the 1980s, following the deaths of Brezhnev and his immediate successors, and the accession to power of an altogether new generation, there is an historic opportunity once again to rid the country of its postrevolutionary burden, and recover the genuine inspiration of 1917 and its socialism with a human face. . . .

Is Gorbachev a leader with the intention or the ability to mobilize the available social forces and carry out the kind of reform that the logic of the revolution requires? In his speeches calling for perestroika and glasnost he has made it plain that he is dedicated to fundamental change of some sort. "I would equate the word restructuring with the word revolution," he declared at Khabarovsk in July 1986. His revolutionary steps have ranged from permitting the election of liberal literary and film leaders, to the release of Andrei Sakharov from internal exile. Mingling with workers at Krasnodar in September 1986, Gorbachev asserted, "If we now retreated from what we have begun, our people would be greatly disappointed. And that would affect everything. We can't allow this to happen."

The ascendancy of Gorbachev has created a situation closely paralleling the era of Khrushchev. This time the tensions between the reformist intelligentsia and the anachronistic party bureaucracy are even more pronounced. Judging by his extraordinary remarks to the writers in June 1986, Gorbachev is quite conscious of the similar alignment of forces. He called frankly upon the intelligentsia to help him offset the inertia of the "administrative layer—the apparatus of the ministries, the party apparatus—that does not want changes" and thereby clear the way for "restructuring" Soviet society. "Society is ripe for a sharp turn," he is reported to have said. "If we retreat, society will not agree to a return. We have to make the process irreversible. If not us, then who? If not now, when?" "Our enemies," he concluded, only fear our democratization. "They write about the apparatus that broke Khrushchev's neck, and about the apparatus that will break the neck of the new leadership."

Ironically, the shift from Stalin's despotism to the present collective leadership has made it more difficult for a reform-minded leader to command change from above. The relationship of the General Secretary to the representatives of the bureaucracy in the Politburo and the Central Committee has become one of mutual vulnerability, illustrated first by the fall of Malenkov[1] in 1955, then by Khrushchev's narrow escape in 1957, and subsequently by the fall of the latter in 1964. Brezhnev never ventured to threaten the interests of the bureaucracy. To be sure, Gorbachev has been able to use his new authority to accelerate the generational renovation of the bureaucracy begun by Andropov in 1982–1983. In the Central Committee installed by the Twenty-Seventh Party Congress, 44% of the members were new. Yet if the leader tries to move too far or too fast to change policy or personnel in the name of reform, and if the Politburo and Central Committee can coalesce in time, he can be removed and replaced. Second Secretary Ligachev, a protegé of Andropov who is ten years older than Gorbachev, has already offered hints that he could be a rallying point for the conservatives if the time comes.

The prospects for a reform that would consummate the moderate revolutionary revival in Russia are further limited by historical circumstances. Thanks to Stalin's postrevolutionary assimilation of the Russian past into the Soviet present, the system still embodies the long Russian tradition of centralized, bureaucratic, and despotic government, endowed by its exclusive official faith with what Gorbachev himself has condemned as an "infallibility complex." As a secret dissident said to me in Moscow a few years ago, "The trouble with the Soviet Union is that we still have too much Orthodoxy." The question is whether any reform, any new

---

[1] Georgii M. Malenkov, Stalin's immediate successor as prime minister, 1953–1955.—Ed.

leadership, even a change of regime, could alter the way in which Russia has been ruled for centuries and continues to be ruled. Perhaps the spirit of 1917 represented such a radical break from the Russian past that it could not be successfully revived and sustained even now.

While politically the Russian historical legacy impedes reform, economically the same legacy makes reform imperative. The Stalinist economic system was a premature imposition on a relatively backward society where capitalism had not had the opportunity to develop the country's industrial potential fully. Even more serious, though not so widely appreciated, was the fact that capitalism had not yet accomplished the concentration and modernization of the country's petty-bourgeois economic sectors—agriculture, trade, and services—that might have made them ready for socialization. Abrupt nationalization in 1918 and its reaffirmation along with the collectivization of agriculture when Stalin ended the NEP [New Economic Policy] in 1929 set these immature sectors back to an extent that they have not even yet recovered from. This error of premature socialization of pre-capitalist sectors has sooner or later been recognized and addressed in most Communist countries that have been sufficiently independent of the Soviet mode (Yugoslavia, Poland, Hungary, China). Steps in the same direction are now being hinted at in the Soviet Union itself, notably by the law of November 19, 1986, legalizing family enterprise.

While the Soviet economy in the sectors noted suffers from revolutionary prematurity, in the industrial sector it suffers from the political anachronism of the Russian tradition of centralism, reinstituted in an extreme form in the Stalinist command economy. The cost of this in the inhibition of initiative and innovation is finally being recognized today in the Soviet Union, as economic growth stagnates and the technological gap vis-à-vis the West steadily widens. The well-known "Novosibirsk Report" of 1983 by the sociologist Tatiana Zaslavskaya put the blame on "the lagging of the system of production relations, and hence of the mechanism of state management of the economy which is its reflection, behind the level of development of the productive forces." State management as practiced since the 1930s, Zaslavskaya observed, reflected "the predominance of administrative over economic methods, of centralization over decentralization." Gorbachev has warned (in the Khabarovsk speech), "There will be no progress if we seek answers to new questions in the economy and in technology in the experience of the 1930s, the 1940s, the 1950s, or even of the 1960s and the 1970s." (He conspicuously left open the 1920s and the NEP for lessons in decentralization.) Here is the front line in the current battle between the Gorbachevian modernizers and the Brezhnevian (and Andropovite) conservatives. The issue will not disappear no matter what happens to the current reformist leadership.

Hovering over all aspects of the reform question, political and economic, there is still the question of the relationship of the Soviet regime to its professed ideology and its actual history. As a postrevolutionary regime still clinging to a revolutionary mythology for its legitimacy, the Soviet regime has been compelled to control all channels of cultural and intellectual expression that might convey doubts about the legitimizing tie with the revolutionary past. This need, reinforced by Stalin's personal mania, has been the basis for the whole system of stultifying dictation maintained since his time over all forms of artistic creation, historical investigation, and speculative thought. It is as though an entire nation were subjected to a pervasive historical neurosis, demanding repression or mythologizing of the regime's own record to fit the psychological needs of a defensive and anxious ruling elite. The price paid by the nation in lost creativity and intellectual apathy has been inestimable.

None of this is necessary. It is possible, as the West European Left has shown, to rethink one's ideological heritage and escape from the burden of historical and philosophical dogmatism. . . . The time has come, as a logical imperative if not as a political possibility, for the Soviet Union itself to recognize that, in the sensational words of Enrico Berlinguer,[2] "The propulsive force that had its origin in the October Revolution has become exhausted."

Reform in Soviet Russia in the sense of a moderate revolutionary revival would not mean the repudiation of socialism. Socialism, in its essence as the overthrow of the power of private property in human relations, is the soul of the Russian Revolution,

---

[2] Leader of the Communist Party of Italy, 1972–1984.—Ed.

even though it may appear to many critics as a lost soul. What reform would require, as Mlynař points out, is a reconsideration of the bureaucratic, centralist, Russian-style socialism that has been maintained ever since Stalin's time as if it were the only conceivable expression of the ideal. Such a reconsideration is clearly the direction of Gorbachev's current efforts, exemplified in his economic reforms, his espousal of glasnost, and his call to breathe life into the local soviets.

There is ample precedent for an anti-bureaucratic socialism in the history of the Communist movement—in the Workers' Opposition in Russia in 1921, in Yugoslavia in a limited way since 1950, in China in diverse ways both during and since the Cultural Revolution—not to mention the West European New Left of 1968. Santiago Carrillo[3] suggested in *Eurocommunism and the State*, "The progress of the socialist movement in the developed capitalist countries may help Soviet society and the Soviet Communists to go beyond that type of state . . . which . . . tends to place itself above its own society and above the societies of other countries, a type of state which tends toward coercion through a series of objective and subjective factors, . . . and make progress in transforming it into a real working people's democracy." In other words, the traditional Soviet notion that the first socialist country shows the way to all others must be reversed.

As a practical matter, despite the exhortations of the European Left, fundamental reform based on a true return to revolutionary beginnings may remain a political impossibility in the Soviet Union, since it requires just that reconsideration of the past that arouses more political resistance and thereby makes the success of reform less likely. But there are underlying circumstances that have not yet had their full effect on the surface of Soviet reality—the pressures and needs of a modern society, the tension between the regime and its revolutionary origins, the impatience of a new generation of leadership. China over the last decade has illustrated how quickly and surprisingly a great nation in the Marxist-Leninist tradition may change under the pressure of such circumstances. To be sure, the more applicable precedents for reform offered by Eastern Europe have had discouraging

---

[3] Leader of the Communist Party of Spain, 1960–1982.—Ed.

outcomes, thanks to Soviet intervention. But if any comparable reform should be attempted within the Soviet Union itself, there is no one to intervene against it.

Andrei Sakharov

The Democratic Vision

Andrei Sakharov, eminent physicist and father of the Soviet hydrogen bomb, lost faith in the Communist regime in the 1960s and became the Soviet Union's most famous democratic dissident. He sent a series of manifestos and memoranda to the Soviet leadership, protesting the dictatorship, the lack of freedom, and the arms race. The only response was harassment by the police, but Sakharov's writings circulated privately in *samizdat* ("self-publishing," by typing carbon copies) and were smuggled out to the West for publicaton. His memorandum of March 1971 and a postscript of June 1972 are excerpted here.

Released by Gorbachev in 1986 from internal exile in the city of Gorky, Sakharov won a seat in the new, semidemocratic Congress of People's Deputies in 1989. He was boldly challenging Gorbachev to move on to real democracy when he died suddenly in December 1989.

The Memorandum

The problems listed [on the following page] appear to me to need urgent consideration.

For brevity's sake they have been expressed in the form of proposals. While recognizing that some of these problems require further study, and conscious that the list is of necessity an incomplete and therefore to a certain extent a subjective one (I have

From *Sakharov Speaks*, edited by Harrison E. Salisbury, pp. 137–144, 147–148, 152–156. Copyright © 1974 by Alfred A. Knopf, Inc. Reprinted by permission of the publisher.

tried to set out several equally important questions in the second half of this memorandum, while several could not be included at all), I nevertheless consider that a discussion of the following proposals by the competent authorities is essential.

1. *Concerning political persecution.* I feel it is high time to consider the pressing problem of implementing a general amnesty for political prisoners; . . . persons convicted on religious grounds; persons confined in psychiatric institutions; persons sentenced for attempting to cross the frontier; and political prisoners given an additional sentence for attempting to escape or for disseminating propaganda in their camp.

Measures should be taken to insure real and widespread public access to the hearings of all legal proceedings, especially those of a political character. I consider it important that all judicial verdicts carried in violation of the principle of public access should be reviewed.

I hold inadmissible all psychiatric [methods of] repression on political, ideological, and religious grounds. I am of the opinion that a law must be passed to protect the rights of persons subjected to compulsory psychiatric hospitalization; resolutions must be passed and the necessary legislative measures introduced to protect the rights of persons assumed to be mentally ill in the course of a prosecution on political charges. In particular, private psychiatric investigation by commissions independent of the authorities should be allowed in both cases. . . .

2. *Concerning publicity, freedom of information exchange, and freedom of beliefs.* A bill concerning the press and the mass media should be submitted for nationwide discussion.

A resolution should be passed calling for greater freedom in the publication of statistical and sociological data.

3. *Concerning nationalities problems and the problem of leaving the country.* Resolutions and laws should be passed fully restoring the rights of peoples deported under Stalin.

Laws should be passed to insure that citizens may easily and without hindrance exercise their right to leave the country and freely return to it. The directives restricting this right and in contravention of the law should be annulled.

4. *Concerning international problems.* We should show initiative and announce (or affirm, unilaterally at first) our refusal to

be the first to use weapons of mass destruction (nucelar, chemical, bacteriological, and incendiary weapons). We should allow inspection teams to visit our territory for effective arms control (assuming that we conclude an agreement on disarmament or partial limitation of certain types of armaments).

In order to consolidate the results of our changed relations with East Germany we should work out a new, more flexible, and realistic position on the question of West Berlin.

We should alter our political position in the Middle East and in Vietnam, and actively seek, through the United Nations and diplomatic channels, a peaceful settlement in the shortest possible time, on the basis of a compromise, with the renunciation by the United States and the USSR of any intervention, military or political, direct or indirect; the promotion of a program of large-scale economic aid on an apolitical, international basis (through the United Nations?); and the proposal that UN troops be widely used to safeguard political and military stability in these areas.

By way of preparation for a discussion of the basic problems of the development and foreign policy of our country I have attempted to formulate a number of theses. Some of them are set out in the form of discussion points. I have tried to give the fullest possible exposition of my views, although I realize that some of the theses will seem unacceptable and others uninteresting or insignificant.

1. Since the year 1950 a number of important measures have been taken in our country to eliminate the most dangerous and ugly features of the previous stage of development of Soviet society and state policies. However, at the same time there do occur certain negative phenomena—deviations, inconsistencies, and sluggishness in the implementation of the new line. It is essential to work out a clearcut and consistent program of further democratization and liberalization, and to take a number of immediate steps as a matter of urgency. This is required in the interests of technical and economic progress, of gradually overcoming our backwardness and isolation from the advanced capitalist countries, and [in the interests of] the prosperity of large sectors of the population, internal stability, and external security. The development of our country is taking place in the extremely difficult

conditions presented by our relations with China. We are faced with serious internal difficulties in the sphere of the economy and the general standard of living, technical and economic progress, culture and ideology.

One must point out the increasingly acute nationalities problem, the complexities of the interrelationship between the Party-state apparatus and the intelligentsia, and of that between the basic mass of the workers, who find themselves relatively worse off with regard to their standard of living and financial status, their prospects for professional promotion and cultural development, and many of whom feel disillusioned with all the "fine words," and the privileged groups of "the bosses," whom the more backward sectors of the workers frequently, and chiefly by virtue of traditional prejudices, identify with the intelligentsia. Our country's foreign policy is not always sufficiently realistic. We need basic decisions in order to prevent possible complications.

2. I venture the opinion that it would be correct to characterize as follows the society toward the creation of which urgent state reforms as well as the efforts of citizens to develop a social conscience should be directed:

The basic aim of the state is the protection and safeguarding of the basic rights of its citizens. The defense of human rights is the loftiest of all aims.

State institutions always act in complete accordance with laws (which are stable, and known to all citizens, institutions, and organizations).

The happiness of the people is safeguarded, in particular, by their freedom of work, freedom of consumption, freedom in their private lives, and in their education, their cultural and their social activities, freedom of conviction and of conscience, and freedom of exchange of information, and of movement.

Openness facilitates the social controls safeguarding legality, justice, and the rightness of all decisions taken, contributes to the effectiveness of the entire system, makes for a scientific and democratic system of government, and promotes progress, prosperity, and national security.

Competitiveness, openness, and the absence of privileges insure an equitable distribution of incentives for the labor, personal capabilities, and individual initiative of all citizens.

There is a definite stratification of society based on type of occupation, nature of abilities, and [social] relations.

The basic energies of the country are directed toward harmonious internal development, with the purposeful deployment of labor and natural resources, and this is the basis of its power and prosperity. The country and its people are always ready to enter into friendly international cooperation and aid within the framework of universal brotherhood, but the society is such that it does not need to use foreign policy as a means of internal political stabilization, or to extend its spheres of influence, or to export its ideas. Messianism, delusions as to the uniqueness of a society and the exclusive merits of its own path, as well as the rejection of the paths of other [societies], are alien to [the ideal] society; organically alien to it also are dogmatism, adventurism, and aggression.

In the actual conditions obtaining in our country in particular, we will only overcome our economic difficulties and improve the people's standard of living by a concentration of resources on internal problems, and, given some additional conditions (democratization, the elimination of our people's isolation in terms of access to information from the rest of the world, and economic measures), this alone will give us any hope of gradually narrowing the gap between ourselves and the advanced capitalist countries, safeguard national security in the event of a deterioration in [our relations with] China, and insure that we have ample opportunity to assist countries in need. . . .

6. *Information exchange, culture, science, and freedom of beliefs.* Freedom of beliefs, the spirit of inquiry, and creative anxiety should be encouraged.

The jamming of foreign radio broadcasts should be stopped, more foreign literature brought in from abroad, the international copyright agreement signed, and foreign travel facilitated, in order to overcome the isolation that is having a pernicious effect on our development.

Resolutions should be passed insuring the real separation of church and state, and real (that is, legally, economically, and administratively guaranteed) freedom of conscience and worship.

A review should be carried out of those aspects of the interrelations between the Party-state apparatus and art, literature, theater, organs of education, and so on that are harmful to the development of culture in our country, reduce the boldness and versatility of the creative endeavor, and lead to conventionality, grayness, and ritual repetition. In the social sciences and the humanities, which play an ever greater role in modern life (philosophy, history, sociology, jurisprudence, etc.), we must insure the elimination of stagnation, a widening of scope in the creative endeavor, an independence of all superimposed opinions, and the use of the entire gamut of foreign experience.

7. *Social policies.* The possibility of abolishing the death penalty should be explored. Special- and strict-regime imprisonment should be abolished, since it conflicts with humaneness. Measures should be taken to perfect the penitentiary system, utilizing foreign experience and the recommendations of the UN.

A study should be made of the possibility of setting up a public supervisory organ to eliminate the use of physical coercion (assault, starvation, cold, etc.) against detainees, persons under arrest or investigation, and convicted persons.

There must be a radical improvement in the quality of education: increased salaries and independence for schoolteachers and college lecturers should be given; less importance should be attached to the formal role of diplomas and degrees; the educational system should be less monolithic; a wider range of subjects should be studied in schools; there should be increased guarantees of the right of freedom of beliefs.

Intensified measures should be taken in the struggle against alcoholism, including the possibility of public control over all aspects of the problem.

Stronger measures should be implemented in the struggle against noise, air and water pollution, erosion, the salting and chemical pollution of the soil. More should be done to preserve forests and wild and domestic animals, as well as to prevent cruelty to animals.

Reform of the health service, expansion of the network of private polyclinics and hospitals; a more important role for doctors, nurses, and health visitors in private practice; salary increases for health-service employees at all levels; reform of the drug industry; general access to modern medicines and equipment; the introduction of X-ray television equipment.

8. *Legal policies.* All forms of discrimination, overt and concealed, with regard to beliefs, national characteristics, etc., should be abolished. . . .

Postscript

The "Memorandum" was sent to the Secretary General of the CPSU [Mr. Brezhnev] on March 5, 1971. It received no reply. I do not think it would be right for me to delay its publication any longer. The "Postscript" was written in June 1972. It contains some additions to and partly replaces the note "Concerning political persecution" mentioned in the text. . . .

As before, I consider that it will be possible to overcome the tragic conflicts and dangers of our time only through the convergence of capitalism and the socialist regime.

In capitalist countries this process must be accompanied by a further improvement in the protection of workers' rights and a reduction in the role of militarism and its influence on political life. In socialist countries it is also essential to reduce the militarization of the economy and the role of a messianic ideology. It is vitally necessary to weaken the extreme forms of centralism and Party-state bureaucratic monopoly, both in the economic sphere of production and consumption, and in the sphere of ideology and culture.

As before, I consider the democratization of society, the development of openness in public affairs, the rule of law, and the safeguarding of basic human rights to be of decisive importance.

As before, I hope that society will evolve along these lines under the influence of technological-economic progress, although my prognoses have now become more cautious.

It seems to me now, more than ever before, that the only true guarantee for the safeguarding of human values in the chaos of uncontrollable changes and tragic upheavals is man's freedom of conscience and his moral yearning for the good.

Our society is infected by apathy, hypocrisy, petit bourgeois egoism, and hidden cruelty. The majority of representatives of its upper stratum—the Party apparatus of government and the highest, most successful layers of the intelligentsia—cling tenaciously to their open and secret privileges and are profoundly indifferent to the infringement of human rights, the interests of progress, security, and the future of mankind. Others, though deeply concerned in their hearts, cannot allow themselves any freedom of thought and are condemned to the torture of internal conflict. Drunkenness has assumed the dimensions of a national calamity. It is one of the symptoms of the moral degradation of a society that is sinking ever deeper into a state of chronic alcoholic poisoning.

The country's spiritual regeneration demands the elimination of those conditions that drive people into becoming hypocritical and time-serving, and that lead to feelings of impotence, discontent, and disillusionment. Everybody must be assured, in deed and not just in word, of equal opportunities for advancement in his work, in education, and cultural growth; and the system of privileges in all spheres of consumption must be abolished. Full intellectual freedom must be assured and all forms of persecution for beliefs must cease. A radical educational reform is essential. These ideas are the basis of many proposals in the memorandum.

In particular, the memorandum mentions the problem of improvement in the material condition and independence of two of the most numerous and socially significant groups of the intelligentsia, the teachers and medical workers. The sorry state of popular education and of the health service is carefully hidden from the eyes of foreigners, but cannot remain secret from those who wish to see. A free health service and education are no more than an economic illusion in a society in which all surplus value is expropriated and distributed by the state. The hierarchical class structure of our society, with its system of privileges, is reflected in a particularly pernicious way in the health service and education. The condition of the health service and of popular education is clearly revealed in the rundown state of public hospitals, in the poverty of the village schools, with their overcrowded classes, the poverty and low standing of the teacher, and the official hypocrisy in teaching, which inculcates in the rising generation a spirit of indifference toward moral, artistic, and scientific values. . . .

The persecution and destruction of religion, which has been carried on with perseverance and cruelty for decades, has resulted in what is undoubtedly one of the most serious infringements of the rights of man in our country. Freedom of religious belief and activity is an integral part of intellectual freedom as a whole. Unfortunately, the last few months have been marked by fresh instances of religious persecution, in particular in the Baltic states.

Seweryn Bialer

Generations of Leadership

One of the most insightful writers on Soviet politics is Seweryn Bialer, professor of political science at Columbia University and a Communist party official in Poland before he defected to the West in the 1950s. Among his many books, *Stalin's Successors*, excerpted here, analyzed the Soviet political leadership under Brezhnev with an eye to his succession. Bialer emphasized the impending abrupt change from the old "Great Purge" generation of leaders—those who rocketed to power during Stalin's purge of party officials in the 1930s—to a "post-Stalin" one, which as we now know provided the initial impetus for Gorbachev's reforms.

The centralization of the Soviet system of administration, the lack of institutional arrangements concerning tenure and removal from high office, the weakness of legitimate channels of control directed upward from lower elites, let alone from outside the elites, the secrecy affecting decision making and the political process—all have worked in the past and, to the extent they are present today, continue to work to effect a tendency toward concentration of individual power within the top Soviet leadership. It is clear, however, that when compared not only to Stalin's dictatorship but also to Khrushchev's dictatorship, the pattern of distribution of power, of conflict and accommodation, prevalent

From Seweryn Bialer, *Stalin's Successors: Leadership, Stability, and Change in the Soviet Union*, pp. 70–71, 88–91, 94–98, 104, 106, 114–116, 124–125. Copyright © 1980 by Cambridge University Press. Reprinted by permission of the publisher.

The Old Regime at work: Brezhnev's Politburo attending the Supreme Soviet, November 1981. *From left: first row,* Chernenko, Kirilenko, Suslov, Tikhonov, Brezhnev; *second row,* Scherbitsky, Grishin, Gorbachev, Pelshe, Kunaev; *third row,* Ponomarev, Romanov, Ustinov, Andropov, Gromyko. (ITAR-TASS/SOVFOTO)

within the top Soviet leadership in the Brezhnev period is different. If Khrushchev's Presidium could be called "collective leadership" as opposed to Stalin's one-man rule, Brezhnev's Politburo
represents this form of leadership in a much more pure and stable
edition, and one much less prone to becoming a transitional stage
between periods of one-man rule. . . .

Those who in the later 1930s and early and even mid-1940s
filled the vacuum left by the Great Purge and occupied openings
created by the expansion of the network of elite positions shared
two interrelated characteristics: Their advancement in the ranks
of bureaucracy was extremely rapid by any standard; and they
were extraordinarily young for the positions to which they advanced. . . .

The survival ratio of the beneficiaries of the Great Purge
during the remainder of the Stalinist era was surprisingly high.
Nothing ever approaching a mass "permanent purge" among the
higher echelons took place in the last decade of Stalin's rule. The
purges were narrow and deliberate in aim. In the Khrushchev
period the beneficiaries of the Great Purge constituted the basic
pool of personnel advancing to leadership positions. Despite the
fact that the turnover of personnel under Khrushchev was considerably higher than under late Stalinism, this stratum was so broad
and so well established on *all* levels of the hierarchies that it
constituted by far the largest group from which replacement came
for the personnel dismissed by Khrushchev from positions of
influence and power. As a result, on the eve of Khrushchev's
ouster, it was this group which still dominated the top leadership
and even middle levels of the diverse elites. The sudden and
almost complete disappearance of the preceding elite generation
in the Great Purge, the simultaneous and very rapid advancement
of a new generation to positions of top and middle responsibility,
and their extremely young age at the midpoint of their careers
made for their inordinate staying power and their tenacity in
dominating the Soviet political scene for so long. . . .

It is primarily the Brezhnev period . . . which accounts for
the fact that the political leadership and elite of mature Stalinism,
the youngest in modern history, who passed through middle age
in the Khrushchev period, has become the old one of today.

The fifteen years of Brezhnev's chairmanship was [a time] of unparalleled bureaucratic stability and, first and foremost, of personnel stability. If Khrushchev brought the Soviet elite the gift of security of life, Brezhnev assured it security of office. Soviet high officials do not fade away; they die in office. Under Brezhnev, turnover on the leadership and elite level was, until recently, lower than in any other period in Soviet history. . . .

. . . The average age of the incumbents of the most powerful body, the Politburo, is today exactly thirteen years higher than it was thirteen years ago in 1965 at the beginning of the Brezhnev period. That is to say, the end result is the same as if no influx into this body had taken place at all. (The same is also true of the top governmental body, the Presidium of the Council of Ministers.) Most importantly, with the possible exception of the 60-year-old Kulakov, who died in 1978, no younger member of the top hierarchy during the Brezhnev period has penetrated the inner core of the Politburo and Secretariat. And equally important is the fact that the presumed heir-apparent to the 73-year-old Brezhnev is either the 73-year-old Kirilenko[1] or the 76-year-old Suslov[2]. . . .

. . . The post-Khrushchev leadership's attempt to stabilize and consolidate the system politically and ideologically has been a response to and a reaction against the cycle of organizational, political, and ideological fluidity in the Khrushchev era, which produced near-chaos.

Now in the last years of Brezhnev's leadership, ossification seems again to have set in. It is reflected in the lack of any attempt at reforms, especially in the economic structure, despite the major pressure of deteriorating economic performance, and in the inertia and lack of major initiatives in domestic policies. Its key reflection, however, and, one suspects, its major source is the ossification of the leadership structure and personnel, especially at the central level.

The superstability of personnel in the middle and late period of Brezhnev's leadership cannot be comprehended as anything

---

[1] Andrei Kirilenko, Politburo member, elbowed aside by Andropov in 1982, died in 1990.—Ed.

[2] Suslov: see p. 48.

other than a deliberate policy of the top leadership followed by their subordinates. We do not know to what extent it is a policy pursued primarily because the old leaders feel comfortable with the well-known faces around them and, as many old leaders have done throughout history, do not want to think about what comes after them. Considering the homogeneity and closeness of the core leadership group, there is little under Soviet conditions that dissenters from this policy in the Soviet leadership and elite, especially younger dissenters, can do to reverse or revise it.

Initially, however, this policy also reflected an unwritten agreement, a compact, between the top leadership and the elite to provide the security denied to them in the past. It reflected the recognition of the greater role and influence of the elite, and it may still reflect it today. This policy was secured by the preservation of the oligarchical nature of the top Soviet leadership and might have been difficult to change without endangering the balance of power and of policy preferences within this leadership. That this policy is satisfactory to the aged members of the Soviet leadership and elite even today is obvious; that it is not looked at askance by its younger members one may doubt.

The gates of the dam have been closed for very long, and there must be a great deal of pent-up frustration and impatience among the younger members of the elite, a frustration which is mitigated to a large extent by the hopes of advancement which they associate with the expected Brezhnev departure and the passing of the old generation. How quickly, of what scope, and how much compressed in time such a replacement will be depends, of course, partly on the vagaries of nature but largely also on the pattern in which the succession will unfold and the political framework in which the succession will take place. . . .

We do not know how much longer Brezhnev will remain in office. We do expect, however, that as long as he does remain his personnel policy will remain basically intact. From the point of view of the coming succession this continuity is fraught with major dangers. As we stated earlier, Brezhnev's personnel policy seems to give little thought and low priority to a gradual preparation of a leadership changeover, a shortsightedness that may have profound destabilizing repercussions. Very major changes of personnel on the leadership and elite level, especially in the central institutions, cannot be avoided in the coming succession under any circumstances. But every year that the Brezhnev succession is delayed and his policy of personnel stability continued, the chance of extraordinarily drastic, massive, and condensed changes within the leadership and elite becomes more and more likely.

Already today there is within the elite a considerable representation of younger members on all levels of power and especially in the middle echelons of the various hierarchies, as well as among the adviser-experts to the leadership. In the highly centralized Soviet system their impact on Soviet policies may well have been circumscribed and dampened by the stability on the top, by the continuing domination of the top places of power on the part of a coterie of old leaders who are afraid of change and actively stifle any initiative for transforming established policies and routines. Assuming that the influx of newcomers to positions of high and intermediate levels of power will accelerate and attain a high level in the coming years, during and partly as a result of the succession, the key question, of course, still remains: How will the newcomers differ from those they replace; how will their style of leadership, their manner of behavior in office, their attitudes, their beliefs, and their actions compare to those of their predecessors?

Those massive replacements at the levels of the top leadership and central elite that will certainly accompany if not the first then the second stage of the upcoming succession, I would argue, will most probably produce disruptions, political conflicts over policies and procedures, and policy changes regardless of the identities of the newcomers to positions of power. Such a prospect is especially likely because on the one hand the succession follows a period of extraordinary and long-lasting stability during which policy differences were submerged in the name of unity, stability, and compromise while bold initiatives, especially on the domestic scene, were lacking; and on the other hand it comes at a time when the Soviet Union begins to face difficult economic choices, when the possibility of satisfying diverse interests and pressures through compromise solutions will be more difficult than in the Brezhnev period.

It is my argument that a high level of circulation of elites, especially when compressed into a short period of time, can by itself be significant in determining the formation of the styles and behavior of the leadership and elites. By breaking the inculcated official routine in a bureaucratic and centralized structure, by undermining the inertia of a set style of work, by disrupting existing and fixed informal ties, and by weakening the vested interests in long-established substantive policies, it provides a setting that facilitates the elaboration of changed modes of political behavior. Yet the key questions still remain: How disposed will the newcomers be to make use of the opportunity to be different; how much pressure will they exert and in what direction in order to achieve a change in the policies and processes of the Soviet government? In short, just how different will they be from their predecessors? . . .

The question then is: Whether and to what extent does the succession and the replacement of large segments of the elites that will probably accompany it coincide with the distinctive differences of the incoming members as a group when compared to the outgoing as a group—that is, irrespective of inevitably diverse personality characteristics within each group? I should like to suggest that in the approaching succession such coincidence does occur, that in addition to the imminent replacement of the top leader and a large part of the highest leadership stratum, the coming decade will witness simultaneously a generational change among Soviet elites. . . .

The new generation is clearly a Soviet generation in its typical and persistent adherence to the cult of the state. One cannot doubt the sincerity of its members' commitment to the basic forms of Soviet political organization, their belief that the system is right and proper for the Soviet Union. At the same time one is not persuaded that they believe this system is suitable or desirable for developed Western societies. If they share with their predecessors a devoted patriotism, they tend to exhibit little of their predecessors' xenophobia, and much less of their fear and deeply rooted suspicion of the outside world. Rather they display a curiosity that surely reflects intense concern with the patent inadequacies in the working of the Soviet system.

One most striking trait of this group is its skepticism about the grander claims of Soviet propaganda concerning the system's merits. Its members display both a well-developed awareness of the system's functional shortcomings and a restless impatience with them and with Soviet backwardness and provinciality in general. They do not disguise their dislike and lack of respect for the old generation.

This new generation seems scarcely touched by traditions of populism and egalitarianism. Grossly materialistic in wants and expectations, it is characterized by highly developed career orientation, cult of professionalism, and elitism. Condescending in attitude toward compatriots and older colleagues, the members of this generation appear self-confident and less sensitive to real or imagined slights. Just as one postulates for the old elite strong bonds of generational solidarity, one can suppose that the members of the new generation are in the process of forming similar bonds. . . .

The basis for generalizing about the modernizing mentality of the new Soviet elite generation is clearly insufficient. Yet from what we have already said about the generation a limited number of tentative hypotheses can be advanced. It is a generation that perceives the inability of the Brezhnev administration in recent years to lay out a direction for Soviet development. It is a generation that deplores the backwardness of Soviet society, the functional deficiencies of the system, the inability of the present administration to make progress in rectifying the situation, and at the same time it probably stands confident in its own ability to do so. It is a generation that is less likely to accept actual or potential international achievements as substitutes for internal development. It is a generation that may be willing to pay a higher price in terms of political and social change *if* persuaded that such a price would assure substantial improvement in the growth and efficiency of the productive and distributive processes. . . .

The Great Purge generation derives overwhelmingly from lower-class origins, with the sons of peasants a dominant component. Born and raised in a small town or village, they entered the white-collar class very early in life, not later than their mid-twenties. Higher education, which was of a narrow technical nature outside the major educational centers, afforded the initial avenue of social mobility. (It should be clear that while most members of this elite generation were chosen from among graduates of technical institutes, their *general* education falls far short of the standards associated with graduates of institutions of higher learning. Their basic, that is pre-institute, education was in most cases an accelerated version of the three Rs.) While trained as engineers and agronomists for the most part, they spent very little time in these occupations. Their political careers commenced very early, usually away from great metropolitan centers, and their advance was very rapid. They became and remained generalists whose key skill was general organization rather than its application to any particular area. . . .

. . . The post-Stalin generation . . . as a whole is very homogeneous. Life and career patterns as well as background characteristics are with very few exceptions repeated from individual to individual. As far as it was possible to establish, industrial workers seemed to form the social base of the post-Stalin elite. The peasant base of recruitment shows a clear decline, while the new Soviet middle class for the first time constitutes a sizable and growing minority. One finds also for the first time a dominant proportion of individuals who spent their youth in large cities and a growing number who attended schools in metropolitan areas.

The youth and early working life of this group reflect the normalization of Soviet living conditions and epitomize typical middle-class patterns. The normal route went from high school to an establishment of higher learning; working life started at the age of 22 to 24 in professional or low managerial positions; regardless of social origin, very few of them were at any time workers or peasants.

Education constitutes the dominant avenue of mobility. With but one exception all individuals in our group finished some form of higher education. Moreover, the education of this elite generation on the average clearly surpasses that of its predecessors in terms of quality. In only two cases were degrees attained through correspondence courses; a sizable minority even acquired graduate degrees. The education of this group still centers almost entirely on technological skills; evenly divided between engineers and agronomists, it also includes for the first time a number of economists. A minority of this group attended the Higher Party School in Moscow at a late point in their party career and in all but one case received important promotions after graduation. . . .

. . . The approaching succession, whatever the form and results of its initial stage, will eventually involve a replacement in the top leadership and the central establishment on a scale much greater than the last two successions and will be combined with an increased generational turnover of the Soviet political elite. This conjunction of successions in both the broad and narrow senses has no precedent in Soviet history. It will be a political development of long-term duration and significance. . . .

The stability and longevity of the existing pattern, however, have been conditional on two internal structural factors: gradualism in major policy changes and gradualism, to say the least, in personnel replacement. We do not know whether the first condition will still obtain in a succession or whether, after the cycle of cautious readjustments and traditionalism of the last decade, the mood of the leadership and the elite will swing toward revitalization and major reforms, just as the frozen conditions of Stalin's Russia were replaced by the flux of the Khrushchev period. Certainly, the key determinant of what will be the dominant tendency in this respect during the succession will crucially depend on whether there is a major increase in the perception by Soviet leaders and the elite of pressures and frustrations stemming from failures or dangers at home or abroad. What we do know, however, is that the second condition—gradualism in personnel replacement—will most probably not obtain.

Changes in the structure of relations within the Soviet political elite were a more important channel for elite change in the last decade than elite replacement. The greater assertiveness of institutional interests, the increase in the operational autonomy of elite organizations, the diffusion of influence from the top leadership, and the relative stability of the balance of countervailing forces within the top leadership stopped, however, very short of institutionalization. They may therefore be partly reversed, even if with difficulty, in the coming succession.

The post-Khrushchev structural innovations may satisfy the present generation of officeholders. But they may not satisfy the next one, which may want not only to broaden its operational autonomy but also to influence the agenda of decision making. Response to social reality always involves a lag: Not only individuals but also groups respond to new conditions on the basis of attitudes and habits developed under old conditions. The situation which future Soviet leaders will face with regard to their major elite institutions will be very different from the ones faced by Stalin's successors. Stalin did not simply control the party, the military, or the planners—he crushed them. Ironically, only now, when Stalin is again becoming an officially "respectable" figure, is the delayed impact of Stalinism on the character of Soviet bureaucracy dissolving. Soviet administrators display today more self-confidence and professional pride than ever before. These qualities are easily reconcilable with an authoritarian outlook toward the society at large but are difficult to fit into a highly restrictive elite structure without endangering its effectiveness.

Tatiana Zaslavskaya

The Old Regime in Crisis

In 1983 a remarkable Soviet document was leaked to the Western press, a memorandum for a very restricted readership, written by the sociologist Tatiana Zaslavskaya of the Institute of the Economics and Organization of Industrial Production in Novosibirsk. Universally known as the "Novosibirsk Report," Zaslavskaya's statement was a probing analysis, clothed in Marxist jargon, of the social and economic crisis that gripped the Soviet Union in Brezhnev's last years and compelled his successors to face the imperative need for reform. Zaslavskaya went on to become an adviser to Gorbachev and currently works in Moscow researching social problems and public opinion.

Over a number of decades, Soviet society's economic development has been characterized by high rates and great stability.

From Tatiana Zaslavskaya, "Report on the Necessity of a Deeper Study in the USSR of the Social Mechanism of the Development of the Economy," translated as "The Novosibirsk Report," *Survey*, vol. 28, no. 1 (spring 1984), pp. 88–92, 94–96, 98–101, 106. Copyright © 1988 by *Survey*. Reprinted by permission of the publisher.

This automatically suggested a notion about the organic nature of its features for the management of a planned socialist economy. However, in the past 12–15 years a tendency towards a noticeable decline in the rate of growth of the national income began to make itself felt in the development of the economy of the USSR. If in the eighth five-year plan the average annual increase was 7.5 per cent and in the ninth it was 5.8 per cent, then in the tenth it fell to 3.8 per cent, and in the first years of the eleventh it was about 2.5 per cent (with the average population growth at 0.8 per cent per annum). This does not provide for either the rate of growth in living standards that is required for the people, or for the intensive technical retooling of production.

Increasing effectiveness and speeding up the rate of development of the economy is of paramount concern for the Party, the people and the scientists. In their analyses of the reasons for the negative tendencies in the economy, separate groups of scientists have placed the emphasis on deterioration in conditions for mining raw minerals, the growing frequency of years of drought, the structural disproportions in the country's national economy (the falling rate of investment, deterioration of transport, insufficient interest on the part of the workers in the results of their labour, the weakness of labour discipline, and so on).

All these factors do indeed play a determined role in the creation of the tendencies under scrutiny, but they bear a particular character while the deterioration of the economic indices takes place in the majority of sectors and regions. Therefore, there is a more general reason at the foundation of this phenomenon. In our opinion, it consists in the lagging of the system of production relations, and hence of the mechanism of state management of the economy which is its reflection, behind the level of development of the productive forces. To put it in more concrete terms, it is expressed in the inability of this system to make provision for the full and sufficiently effective use of the labour potential and intellectual resources of society.

The basic features of the present system of state management of the economy of the USSR (and thus of the system of production relations to which it gives rise) were formed roughly five decades ago. Since that time, this system has repeatedly been readjusted, renewed and improved, but not once has it undergone a qualitative restructuring which would reflect fundamental changes in the state of the productive forces.

The most important features of the system of state management of the Soviet economy, noted in the scientific literature, include: a high level of centralization in economic decisions, the character of production planning being based on direct indicators, the weak development of market relations (the prices of goods in demand and the means of production bear no relation to their social value; the centralization of supplies of materials and technology to enterprises, the absence of a market for production, and so on), the centralized regulation of all forms of material incentives for labour, the prevalence of the branch over the territorial principle of management, lack of departmental liaison in the management of the economy by branch and sub-branch, restrictions on economic rights, and consequently also on enterprises' economic responsibility for the results of their economic activity, restriction on all aspects of informal economic activity by the population in the areas of production, services and exchange. All these features reflect the predominance of administrative over economic methods, of centralization over decentralization. . . .

. . . The system of centralized . . . economic management . . . correspond[s] for the most part to the level of development of the productive forces of Soviet society in the 1930s. The material and social base of large-scale socialist production at that time was only just beginning to take shape, and the level of real socialization of labour remained comparatively low. The links between the branches, enterprises and regions were as yet easily "overseen" from the centre and could be regulated "from above." An overwhelming number of workers in industry had only recently left their villages and had a weakly developed sense of their rights, and no claims to participation in management. For the majority of them material incentives predominated at work over social and spiritual ones. Being relatively undeveloped, they were a convenient object of management. . . .

However, decades have passed since then, in the course of which the political and economic situation of Soviet society has radically changed. The present state of its productive forces is different from the 1930s not only quantitatively (in terms of scale),

but qualitatively (in terms of new "procedures" and "generations"). The branch, departmental and territorial structure of the
national economy has become much more complex, the number
of its links has grown colossally and even more its technological,
economic and social ties. The structure of the national economy
long ago crossed the threshold of complexity when it was still
possible to regulate it effectively from one single centre. Regional,
branch and economic disproportions in the national economy of
the USSR, which emerged and can be observed in the past five-
year plans, are growing relentlessly; and, more than anything else,
indicate the exhaustion of possibilities for centrally-administered
economic management, the necessity for more active use of "automatic" regulators in balancing production, linked to the development of market relations. In this situation, the scientists' tardiness
in stating their position on the direct social nature of socialist
labour and the "special" nature of socialist commodity and monetary relations has been a poor turn to society.

Important changes have also taken place in the social type
of worker in the socialist economy. The level of his education,
culture, general information, and awareness of his social position
and rights, has grown incomparably. The main body of skilled
workers, on whom above all the effectiveness of the production
process depends, nowadays has a rather wide political and economic horizon, is able to evaluate critically the leaders' economic
and political activities, accurately recognizes its own interests and
can defend them if necessary. The spectrum of needs and interests
of workers is today more abundant and broader than that of
workers in the 1930s; moreover, in addition to economic, it includes social and spiritual needs. It testifies to the substantial
increase in the level of the workers' personal development, but
at the same time it is an indication that they have become a much
more complex object of management than previously.

The change in the predominant social type of worker would,
in turn, not have been possible without substantial changes in
the socio-economic conditions of the people's sphere of activities.
The democratization of political life, the broadening and constitutional bolstering of individual rights, the universal issue of pass-
ports and equalizing of civil rights for every group within the
population, a sharp improvement in the standard of living, the

introduction of social welfare for sickness and old age, and also the beginning of labour shortages in recent years in the majority of sectors and regions in the country—all these assisted a significant broadening of economic freedom in the workers' behaviour and, as a result, the role of subjective factors in economic development increased.

Finally, there has been a qualitative change, in the course of the period in question, in the material and technical base of production and the demands made by it on human labour. The size and value of the means of production used by this labour and its technical armoury have grown many times. As a result, on the one hand the level of productive labour has greatly increased, but on the other, the scale of damage inflicted upon society through careless labour, violations of labour and technology discipline, irresponsible attitudes to technology etc., have also risen. The widespread application in many sectors of the economy of complete technological systems, the increase in the specific weight of labour given over to the functions of adjustment, control and regulation, and improvement of technological concerns have noticeably increased the demand for qualifications, reliability and responsibility in human labour, for workers' personal involvement in plan fulfilment, and so on. . . .

The overall results of all these advances are, on the one hand, an increase in the technological demands made on the labour behaviour of the workers, and on the other, a decrease in the effectiveness of centralized production management, based on the administrative regulation of the activities of the lower-ranking links by the higher. Based on the expectation of a relatively low level of development in the workers, this system appears unable to regulate the behaviour of more developed (in personal terms) and economically free workers, unable to make sufficiently effective use of their labour potential and intellectual resources, unable to ensure a high level of labour, production and plan discipline, high quality work, effective use of technology, or to assure positive modes of conduct in the managers, accountants and supply technicians.

As we see it, all this testifies to the fact that the present system of production relations has substantially fallen behind the level of development of the productive forces. Instead of enabling their accelerated development, it is becoming more and more of a brake on their progressive advancement. One outcome of this is the inability of production relations to provide modes of conduct for workers in the socio-economic sphere that are needed by society. Let us look at this question in greater detail. . . .

Motivated by individual and group interests, the socio-economic behaviour of the workers has a substantial influence on practically all aspects of the economy and is therefore one of the sources of spontaneity in its development. The role of the spontaneous, that is, not regulated, behaviour of the workers in the development of the socialist economy has many ramifications. Several aspects of it often infringe upon its planned character, cause disproportions and lower the rate of production development. But other aspects testify to the release of the workers' creative forces, to the raising of their labour activity and to making active use of social reserves in production effectiveness. The management of the workers' economic behaviour is thus a complicated affair.

Within the framework of this problem, one can distinguish two tasks, each demanding a different approach. The first lies in determining, from the point of view of public interests, the optimum sphere of individual behaviour for workers in each field of their socio-economic activities which are not regulated "from above." The second task is indirectly to provide modes of socio-economic behaviour for workers, in the sphere of choice left to them, which are in line with public interests.

The determination of the first task is connected with the fact that the boundary between the activity *per se* and its subjective aspect—behaviour—is not fixed. It depends on how strictly the given activity is regulated. As an example, where labour discipline is weak, the workers have the possibility of working only part of the time allocated, of being absent from work, of permitting stoppages, of drinking alcohol at their place of work, and so on. The least disciplined section of workers takes advantage of this opportunity, while the main nucleus of skilled workers works honestly. Under these conditions, the use made of work hours is an important indication of workers' behaviour at work.

The introduction of order, the raising of the demand for labour discipline, the strengthening of control over the use of work hours, change the situation: the regular attendance of the workers at their place of work becomes the norm and by the same token ceases to reflect the peculiarities of their individual behaviour. Today, their individual relationship to work manifests itself in the varying degrees of care and attention which they give to it and, consequently, in the uneven quality of the produced goods. Stricter regulation of the quality of output leads to a further narrowing in the scope of the workers' labour behaviour, which is restricted, for example, by differences in the expenditure of raw materials, energy, goods, in different degrees of participation in management and rationalization activities, etc.

On the whole, the more strictly regulated the working and economic activity is from without, the narrower the sphere of individual behaviour of those who execute it, and, so it seems, the less the influence of personal behavioural factors on the development of production. But what is the actual dependency between the rigour of administrative regulation of activity and the effectiveness of the development of the economy? Is it, indeed, that the more strictly controlled the aspects of the workers' activity, the more successful its results? For a whole number of reasons, this question has to be answered in the negative.

First, the administrative regulation of labour and of other economic activities has a centralized character and, in the majority of cases, is carried out without taking into account the conditions of specific regions, sectors and enterprises. And since these conditions vary, the practical fulfilment of regulating rules and norms runs across great difficulties in the provinces and does not always lead to favourable results.

Second, the increasing severity in regulating activity strengthens the need to observe established rules in administrative control; this is fraught with the increase of non-productive labour and the deterioration of the economic indices of the enterprises. Therefore, in practice, there is often no control on a daily basis over the observation of these rules, and they are flouted. As a result, not only is the actual leeway for workers' free behaviour not curtailed, but sometimes it increases noticeably. There often arises a paradoxical situation whereby the opportunity for a positive show of initiative by the workers is reduced by multiple administrative restrictions to naught, while the spectrum of anti-social modes of behaviour remains rather broad.

Third, although the strengthening of the administrative regulation of activities helps the elimination of certain negative modes of behaviour, it almost inevitably also leads to the undermining of creative elements of labour, a restriction on economic and technical initiatives by the workers, the deflection of their personal interests to the realm of the family, leisure pursuits, their own household, and so on. Anyway, to transfer the economy from a path of extensive development to one of intensive development can only be done in conditions where all available social reserves and all creative potential of the workers are realized.

Thus, it is in the interests of socialist society, while regulating the key aspects of the socio-economic activity of the workers, to leave them a sufficiently wide margin of freedom of individual behaviour. Hence the necessity for directing behaviour itself, i.e., the subjective relationship of the workers to their socio-economic activity. Administrative methods of management are powerless here. The management of behaviour can only be accomplished in an oblique fashion, with the help of incentives which would take into account the economic and social demands of the workers and would channel their interests in a direction which would be of benefit to our society. Moreover, to be able to control behaviour, it is not enough to provide the correct direction for each class or social group's interests. It is necessary to aim, on the one hand, at the coordination of public, collective and individual interests of workers "along vertical lines," and on the other, at the integration of the interests of classes and groups, which interact as it were on the "horizontal" plane.

The realization of these tasks presupposes a serious reorganization of the system of state management of the economy and especially the rejection of administrative methods of management with a high degree of centralization of economic decision-making, and the subsequent complex transition to economic methods of regulating production.

The urgent need for reorganizing the system of state management of the economy was realized in theory by the Party a long time ago, and this was reflected in numerous resolutions made by the Party over the past decade; in particular in the resolutions of the 24th, 25th and 26th CPSU [Communist Party of the Soviet

Union] congresses, and in those of the November 1979, October 1980 and May 1982 Plenums of the CC [Central Committee] of the CPSU. In a speech at the November (1982) Plenum of the CC of the CPSU Comrade Yu. V. Andropov again stressed that "it is necessary to create conditions—economic and organizational—such that would stimulate top quality productive labour, initiative and enterprise. And, conversely, bad work, inactivity, and irresponsibility must, in the most direct and irredeemable fashion, affect the material rewards, the work situation and the moral authority of the workers."

However, while the problem is not solved, and the present system of management of the economy stubbornly retains its existing features, Party documents note the necessity of decisively overcoming this. Resolutions made about this matter are slowly being realized in a compromise fashion, as though coming up against hidden opposition. In the face of this, periods of more or less successful progress in the intended direction are from time to time replaced with "ebbs"—a return to administrative methods of management which ignore the demands of economic laws. . . .

. . . The concrete system of management of the national economy, reflecting this or that modification in production relations, brings about a corresponding distribution of influence among social groups, central and regional economic departments, organs of regional and territorial management, ministries and associations, associations and enterprises, etc. Therefore, a radical reorganization of economic management essentially affects the interests of many social groups, to some of which it promises improvements, but to others a deterioration in their position.

By virtue of this, attempts at improving production relations, bringing them into greater correspondence with the new demands of productive forces, attempts undertaken by the higher organs of power, cannot run their course without conflict. The successful resolution of this task is only possible on the basis of a well thought out socialist strategy being brought into play, a strategy that would simultaneously stimulate the activity of groups interested in changing present relations and block the actions of groups capable of obstructing this change. The attempts to reorganize the management of the national economy, undertaken during the last five-year plan, did not take into consideration the social aspects of the process of improving production relations under socialism, and this was one reason, so it seems to us, for their lack of success. . . .

Any serious reorganization of economic management must be accompanied by a certain redistribution of rights and responsibilities among various groups of workers. Thereby, the expansion of every group's rights is, as a rule, combined with an increase of responsibilities; and a decrease of responsibilities goes hand in hand with a reduction of rights. Because of this, the attitude of the majority of groups to possible transformations in production relations, and to the economic mechanism which is their reflection, is not unambiguous.

Thus, a good number of workers in the central organs of management, whose prospective role ought to be increased, is afraid that its responsibilities will become substantially more complicated, as economic methods of management demand much more of highly qualified cadres than do administrative methods. The guarded response of this group of workers to the idea of a transition to and a consistent implementation of economic methods of management often manifests itself in unfounded assertions, as though such transition was going to undermine the centralized motive power in the development of the socialist economy, or to reduce the real importance of the plan.

The reorganization of production relations promises a substantial narrowing and simplification in responsibilities for workers in departmental ministries and their organs. However, it is pregnant with just as significant a reduction in their rights, in their economic influence and also in the number of their apparatuses: the liquidation of many departments, administrations, trusts, branches etc. that have grown like mushrooms in recent decades. Naturally, such a prospect does not suit the workers, who at present occupy numerous "cosy niches" with ill-defined responsibilities, but thoroughly agreeable salaries.

Logically speaking, the group which must be most interested in the transition to economic methods of management is the managerial "staff" of the enterprises (associations), whose rights it has been proposed to widen sharply, and in the second place, the ordinary workers and ITR (Engineering and Technical Workers), who could use their individual capabilities more fully, work more effectively and receive a higher salary. However, in practice both these groups are not homogeneous in their subjective attitude to the projected reorganization of the economic mechanism. The more qualified, energetic and active representatives of these groups reckon that they are not working at full strength now. They want to realize themselves more fully in their work, to have better living conditions, and thus they support ideas about the intensification of the economy. In contrast to this, the more apathetic, the more elderly and the less qualified groups of workers are worried that they will have to "pay for it" if their rights are broadened and their salaries increased, with a sharp growth in their obligations, increasing labour intensity, and more economic responsibility for the results. And this is not at all to many people's taste, the more so since the system of production relations which has been in operation over the course of many decades has formed a predominantly passive type of worker, who bears witness to the famous principles of "I need no more than anybody else" and "that's no concern of mine."

From what has been said it is evident that the social necessity of improving production relations, and likewise the system of economic management thereby reflected, will not find a clear and precise echo in the interests of many social groups. Therein resides the social reason for the high stability of the rigidly central-ized, predominantly administrative, system of management of the economy, whose ineffectiveness was long ago recognized by the Party and reflected in its resolutions. . . .

. . . It is impossible to improve the mechanism of economic management, arrived at many years ago, by gradually replacing the more outmoded of its elements with more effective ones. Evidently, one should recognize that the discreet replacement of concrete systems of production relations in the process of the development of the communist order means that such a change will come about rather infrequently, but for that it is a complex and deep matter.

It is natural that socialist society can decide on such a serious transformation of production relations only under the influence of objective necessity, with a clearly established aim and reliable means of achieving it. We have already spoken about the first aspect of this question: there is a need for a transformation of production relations and the system of economic management, and its aims are sufficiently clear. The economic aim of the transformation lies in raising the effectiveness and rate of development of the national economy, and the social aim is in the elimination of obstacles to the social, professional and individual development of the workers, in the formation of a genuinely socialist attitude to labour among the workers. However, the means for achieving these aims are as yet clear only in general outline, rather as directions for principles than as decisive forms of transformation to new production relations. . . .

. . . The building of a concrete mechanism of national economic management based on economic incentives, remains a matter for the future. The social aspects of reforming economic management are as yet especially weakly worked out: concrete means for coordinating public, group and personal worker interests, methods for the provision of positive forms of economic behaviour, means of activating workers' participation in the management of production and society. Hence, there are new and great tasks confronting sociology, and in particular that branch of it which we are trying to develop under the name of "economic sociology." The central object of this scientific discipline is the social mechanism of economic development. . . .

In the light of what has been said, we must admit that the social mechanism of economic development as it functions at present in the USSR does not ensure satisfactory results. The social type of worker formed by it fails to correspond not only to the strategic aims of a developed socialist society, but also to the technological requirements of contemporary production. The widespread characteristics of many workers, whose personal formation occurred during past five-year plans, are low labour- and production-discipline, an indifferent attitude to the work performed and its low quality, social passivity, a low value attached to labour as a means of self-realization, an intense consumer orientation, and a rather low level of moral discipline. It is enough to mention the broad scale of activity of the so-called "touts," the rampant spread of various "shady" deals made at public expense, the development of illegal output, of irregular registrations, of procuring wages which are not dependent on the results of labour.

It is our conviction that both the expansion of these negative phenomena and the lowering of the rate of growth of production come about as a result of the degeneration of the social mechanism of economic development. At present, this mechanism is "tuned" not to stimulate, but to thwart the population's useful economic activity. Similarly, it "punishes" or simply cuts short initiatives by the chiefs of enterprises, in the sphere of production organization, aiming at the improvement of economic links. Nowadays, higher public value is placed not on the activities of the more talented, brave and energetic leaders, but on the performances of the more "obedient" chiefs, even if they cannot boast production successes.

An important source of social tension in the economic structure is not only the "inharmoniousness," but also the clash of interests between vertically aligned groups: between workers and foremen; foremen and the chiefs of enterprises; chiefs of enterprises and administrators in the ministries.

Finally, the centralized system of rules and norms of economic activity, which was created over the course of decades, has now become tangled to an unbelievable degree and many of its elements have become outdated. The "economic labyrinth," called upon to direct the workers' behavior in the channel needed by society, actually consists of a multitude of "saps" and "manholes," which allows the achievement of the same income by a significantly easier route. This not only extensively promotes undesirable practices, but also the formation of a type of worker who is alien to genuinely socialist values.

Archie Brown

The Succession and Reform

Archie Brown, Fellow of St. Antony's College, Oxford, is the most prominent British authority on the history of the Soviet leadership.

From Archie Brown, "Power and Policy in a Time of Leadership Transition, 1982–1988," in *Political Leadership in the Soviet Union*, Archie Brown, ed., pp. 164–173, 175–177, 180–184. Copyright © 1989 by Macmillan. Reprinted by permission of the publisher.

He has closely chronicled the dramatic transition from the political immobilism of the Brezhnev years to the dynamic era of Gorbachev. This selection is from a paper that Professor Brown presented at the 1985 World Congress of Soviet Studies and subsequently updated, in which he emphasizes the role of personalities and personal politics in opening the way to reform.

The death of Mikhail Suslov in January 1982 . . . , at the age of seventy-nine, was a major event. It removed one sizeable barricade from the path of reform and it also led to an intensified struggle for power and over policy among those who remained in the Soviet leadership. . . .

. . . Suslov had been an important figure in Moscow for a decade before Leonid Brezhnev arrived there (he was already a Secretary of the Central Committee and, concurrently, editor of *Pravda* in Stalin's time) and there were many people in high places with connections to him. His patronage over many years had been a major factor in ensuring that his voice remained to the end an influential one. His seniority in the leadership, together with the fact that he was obviously not one of Brezhnev's placemen but a figure of independent standing in the Politburo, made his support for Brezhnev's occupancy of the General Secretaryship and his broad acquiescence with the policies pursued by the Brezhnev group all the more valuable for the latter.

Suslov's death not only removed a key figure in Soviet decision-making but also raised the question of which leadership contender, at a time when Brezhnev's own declining health was becoming increasingly evident, would be the main beneficiary of the institutional powers Suslov had perforce vacated. Andropov, who had been shunted aside from the direct line of party advancement in 1967 with his move to the chairmanship of the KGB [secret police], clearly saw this as his opportunity to make a decisive comeback and put himself in line for the party leadership. . . .

. . . Andropov immediately began to wield a greater influence over policy (beginning an anti-corruption drive which he was to pursue with greater political resources at his disposal once he had become General Secretary) and especially a much enhanced power over party cadres than he had enjoyed as Chairman of the KGB. . . .

The state of Brezhnev's health was an important factor in the political equation. Although fulsome tributes continued to be paid to him so long as he was alive, he could no longer wield as much day-to-day power as he did a few years earlier. The serious candidates for the succession turned out to be Andropov and Chernenko. It was always likely that the next General Secretary would come from the ranks of the senior secretaries. That appeared probable at a time when the Soviet system had been headed by only three General Secretaries, and now that the number has doubled to six (all of whom were both Politburo members and Secretaries of the Central Committee before obtaining the top party post) it all the more clearly holds good. . . .

The real choice of General Secretary is made by the full members of the Politburo. The Central Committee has thus far never turned down the Politburo's nominee for the General Secretaryship, even though that person takes office only from the time that the Central Committee gives its imprimatur to the Politburo's selected candidate. There was, of course, the exceptional occasion—the "anti-party group" crisis of 1957—when the Central Committee failed to uphold the majority in the Politburo (or Presidium of the Central Committee, as the Politburo was known at that time) after most Politburo members had agreed that they should oust Khrushchev. But at the stage at which the Central Committee first elects a General Secretary, there is no evidence to suggest that alternative candidates were even voted on. The plenary sessions which elected Andropov, Chernenko and Gorbachev within the space of three years affirmed decisions taken in essence elsewhere. . . .

Andropov had the advantage that he could appeal to both the disciplinarian and reformist tendencies within the party. His former headship of the KGB did him no harm at all in the eyes of many of the disciplinarians, although reformers, too, could readily agree with Andropov's speech on the anniversary of Lenin's birth in April 1982, with its tough line on the need to uproot embezzlement and bribery. In a remarkable book, edited by the historian, Yuriy Afanas'ev, and published in Moscow in 1988, Academician Andrey Sakharov—after castigating the KGB for the part it played in Brezhnev's time as an instrument of repression of dissidents—goes on to observe: "On the other hand, precisely the KGB, thanks to its elite character, turned out to be almost the single force not touched by corruption and therefore in opposition to the mafia. This duality was reflected in the personal fate and position of the leader of the KGB, Yu. V. Andropov."

Andropov's April speech made a few concessions to the views of reformers, such as his acceptance that Soviet society—in common with every other—contained different points of view and different interests, a point made, however, in the context of rejecting the application of the concept of pluralism to Soviet society. Andropov's appeal to reformers rested less on his activities in the most recent period than on the reputation he had earned as head of the Socialist Countries Department of the Central Committee between 1957 and 1967 and on the known views of the people he chose to be his consultants in the Central Committee apparatus during those years—among them, Georgiy Arbatov, Oleg Bogomolov, Aleksandr Bovin, Fedor Burlatsky, Lev Delyusin and Georgiy Shakhnazarov. Despite varying degrees of caution or boldness among them, and the varying constraints imposed on them by the posts they subsequently held, all of these people, who hoped to see Andropov succeed Brezhnev, continued to be identified with the reformist tendency in Soviet politics. . . .

The disciplinarians and the reformers within the leadership could agree that they did not want [Brezhevism]. They were also in agreement on the need for a strong leader. After the long years of cosy, and frequently corrupt, relationships under Brezhnev, only a leader possessing clear authority would have much chance of reinvigorating the system and society. Andropov looked as if he could become such a leader; Chernenko did not.

Nevertheless, the struggle for the succession between Andropov and Chernenko was a close-run thing. There is no definitive account of the voting in the Politburo which saw Andropov emerge as their nominee, but the Brezhnev group rallied to Chernenko, while the Politburo heavyweights sided with Andropov. . . .

Andropov made clear from the outset that he intended to make full use of his new authority and there could be no shadow of doubt, as there had been after the death of Stalin and, to a lesser degree after the fall of Khrushchev, concerning who was the new top leader of the country. With his strong background in international affairs (having been successively an official of the Ministry of Foreign Affairs, head of the Socialist Countries Department of the Central Committee, head of the KGB, and a senior secretary of the Central Committee), Andropov immediately took charge of the discussions which were conducted with various statesmen who arrived in Moscow for Brezhnev's funeral. There was to be a complete contrast with this fifteen months later when [Foreign Minister Andrei] Gromyko, rather than Chernenko, took the leading part in similar discussions with those who were attending Andropov's funeral. . . .

So far as concrete policy changes were concerned, the earliest to be implemented related to the disciplinarian rather than the reformist aspect of Andropov's dual approach. There was a crackdown on excessive alcohol consumption and on absenteeism (with police checks on shoppers and patrons of hairdressing salons to see which of the customers who were there should have been working at the time), but only the first faltering steps towards economic reform were taken.

Andropov's style as General Secretary was, nevertheless, brisk and business-like. He observed in one of his earliest speeches that "a disposition to action rather than rhetoric" was what was now needed in the Soviet Union. He was cautiously putting economic reform on the political agenda when he spoke in one of his first utterances as General Secretary of the need to move in a practical way to a decision on how to extend the independence of associations and enterprises. A number of "experiments" were conducted, whereby in selected industries, enterprises were given expanded rights and were less subject to the detailed tutelage of their ministries. Although Andropov did not use the word "reform," it is probable that the experiments were intended to show that reform was necessary, for there is an artificiality in the Soviet context in choosing certain enterprises, under the jurisdiction of particular ministries, and giving them rights not accorded to others. In one way or another, they become the object of special treatment and their performance can be only a very inadequate guide to the likely effects of comprehensive reform of the entire economic system. As it was, the ministries did not play by the rules and indulged in the petty tutelage they were now supposed to eschew. Nevertheless, the very fact that these enterprises were under special scrutiny no doubt helped to produce the higher rates of growth of labour productivity and of contract fulfilment, which were reported, so that the experiment could be judged a "qualified success." That the judgment was made in August 1984, less than eight months after five ministries had been put on such an experimental footing, suggests that it was intended from the outset by Andropov—and by Gorbachev, whose responsibilities, under Andropov, were extended to embrace not just the agricultural sector of the economy but the economy as a whole—to provide support for those who wished to move in the direction of reform. . . .

Andropov made a substantial start to changing the composition of the Soviet leadership—more changes than were, in fact, made during the first fifteen months of any previous General Secretaryship. (This was, however, a short-lived record. By the end of his first year Gorbachev had secured more personnel change at the top.) Immediately after Andropov's death, the top leadership team as a whole—the full and candidate members of the Politburo and the Secretaries of the Central Committee—consisted of twenty-three people. More than a sixth of them (Vitaliy Vorotnikov, Nikolay Ryzhkov, Egor Ligachev and Viktor Chebrikov) were brought into it during Andropov's brief tenure of the General Secretaryship, while a quarter of the members of the Politburo (Geydar Aliev, Mikhail Solomentsev and Vorotnikov) received their promotions to full membership during Andropov's fifteen months at the helm. In addition, over a fifth of the Moscow-based members of the Council of Ministers of the USSR, more than a fifth of the regional party secretaries and over a third of the heads of departments in the Central Committee were replaced. Andropov began a process of rejuvenation which has continued under Gorbachev. . . .

The brief Andropov era (which came to an end in February 1984) was an ambiguous one. There was little sign of the cultural liberalisation which was to be such an important feature of Gorbachev's General Secretaryship in the second half of the 1980s, but social scientists with ideas for reform were given more encouragement than they had received in Brezhnev's time, not least from

Gorbachev with his extended responsibilities for the economy within the Secretariat. It is clear, however, that Andropov's combination of discipline and more open mind about reform evoked a far from uniform response within the higher echelons of the party and state. In addition, his rejuvenation policy (in contrast with Brezhnev's "stability of cadres") posed a threat to many members of the Soviet political elite. Thus, though that body was divided and though the choice of Chernenko was greeted with something close to despair by many party intellectuals, the Politburo turned to the seventy-two-year-old Chernenko rather than to Gorbachev (then still a month short of his fifty-third birthday and, therefore, almost outrageously young in the eyes of those who had grown old in office under Brezhnev and had been lucky enough to live longer than Andropov).

Chernenko was at the time of Andropov's death the most senior of the senior secretaries in the sense that he had served for longest as a joint member of the Politburo and the Secretariat of the Central Committee. It was he, moreover, who had chaired Politburo meetings during Andropov's long absences through illness. When it became clear that the real choice facing the Soviet selectorate was between this elderly protégé of Brezhnev and the much younger Gorbachev, who had been far closer to Andropov and who might at the very least be expected to pick up Andropov's new broom and wield it with still greater vigour, there was a majority in the Politburo and within the Central Committee as a whole ready to settle for a quieter life.

With Chernenko's election to the General Secretaryship, only two other senior secretaries were left in the Politburo, Gorbachev and [Grigory] Romanov. Until the number of departments of the Central Committee was drastically reduced in late 1988, the greatest power (after that which was concentrated in the General Secretary's hands) devolved to the senior secretaries, who each supervised the work of several of the departments (more than twenty in number) of the Central Committee. With only two senior secretaries, the supervisory responsibilities at the disposal of Gorbachev and Romanov were unusually great. Gorbachev had, however, enjoyed a sufficiently strong position in the Politburo under Andropov that on the latter's death he was able to strike a much better deal than Romanov. As a price for not attempting to marshall all the forces unhappy about Chernenko's elevation to the party leadership, he was accorded an extraordinary range of supervisory responsibilities within the Secretariat, so that these now embraced foreign policy as well as party appointments, the economy and ideology. He became, quite clearly, the *de facto* second secretary and the "heir apparent" to Chernenko. That he was in the number two slot gained in significance from the fact that Chernenko was the first person ever elected party leader when already a septuagenarian. . . .

There is no doubt that Gorbachev was the logical successor to Chernenko, not only in terms of his ability but on account of the functions he had already been performing during Chernenko's period as top leader. Gorbachev, as the "second secretary," was in day-to-day charge of the running of the Secretariat. This was made abundantly clear by Gromyko in his speech recommending Gorbachev for the General Secretaryship to the Central Committee plenum which met after Chernenko's death. "He led the Secretariat," said Gromyko, who went on to provide the even more important information that Gorbachev had chaired the Politburo on those occasions when Chernenko was too ill to attend: "He also took the chair at sessions of the Politburo in the absence of Konstantin Ustinovich Chernenko." Gromyko added that, in his capacity as chairman, Gorbachev had performed "brilliantly."

All that notwithstanding, enough evidence has emerged since then for it to be now clear that Gorbachev's elevation to the General Secretaryship in succession to Chernenko did not go uncontested. Those who tried to block Gorbachev's path were no doubt worried about the prospects of their holding on to their own posts should he become leader. They may also have had at least an uneasy awareness of how radical a reformer, by the standards of previous General Secretaries, he might be. They were given notice of it in an important speech which Gorbachev delivered in December 1984, that set out quite a number of the reformist themes he was later to invest with greater substance.

Two of the main sources of evidence of division in the ranks of the leadership over Gorbachev's succession come from different points of the Soviet political spectrum. The first to cast light on it was the playwright Mikhail Shatrov, an ardent anti-Stalinist and a supporter of Gorbachev and of radical reform. Writing in the Soviet weekly journal, *Ogonek*, in 1987, Shatrov explicitly stated that from the point of view of the interests of socialism there was no alternative to the choice of Gorbachev and acceptance of the idea of "the necessity and possibility of democratic renewal of the country," but that in real life there *had* been a choice. Without actually naming Viktor Grishin, who at that time was seventy years of age and the First Secretary of the Moscow Party organisation, and one of the longest-standing members of the Politburo, Shatrov made it clear to the readers of *Ogonek* that it was Grishin who was being put forward as the alternative to Gorbachev.

If, as seems likely, Shatrov was right that the candidacy of Grishin was being promoted, then the idea of someone who was not already a senior secretary becoming General Secretary could at least be entertained by some members of the Politburo. The fact, however, that Grishin's bid for the leadership failed served only to underline the advantages which accrue to a senior secretary—and especially to one already supervising party cadres. The only other senior secretary, Romanov, did not control nearly as much of the apparatus or have as many friends as Gorbachev and, given that he was poles apart from Gorbachev both temperamentally and in political outlook, it was in his interests to support the distinctly conservative and complacent Grishin, under whom the balance of power within the Secretariat could have been tilted away from Gorbachev and towards Romanov and have put the latter in line for the succession to Grishin.

In an interview with a Finnish journal (which he subsequently partly disowned after it had become a source of embarrassment to him), Shatrov was quoted as saying that the Politburo was actually evenly split between Gorbachev and Grishin and that only the casting vote of Andrey Gromyko, who was in the chair, gave victory to Gorbachev. However, while it seems certain that Grishin had his supporters, there is not yet enough corroborating evidence to confirm that the contest was quite as close as Shatrov is cited as suggesting. His reported statement that initially "the Politburo voted evenly 4–4" for Gorbachev and Grishin cannot, however, be ruled out of court, since of the ten voting members of the Politburo, two were abroad at the time of Chernenko's death. Less than a day elapsed between Chernenko's death at twenty past seven in the evening (Moscow time) on 10 March and Gorbachev's election by the Central Committee as the new General Secretary late the following afternoon. This was a much faster election of a new leader than occurred after the death of either Brezhnev or Andropov.

The two Politburo members who were out of the country when Chernenko died were Vladimir Shcherbitsky and Vitaliy Vorotnikov. Shcherbitsky was in the United States and Vorotnikov in Yugoslavia; both of them returned to Moscow only on 11 March, almost certainly too late to take part in the pre-selection of Gorbachev by the Politburo which preceded his election by the hurriedly-convened Central Committee plenum. . . .

. . . Gromyko, . . . , whose speech proposing Gorbachev to the Central Committee on 11 March was a panegyric entirely out of keeping with his normal low-key style, does seem to have been a crucial political actor. Apart from him, Gorbachev's supporters (if the Politburo members in Moscow at the time really did split 4–4) would be Aliev and Solomentsev, neither of whom could be regarded as more than conditional allies. . . .

Shatrov's testimony of division in the leadership over the election of Gorbachev received corroboration in 1988 from a very different source, Egor Ligachev . . . , in the course of his speech in July 1988 to the Nineteenth Conference of the Soviet Communist Party. . . . Ligachev observed that "absolutely different decisions" could have been taken at the March 1985 plenum and that there had been "a real danger" of that. In a passage from his speech which was omitted from *Pravda* he said: "And others would be sitting here, if there could be a party conference at all. And I think, what would have become of the country afterwards?" The reason why "the only correct decision"—that is, the election of Gorbachev—was taken at the March plenum, according to Ligachev, was "the positions firmly adopted by members of the Politburo Chebrikov, Solomentsev and Gromyko and a large group of *obkom* [regional party committee] first secretaries." Ligachev's reference to those names in particular had significance for the politics of 1988 as well as for 1985. None of the three people he mentioned could be regarded as radical reformers, any more than he himself could, and he was attempting to remind Gorbachev, and to tell the entire party, that Gorbachev was holding his present high office only because these sound and solid party veterans had put him there. As a tactic, it did not have quite the effect Ligachev desired, for within three months he himself had been demoted, Gromyko and Solomentsev had been pensioned off and Chebrikov had been moved out of the chairmanship of the KGB.

In the present context, however, the point is that all four men were allies of Gorbachev at the time of his succession, albeit conditional allies. They were—as was Gorbachev himself—people who had owed at least some of their advancement, whether in rank or in the expansion of their power and functions, to Andropov. To the very limited extent to which they constituted a group, it was an "Andropov group" rather than a "Gorbachev group" or—if one includes (as Ligachev, for his own reasons, did not) more enthusiastic Gorbachev supporters such as Eduard Shevardnadze, at that time a candidate member of the Politburo—they may be seen as a coalition for which the term "Andropov–Gorbachev group" would not be out of place. . . .

It is reasonably clear that Gorbachev did not come to the leadership with a complete blueprint for economic and political reform. Since one of his more important characteristics is a relatively open mind, his views have naturally developed both in the light of advice he has received since becoming General Secretary and on the basis of the concrete experiences—some of them harsh, such as the Chernobyl nuclear power plant disaster—of Soviet society over the past few years. Yet Gorbachev was already familiar with the diagnoses of such serious Soviet reformers as Tat'yana Zaslavskaya and Abel Aganbegyan before he became General Secretary and had accepted much from their critiques of what was wrong with the Soviet economy and society. It is "not accidental" (to use a popular Soviet phrase) that both Aganbegyan and Zaslavskaya moved from Novosibirsk to Moscow after Gorbachev became party leader.

In a speech delivered in December 1984, . . . many of Gorbachev's reformist ideas and some of the key concepts of the Gorbachev era were given an early airing. It is true that he did not use the actual word "reform," but other terms and notions which were to become familiar once he had established himself as General Secretary were there already—not only *uskorenie* [acceleration] but "the human factor," stress on the variety of interests to be found within Soviet society, *perestroika*, *glasnost'*, self-management (*samoupravlenie*) and "commodity–money relations," to name but a few.

Indeed, a careful reading of that speech, published three months before Gorbachev became General Secretary, suggests that he already saw the need for far-reaching economic reform and that he was aware of the necessity for political change. Explicit support for "reform" and for "market relations" did not come until 1986, for both concepts had been taboo in leadership circles since Kosygin's relatively modest reform launched in 1965 was watered down and finally jettisoned in 1968. The conjunction in that year of political and economic reform in Czechoslovakia frightened Soviet conservatives into condemning themselves and their country to an "era of stagnation," as the years of Brezhnev's ascendancy have come to be known in the Gorbachev period. . . .

The December 1984 speech also marked a turning-point in the public elaboration of Gorbachev's view of *glasnost'*. As early as 1974, he had used the term *glasnost'*, but then only in the limited sense of giving publicity to advanced methods of agricultural work. By 1978 he was using the term in the context of the need to expand socialist democracy and take account of public opinion. But it was in his programmatic speech three months before Chernenko's death that he gave the most central place to *glasnost'* that it was to occupy until he delivered the Central Committee's Political Report to the Twenty-Seventh Party Congress in February 1986. By December 1984, *glasnost'* was, for Gorbachev, "an inalienable aspect of socialist democracy and a norm for all social life." Giving broad, prompt and open information was, he said, testimony to faith in people and indicated respect for their intellect and feelings. He linked *glasnost'* in the work of party and state organs to the struggle against bureaucratism, to more thoughtful decision-making in party and state bodies and to the supervision of the fulfilment of decisions.

It is quite true that Gorbachev's reform proposals became more specific and far-reaching in each successive year between

1985 and 1988 and that his political rhetoric also became more radical as time went on. But it is a mistake to think that he had no interest in economic reform, *glasnost'* or democratisation until 1986 or 1987. It is of interest that in some respects Gorbachev's speech three months before Chernenko died is even more reformist in tone than his speeches in 1985 after he became General Secretary in March. The explanation is straightforward. Given Chernenko's declining health, Gorbachev in December 1984 was relatively free to set his own agenda when speaking primarily for himself. Once he became General Secretary, every policy pronouncement was going to be regarded as committing the leadership collectively, and even most of Gorbachev's allies in the leadership in March 1985, not to speak of his opponents (who could not be removed at once), had less radical conceptions than he of the general direction in which the Soviet Union should be moving.

Thus, while Soviet policies in recent years have changed partly as the ideas of Gorbachev and others in the Politburo have evolved, they have developed still more strikingly in pace with Gorbachev's consolidation of his power within the leadership. The first regular plenum of the Gorbachev era—that of April 1985, which is hailed in the Soviet Union as the beginning of *perestroika* and of a change of course—saw promotions of three people to full membership of the Politburo, all men who had been brought into the leadership by Andropov and who had supported Gorbachev the month before: Ligachev, Ryzhkov and Chebrikov. This did not, however, as was to become clearer later in the cases of Ligachev and Chebrikov, mean that they had as bold a vision of the kind of changes needed as had Gorbachev. At the same plenum, Marshal Sokolov, who had succeeded Ustinov as Minister of Defence the previous December, attained candidate membership of the Politburo, and Viktor Nikonov, who had been a deputy Minister of Agriculture of the USSR and then Minister of Agriculture for the Russian republic while Gorbachev was overseeing agriculture in the Secretariat, became a Secretary of the Central Committee with responsibility for agriculture. In view of his speciality, he could have entered the leadership only with Gorbachev's blessing and as his ally, though neither then nor later was he to show much sign of being as imaginative a reformer.

Other important changes of personnel and function followed fast. At the beginning of July 1985 Romanov paid the price for trying to stop Gorbachev becoming General Secretary and was unceremoniously pensioned off even though he was still below the average age of the Politburo. At the same time, the elevation of Eduard Shevardnadze to full Politburo membership brought Gorbachev his first genuinely like-minded colleague on that body. By securing for Shevardnadze the post of Foreign Minister, Gorbachev made a very shrewd move. He assured his own leading role in foreign policy by choosing someone with less experience of international affairs than he possessed himself, one with whom he could co-operate closely and someone who, once he had learned the job, was to demonstrate great political and diplomatic skill and make his own distinctive contribution to policy innovation and to the Soviet Union's much enhanced international image by the later 1980s. The same plenum saw the elevation to the Secretariat of the Central Committee of Lev Zaykov, whose further promotion was to be fast but whose political position has been more cautious than that of Gorbachev himself. The July plenum also brought the election of another new Central Committee Secretary, Boris Yeltsin, ironically (in view of their later feud) on the recommendation of Ligachev, though he must have been known also to Ryzhkov from the time when they both worked in Sverdlovsk and Yeltsin presumably received the latter's support too. . . .

. . . Gorbachev's Political Report to the Twenty-Seventh Party Congress (which, of course, required prior Politburo and Central Committee approval) became the most interesting and forthright since Khrushchev's report at the Twenty-Second Congress in 1961. . . . One speech which caused a stir and which foreshadowed some changes which were to be made after its author had already fallen from political favour was that by Yeltsin, who criticised the fact that the Central Committee apparatus had gradually come to resemble the organisation of Gosplan and of the Council of Ministers. In calling for the restructuring of the Central Committee's economic departments, he may well have been in tune with ideas of Gorbachev which the latter was not yet strong enough to carry through the Politburo, since such an administrative reform did indeed take place in 1988. In what, at least in retrospect, can be seen as the first sign of a rift between Yeltsin and Ligachev, the Moscow Party First Secretary also expressed discontent in his Congress speech with the performance of the Department of Organisational–Party Work. Since the senior Secretary supervising that department was none other than Ligachev, the implied rebuke from a more junior member of the leadership team at such a major party forum could have done nothing to endear Yeltsin to Ligachev. . . .

   . . . The most significant changes, . . . which notably strengthened Gorbachev's position, were in the Secretariat. No fewer than five new Secretaries were elected, all of them potential allies of Gorbachev and two of them particularly close to him. The five included the first woman in the top leadership team since 1961 when Ekaterina Furtseva lost the Politburo membership she had held for the previous four years. Aleksandra Biryukova, after seventeen years as a Secretary of the Central Council of Trade Unions, was one of the few women in 1986 in a senior enough political position to be considered for a Secretaryship of the party Central Committee, given both the conventions about career profile and the sense of hierarchy which have governed entry to the top leadership team. . . .

The two most valuable elevations to the Secretariat from Gorbachev's standpoint were, however, those of Aleksandr Yakovlev and Georgiy Razumovsky. There is no reason to suppose that Gorbachev had known Yakovlev before he visited Canada in 1983, where Yakovlev had been serving as Soviet Ambassador for ten years after losing favour as acting head of the Department of Propaganda of the Central Committee for showing excessive zeal in criticising Russian nationalism. But Gorbachev and Yakovlev formed both a personal and political friendship from that time onwards, and very shortly after Gorbachev's return home Yakovlev was recalled to Moscow and given the influential position of Director of the Institute of World Economy and International Relations (IMEMO), from which he moved in 1985 to the headship of his old Central Committee department, that of Propaganda. Both then, and, still more, once he gained increasing authority in the Secretariat, Yakovlev has been a key supporter of the extension of *glasnost'* in Soviet cultural and political life, and a convinced and influential reformer. . . .

By the time he had completed one year as General Secretary, Gorbachev had presided over by far the largest turnover in the top leadership team ever to be affected so early in the incumbency of any Soviet party leader. Not all of the people promoted were as prepared for far-reaching reform as he himself was, but in the Secretariat—to a greater extent than in the Politburo—he had already begun to build real support. The actual turnover figures are remarkable. In March 1986, as compared with March 1985, five out of the twelve full members of the Politburo were new and five out of the seven candidate members had not been there a year earlier. Of the seven Secretaries of the Central Committee not holding either full or candidate membership of the Politburo, no fewer than six were newcomers, and if the Secretariat is considered as a whole, seven out of eleven had not been there a year before. This was a striking break with the pattern of substantial continuity of Politburo and Secretariat membership which had marked the earliest period of other General Secretaryships, and it helped to pave the way for the more substantial policy innovation which was to follow. . . .

The plenary session of the Central Committee which was eventually held in January 1987 should, in fact, have taken place in 1986. But the radicalism of the reform proposals Gorbachev wished to bring to it led to fierce resistance and argument. The second of the two plenums actually convened in 1986 was held in June, and there should be a gap of no more than six months between plenary sessions. Gorbachev himself noted in February 1987, in a speech to the Eighteenth Congress of the Soviet Trade Unions, that the plenum which took place in January had been postponed three times. He also hailed it as a historic turning-point. "After the January 1987 Plenary Meeting of the CPSU Central Committee," Gorbachev observed, "it was no longer possible to deny that this country has actually entered a period of bold and far-reaching reforms."

Among the most important elements in Gorbachev's speech was his emphasis on the need for competitive elections within the party and for deputies to soviets. The following month, addressing leading figures in the mass media, he said: "The main idea of the January plenum . . . is the development of democracy. To develop democracy in the economy, in politics and in the party itself, but on a socialist basis." At the January plenum, Gorbachev observed that the promotion of non-party members to leading positions was an "important aspect of the democratisation of public life." He also made his most forthright reference thus far to the influence of the dead hand of Stalinism on Soviet ideology when he said that Soviet socialist theory had remained largely fixed "at the level of the 1930s and 1940s" when "vigorous debates and creative ideas disappeared . . . while authoritarian evaluations and opinions became unquestionable truths." . . .

In his speech to the June plenum Gorbachev took up the theme of "radical reform" of the Soviet economic system in more detail than ever before, and the resolutions adopted by the plenum finally put a reform which would include a significant market element (somewhat akin to the first stage of the Hungarian economic reform) firmly on the political agenda. Gorbachev criticised by name a number of officials responsible for economic policy, including Nikolay Talyzin, the Chairman of Gosplan [the State Planning Commission], who in 1988 was to lose his chairmanship of that body, though he kept the candidate membership of the Politburo he had been accorded in 1985. Referring to the view of "some comrades" that since *perestroika* had to be a long-term policy, it could be "implemented at a leisurely pace" and "without troubling oneself much at all," Gorbachev observed: "We have lost years, even decades that way." He also defended the collective and family contract system in agriculture against its critics.

Gorbachev gave his most sombre assessment thus far of Soviet economic failure in the late 1970s and the 1980s, observing that "the gulf in comparison with the most developed countries began to widen and not in our favour." He attacked the rigid centralism of the ministerial system and justified different forms of ownership—above all, co-operative ownership—while denying that any of this meant a departure from the principles of socialism. Instead, he emphasised the extent to which ideas about socialism and the economy were constantly developing and being enriched by taking account of historical experience and objective conditions. Gorbachev justified the new Enterprise Law, intended to devolve far greater powers to the economic enterprise, and called for a "radical reform of the price mechanism" which would, among other things, expand the use of contractually agreed, as distinct from centrally fixed, prices.

He faced up to the fact that some factories would have to close if the economic reform were to be taken seriously and that workers' security in the particular job they were then doing would have to go. At the same time he emphasised the "constitutional right to work," thus indicating redeployment rather than unemployment. The essence of the economic reform announced by Gorbachev was rather simple: it was to start taking seriously the law of supply and demand. One of the major aims of the reform would be to expand the ways in which production in both state and new co-operative enterprises would be determined by consumer needs and choice, since "simply filling warehouses" with goods no one wanted to buy was "not only extravagant but also absurd" and it was "better to close down such production."

The June 1987 plenum produced a commitment to more radical economic reform than the party had accepted hitherto, but bold speeches and good resolutions could not by themselves facilitate the enormously difficult task of implementing the reform in practice. How difficult the implementation would be (with even convinced economic reformers worried about the social and political consequences of removing the enormous food subsidies in a move towards market prices) was still clearer by the end of 1988.

The plenum was also the occasion of further significant personnel changes, including the promotion of no fewer than three people to the ranks of the senior secretaries. The three thus elevated were Yakovlev, Nikonov and Slyun'kov, the first two Gorbachev loyalists, though only Yakovlev of the trio could be seen as a key figure in attempting to push political and economic reform into hitherto unexplored terrain. . . .

It would obviously be wrong to see everything innovative that happened in the Soviet Union during the first years of the Gorbachev era—even in 1987 and 1988, by which time Gorbachev's position within the leadership was stronger than it had been at the outset of his General Secretaryship—as a result of the conscious choice either of the individual top leader or of the top leadership team collectively. The leadership decision, however, to embrace the idea of political and economic reform and to promote *glasnost'* made a huge contribution to changing the political climate. Such a new orientation opened up space for cultural and political initiatives which were soon forthcoming, not least from the creative intelligentsia, many of whose representatives were more than ready to break the bonds of censorship and self-censorship.

Perestroika has also, of course, had unintended consequences as well as intended and partly intended ones. The national stirrings—and especially those which erupted in early 1988 into violence between Azeris and Armenians over the disputed territory of Nagorno-Karabakh—fall most clearly into the former category. What is noteworthy in the present context, however, is that faced with national[ity] problems (themselves not new but a matter of long-standing and long-suppressed grievances and tensions coming into the open) and with widespread domestic concern over stagnating (or even deteriorating) living standards, the Soviet leadership did not retreat into the familiar, heavily authoritarian methods of managing national[ity], economic and political relations. Instead, Gorbachev and the more reform-minded among his colleagues in the Politburo attempted to keep up the momentum of change and to channel even the "contradictions" into constructive reform.

Whether the leadership could, by choosing the reformist path, continue to preside over not-so-gradual change of the Soviet system or whether, in the face of difficulties, it (or its successors) would either resort to a resassertion of conservative Communist values or lose control and be faced by the disintegration, rather than reform, of the Soviet state had by the end of 1988 become live issues. That such questions could be raised was an indication of the seriousness of the change in policy and in Soviet society which had already taken place.

Amid much that was unfamiliar, there were, however, familiar features of Soviet leadership politics at work. Like all Soviet General Secretaries before him except Chernenko, whose timespan of thirteen months at the top was the shortest on record, Gorbachev had used his influence over appointments to strengthen his power. His impact on policy and his support within the leadership were substantially greater in his fourth year than in his first year as party leader, social ferment and unresolved problems notwithstanding. To a certain extent Gorbachev was using traditional methods to bring about far from traditional policy outcomes. This was a demonstration once again that substantially greater political resources are concentrated in the office of General Secretary than in any other within the Soviet system. Previously the powers of that office had been used much more often to frustrate than to facilitate the endeavours of Soviet reformers, but in the second half of the nineteen-eighties the reformist disposition, political skill and determination of a Gorbachev in the top leadership post constituted a necessary, albeit not a sufficient, condition (since there were other stimuli and social forces at work) for the most dramatic policy innovation to take place so early in any General Secretaryship in Soviet history. In the past the concentration of great power in the hands of the Soviet leader has been at worst a catastrophe and at best a mixed blessing, but the strengthening of Gorbachev's position was welcomed by a majority of active supporters of *perestroika*. The consolidation of his power within the structures of the party and state gave hope to those who preferred reform to reaction and evolutionary change to destabilisation.

Mikhail Gorbachev selling *perestroika* to the public, May 1985. (ITAR-TASS/SOVFOTO)

PART

II Perestroika, 1985–1988

Mikhail Gorbachev

The Revolutionary Promise

A year and a half after he assumed power and launched perestroika, Gorbachev took a long vacation to rethink the past, present, and future of the Soviet Union. Perestroika, he asserted in the book he wrote during this time of reflection, was a kind of revolution. It aimed to recapture the original spirit of the Revolution of 1917 and marry socialism with democracy in order to revitalize Soviet society after the "era of stagnation" under Brezhnev. Gorbachev clung to this vision to the very end of his leadership of the Soviet Union in 1991.

From Mikhail Gorbachev, *Perestroika: New Thinking for Our Country and the World*, pp. 17–19, 21–22, 24, 33, 36–38, 49–51, 54, 56, 81–86, 253–254. Copyright © 1987 by Harper & Row. Reprinted by permission of the publisher.

Perestroika is no whim on the part of some ambitious individuals or a group of leaders. If it were, no exhortations, plenary meetings or even a party congress could have rallied the people to the work which we are now doing and which involves more and more Soviet people each day.

Perestroika is an urgent necessity arising from the profound processes of development in our socialist society. This society is ripe for change. It has long been yearning for it. Any delay in beginning perestroika could have led to an exacerbated internal situation in the near future, which, to put it bluntly, would have been fraught with serious social, economic and political crises. . . .

. . . In the latter half of the seventies—something happened that was at first sight inexplicable. The country began to lose momentum. Economic failures became more frequent. Difficulties began to accumulate and deteriorate, and unresolved problems to multiply. Elements of what we call stagnation and other phenomena alien to socialism began to appear in the life of society. A kind of "braking mechanism" affecting social and economic development formed. And all this happened at a time when scientific and technological revolution opened up new prospects for economic and social progress.

Something strange was taking place: the huge fly-wheel of a powerful machine was revolving, while either transmission from it to work places was skidding or drive belts were too loose.

Analyzing the situation, we first discovered a slowing economic growth. In the last fifteen years the national income growth rates had declined by more than a half and by the beginning of the eighties had fallen to a level close to economic stagnation. A country that was once quickly closing on the world's advanced nations began to lose one position after another. Moreover, the gap in the efficiency of production, quality of products, scientific and technological development, the production of advanced technology and the use of advanced techniques began to widen, and not to our advantage. . . .

An absurd situation was developing. The Soviet Union, the world's biggest producer of steel, raw materials, fuel and energy, has shortfalls in them due to wasteful or inefficient use. One of the biggest producers of grain for food, it nevertheless has to buy millions of tons of grain a year for fodder. We have the largest number of doctors and hospital beds per thousand of the population and, at the same time, there are glaring shortcomings in our health services. Our rockets can find Halley's comet and fly to Venus with amazing accuracy, but side by side with these scientific and technological triumphs is an obvious lack of efficiency in using scientific achievements for economic needs, and many Soviet household appliances are of poor quality.

This, unfortunately, is not all. A gradual erosion of the ideological and moral values of our people began.

It was obvious to everyone that the growth rates were sharply dropping and that the entire mechanism of quality control was not working properly; there was a lack of receptivity to the advances in science and technology; the improvement in living standards was slowing down and there were difficulties in the supply of foodstuffs, housing, consumer goods and services.

On the ideological plane as well, the braking mechanism brought about ever greater resistance to the attempts to constructively scrutinize the problems that were emerging and to the new ideas. Propaganda of success—real or imagined—was gaining the upper hand. Eulogizing and servility were encouraged; the needs and opinions of ordinary working people, of the public at large, were ignored. In the social sciences scholastic theorization was encouraged and developed, but creative thinking was driven out from the social sciences, and superfluous and voluntarist assessments and judgments were declared indisputable truths. Scientific, theoretical and other discussions, which are indispensable for the development of thought and for creative endeavor, were emasculated. Similar negative tendencies also affected culture, the arts and journalism, as well as the teaching process and medicine, where mediocrity, formalism and loud eulogizing surfaced, too.

The presentation of a "problem-free" reality backfired: a breach had formed between word and deed, which bred public passivity and disbelief in the slogans being proclaimed. It was only natural that this situation resulted in a credibility gap: everything that was proclaimed from the rostrums and printed in newspapers and textbooks was put in question. Decay began in public morals; the great feeling of solidarity with each other that was forged during the heroic times of the Revolution, the first five-year plans, the Great Patriotic War and postwar rehabilitation was weakening; alcoholism, drug addiction and crime were growing; and the penetration of the stereotypes of mass culture alien to us, which bred vulgarity and low tastes and brought about ideological barrenness increased. . . .

An unbiased and honest approach led us to the only logical conclusion that the country was verging on crisis. This conclusion was announced at the April 1985 Plenary Meeting of the Central Committee, which inaugurated the new strategy of perestroika and formulated its basic principles.

I would like to emphasize here that this analysis began a long time before the April Plenary Meeting and that therefore its conclusions were well thought out. It was not something out of the blue, but a balanced judgment. It would be a mistake to think that a month after the Central Committee Plenary Meeting in March 1985, which elected me General Secretary, there suddenly appeared a group of people who understood everything and knew everything, and that these people gave clear-cut answers to all questions. Such miracles do not exist.

The need for change was brewing not only in the material sphere of life but also in public consciousness. People who had practical experience, a sense of justice and commitment to the ideals of Bolshevism criticized the established practice of doing things and noted with anxiety the symptoms of moral degradation and erosion of revolutionary ideals and socialist values. . . .

. . . Not only theory but the reality of the processes under way made us embark on the program for all-round democratic changes in public life which we presented at the January 1987 Plenary Meeting of the CPSU Central Committee.

The Plenary Meeting encouraged extensive efforts to strengthen the democratic basis of Soviet society, to develop self-government and extend glasnost, that is openness, in the entire management network. We see now how stimulating that impulse was for the nation. Democratic changes have been taking place at every work collective, at every state and public organization, and within the Party. More glasnost, genuine control from "below," and greater initiative and enterprise at work are now part and parcel of our life.

The democratic process has promoted the entire perestroika, elevated its goals and has made our society understand its problems better. This process allowed us to take a wider view of economic issues, and put forward a program for radical economic reforms. The economic mechanism now well fits the overall system of social management which is based on renewed democratic principles.

We did this work at the June 1987 Plenary Meeting of the CPSU Central Committee, which adopted "Fundamentals of Radical Restructuring of Economic Management." Perhaps this is the most important and most radical program for economic reform our country has had since Lenin introduced his New Economic Policy in 1921. The present economic reform envisages that the emphasis will be shifted from primarily administrative to primarily economic management methods at every level, and calls for extensive democratization of management, and the overall activization of the human factor.

The reform is based on dramatically increased independence of enterprises and associations, their transition to full self-accounting and self-financing, and granting all appropriate rights to work collectives. They will now be fully responsible for efficient management and end results. A collective's profits will be directly proportionate to its efficiency. . . .

Perestroika is closely connected with socialism as a system. That side of the matter is being widely discussed, especially abroad, and our talk about perestroika won't be entirely clear if we don't touch upon that aspect.

Does perestroika mean that we are giving up socialism or at least some of its foundations? Some ask this question with hope, others with misgiving.

There are people in the West who would like to tell us that socialism is in a deep crisis and has brought our society to a dead end. That's how they interpret our critical analysis of the situation at the end of the seventies and beginning of the eighties. We have only one way out, they say: to adopt capitalist methods of economic management and social patterns, to drift toward capitalism.

Glasnost: new papers spring up, 1987–1990. (ITAR-TASS/SOVFOTO)

They tell us that nothing will come of perestroika within the framework of our system. They say we should change this system and borrow from the experience of another socio–political system. To this they add that, if the Soviet Union takes this path and gives up its socialist choice, close links with the West will supposedly become possible. They go so far as to claim that the October 1917 Revolution was a mistake which almost completely cut off our country from world social progress.

To put an end to all the rumors and speculations that abound in the West about this, I would like to point out once again that we are conducting all our reforms in accordance with the socialist choice. We are looking within socialism, rather than outside it, for the answers to all the questions that arise. We assess our successes and errors alike by socialist standards. Those who hope that we shall move away from the socialist path will be greatly disappointed. Every part of our program of perestroika—and the program as a whole, for that matter—is fully based on the principle of more socialism and more democracy. . . .

We will proceed toward better socialism rather than away from it. We are saying this honestly, without trying to fool our own people or the world. Any hopes that we will begin to build a different, nonsocialist society and go over to the other camp are unrealistic and futile. Those in the West who expect us to give up socialism will be disappointed. It is high time they understood this, and, even more importantly, proceeded from that understanding in practical relations with the Soviet Union.

Speaking so, I would like to be clearly understood that though we, the Soviet people, are for socialism (I have explained above why), we are not imposing our views on anyone. Let everyone make his own choice; history will put everything in its place. Today, as I told a group of American public figures (Cyrus Vance, Henry Kissinger, and others), we feel clearly as never before that, due to the socialist system and the planned economy, changes in our structural policy come much easier for us than they would in conditions of private enterprise, although we do have difficulties of our own, too.

We want more socialism and, therefore, more democracy.

As we understand it, the difficulties and problems of the seventies and eighties did not signify some kind of crisis for socialism as a social and political system, but rather were the result of insufficient consistency in applying the principles of socialism, of departures from them and even distortions of them, and of continued adherence to the methods and forms of social management that arose under specific historical conditions in the early stages of socialist development.

On the contrary, socialism as a young social system, as a way of living, possesses vast possibilities for self-development and self-perfection that have yet to be revealed, and for the solution of the fundamental problems of contemporary society's scientific, technological, economic, cultural and intellectual progress, and of the development of the human individual. This is indicated by the path our country has taken since October 1917, a path that has been full of innumerable difficulties, drama and strenuous work, and at the same time full of great triumphs and accomplishments. . . .

Perestroika is a word with many meanings. But if we are to choose from its many possible synonyms the key one which expresses its essence most accurately, then we can say thus: perestroika is a revolution. A decisive acceleration of the socio-economic and cultural development of Soviet society which involves radical changes on the way to a qualitatively new state is undoubtedly a revolutionary task.

I think we had every reason to declare at the January 1987 Plenary Meeting: in its essence, in its Bolshevik daring and in its humane social thrust the present course is a direct sequel to the great accomplishments started by the Leninist Party in the October days of 1917. And not merely a sequel, but an extension and a development of the main ideas of the Revolution. We must impart new dynamism to the October Revolution's historical impulse and further advance all that was commenced by it in our society.

Of course, we don't equate perestroika with the October Revolution, an event that was a turning point in the thousand-year history of our state and is unparalleled in force of impact on mankind's development. And yet, why in the seventieth year of the October Revolution do we speak of a new revolution?

Historical analogy may be helpful in answering this question. Lenin once noted that in the country of the classical bourgeois revolution, France, after its Great Revolution of 1789–93, it took another three revolutions (1830, 1848 and 1871) to carry through its aims. The same applies to Britain where, after the Cromwellian Revolution of 1649, came the "glorious" Revolution of 1688–9, and then the 1832 reform was necessary to finally establish the new class in power—the bourgeoisie. In Germany there were two bourgeois-democratic revolutions (1848 and 1918), and in between them the drastic reforms of the 1860s, which Bismarck carried out by "iron and blood."

"Never in history," wrote Lenin, "has there been a revolution in which it was possible to lay down one's arms and rest on one's laurels after the victory." Why then should not socialism, called upon to carry out even more profound socio-political and cultural changes in society's development than capitalism, go through several revolutionary stages in order to reveal its full potential and finally crystalize as a radically new formation? . . .

Perestroika is a revolutionary process, for it is a jump forward in the development of socialism, in the realization of its essential characteristics. From the outset we realized that we had no time to lose. It is very important not to stay too long on the starting line, to overcome the lag, to get out of the quagmire of conservatism, and to break the inertia of stagnation. This cannot be done in an evolutionary way, by timid, creeping reforms. We simply have no right to relax, even for a day. On the contrary, day after day we must add to our effort, build up its pace and its intensity. We must withstand the stresses, what cosmonauts call big overloads, at the initial phase of restructuring. . . .

Like revolution, perestroika is not something you can toy with. You must carry things through to the end and make progress every day so that the masses can feel its results and the process can continue gathering momentum both materially and spiritually.

When we call our measures revolutionary, we mean that they are far-reaching, radical and uncompromising, and affect the whole of society from top to bottom. They affect all spheres of life and do so in a comprehensive way. This is not putting new paint on our society or dressing up its sores, but involves its complete recovery and renewal.

Politics is undoubtedly the most important thing in any revolutionary process. This is equally true of perestroika. Therefore we attach priority to political measures, broad and genuine democratization, the resolute struggle against red tape and violations of law, and the active involvement of the masses in managing the country's affairs. All this is directly linked with the main question of any revolution, the question of power.

We are not going to change Soviet power, of course, or abandon its fundamental principles, but we acknowledge the need for changes that will strengthen socialism and make it more dynamic and politically meaningful. That is why we have every reason to characterize our plans for the full-scale democratization of Soviet society as a program for changes in our political system. . . .

. . . The restructuring effort started with the Party and its leadership. We began from the top of the pyramid and went down to its base, as it were. Still, the concept of "revolution from above" doesn't quite apply to our perestroika; at least it requires some qualifications. Yes, the Party leadership started it. The highest Party and state bodies elaborated and adopted the program. True, perestroika is not a spontaneous, but a governed process. But that's only one side of the matter.

Perestroika would not have been a truly revolutionary undertaking, it would not have acquired its present scope, nor would it have had any firm chance of success if it had not merged the initiative from "above" with the grass-roots movement; if it had not expressed the fundamental, long-term interests of all the working people; if the masses had not regarded it as their program, a response to their own thoughts and a recognition of their own demands; and if the people had not supported it so vehemently and effectively. . . .

I recall a meeting in June 1986 with the personnel of the apparatus of the CPSU Central Committee. It concerned perestroika. I had to ask them to adopt a new style of working with the intelligentsia. It is time to stop ordering it about, since this is harmful and inadmissible. The intelligentsia has wholeheartedly welcomed the program for the democratic renewal of society.

Congresses of creative unions of film-makers, writers, artists, composers, architects, theatrical figures and journalists have been held. They were marked by heated debate. All the congresses sincerely supported perestroika. The participants severely criticized themselves; many former top union officials were not elected to leading bodies, nor were the loudmouths. Instead, eminent, authoritative people were elected to head the unions.

I told those who found the debates too heated that they should not be surprised or become indignant, that these congresses should be accepted as a normal, albeit new, phenomenon. Democratization is taking place everywhere, acquiring acute forms at times. Someone objected, claiming that it would be difficult to work in an environment where each individual is his own philosopher, his own foremost authority, and believes that only he is right. I replied that it is far worse to be dealing with a passive intelligentsia, and with indifference and cynicism. . . .

The intelligentsia is imbued with a sense of civic responsibility, and it has eagerly shouldered a large share of the restructuring effort. Our intelligentsia has, along with the Party, got down to change. Its public-spirited stand is manifesting itself more and more strongly, and we have a vested interest in this activity; we appreciate everything—the way it joined the effort after April 1985, its enthusiasm and its desire to help the restructuring of society. We hope that this contribution by the intelligentsia will continue to grow. The intelligentsia is rising to a new level of thinking and responsibility. Its guidelines coincide with the political course of the CPSU and the interests of the people.

How has perestroika been developing in the economy?

I must say, frankly, that all our efforts toward changing the structure of the national economy, transferring it on to the track of intensive development, and accelerating scientific and technological progress prompted even more urgently the need for a radical reform of the economic mechanism and for restructuring the entire system of economic management.

Socialism and public ownership, on which it is based, hold out virtually unlimited possibilities for progressive economic processes. For this, however, we must each time find the most effective forms of socialist ownership and of the organization of the economy. Of prime importance in this respect is for the people to be the true master of production, rather than a master only in name. For without it, individual workers or collectives are not interested, nor can they be interested, in the final results of their work.

It is Lenin's idea of finding the most effective and modern forms of blending public ownership and the personal interest that is the groundwork for all our quests, for our entire concept of radically transforming economic management. . . .

I would say that the concept of economic reform, which we submitted to the June Plenary Meeting, is of an all-embracing, comprehensive character. It provides for fundamental changes in every area, including the transfer of enterprises to complete cost accounting, a radical transformation of the centralized management of the economy, fundamental changes in planning, a reform of the price formation system and of the financial and crediting mechanism, and the restructuring of foreign economic ties. It also provides for the creation of new organizational structures of management, for the all-round development of the democratic foundations of management, and for the broad introduction of the self-management principles. . . .

. . . We should start with enterprises and amalgamations, the main link in the economic chain. We should start with finding the most effective economic model for them, then create the optimum economic conditions, extend and consolidate their rights, and only on that basis introduce fundamental changes in the activity of all higher echelons of economic management.

As we determined that sequence of the restructuring effort, we bore in mind that it is there, at enterprises and amalgamations, that the main economic processes are taking place, that material values are being created, and scientific and technological ideas are materializing. It is the work collective that gives a tangible shape to economic and social relations, and it is in the work collective that personal, collective and social interests of people are interlinked. The work collective largely determines the social and political atmosphere countrywide.

We also took into consideration our past experience, in which repeated attempts to reform the upper management levels without support from below were unsuccessful because of the stubborn resistance of the management apparatus, which did not want to part with its numerous rights and prerogatives. We have recently encountered that resistance, and still encounter it now. Here too, as in all other areas of restructuring, we must combine what comes from above with the movement from below, i.e., give the restructuring effort a profoundly democratic nature.

What is the main shortcoming of the old economic machinery?

It is above all the lack of inner stimuli for self-development. Indeed, through the system of plan indices, the enterprise receives assignments and resources. Practically all expenses are covered, sales of products are essentially guaranteed and, most importantly, the employees' incomes do not depend on the end results of the collective's work: the fulfilment of contract commitments, production quality and profits. Such a mechanism is likely to produce medium or even poor quality work, whether we like it or not. How can the economy advance if it creates preferential conditions for backward enterprises and penalizes the foremost ones?

We can no longer run our affairs like that. The new economic mechanism must put matters right. It must become a powerful lever, a motivating force for resourceful quality performance. Every enterprise must proceed from real social demands to determine production and sales plans for itself. Those plans must be based not on numerous detailed assignments set by higher bodies, but on direct orders placed by government organizations, self-accounting enterprises and trade firms for specific products of appropriate quantity and quality. Enterprises must be put in such conditions as to encourage economic competition for the best satisfaction of consumer demands, and employees' incomes must strictly depend on end production results, on profits. . . .

The restructuring doesn't come easily for us. We critically assess each step we are making, test ourselves by practical results, and keenly realize that what looks acceptable and sufficient today may be obsolete tomorrow.

The past two and a half years have given us a great deal. The coming years, and maybe even months, will see fresh unconventional moves. In the course of the restructuring we are expanding and clarifying our notions about the yesterday, today, and tomorrow of socialism. We are discovering ourselves anew. This was and is being done, as I've said already, not to catch the imagination, nor to "gain affections," nor to win applause. We are motivated by the ideas of the 1917 October Revolution, the ideas of Lenin, the interests of the Soviet people.

We believe that the fruits of the restructuring will benefit international relations, too, including Soviet–American relations. New political thinking is an imperative of the times. . . .

We are all students, and our teacher is life and time. I believe that more and more people will come to realize that through RESTRUCTURING in the broad sense of the word, the integrity of the world will be enhanced. Having earned good marks from our main teacher—life—we shall enter the twenty-first century well prepared and sure that there will be further progress.

We want freedom to reign supreme in the coming century everywhere in the world. We want peaceful competition between different social systems to develop unimpeded, to encourage mutually advantageous cooperation rather than confrontation and an arms race. We want people of every country to enjoy prosperity, welfare and happiness. The road to this lies through proceeding to a nuclear-free, non-violent world. We have embarked on this road, and call on other countries and nations to follow suit.

Abel Aganbegyan

Market Socialism

The initial target of perestroika was the Soviet economy, and no one else had more influence on Gorbachev at this stage than the economist Abel Aganbegyan, head of the same institute in Novosibirsk where Tatiana Zaslavskaya worked. Like much other Soviet writing of this period, Aganbegyan couched his criticisms and recommendations in rather abstract language, which requires some reading between the lines. But his main message is clear: the Soviet Union

From Abel Aganbegyan, *The Economic Challenge of Perestroika*, Edited by Michael B. Brown; introduced by Alec Nove; translated by Pauline M. Tiffen, pp. 1, 6, 20–24, 31–32, 38–39, 125–128, 131–133, 135, 136, 224–227. Indiana University Press. Copyright © 1988 by Abel Gezevich Aganbegyan; English translation © 1988 by Hutchinson Education. Reprinted by permission of the publisher.

should return to the model of Lenin's New Economic Policy of the 1920s and reconcile market economics and socialist planning to get the country moving.

The new economic strategy of development for our country proclaimed by M. Gorbachev in April 1985 at the Plenary meeting of the Central Committee of the Communist Party of the Soviet Union (CPSU) is summed up in the new political concepts of *"uskorenie"* (acceleration), *"perestroika"* (restructuring) and *"glasnost"* (openness).

At the root of this new economic strategy lies the concept of uskorenie, the acceleration of social and economic development. This revolutionary strategy is in contrast to the tendency of *zamedlenie*, the slowing down of development of the last 15 years. . . .

Perestroika . . . signifies profound qualitative changes. *Perestroika* is inevitable when existing economic conditions do not respond to new conditions, formed by the needs of the development of society and the demands of the future. Here it is necessary to change the economic system, to transform and renew it fundamentally. For this transformation restructuring is necessary not just of individual aspects and elements, but of the whole economic system, all aspects and all elements together, in order to achieve a qualitative leap. The essence of the matter is that this is a revolutionary form of change in contrast to an evolutionary form. The term *perestroika* expresses a revolutionary qualitative transformation. This term is many-sided, synonymous in many ways with terms such as radical reform, major reconstruction, radical change, transition to new quality and a breakthrough.

Perestroika in our society affects everything and everyone. It is universal, many-sided and all-embracing. It is not only in the economy that profound reforms are being undertaken. We are also rebuilding our political system, ideology, party work—the whole superstructure rooted in the economic base of society. As an economist I will speak of *perestroika* in the economy. It should be emphasised that it is extraordinarily important that economic reform does not occur in isolation from other sectors of social life but strengthens the transformation of these sectors. . . .

. . . The existing system of economic management does not correspond to new conditions, to the goal of the acceleration of socio-economic development. Indeed the existing system of management is out of date and acts as a brake on the development of the economy.

All other efforts to transform the economy are now coming up against the absence of solutions to the problems of management in the working of the economic mechanism. At present this mechanism encourages extensive and impedes intensive development. It further complicates the problem by making scientific and technological progress unprofitable and failing to guarantee advantage to those who raise the quality of production. It encourages new construction but makes work on technical reconstruction unprofitable. This system hoards the depreciation funds, perpetuates the output of old products, and does not push enterprises to renew their funds and products. It hinders *perestroika*.

The existing system of economic management, based on the command system, represses democracy, initiative and the creativity of workers and does not encourage the potential for work or social activity. It does not make workers interested in the final product of their labour. The unjustifiable levelling of wages, the shortages, the gap between supply and demand for individuals and society, the residual principle in the allocation of resources for the development of the social sector—these are all products of the old economic system.

A chief characteristic of the existing system of management is the predominance of administrative methods, with economic methods having only secondary significance. This system has been formed over a long period of Soviet history. In the ups and downs of history the state used its administrative power to achieve its priorities. With the transition of the country to industrialisation at the end of the 1920s and early 1930s it became a priority to distribute resources away from agriculture and consumer goods and into heavy industry. . . .

From the beginning of the 1930s economic methods of management were curtailed. Trade between production units was replaced by centralised allocation of resources, and the market contracted. The primacy of production was established along with the secondary role of the consumer. Financial reforms at the beginning of the 1930s ended commercial credit and erased the differences between direct finance and credit financing. Rather than self-financing, the external budget control method of financing prevailed. The work done by enterprises was determined by directives, which year after year became more detailed. Financial accountability became a formality; prices were virtually irrelevant and many branches were unprofitable. Losses were hidden in the form of subsidies from the state budget.

Administrative methods were extended to official employment policy. All managers were appointed from the top down. Assessment of work was made according to the degree to which the plan had been fulfilled. Army-like disciplinary methods were propagated. These administrative methods of management became more brutal during the Second World War (1941–1945), when a large part of industry was evacuated to the Urals and Siberia from the western and central regions of the country occupied by the fascists. . . .

. . . In the period 1953–57, after Stalin's death, and also during the economic reforms of 1964–65, attempts were made to introduce economic methods of management more widely. But these attempts were not all-embracing and touched only individual branches and sectors of the economy. Despite isolated positive results, there were few successes at that time. Ultimately, a relapse occurred back to administrative management and command systems.

With the development of productive forces, the unfolding of the scientific and technological revolution, the strengthening of socioeconomic factors in economic development, the administrative system of management began to stand in ever greater contradiction to the growing needs of the development of society and finally came into sharp and protracted conflict with them. The situation worsened at the beginning of the 1970s, when the potential of extensive development through growth of resources began to decline, when a new stage of the scientific and technological revolution began and the needs of the population grew significantly. In this period the system of management of the economy began to act as a serious brake on development. As a result, towards the end of the 1970s and beginning of the 1980s [a] crisis arose. Stagnation had occurred in the economy. The standard of living had stopped rising.

It became clear that this could not continue, that fundamental change was needed. A major element of *perestroika* in the economic sector is the radical reform of management of the whole economic system. It has necessitated two long years to work out the direction of this reform, conducting numerous economic experiments to test the elements of the new economic system. This period is now behind us. The June 1987 Plenary completed the working out of a new integrated management system. An expanded programme of *perestroika* of the economic system was accepted. The essence of this *perestroika* lies in the transition from administrative to economic methods of management. For this the basic element in production is the transfer of associations and enterprises to full economic accountability, self-financing and self-management. The dynamic development is economic democracy, the workers being widely involved in management, and now able to elect their own economic managers.

Transition to economic methods greatly increases the role of prices, finance and credit and enhances motivation and incentives to work. Therefore, the immediate task of *perestroika* of management is the fundamental reform of the pricing system and the financial credit system. This will create the preconditions for a broad and universal transition from centralised allocation of funds for the supply of goods to numerous options for trade between units of production. Simultaneously, a direct relation is established between the size of the enterprise wage fund together with its material incentive fund and the end results of the workers' labour. Changes in the structure of rates and wages are taking place. A broad transition is occurring towards collective forms of organisation and work incentives. Work collectives have received the right to determine wages.

All this requires radical changes in the central system of planning and management. Instead of detailed directives of tasks, planning is being concentrated on the establishment of norms of economic proportions with economic incentives, while a system is being developed for consumers to order products from producers. Among these consumers will be state organisations, placing state orders.

The activity of the various ministries and regional authorities will also change fundamentally. The ministries will refrain from detailed regulation and trivial involvement in the activities of enterprises, to become the planning, economic and scientific and technological headquarters of industry. The role of regions in management will be greatly strengthened. The formation of local budgets will be changed to a system of economic proportions. Regional management bodies concerned with economic activity are being created as departments of local authorities. . . .

Democratisation of the whole of our society including the development of *glasnost* is an important aspect of *perestroika*. As it applies to the economy, debate is proceeding on an increased role for workers' collectives in the resolution of economic questions, and in the transition to self-management. In the Law on Socialist Enterprises, workers' collectives have been granted extensive rights in framing the plans of economic development for their enterprise, deciding on the way incentives should be offered, on work conditions and salaries, and the social development of their collective.

Of particular significance is the right of workers' collectives to choose their economic leaders, at brigade, enterprise and association level. Earlier, under the administrative system, directives on the conduct of the plan, even the smallest details, were handed down from above. Now, with full economic independence and self-accounting, the welfare of the collective depends above all on work organisation and levels of productivity. Its leader, as head of the working collective, must take the lead in striving for higher efficiency and productivity.

Perestroika is a difficult and painful process. Its success is determined by the socio-political climate of the society in which it occurs. The most complex question concerns the *perestroika* of people's thinking and consciousness. For, the consequence of *perestroika* in thinking and consciousness defines the way they work towards the transformation of society. Karl Marx wrote: "An idea becomes a material force when it takes hold of society." The idea of *perestroika* must come to grip society for *perestroika* to move into gear. But how can this transition to a new way of thinking and an understanding of new tasks be assured? Here the media of mass information are of inestimable help. *Glasnost*, truth, criticism and self-criticism are the instruments that will effectively prepare for the new consciousness. Change in the sphere of ideology is thus the inspiration for *perestroika* of the economy and of other parts of society.

This is what is happening in our country now. Enormous changes are apparent in publishing, television programmes, the activities of writers, film makers and theatre directors. Freedom of expression has been expanded. Ongoing changes are being analysed critically and past experiences are being assessed. All this is directed at working people. Everyone feels that it has become easier to breathe, and that the socio-psychological climate in the country is receptive to *perestroika*. Thus *glasnost* is working and encouraging reform of the economy. . . .

In the end we have to move from a command economy with mainly administrative methods of management, towards a democratic, independent, self-managing economy, to an economy in whose management the broad masses of working people are actively participating. All this will fundamentally change the look of our economic system. The advantages of socialism within our economy will become apparent. We want a highly efficient economy, to reach the highest productivity levels in the world, to be at the forefront in technology and quality of production and at the same time to avoid unemployment, preserve the short working day and strengthen the social achievements of working people all on a broad democratic foundation.

It is towards the achievement of these goals that the CPSU Programme, adopted at the XXVII Party Congress [February–March 1986], is orienting our society. Its goals cannot be achieved in the short term. The largest leap is to be made in the period up to the year 2000. By this time the material technical base of our society will be renewed. The scientific technological revolution will have unfolded widely in the country and, using its achievements, we should advance to the foremost position in the world. But our backwardness compared to the most developed countries in the world is too great to be overcome before the end of the century. Thus in terms of productivity we are two and a half to three times behind the USA and two to two and [a] half times behind other developed Western countries. . . .

In the journal *Novyi Mir* [New World] a piece appeared recently from the Soviet economist Popkova entitled "Whose pies are lighter?" Although confused and seeming like a stream of consciousness the piece defined the nature of socialism as being a centralised society in which the market must not be developed and used to meet people's needs more fully and so end shortages. The market, the author asserted, is a characteristic of capitalism and only under capitalism can shortages be avoided and the market come to be full of goods. The author concludes that there is no third alternative. This primitive view of a socialist economy is fairly widespread in the Soviet Union and more so in the West. In our opinion, this point of view is wrong and contradicts not only theory but practice. . . .

. . . Commodity production and money existed before capitalism and exist under socialism as well. Commodity production and market relations arise when producers are individualised and there is a division of labour. In such conditions goods are exchanged to meet social needs. Under socialism the division of labour is well developed and deepens and widens further according to the degree of development of the productive forces. Within the framework of public ownership, which predominates in the Soviet economy, the individualising of enterprises and economic organisations is relative. This is linked to the fact that common public ownership gives the rights of possession, use and distribution of resources to individual enterprises and organisations in managing their businesses. In the recent Law on State Enterprises it is laid down that the state is not responsible for the debts of enterprises, but neither are enterprises under obligation to answer for the debts of the state. By law enterprises are accordingly being transferred to full self-accounting, self-financing and self-management.

Under socialism there exist also cooperative enterprises and organisations, including collective farms, based on another cooperative form of socialist ownership. Once, quite unjustified efforts were made in the Soviet Union to abolish cooperatives. Now cooperatives are reviving in industry, trade and other sectors and continue to develop in agriculture. Cooperatives, as a flexible form of organisation of collective labour, have some definite advantages and a promising future. . . . Self-employment, which is to be developed in socialist conditions, is individualised by its very nature and assumes separation of producers, the division of labour and the exchange of commodities. . . .

. . . In the exchange of commodities relations are established between people. These can be between private capitalist owners or monopolies and the population, as is characteristic of capitalism, or between socialist enterprises or cooperatives and the population as under socialism. Commodity production, the market and market relations in the socialist conditions of the Soviet Union, vary greatly. But in contrast to capitalism commodities and money relations are not universal categories. Land and natural resources cannot be bought and sold. Since there is no unemployment and the economic base of society accords with socialist ownership, there is no labour market. A market for capital is not envisaged as part of *perestroika*. There are no plans for a Soviet stock exchange, shares, bills of exchange or profit from commercial credit.

A socialist market is a government-regulated market. Through the prescription of set economic proportions, fixed wages and a system of state finance and credit, the monetary income of the population is regulated. On the other hand, prices for most essential products are also to be set by state bodies. Major capital investment and other economic levers and stimuli are in the hands of the state and can be directed at greater or lesser production of certain goods and thus have a major influence on the market.

Up to now the market in the Soviet Union has been both restricted and deformed. Most means of production have been centrally allocated by the state through a material and technical supply system. They are not freely bought and sold. The market is still one in which there are persistent shortages and consumer demand, especially for high quality goods, is not being met. The system of pricing is excessively rigid and centralised, so that prices may not reflect reality because they do not correspond to the costs incurred and efficiency in the production of the goods. Since in the past, many types of cooperatives were not permitted to develop and self-employment was not encouraged, representation of commodity producers in the market was incomplete. In such a distorted marketplace the grey economy became widespread with its uncontrolled mechanism for distributing goods and incomes. The so-called black market also grew and speculation became increasingly rife.

During *perestroika* market relations in the USSR will be deepened and broadened. Above all the market is set to more than double in size thanks to the transition from centralised material and technical supply to wholesale trade in means of production, including direct commercial links between enterprises. In this way a well-developed market in the means of production will be created, and the proportion of centrally set prices will be substantially reduced. Centralised pricing will be retained only for the most essential products, to control their rate of growth and to stave off inflation. At the same time the scope of contracted and free prices will grow significantly. . . .

The development of cooperatives and of self-employment will supply the socialist market with many goods, and bring the higher flexibility and competitive potency needed to satisfy social needs. The essential attribute of a market is consumer choice. The advantage of a market is lost when monopoly occurs. To give the market its economic effectiveness, competition between producers making similar or the same goods is crucial. Under *perestroika* this question is being given special attention. Monopoly of particular lines of production has to be ended and parallel enterprises or economic organisations created. When designating enterprises as economically effective we now apply the term "economic emulation," to express the distinctive form of competition between enterprises in Soviet conditions. The growing socialist economy can never become capitalist. Since there is no hired labour, business-owners, exploitation and commodities are not a universal category. There will not be an uncontrolled market. In the light of this the relationship between the plan and market must be examined.

A socialist economy is by its nature planned. Indeed it is based on socialist ownership with state ownership as its main form. The means of production of society, particularly the land, material wealth and enterprises belong to the whole people, through which their administrative bodies systematically manage them and seek to make good use of them.

Thus the social formation of a planned economy from top to bottom as in Soviet society is overriding and universal. This formation will be conserved even with *perestroika*, but it will take on some new features and, most importantly, new forms to implement the realisation of a planned economy. Planning for the development of the economy will in part be realised through the market. In the market place commodities obtain the social recognition of the consumer—they are bought or rejected. Social valuation is given to the production costs of the goods. Thus the market place acts as a key additional regulator of production within socialist society.

People ask the following question: is the development of a socialist market a step on the road to capitalism? From the above it will be quite evident that the answer to this question is categorically "no!" We are not developing capitalist production, but a socialist market with a new content and system of operation in a socialist economy. . . .

In our radical reform of management the relationship of plan and market is being fundamentally changed. It is changing because the whole centralised system of planning is being looked at differently. It is changing because the market sector is being developed and extended and a new unity and interaction of plan and market is beginning. Plans are being implemented by proportional norms and contracts and not by commands.

In the new system of economic management prices become a basic point of reference. Enterprises and associations will evaluate the results of their work through the pricing of their products. The existing system of prices does not give a true valuation because prices do not reflect social costs and the economic efficiency of production. Up to now this common denominator has been lacking in the Soviet Union. . . .

To ensure that production really leads to the satisfaction of consumer needs a number of measures are proposed to strengthen the influence of the consumer on the technical level and quality of production. One of the main impediments to scientific technological progress lies in the existence of shortages. And these shortages are not primarily caused by too little being produced. Their main underlying cause rests in the lack of any real feedback between consumer and producer. In other words shortages are generated by the working of the economic system. . . .

The decisive principle to underlie future distribution policy will be social justice. The current differentiation in incomes and standards of living and lifestyles of different strata of the population is not very large. If one takes the poorest decile of families and the top decile then the current difference between their incomes is about three to one. In the capitalist countries there are super-rich capitalists and in contrast the very poor. The differences between these two poles in capitalist society are incomparably greater. The guaranteed right to work in the USSR, the absence of unemployment and of the large proportion of the population living on low levels of unemployment benefit that occur in capitalist societies, help greatly to reduce the differences. Thanks to this social protection, Soviet working people are already convinced that they can look forward to a secure future. As people's needs are increasingly fully met, this conviction can only be strengthened.

The radical reforms proposed for management will give a qualitatively new impetus to the whole Soviet economy. This will aim at subordinating production to the demands of the consumer, stimulating both high cost-effectiveness and quality, technological innovation and individual worker involvement. Mechanisms are to be created and refined for accelerating the socio-economic development of the country and removing any barriers and impediments which hinder development.

This renewal of the economy will elevate the role and significance of the Soviet Union in the world. Currently, according to the figures of Soviet statistical authorities, the national income of the USSR is about 66% of the US level, while Western economists usually quote figures of 50%–55%. During the last 25 years the national product in the USA has been growing at less than 3% annually. This indicator for the USSR will in [the] future, according to our estimate, be about 5% a year. With these differing rates the Soviet national income by the year 2000 will closely approach that of the USA. If per capita income is taken, the Soviet lag will be more marked, insofar as there are less than 240 million people in the USA and more than 280 million in the USSR. At present rates, the population in the USSR is growing one and a half times faster than in the USA (in 1986 the population of the USSR increased by 1.02% and of the USA by 0.7%). Since a larger volume of labour and material resources is used in the USSR the indicator of cost-effectiveness for the Soviet Union will continue to lag behind the USA, although the difference will be reduced sharply. While productivity over the last 25 years rose in the US economy on average by less than 2% a year, and should increase at roughly this rate in the future, the proposed annual growth in labour productivity in the USSR is roughly 6% per annum. The gap will therefore be narrowing. An issue of especial concern for the USSR is the attainment of leading positions in the world in technology and quality of production. The fundamental technological reconstruction which is being implemented in the economy, the programme to advance machine-building, and the economic and administrative measures to improve the quality of production and its competitiveness are all aimed at this goal.

With the growth of social production in the USSR, its international relations will be developed and deepened, in the first place with socialist countries on the basis of economic integration and the implementation of the Comprehensive Programme of Scientific and Technological Progress for the CMEA[1] members. I believe that in the near future the Soviet Union will overcome the decline that has occurred in international trade with capitalist and developing countries (caused by the sharp drop in the prices of oil and of several other raw materials) and that the country will begin to expand dynamically its economic relations with these countries. We hope that joint ventures with foreign companies on the territory of the USSR will become widespread and will develop effectively. In a word, the USSR will increasingly come to be included in the international division of labour. . . .

. . . The fundamental *perestroika* of Soviet society and first of all of its economy is a continuation of the Great October Socialist Revolution. This is not only because what is occurring under *perestroika* is revolutionary, but because it is aiming to raise the standard of living of Soviet society to a qualitatively new level, in line with its renewal and transformation according to socialist principles. The *perestroika* is a continuation of the October Revolution also in a more profound sense. The October Revolution began the transition to socialism including the setting up of a

---

[1] Council for Mutual Economic Assistance, the Communist bloc trading organization.—Ed.

socialist economy. Socialism was eventually victorious and socialist relations have come to hold sway completely in Soviet society. The October revolution, in this way, established a base for the socialist system which we consider to be better than the capitalist system.

Socialism must, however, demonstrate its higher economic and social efficiency by its evident advantages. The ongoing *perestroika* in the USSR is aimed precisely at disclosing the advantages of socialism. Lenin said that socialism must ensure a higher level of productivity than capitalism. This has still not been achieved. Only now during *perestroika* is this goal put on the agenda as a practical, albeit long-term task. *Perestroika* must carry Soviet society to a qualitatively new state, when thanks to the advantages of socialism we will surpass the capitalist countries in productivity and other indicators of cost-effectiveness, in quality of production and the level of technology. As the most progressive society, in stimulating scientific and technological progress, we must have the best, the most effective material and technological social base and be at the forefront of scientific and technological advance. Under socialism the best achievements of science and technology must be applied more widely than under capitalism, since there are not the same economic barriers for the application of scientific and technological progress.

On the basis of higher cost-effectiveness we aim to achieve the highest standard of living in the world—in all the component parts: diet, consumer goods, housing, social sector services and, of course, by rendering the population healthier and with a higher average life expectancy. Socialist society must be more educated, more intellectual, more spiritually and morally committed. This is to be achieved with *perestroika* and with the wholesale revision of social relationships.

Walter Laqueur

Glasnost

A key aspect of Gorbachev's reforms was the concept of glasnost ("openness" or "publicity"): the press and cultural life would be freed up so as to expose the abuses of the past and put pressure on the bureaucracy to move forward. As described by Walter Laqueur of the Center for Strategic and International Studies in Washington, D.C., glasnost proceeded unevenly and step-by-step in Soviet publishing, cultural life, history writing, and unofficial discussion groups, as the reformers gradually gained ground against the conservatives in the Communist party between 1986 and 1988.

Glasnost came as a surprise to most observers of the Soviet Union, and there has been much admiration for those who have initiated a more truthful policy after many decades of official and unofficial mendacity. *Glasnost* means self-criticism; it implies that the ever-widening gap between words and deeds is admitted. Such an approach demands courage; it would undoubtedly be far easier and politically less risky to continue with the old habits. It is therefore not astonishing that there is obstinate resistance against *glasnost* inside the Soviet Union. Nor is its future assured in view of the many vested interests opposing it.

But *glasnost*, however intrinsically important, is an approach, a style; it is not the substance of Soviet politics. This has frequently been misunderstood in the West, especially with regard to foreign policy. Time and again it has been asked why the Soviet leadership continued or adopted a certain policy even though, as Western observers saw it, it contradicted *glasnost*. The short answer is that *glasnost per se* does not aim at basic, structural changes in the Soviet system and has nothing to do with the aims of Soviet foreign policy. It wants to make the system work better, more efficiently. There has been a certain amount of "new thinking" (another of the new key words) on foreign policy which may lead eventually to radical change. But this, in any case, is not *glasnost*. . . .

It seems to have been clear to Gorbachev from the beginning that institutional changes would not suffice to get the country moving again; attention had to be given to the "human factor." This meant above all imposing stricter discipline, stamping out corruption and indifference. But it also meant the active participation of the masses, which is to say some kind of democratization, some electoral reform, and *glasnost*.

Gorbachev's frustration during his first year of office must have driven him toward greater emphasis on spiritual, political, cultural, and moral regeneration, the realization that *perestroika* would not work but for something akin to a cultural revolution, within, of course, strict limits. Hence his appeal at the January 1987 plenum to "develop democratization, to involve people's energy and interest in all the processes of our lives. This is the most important thing, the main point of everything, comrades." Thus 1987 became the year of *glasnost* but it also rallied the forces opposed to it. . . .

By February 1987 Gorbachev seems to have reached the conclusion that the historians, too, needed some *glasnost*. In a speech to leading representatives of the Soviet mass media he said, "There should be no forgotten names or blanks either in history or literature." And again: "Those who made the revolution must not be pushed in the background. . . . It is immoral to forget or pass over in silence large periods in the life of our people." Gorbachev's moral qualms were not shared by most of his Politburo colleagues, whose interest in the importance of history was less pronounced, or who saw more clearly than he did the dangers of opening the sluice gates of historical truth. . . .

. . . Up to 1985, Stalin's crimes were belittled in the history books; on the other hand his great merits in peace and war were frequently mentioned in the press, in books, and in movies; his hundredth birthday (December 1979) was duly commemorated. Thus for twenty years after Khrushchev's fall some of the modest concessions to historical truth were again unmade or whittled down. And it is important to stress that even at the height of the de-Stalinization campaign it had been the custom to use euphemisms—"repression" stood for muder, "cult of the personality" for totally arbitrary rule and glorification of a leader without precedence in modern history. Many of Stalin's victims were rehabilitated only in a legal sense; they were found not guilty of the charges that had been brought against them at the time—such as of having poisoned wells in the Ukraine on behalf of the Gestapo, or the British or Japanese secret services. But they were not rehabilitated politically: Stalin and his henchmen had been right in removing them from positions of influence, but it had been wrong to bring fantastic charges against them and to execute them. Brezhnev and his colleagues were great believers in letting bygones be bygones; unlike some Shakespearean heroes their nights were not interrupted by the appearance of ghosts from the past.

A Soviet historian trying to write the history of his country faced insurmountable difficulties. He could not write about the 1930s, for, all other considerations apart, access to the archives was minimal. But he could not write about the postwar period either, again because there was no access to the sources and because of Khrushchev, who had become a nonperson. The ideal history book was one which mentioned no names. . . .

The call for *glasnost* made little impression on Soviet historians during 1985 and 1986. There were no major changes in the professional literature; Soviet historians either thought that there was no need for revaluations or, more likely, having no clear lead from the party authorities (but accustomed to being told what to do), they preferred to wait and see.

In the meantime, however, the initiative of confronting the past was taken up by playwrights, filmmakers, novelists, and journalists. . . .

Increasingly, the historians faced a totally unprecedented situation: there were two (or even more) versions on topics such as the revolutions of 1917, collectivization, industrialization, the purges and Stalin's role in the Second World War—in other words, all the important issues in the history of their country. Worse yet, there were some voices from within the profession claiming that the state of Soviet historiography was exceedingly bad. . . .

Eventually Gorbachev modified his stand, perhaps under the influence of his advisers and friends. In a speech to the Central Committee in January 1987 he said that the causes of the present situation went back far into the past; and in July 1987, talking to key figures in the media, he declared that "we shall never be able to forgive and forget what happened in 1937–38." This theme reappeared in his speech commemorating the seventieth anniversary of the October revolution.

This was as far as Gorbachev was willing to go, but his followers expected more. Throughout 1987, right up to his speech in November, there had been high expectations that very soon the green light would be given for a wholesale rewriting of Soviet history; Bukharin, Zinoviev, Kamenev, perhaps even Trotsky, would be politically rehabilitated; a fairer approach would prevail vis-à-vis the Mensheviks and other left-wing opponents of the Bolsheviks. Some of these predictions appeared in interviews given by Soviet literary figures to Western journalists, and great was the disappointment when nothing quite so dramatic happened.

Why was it so difficult to make concessions to historical truth? Gorbachev, after all, must have felt closer in many respects to Bukharin's views than to Stalin's. And Bukharin had almost been rehabilitated thirty years earlier under Khrushchev. The short answer is that this would have been possible only on the basis of a radical reassessment of Stalinism, and this still seemed very difficult for political reasons. . . .

The treatment of Trotsky is the litmus test of *glasnost* in Soviet historiography, precisely because for so many years he had been treated as the archvillain: he was Satan, Judas, Lucifer, the main traitor, the incarnation of all evil. One should have thought that almost half a century after his assassination it ought to have been possible to publish the truth about him. Since Trotskyism as a political movement had never constituted a real danger to Soviet power, what made a reexamination of Trotsky's role so difficult? True, he could now appear in some plays and novels—not as a collaborator with the Gestapo but merely as a doubtful character, a man who had never been a true Bolshevik, and who had almost always been wrong. This raised new questions. For if Trotsky had been both incompetent and unreliable, how to explain that the infallible Lenin had entrusted him with leading positions in party and state? . . .

The miraculous years of Soviet literature, 1987 and 1988, were a new "golden age," the richest harvest ever. In the words of one critic it was more than a second thaw; it was a true cultural blossoming, unfettered (or almost unfettered) by the dead hand of censorship. These were years of enormous spiritual ferment and creative openness such as a much-suffering Soviet culture had not known for six decades. As the German humanist of the Renaissance had written, "*Iuvat vivere*"—"It is a joy to be alive." But not everyone shared this joy and some, in fact, were firmly convinced that Satan and the forces of evil were about to destroy all that was still good in Russia.

The fact that the literary magazines after years of almost unmitigated drought suddenly became very interesting would not have been considered a matter of paramount importance in almost any other country. But in Russia literature always had a function and an impact more powerful than elsewhere. There had been more freedom of expression in Russian literature under the Tsars than in any other field. As Belinski[1] had written in an often quoted letter 150 years earlier, in literature alone, despite Tartar censorship, is there life and a forward movement. Something of interest, however slight, could usually be found in one of the literary magazines. . . .

The differences in the degree of *glasnost* were so striking that one looks for specific causes and explanations. Did the ferment proceed on orders from above, or was it spontaneous, or perhaps a mixture of the two? The pattern was far from clear. In some fields there was a great deal of movement, in others hardly any at all. This is true, for instance, with regard to the "party sciences" such as philosophy, history, and economy; there was a reshuffle in the editorial board of *Questions of History* but it came late in the day (January 1988). How to explain that some institutions and their organs became more liberal whereas others hardly changed or even opposed change?

[1] Vissarion Belinski (1811–1848), radical Russian literary critic.—Ed.

All appointments had to be approved by the party, and seen in this light the element of chance was minimal. The instruction given was: let the intellectuals and the artists have some more freedom. But some did not want more freedom and, on the other hand, in two specific cases something akin to a palace revolution took place and the old guard was unceremoniously ousted.

First there was the revolt of the Soviet moviemakers at the fifth congress of their union (May 1986). The situation in this field had been particularly bad, even though more movies were being produced than in Stalin's last years, when the industry had come to a virtual standstill. But the quality was low, and this expressed itself in steadily decreasing cinema attendance. Slightly unconventional films were either heavily censored or altogether shelved. Leading directors such as Tarkovski made their homes abroad; others were ostracized. A small clique decided what should be produced and by whom and how widely it should be distributed. When the elections to the secretariat of this organization—usually a formality—took place on the last day of the conference in 1986, Lev Kulizhanov, secretary general for the past twenty years, was replaced by Elem Klimov, a moviemaker of the avant-garde who had been in deep trouble for years with the censors. Two-thirds of the seats in the new executive also went to the rebels. In some ways it was a generational revolt—of those in their late forties and early fifties against those about ten years older who had dominated the scene during the Brezhnev era and even before. But the decisive issue was whether the moviemakers would have more creative freedom.

There had been rumblings even before the congress, such as bitter complaints in some leading newspapers about the dead hand of the censor (Goskino) which stifled all creative activity. The revolution in the union of moviemakers caused misgivings in the ranks of orthodox party leadership: What if the apparently spontaneous uprising would spread? Was it not a dangerous omen if a professional union slipped out of direct party control? But since at the time of the coup several leading representatives of the Central Committee, including Alexander Yakovlev, had been present, it must be taken that Klimov and his supporters had at least tacit approval from some party leaders. And when Gorbachev was approached in the weeks after, he explained to his apprehensive comrades that he regarded the upheaval among the filmmakers as a healthy development and that there was no room for fear and overreaction.

The revolution in the Soviet theater was equally sudden and in some respects even more far-reaching: At the time of the fifteenth congress of the all-Russian theater society (VTO) in October 1986, one of its members, Oleg Efremov, head of the Moscow Arts Theatre (Mkhat), got up and suggested the establishment of a new organization of Soviet theater workers. He received the support of a majority of those present and the new organization came into being soon after.

Such administrative reorganization may appear to Western observers of no particular significance, but in the Soviet context it was of very considerable importance. For according to established practice every Soviet theater had to have its repertory confirmed in Moscow. It was totally dependent on the decision of party officials with little or no competence in the field. It was defenseless against regional party secretaries who, for one reason or another, wanted to ban a certain play, even if it was performed elsewhere in the Soviet Union.

The old generation had done nothing to defend theater workers against such intervention and censorship, whereas the new union was created specifically for the purpose of defending theatrical art against arbitrary administrative interference. Even those who had been accused in previous years of being "modernists" or "subjectivists" were now given the opportunity to stage their plays in their own new theaters or within the framework of old established ones. . . .

A review of the cultural scene during the heyday of *glasnost* shows a contradictory picture: great changes in some fields and hardly any in others. . . . At times the conservatives must have felt misgivings about the future, but so did their antagonists. No one could be certain how far *glasnost* would go and how long it would last. Remembering past experiences, the reformers felt behind them the lengthening shadow of the gunman. Thus the situation in the arts, the sciences, and the media resembled the state of affairs in general. There was hope for more freedom but there was also great resistance to change, and there was no certainty that *glasnost* had come to stay. But there was greater courage than at any time in the past on the part of writers and artists, of composers and moviemakers, greater readiness to defend cultural freedom. And this was perhaps the most encouraging aspect of *glasnost* in the cultural field.

With the rise of *glasnost* it was widely believed in the West that Gorbachev's reforms would lead to a renaissance of left-wing, liberal democratic thought in the Soviet Union. The new Soviet ideology would seek its roots in the ideals of the Enlightenment, the French Revolution, and the democratic tradition of the Russian radical movement of the last century. Gorbachev and his supporters looked back with nostalgia to the early years after the revolution of 1917, the age of enthusiasm and relative freedom, a period of cultural experimentation when the skies of Russia had been bluer and the sun had been shining brighter than anywhere else, when Russian books, films, and educational ideas had attracted the attention and the support of men and women of goodwill all over the globe.

It should have been clear, however, that greater freedom would give rise to a variety of schools of thought. Neo-Stalinism still had its admirers. Other searchers for historical roots derived their inspiration from the Russian nationalist tradition, from the Slavophiles and their nineteenth-century rejection of Western ideas and modernism.

The reemergence of a "Russian party" as a serious contender should not have come as a surprise. The democratic experiment in Russian history had lasted for less than a year, from March to November 1917. Attitudes toward the West had always been ambivalent and there had been few true "Westerners" in Russian intellectual history. The victory of Marxism had been considered at one time the final triumph of Westernism in the long dispute with the East for Russian soul. But victories in history are seldom final, and over the next three generations Marxism with its progressive internationalist and modernist elements was tried and found wanting.

Thus the outlines of a new Russian ideology emerged in the search for a new equilibrium. If the old optimism had vanished; if there were universal complaints about the disappearance of

goodness and compassion, of warmth and conscience; if material-
ism, naked egoism, and general moral anarchy were said to have
prevailed, the cause seemed only too clear to many: it had been
a fatal mistake to stamp out the prerevolutionary "accursed" past,
to use Lenin's famous phrase. . . .

Throughout history there have been liberal and conservative
movements, parties of the left and the right, nationalist and internationalist. It would be a miracle if Russia alone were exempt
from such diversity of political opinion. Seen in the context of
seventy years of Soviet history, the right-wing reaction against
the "left-wing excesses" of the twenties and thirties seems almost
inevitable. Conservative policies have been advocated and conducted for decades in the Soviet Union under a left-wing veneer
which has become progressively thinner. For having made Russia
strong in military power and influence, the right is indebted to
Stalin, and, within limits, also to his successors. But the conservatives could not relish the Stalinist domestic system, nor could
they accept Marxist-Leninist ideology even though most of the
time all that was expected of them was routine lip service. They
agreed with the neo-Stalinists on a wide range of issues. But
they also had ideas and idols of their own which could not be
accommodated in a Marxist-Leninist system, however leniently
interpreted. They had common enemies, but their alliance still
remained fragile.

For all one knows, the "Russian party" could make a contribution in a Russia liberated of old shackles and shibboleths. But as
so often happened in Russia's past, the trend toward exaggeration,
fanaticism, and extremism, the historical bane of the Russian
left, has its counterpart on the right, and now, it would appear,
more strongly than ever.

The revelations of the *glasnost* era had a staggering effect,
but not because the truth about the Soviet past and present had
been totally unknown in Russia and abroad; the great innovation
was the fact that it was now possible to talk and write openly
about what had been tabu only yesterday. *Glasnost* caused a state
of euphoria, but more among people outside Russia, for Soviet
citizens had learned from bitter experience that what had been
given by the state could be taken away at almost any time. Few

in the Soviet Union dared openly to oppose *glasnost;* everyone paid lip service to it. But there was little enthusiasm for *glasnost* among the political bosses and there is no denying that for them it had been much easier to run the country under the old system. Nor was *glasnost* as yet deeply rooted among wide sections of the population. . . .

However, the more *glasnost* there was, the greater the resistance against it, and it did not come only from minor party secretaries in distant parts of the Union or from conservative writers who feared for their reputation and royalties. Opposition to *glasnost* came also from inside the Politburo. Enthusiasm for greater openness among Gorbachev's colleagues had never been overwhelming; they certainly used the term much less frequently than the general secretary. The most highly placed "braker" was Ligachev, the second man in the Soviet leadership in 1986–87. . . .

In July 1987 he turned to the writers and editors of literary magazines. *Glasnost* was throwing up too much froth and filth, he said; there was a danger that the classical writers of the Soviet period (meaning the likes of Sholokhov[2]) would be neglected. The media should take a stronger ideological stand against immorality, vulgarity, and Western mass culture. There should be less clannishness *(groupovshina)* among the writers; the artistic unions had asked for more freedom, and now it appeared that they did not know what to do with it. He did not actually suggest that the freedom should be taken away but his views were usually quite close to the criticism of the right-wing writers. Ligachev no doubt supported their stand, nor was it surprising that in the month that followed the conservatives far more often invoked his authority than the *glasnost* speeches of Gorbachev. Ligachev's warnings culminated in a speech in August 1987: "Abroad and in some places in our midst there are attempts to call into question the whole course of the construction of socialism in the Soviet Union, to represent it as a chain of never-ending mistakes, to disregard the historical feat of the people that created a mighty socialist power, and to do all this by referring to the facts of groundless repression. . . . After all, in the thirties the country reached

---

[2] Mikhail Sholokhov (1905–1984), leading Stalinist novelist.—Ed.

second place in the world in industrial output, agriculture was collectivized and unprecedented heights were reached in the development of culture, education, literature and the arts." . . .

Yet Gorbachev was by no means for unconditional *glasnost* either. Yakovlev, another member of the Politburo and a close Gorbachev supporter, had said that critical statements must be assessed by only one criterion: do they correspond to the actual state of affairs? Gorbachev usually opened his definitions in a similar sweeping way but later on introduced some reservations. Thus in a meeting with leading media figures in January 1988, he said: "I stress once again: we are in favor of *glasnost* without reservations and limitations. But for *glasnost* in the interest of socialism. And we solemnly reply to the question whether *glasnost* criticism and democracy are in the interests of the people—they are limitless." One year earlier in a similar meeting with key media figures he had taken exactly the same line. Openness, self-criticism were not a tactic but a matter of principle; they "have become the norms of our life," or, in Yakovlev's words, "our collective return to truth." But, again in Gorbachev's words, "Criticism must always be true to party ideology and based on the truth, and this depends on the party-mindedness of the editor." Sorely tried Soviet editors with a longer memory would ask, like Pontius Pilate, "What is truth?" and a few might well remember that Joseph Stalin in his time had also admonished writers to write the truth and nothing but the truth.

Thus the limits of *glasnost* were clearly stated. It was to be not openness *per se* as a supreme value and a right of the people, but openness within a political framework, "socialism" as defined by the Politburo. . . .

The sprouting of the "informal groups" was one of the characteristic features of the era of *glasnost*; a few people would gather from time to time to discuss current events or to engage in activities of common interest. Sometimes these were friends or neighbors; at other times their place of work provided the outward framework. Some were interested in public affairs; others set themselves more narrow aims. This was in stark contrast to previous decades when the Communist Party and its various branches had a monopoly on organization and no spontaneous activity was possible.

The existence of such a monopoly was one of the essential features of the Communist regime; it was also the reason for the mushrooming of the informal groups once the reins were loosened. As a close observer noted, this new and startling phenomenon was the direct result of the bureaucratization of public life, of the absence of all and any initiatives, except those which had been imposed from above.

By August 1987 more than a thousand such circles were said to exist in Moscow alone. But no one knew for certain and it could have been ten times as many; in any case, their number continued to grow. . . .

What was the specific character of these groups? How strong were they, and what was the response of the authorities? The coordinating meeting in August gave a general idea of the aims and activities of the various political clubs. It appeared that all groups except Pamyat[3] were quite small; their number of militants was perhaps fifteen to thirty in most cases, though a greater number of sympathizers would from time to time attend their lectures and discussions. . . . A few groups advocated left-wing socialist or Marxist ideas such as Obshina and the radio club Alie Parus; Obshina opposed the presence of Democracy and Humanism at the coordination meeting. Obshina announced that it accepted the leading role of the Communist party in society and would not break the law. But if they accepted the leading role of the party, why not work for *perestroika* from within? There was no clear answer. There was a small New Left in Moscow and Leningrad following with passionate interest ideas and political developments among the West European Communist parties and also in Hungary. They argued that it was premature to jettison socialism since it had never been given a real chance in Russia. Support for this New Left seems to have been greater in the United States and among Western European sympathizers than inside the Soviet Union. . . .

More radical and more representative was the founding meeting in April 1988 of a group called the Democratic Union, which intended to provide a platform for new political parties to be

---

[3] *Pamyat* ("memory"), a nationalist and anti-semitic organization set up in the mid-1980s.—Ed.

established in the Soviet Union. The authorities arrested some of the leaders of the new group, albeit only for a week, showing that there was no intention to make concessions to the demands of the "Union" such as the abolition of the KGB, changes in the constitution, or indeed political pluralism.

Lastly, suggestions were made by spokesmen for the reform wing inside the party to establish a "Popular Front" or "Union" to promote *perestroika*, in which party members and those belonging to some informal groups could work side by side. However, these proposals encountered suspicion and resistance among the party leadership and no progress was made. . . .

Glasnost has opened one of the most fascinating chapters in Russian cultural history. The choice of words is deliberate, both the emphasis on history and the stress on "cultural" (albeit in a wide sense). Whether *glasnost* will have a lasting impact on the political future of the country is uncertain and, in any case, cannot be answered today. Under *glasnost* complaints about many aspects of Soviet society have been voiced in a way that was unthinkable even a few years ago; cultural controls and restrictions have been either lifted or loosened; books have been published, plays and movies performed, pictures and sculptures exhibited, that were banned for many years. Informal societies have sprung up outside the party and the officially sponsored organizations, freely (or almost freely) discussing topics that were formerly tabu.

It was as if a wave of pent-up energy suddenly found release; it has been compared to the exhilarating effect of inhaling oxygen on one hand and on the other to a thaw of seemingly unmeltable ice. . . .

The party and state bureaucracy was as little prepared for *glasnost* in 1987 as the Tsarist bureaucracy had been in 1905. Some party secretaries were more liberal than others, but the whole style of the administration was authoritarian, accustomed to rule by order and decree. They were prepared for criticism from above but they had not been trained, and were not psychologically ready, to cope with criticism from below. There was a group of party officials, men and women of Gorbachev's generation, communicators such as Yakovlev, Burlatski, or Bovin, who strongly believed that political and psychological de-Stalinization had not gone far enough under Khrushchev. They were repelled by the persistence of make-believe and mendacity. They sincerely believed in Communism with a human face and without too many unnecessary lies. But these were people active in the center in Moscow, and it was easier to be a liberal there than in Verkhne Udinsk. They certainly did not carry the majority with them, not in the higher party institutions, not in the lower ranks, not in the country at large, not apparently among the largely apolitical youth. Their main support came from the intelligentsia, an important social group, to be sure, numbering millions of people with considerable influence in view of their access to the media. But even the intelligentsia was split, as had been the case in Tsarist Russia. . . .

Was true *glasnost* really compatible with a one-party system and total control of internal security and propaganda? Even under *glasnost* the head of the KGB was telling the media not only what not to publish but also on what to concentrate. True, it could be argued that there was a great difference in comparison with the past. Whereas in bygone days any such speech would have produced fear, trembling, and immediate compliance, in the age of *glasnost* there would be less fear and only partial compliance. Chebrikov, the head of state security in 1988, was certainly not a Yezhov or a Beria,[4] only a servant of the party and the state. But he obviously must have felt that his position entitled him to make pronouncements of this kind, and this raised wider issues. As one Soviet citizen put it, would de-Nazification have been possible with the Gestapo still in place? True, it was a much more enlightened Gestapo under new management and different personnel, among some of whom there was apparently sympathy for *glasnost*—within limits. . . .

. . . *Glasnost* is not irreversible, as long as there are no democratic guarantees; what has been given can be taken away. It seems likely that the farther limits of *glasnost* have been reached and that in the years to come there will be no major progress beyond them. There could well be a partial retreat, a more narrow redefinition of these limits.

[4] Nikolai Yezhov and Lavrenty Beria were heads of the secret police, 1936–1938 and 1938–1953, respectively.—Ed.

Glasnost has meant plain speaking about shortcomings of Soviet politics, society, and other aspects of life. But what if the revelations and the debates do not lead to an improvement? *Glasnost* was based on hope; it was felt by many like a breath of fresh air, after the suffocating years of stagnation. But if the changes do not materialize, the hopes are bound to fade and the air will again get stale.

It is unlikely that the reforms of Soviet society will be a full success within the next five or ten years. The economic and social problems are structural; the political shortcomings are rooted deeply in the past. Something akin to a cultural revolution would be needed to effect real change. Such revolutions have occurred but rarely in history, and there are no signs that anything of this kind will take place in the Soviet Union in the near future. The situation may have been precritical (in Gorbachev's words), but it is not critical enough for truly radical change. There will no doubt be minor improvements, as the result of what some economists call the "new broom" effect, of greater energy and new initiatives emerging from the top leadership. But the newness of the broom passes with every year, and what then?

Glasnost will increasingly be in danger because it makes governing the country more difficult than in the past. All kinds of tensions, national and social, which were suppressed before are coming to the fore. There are bound to be clashes and disorder, and this will play into the hands of those who were arguing all along that the Soviet people are not ready now, and will perhaps not be ready for generations to come, for political freedom. The authoritarian style, which has prevailed through virtually all its history it will be said, is the only one befitting it, an enlightened authoritarianism to be sure, but not a system based on freedom and broad, voluntary popular participation. The greater the problems that will face the Soviet leadership in the years to come, the greater the temptation to return to the past style.

Paul Goble

Ferment Among the Minorities

As Gorbachev and his supporters attempted to accelerate reform through glasnost and democratization, the national minorities who made up nearly half the Soviet population seized the opportunity to press for autonomy and ultimately independence. In a 1990 symposium at Georgetown University, Paul Goble, then a U.S. Department of State adviser on the Soviet nationalities, assessed perestroika in the light of this upsurge of the minorities. His paper was published in book form together with the rest of the symposium proceedings in 1991.

The pre-1917 Russian empire . . . was built before the nation at its center was fully consolidated, thus leaving open the question of the boundaries of identity for the metropolitan country and its periphery. Second, economic marginality and foreign threat led to an absorption of society by the state—that is, to the politicization of all relationships. Third, expansion was justified in terms of a radical messianism that sanctioned unexpected cruelty but opened the way for integration of those who accepted its terms. Fourth, the empire was organized not along ethnic or political lines but, rather, for purposes of administrative convenience. And fifth, the central authorities pursued a highly differentiated approach to different ethnic communities under the imperial domain, depending on political calculation and ethnic distance from the dominant community. Thus, some nationalities were seriously repressed, while others enjoyed special protection and still others were excluded from the direct attention of the center.

Paul Goble. "Imperial Endgame: Nationality Problems and the Soviet Future," from *Five Years that Shook the World: Gorbachev's Unfinished Revolution*, Harley D. Balzer, ed., pp. 93–103. Copyright © 1991. Reprinted by permission of Westview Press, Boulder, CO.

Such an autocratic arrangement worked under conditions of underdevelopment and premodern social relationships. But the rise of capitalism and the expansion of communication and education undermined the traditional relationships and by the end of the nineteenth century had made the old order untenable. Several large Western nationalities such as the Poles, the Finns, and the Ukrainians were actively seeking independence; others were demanding one or another form of autonomy or, at the very least, recognition from a regime that steadfastly refused to identify people on the basis of nationality alone—religion and language, yes; but not nationality in most cases.

World War I and then the February 1917 revolution accelerated these changes, leading to demands both for recognition of the nationality principle by all groups, including the Russians, and for independence by an increasing number of ethnic communities. In the ensuing chaos, many successfully achieved independence for a brief period, all were able to achieve recognition of the nationality principle for state arrangements, and some were able to win genuine independence. Had this process proceeded without interruption, the Russian empire would have developed as the Austro-Hungarian one did; and most [nationalities] would have achieved some form of democratic or guided democratic regimes. But as everyone knows, that did not happen.

In ethnic terms, the October 1917 revolution was a profoundly reactionary movement. In the name of socialist internationalism, and with the aid of a powerful army fed simultaneously by ideology and xenophobic anger at foreign intervention, Moscow reconquered the empire, and reordered it at the same time. This reordering took the form of and was reflected in three developments: the creation of a new form of official nationality that required individuals to identify themselves in ethnic terms—something that many people had never done before and that had the effect of intensifying this form of identity; the establishment of pseudo-statehood for the largest nationalities, which were thus given the institutionality of independence without its realization; and the increase of the Russian nationality from 43 per cent of the population immediately before 1917 to more than 60 per cent in 1921 as a result of the departure of Poland, Finland, the Baltic states, and two provinces in Turkey.

Pseudo-statehood and Russian numeric preponderance were central to the elaboration of the repressive Stalinist system, which lasted with only relatively minor modifications until recently. On the one hand, the non-Russians received institutions that could only encourage them and threaten the Russian core with devolution or even dissolution; on the other hand, the Russians, who had also undergone the nationalizing experience, felt that they should be the beneficiaries of these changes. Stalin offered the Russians a Faustian bargain: They could hold the empire but only at the price of denying some of their own aspirations, since to flaunt those openly would render maintenance of their control impossible. The Russians also had to be willing to subject themselves to greater repression than otherwise would have been necessary. In short, the Russians were offered the choice of being free or being powerful; not surprisingly, they chose the latter at the behest of Stalin and thus became the sociological basis of the Stalinist state.

In 1985, the Stalinist system remained more or less in place, although there was some sense that it could not endure much longer. Still, most Soviet leaders were confident that the system would somehow endure and that in any case it was not threatened with collapse. In 1990, only five years later, Mikhail Gorbachev has conceded that the nationalities crisis threatens both his reforms and the integrity of the Soviet Union. Some junior officials are even more explicit. For instance, Vyacheslav Mikhailov, the CPSU Central Committee official responsible for overseeing ethnic developments, has conceded that the Soviet Union "will not survive in its present form" and that it definitely will be "smaller than it is today." He has also suggested that the "critical period" for the country would be the last months of 1990. How did things come to such a pass so quickly? . . .

The most powerful force, and the one that conditions all the others, is the massive social change that the Soviet state has sponsored throughout the USSR. Its policy of mass mobilization not only transformed the country's economy but also brought more ethnic groups into contact with one another. In 1917, relatively few Soviet citizens lived in ethnically mixed regions; now more than one Soviet citizen in five lives in an area dominated by people of another ethnic group. That experience of strangeness is perhaps the most ethnically sensitizing of all. Moscow's policy of promoting equalization among the nationalities had the effect of eliminating one of the most potent arguments for Russian dominance. Non-Russians who might have been willing to accept a Russian role when they lacked the necessary cadres were no longer quiescent once they acquired their own intelligentsias. Moreover, the rise of non-Russian intelligentsias created a political class that by the 1980s could not be absorbed by the slowing Soviet economy, thus leading to a situation familiar to many Third World countries. And the system's promotion of growth—which has often been more rapid on the periphery than at the center—launched a revolution of rising expectations that both the system's own inefficiencies and its inability to move from secondary to tertiary and quaternary economic arrangements would not allow it to meet. As a result, frustration levels rose; and these frustrations were invested with ethnic meaning. . . .

. . . Gorbachev's role should not be underestimated. In this connection, I want to focus on three matters: what he brought to the job in ethnic terms; how his general policy thrusts had unintended consequences given the country's ethnic mosaic; and, finally, how his specific nationality policies have backfired in ways that he neither expected nor desired.

To a remarkable extent, Gorbachev is a Soviet man, perhaps the last Soviet man. He spent most of his career in an ethnically homogeneous environment and, with rare exceptions, has surrounded himself with people like himself. In contrast with his predecessors, he had little experience with ethnicity, little interest in it, and even less patience with ethnic aspirations. Gorbachev is the first Soviet leader since Lenin to have come to power without ever having worked in a non-Russian region of the country; and he is the only Soviet ruler who had never written an article or given a speech on nationality issues before his elevation. In sum, he does not think in ethnic terms, and—as his experience with the RSFSR Supreme Soviet in the spring of 1990 showed—cannot credibly present himself even as a Russian. On the contrary, he is a modern rationalist who identifies with the Soviet system. Unfortunately for him, rationality and Sovietism are not sufficient in a country of more than one hundred ethnic groups.

In keeping with his earlier inattention to ethnicity, Gorbachev neither focused on it during the first years of his reign nor developed policies designed to cope with the country's ethnic mix. Instead, he launched a series of broad policy thrusts, each of which made rational sense and would have worked if the country had been monoethnic, but all of which had serious repercussions in a multiethnic society. Here I would like to consider five of these policy thrusts.

Reduction in Coercion and the Rise of Glasnost

By reducing coercion, Gorbachev hoped to free up public activism. That he has certainly done. But he has also transformed the role of intermediate political leaders (i.e., the heads of union republics) from representatives of the center to mobilizers of the people and representatives of their wishes. Prior to Gorbachev, republic party leaders were Moscow's men on the scene, ready to do Moscow's bidding and to use force to impose central policy. Now, in the absence of coercion, they must represent the population, thereby giving national content to the pseudo-institutions that Stalin created and setting the stage for imperial devolution. Moreover, in allowing greater press freedom, Gorbachev failed to recognize that the Soviet media are divided along ethno-territorial and ethno-linguistic rather than functional lines. As a result, any expansion in press coverage will reflect a nationality bias and promote nationality sensitivities—because there is no issue that does not look different to different parts of the population.

The Cult of Rationality

Gorbachev is a committed rationalist. Unfortunately for him, that stance has ethnic consequences. His attacks on Marxism-Leninism and on Soviet history have deprived the Soviet state of its ideological legitimacy—proletarian internationalism, after all, was the only real justification for the state to retain its current size. And his elimination of affirmative action for non-Russians and of reserved slots for Russians angered both groups, disappointing those who had expected to retain if not improve on their current ethnic situation. Judging people on meritocratic criteria may improve efficiency, but the careful balance implied by the

Stalinist synthesis outlined earlier is unfortunately called into question in the process.

Economic Collapse

Gorbachev has overseen perhaps the worst Soviet economic recession since World War II, and his continued tinkering with the economy has created new classes of winners and losers. Each of these developments has had ethnic consequences as well—in the first case, by leading virtually every group to invest economic difficulties with ethnic meaning; and in the second, by prompting the newly disadvantaged first to see a conspiracy behind the shift to market forces and then to resist them as such.

"New Thinking" in Foreign Policy

Gorbachev's new approach to foreign policy has had serious consequences for the cohesiveness of the country. As one Novosti correspondent put it, "no one can say how long the 'welded forever' Soviet Union would have lasted" had it not been for the "psychology of a beleaguered nation with a common destiny" that was promoted by the cold war. Once that discipline was lost, more and more non-Russians began taking a new look at their country, and Russians increasingly did so as well. It is not only the United States that would suffer by being deprived of an enemy, as Georgiy Arbatov[1] had threatened. Moreover, Gorbachev's decision not to prevent the collapse of Communist power in Eastern Europe—the outer empire—raised the question of whether he would be willing to defend the inner empire as well. Baltic moves in early 1990 cannot be understood outside the context of what happened six months earlier in Eastern Europe.

Holding Elections

Perhaps the most ethnically significant (if ethnically unappreciated) of Gorbachev's policies was his decision to allow republic governments to be elected when he himself had never faced a competitive public election. Indeed, by holding elections in the three Slavic republics on March 4, 1990, Gorbachev allowed the

---

[1] Arbatov, director of the Institute of the USA and Canada in Moscow.—Ed.

creation of legitimate governments in the heartland at a time when he had not been similarly legitimated himself. That decision not only weakened his authority; it also meant that these new republic leaders had to seek out nationalist themes in order to legitimate themselves. Boris Yeltsin is no accident; he is the unintended consequence of Gorbachev's own policies.

If Gorbachev did not want to focus on ethnic issues initially, he soon found that he had no choice, given the nationalist upsurge throughout the country. His initial reaction, however, underscored the extent to which he failed to understand the situation: In early 1988, one of his aides insisted that ethnic unrest would boost perestroika, a line repeated by some in the West. But Gorbachev gradually came to understand that he had to focus on the issue and to adopt policies to cope with nationalist aspirations. According to one Soviet writer, this change began in 1987 and was fully in evidence in 1988 and 1989. Unfortunately for Gorbachev, his earlier inattention was fully in evidence here as well. . . .

To make some sense of this confusing mosaic we have to divide the nationalities according to the way they are perceived in Moscow. Roughly, there are five categories. The first consists of the fourteen non-Russian Union Republics, whose population amounts to 40–45 percent of the total. These, in turn, can be broken down into four basic groups, defined by what they want. The first are the Balts, who actively want independence and are working toward it. The second are the three Republics of the Soviet West—Moldova, Ukraine, and Belorussia. Now that a revolution has occurred in Romania, some Moldovans want to become Romanians. (When Ceauşescu was in power, not even Romanians wanted to be Romanians.)

Ukraine is divided into three parts. . . . The citizens of the extreme west, who constitute one-sixth of the population, probably want to achieve complete independence. But the much larger eastern portion of the Republic has given us such well-known Ukrainian nationalists as Nikolai Ryzhkov[2] and Nikita Khrushchev. I do not think that Ukraine is going to be making the kinds of demands for total separation that we've seen in the Baltics.

[2] Ryzhkov, Soviet prime minister under Gorbachev, 1986–1990.—Ed.

I would argue that the great unheralded national movement is the one in Belorussia. There is enormous anger over the authorities' lies about the consequences of Chernobyl, and about the failure of the local authorities to permit the emergence of a People's Front. The headquarters of the Belorussian people's front had to be established in Riga, Latvia. The organization managed to turn out 100,000 people for a demonstration that included the slogan: "Ingrelia, let us Romanize our leaders," by which they meant to follow the Romanian example in deposing Ceauşescu. The demonstrators took control of Minsk television and radio for nearly four hours to broadcast their story. The Belorussian situation is potentially explosive. The movement is not structured: The level of institutionalization is considerably below the level of mobilization in Belorussia.

Next are the peoples of the republics of the Caucasus, all of whom hate Moscow almost as much as they hate one another. Everybody thinks that these three Republics—Georgia, Armenia, and Azerbaijan—are all pushing for independence. Certainly all of them want a new deal with Moscow. But I would argue that none of them wants independence in the short term. Independence would shrink Georgia by 50 percent in size and 60 percent in population; and it would be reduced to a state that would not be viable at all because of the minorities around it and within its borders, all of whom don't like the Georgians. The Armenians might have a vision of what could happen to them wedged between Azerbaijan and Turkey, and they continue to be worried about that. Both Moscow and Teheran have a vested interest in not letting Azerbaijan become the focal point for the 12 to 15 million ethnic Azerbaijanis in Iran.

The point is not that these people are going to stop pressing their demands, but, rather, that they're not likely to be granted independence, and that it might not be their best option.

To those in the West who, following the demonstration by the women of Stavropol krai, said that Azerbaijan had the potential to become a domestic Afghanistan, I would respond that it took fewer than 5,000 troops, when Moscow finally got around to sending them, to restore some semblance of order in that republic. The Soviets didn't do nearly so well with 100,000 troops in Afghanistan.

Finally, there is Central Asia, where widespread communal violence continues, with Muslims killing Muslims. The violence is likely to worsen with Russians leaving Tadzhikstan at the rate of about 5,000 a month and departing the other Central Asian republics at only a slightly lower rate.

The next category of nationalities is the one that gives Moscow the most grief, because Moscow doesn't have any good answers for its constituents—the various "punished peoples." These include the Germans, the Crimean Tatars, and the Meshkhetians who were deported by Stalin and who certainly can't go home again. The Germans can't go back to the Middle Volga, the Crimean Tatars can't go back to Crimea and the Meshkhetians can't go back to Georgia, because the people who now live in these places don't want them back. Precisely because they are relatively small in number and because they lack political institutions, the kind of activities they engage in will be extra-systemic and tend toward violence, especially in the case of the Meshkhetians but, to a lesser extent, the Crimean Tartars as well. The Germans are going to join the reunited Germany as quickly as they possibly can.

The third big group of nationalities comprise the 60 million Soviet citizens who live outside their home ethnic territories. This group represents Gorbachev's second biggest problem. One consequence of the devolution of authority and power in the Soviet Union from Moscow to the republics was a change in the basis of nationality oppression in the USSR. If hitherto the Russians were oppressing non-Russians, the non-Russians are now oppressing minorities. And they are not suppressing only the Russians. For a good example of what human rights is not about, look at what the Lithuanians have been doing to the Polish minority in Lithuania [i.e., denying them any autonomous government].

Now that these groups are at risk, Moscow's general failure to come to their aid means that people are moving back to their "home" republics. There are now between 750,000 and one million refugees in the Soviet Union—not just from Armenia and Azerbaijan, but from many other areas as well. These population movements constitute an enormous problem. And to the extent that the republics become more ethnically homogeneous, which is what refugee movements tend to promote, Moscow will find it increasingly difficult to manage the situation.

The fourth group of nationalities . . . is composed of the micro-nationalities of the Far North in Siberia. In April 1990 they convened their first All-Union Conference to create institutions intended to pressure the government. While these 38 or 39 groups, who number fewer than a quarter of a million in toto, would not seem to constitute a large problem, they are strategically located. They enjoy enormous support from some key Russian leaders, who see them as local tenants for the only pure part of Russia that is left. And they are in a position right now to cause some very serious policy difficulties. . . .

Finally, there are the Russians. The Russians are very angry. From their point of view they have not done very well. They see themselves as having carried an enormous burden. Now that they have experienced a real election, they have a real Supreme Soviet and a president—a new president with power equivalent to a U.S. governor who controls everything west of the Mississippi River. Their potential for causing trouble for the center is very great. Increasingly, the Russians are against everything, not for something. This tendency was reinforced by the way in which the elections were conducted.

One of the biggest challenges for the Russians may be to hold the Russian Republic together. Increasingly, there are demands for the formation of an Independent Siberian Union Republic, or even an Independent Siberia. The leader of that movement is someone who, as the newspaper *Novosibirsk* put it, was arrested eight years ago for calling for a Siberian Union Republic. Now, he has been elected to the legislature for calling for the same thing.

Historically, both Soviet writers and Western students of Soviet society have discussed the nationality problems of the USSR as a question, implying that there is a single answer to the issue that will allow it to be solved. More recently, the possibility that there may be multiple answers has come to be appreciated. But at least there is still a tendency to assume that there are answers.

Elsewhere, I have argued that nationality developments are tending in three main directions: toward independence, toward federalism, and toward cofederalism. I have also argued that Moscow has five main tools to manage and contain the process: coercion, devolution, the elaboration of a new ideology, economic revival, and charismatic appeals by the leadership. Moreover, I have suggested that only coercion and devolution are immediately available, and that independence and cofederalism are the most likely outcomes. Such conclusions highlight the extent to which I, too, have been a prisoner of the old conceptions.

Here I would like to suggest that the future is likely to be far more complicated than has been adumbrated by Gorbachev. The Soviet empire is likely to devolve into a series of cross-cutting alliances for a variety of specific purposes. Some republics will achieve political independence but will be locked in military and economic alliances, others will have less political freedom but greater economic autonomy, and so on. Gorbachev is correct in saying that the future will not be like the past, but even he has not gone far enough. The end of the Soviet empire will mean the elaboration of a new state system—one in which the USSR may resemble the Warsaw Pact and Comecon [the Council for Mutual Economic Assistance], and in which creative new arrangements are likely. Any effort to impose a single common outcome will fail.

Nina Andreyeva

The Conservative Reaction

In March 1988 the conservative Communist newspaper *Sovetskaya Rossiya* printed a long letter, purportedly written by a Leningrad chemistry teacher, Nina Andreyeva, but probably inspired or edited

Nina Andreyeva. From "I Cannot Forgo Principles," *Sovetskaya Rossiya*, 13 March 1988. English translation, *Current Digest of the Soviet Press*, vol. 40, no. 13. Translation Copyright © 1988 by *Current Digest of the Soviet Press*, published weekly at Columbus, Ohio. Reprinted by permission of the Digest.

by anti-perestroika functionaries in the Communist party. The letter attacked perestroika and glasnost and focused on the country's positive achievements under Stalin. There were also anti-Semitic overtones expressed by code words such as *militant cosmopolitanism*, implying unpatriotic Jews. The Andreyeva letter was widely considered the opening shot in a conservative counteroffensive against perestroika, or even the beginning of a coup d'état, until an article in *Pravda* (reportedly written by Politburo member Alexander Yakovlev) confirmed that the reformers were still in control.

Like many others, I am an adviser for a group of students. In our days, after a period of social apathy and intellectual dependence, students are gradually beginning to be charged with the energy of revolutionary changes. Naturally, debates arise—about the paths of restructuring and its economic and ideological aspects. Openness, candor and the disappearance of zones closed to criticism, as well as emotional fervor in the mass consciousness, especially among young people, are frequently manifested in the posing of problems that, to one extent or another, have been "prompted" by Western radio voices or by those of our compatriots who are not firm in their notions about the essence of socialism. What a wide range of topics is being discussed! A multiparty system, freedom of religious propaganda, leaving the country to live abroad, the right to a broad discussion of sexual problems in the press, the need for the decentralization of the management of culture, the abolition of compulsory military service. Among students, a particularly large number of arguments are about the country's past. . . .

. . . Too many things have turned up that I cannot accept, that I cannot agree with. The constant harping on "terrorism," "the people's political servility," "uninspired social vegetating," "our spiritual slavery," "universal fear," "the entrenched rule of louts"—It is from these mere threads that the history of the period of the transition to socialism in our country is often woven. Therefore, it comes as no surprise, for example, that in some students nihilistic views are intensifying, and ideological confusion, a dislocation of political reference points and even ideological omnivorousness are appearing. Sometimes one hears assertions that it is time to call to account the Communists who supposedly "dehumanized" the country's life after 1917.

At the February plenary session of the Central Committee, it was emphasized once again that it is urgently necessary for "young people to learn the class vision of the world and gain an understanding of the connection between common human and class interests. This includes an understanding of the class essence of the changes taking place in our country." [Ye. K. Ligachev] . . .

In talking with students and pondering crucial problems with them, I automatically come to the conclusion that a good many distortions and one-sided views have piled up in our country, notions that obviously need to be corrected. I want to devote special attention to some of these things.

Take the question of the place of J. V. Stalin in our country's history. It is with his name that the entire obsession with critical attacks is associated, an obsession that, in my opinion, has to do not so much with the historical personality itself as with the whole extremely complex transitional era—an era linked with the unparalleled exploits of an entire generation of Soviet people who today are gradually retiring from active labor, political and public activity. Industrialization, collectivization and the cultural revolution, which brought our country into the ranks of the great world powers, are being forcibly squeezed into the "personality cult" formula. All these things are being questioned. Things have reached a point at which insistent demands for "repentance" are being made on "Stalinists" (and one can assign to their number whomever one wishes). Praise is being lavished on novels and films that lynch the era of tempestuous changes, which is presented as a "tragedy of peoples." . . .

. . . Together with all Soviet people, I share the anger and indignation over the large-scale repressions that took place in the 1930s and 1940s through the fault of the Party and state leadership of that time. But common sense resolutely protests the monochromatic coloring of contradictory events that has now begun to prevail in certain press organs.

I support the Party's call to uphold the honor and dignity of the trailblazers of socialism. I think that it is from these Party and class positions that we should assess the historical role of all Party and state leaders, including Stalin. In this case, one must not reduce the matter to the "court" aspect or to abstract moralizing by people far removed from that stormy time and from the people who lived and worked then. Indeed, they worked in such a way that what they did is an inspirational example for us even today. . . .

From long and frank discussions with young people, we draw the conclusion that the attacks on the state of the dictatorship of the proletariat and on the leaders of our country at that time have not only political, ideological and moral causes but also their own social substratum. There are quite a few people who have a stake in broadening the staging area of these attacks, and not just on the other side of our borders. Along with the professional anticommunists in the West, who long ago chose the supposedly democratic slogan of "anti-Stalinism," there live and thrive the descendants of the classes overthrown by the October Revolution, by no means all of whom have been able to forget the material and social losses of their forebears. One must include here the spiritual heirs of Dan, Martov and others in the category of Russian Social Democratism, the spiritual followers of Trotsky or Yagoda,[1] and the descendants of the NEPmen,[2] the Basmachi [participants in armed resistance to Soviet rule in Central Asia in 1918–1924—Trans.] and the kulaks, who bear a grudge against socialism. . . .

Recently, one of my students startled me with the revelation that the class struggle is supposedly an obsolete concept, as is the leading role of the proletariat. It would be all right if she were the only one maintaining such a thing. But, for example, a furious argument broke out recently over a respected academician's assertion that the present relations between states of the two different social and economic systems are devoid of class content. I admit that the academician did not deem it necessary to explain why for several decades he had written the exact opposite—that peaceful coexistence is nothing other than a form of class struggle in the international arena. It turns out that the philosopher has now repudiated that notion. Well, views do change. However, it seems to me that the duty of a leading philosopher does enjoin him to

[1] Genrikh Yagoda: secret police chief, purged in 1938—Ed.
[2] Private businessmen during the NEP.—Ed.

explain, at least to those who have learned and are learning from his books: What—does the international working class today, in the form of its state and political organs, really no longer act as a countervailing force to world capital? . . .

The first, and deepest, ideological current that has already revealed itself in the course of restructuring claims to be a model of some kind of left-liberal dilettantish socialism, to be the exponent of a humanism that is very true and "clean" from class incrustations. Against proletarian collectivism, the adherents of this current put up "the intrinsic worth of the individual"—with modernistic quests in the field of culture, God-seeking tendencies, technocratic idols, the preaching of the "democratic" charms of present-day capitalism and fawning over its achievements, real and imagined. Its representatives assert that we have built the wrong kind of socialism and that only today, "for the first time in history, has an alliance come about between the political leadership and the progressive intelligentsia." . . .

It is the champions of "left-liberal socialism" who are shaping the tendency to falsify the history of socialism. They suggest to us that in the country's past only the mistakes and crimes are real, in doing so keeping quiet about the supreme achievements of the past and the present. Laying claim to complete historical truth, they substitute scholastic ethical categories for social and political criteria of the development of society. I would very much like to understand: Who needs, and why, to have every prominent leader of the Party Central Committee and the Soviet government compromised after he leaves office and discredited in connection with his actual or supposed mistakes and miscalculations, made while solving some very complex problems on roads uncharted by history? Where did we get this passion for squandering the prestige and dignity of the leaders of the world's first socialist country?

Another special feature of the views of the "left-liberals" is an obvious or camouflaged cosmopolitan tendency, a sort of nationality-less "internationalism." I have read somewhere that when, after the Revolution, a delegation of merchants and factory owners came to the Petrograd Soviet to see Trotsky "as a Jew," complaining of oppression by Red Guards, he declared that he was "not a Jew but an internationalist," which thoroughly bewildered the supplicants.

For Trotsky, the concept of the "national" meant a kind of inferiority and narrowness in comparison to the "international." That's why he emphasized the "national tradition" of October, wrote about "the national element in Lenin," maintained that the Russian people "had received no cultural legacy," etc. For some reason, we are ashamed to say that it was the Russian proletariat, which the Trotskyists slighted as "backward and uncultured," that carried out, in Lenin's words, "the three Russian Revolutions," or that the Slavic peoples were in the vanguard of mankind's battle against fascism.

Of course, what I have said does not signify any disparagement of the historical contribution of other nations and nationalities. It only, as the current saying goes, ensures a full measure of historical truth. When students ask me how it could have happened that thousands of villages in the Non-Black-Earth Zone [northern Russia] and Siberia have become deserted, I reply that this, too, is the high price paid for victory [in World War II] and the postwar rehabilitation of the national economy, as is the irretrievable loss of large numbers of monuments of Russian national culture. I am also convinced that the pacifist erosion of defense and patriotic consciousness, as well as the desire to list the slightest manifestation of national pride by Great Russians under the heading of great-power chauvinism, stem from disparagement of the significance of historical consciousness.

Here is something else that alarms me: Militant cosmopolitanism is now linked with the practice of "refusenikism"—of "refusing" socialism. Unfortunately, we suddenly think of this only when its neophytes plague us with their outrages in front of Smolny or under the Kremlin's walls. Moreover, we are somehow gradually being trained to see this phenomenon as an almost inoffensive change of "place of residence," not as class and nationality betrayal by persons most of whom have been graduated from higher schools and graduate schools at public expense. In general, some people are inclined to look at "refusenikism" as some kind of manifestation of "democracy" and human rights," feeling that the talents of those involved have been prevented from blossoming by "stagnant socialism." Well, if over there, in the "free world," their tireless enterprise and "genius" aren't appreciated and selling their conscience doesn't interest the special services, they can come back—. . . .

Whereas the "neoliberals" are oriented toward the West, the other "alternative tower" (to use Prokhanov's expression), the "guardians and traditionalists," seeks to "overcome socialism by moving backward"—in other words, to return to the social forms of presocialist Russia. The spokesmen for this unique "peasant socialism" are fascinated with this image. In their opinion, a loss of the moral values that the peasant community had accumulated through the dim haze of centuries took place 100 years ago. The "traditionalists" have rendered undoubted services in exposing corruption, in fairly solving ecological problems, in combating alcoholism, in protecting historical monuments and in countering the dominance of mass culture, which they rightly assess as a psychosis of consumerism.

At the same time, the views of the ideologists of "peasant socialism" contain a misunderstanding of the historical significance of October for the fatherland's fate, a one-sided appraisal of collectivization as "frightful arbitrary treatment of the peasantry," uncritical views on religious-mystical Russian philosophy, old tsarist concepts in scholarship relating to our country's history, and an unwillingness to see the postrevolutionary stratification of the peasantry and the revolutionary role of the working class. . . .

The difficulties in the upbringing of young people are deepened still more by the fact that unofficial [*neformalny*] organizations and associations are being created in the pattern of the ideas of the "neoliberals" and "neo-Slavophiles." In some cases, extremist elements capable of provocations are gaining the upper hand in the leadership of these groups. Recently, the politicization of these grass-roots [*samodeyatelny*] organizations on the basis of a pluralism that is far from socialist has been noted. Frequently the leaders of these organizations talk about "power-sharing" on the basis of a "parliamentary regime," "free trade unions," "autonomous publishing houses," etc. In my opinion, all this makes it possible to draw the conclusion that the main and cardinal question in the debates now under way in the country is the question of recognizing or not recognizing the leading role of the Party and the working class in socialist construction, and hence in restructuring—needless to say, with all the theoretical and practical conclusions for politics, the economy and ideology that stem therefrom. . . .

Today, the question of the role and place of socialist ideology has taken on a very acute form. Under the aegis of a moral and spiritual "cleansing," the authors of opportunistic constructs are eroding the boundaries and criteria of scientific ideology, manipulating openness, and propagating an extrasocialist pluralism, which objectively impedes restructuring in social consciousness. This is having an especially detrimental effect on young people, something that, I repeat, we higher-school instructors, schoolteachers and all those who deal with young people's problems are distinctly aware of. As M. S. Gorbachev said at the February plenary session of the CPSU Central Committee: "In the spiritual sphere as well, and perhaps in this sphere first of all, we must be guided by our Marxist-Leninist principles. Comrades, we must not forgo these principles under any pretexts."

We stand on this, and we will continue to do so. We have not received these principles as a gift: We have gained them through suffering at decisive turning points in the history of the fatherland.

Robert Sharlet

The Rule of Law

As perestroika unfolded, Gorbachev felt the need for a power base distinct from the party apparatus and for new legitimacy based on constitutionalism and government according to law. Robert Sharlet, professor of political science at Union College in Schenectady, New

From Robert Sharlet, *Soviet Constitutional Crisis: From De-Stalinization to Disintegration*, pp. 86–95, 98–101, 105–107, 109. Copyright © 1992 by M. E. Sharpe, Inc. Reprinted by permission of the publisher.

York, and an expert on Soviet law, has charted the development of legal thinking in Russia before, during, and after the Gorbachev era. He emphasizes Gorbachev's political pragmatism and the growing difficulties the Soviet reformers had in working out a stable but plausible basis for political authority.

Gorbachev's most dramatic departure from previous post-Stalin reform initiatives was not simply the scope of his program, but the change of venue for its proposed realization. As he gradually shifted the locus of his power from the party to the state, the Soviet Constitution became the principal framework for the articulation of the reform objectives. A constant refrain of Gorbachev and the reformers was the need to institutionalize the changes to ensure the "irreversibility" of restructuring. The main medium to achieve this goal became constitutional law, long just another instrument of party rule.

By 1987, the tenth anniversary year of the 1977 USSR Constitution, the document had been amended only once, a minor amendment in 1981. The following year, in late 1988, nearly one-third of the Constitution was amended. A year later, many of the new and revised constitutional clauses were re-amended. The year 1990 was an even more productive year for constitutional reform. As part of Gorbachev's transfer of power from the party to the state, he engineered the revision of Article 6, depriving the party of its political monopoly over the Soviet system. To offset the consequential decline of his own power as party leader, Gorbachev then pushed through the legislative process the constitutional creation of the office of an executive presidency of the Soviet state. In most Western constitutional systems, these systemic changes alone would represent an extraordinary development, nearly the equivalent of the constitutional transition from the Fourth to the Fifth French Republic under De Gaulle in 1958. . . .

Basically, since the 19th Party Conference in 1988, Gorbachev had sought to create a socialist *pravovoe gosudarstvo*, a term that can be literally translated as "a legal state" or interpretively as "a law-based state." In this sense Gorbachev was building on cumulative political and legal development. The post-Stalin period had witnessed a contraction of prerogative rule, or the so-called administrative-command system, and the progressive expansion of normative means of governance, or the legal order. Khrushchev, through de-Stalinization and criminal justice reforms in the 1950s and early 1960s, and Brezhnev by continuing the law reform process and producing the new USSR Constitution of 1977, had sequentially laid the foundations for Gorbachev's proposal for a law-based state. The net result of the preceding developments, however, was a constitutionalized bureaucracy behind which the party still exercised its unlimited rule over Soviet society.

Gorbachev's idea was far more radical: to build a law-based state in the USSR as both a product of perestroika and the housing for a restructured Soviet system within which the party's rule would be limited by the boundaries of constitutional action. A source of confusion was that Gorbachev had not clearly and consistently sorted out what kind of new state he sought to develop. Would it be merely a state based on law as against unchecked party commands, or a liberal state, with laws protecting individual and group rights? Whatever the future held, Gorbachev's preferred route was via constitutional reform, which, unfortunately, led the USSR into a political labyrinth. In order to establish constitutional supremacy, Gorbachev had to concede to the public various degrees of freedom and a range of individual and collective choice. The unintended consequence was that the long-hoped-for culmination of the country's quest for constitutional order degenerated into constitutional disorder in the 1990s. . . .

Due to the success of the policies of glasnost and democratization and other legal enactments, as well as a constant flow of additions to the legislative agenda, it soon became apparent that the existing constitution could not accommodate the vast restructuring program. Without waiting for promised laws, individuals and groups had begun to appropriate to themselves implied *de facto* rights of a freer press, a wider range of permissible speech, and the virtually unprecedented acts of forming independent groups and taking causes to the streets. Policy statements were outstripping legal empowerment as permitted behavior began to render numerous clauses of the Constitution, especially in the political and rights sections, unreflective of the emerging reality. Proposed new legislation on the courts and due process, not to mention a promised statute on the KGB, implied the future prospect of major constitutional surgery at the very least. In this context it was evident to Gorbachev that an entirely new constitution would be needed. Accordingly, a Constitutional Commission was appointed to draft what was supposed to have become the fifth Soviet constitution since 1918.

Initially, the task of creating a new constitution, a new fundamental law of the land, appeared within reach. The division of the leadership and strategic elites into reform and conservative factions, however, greatly complicated the process of finding a consensus and slowed the drafting process. The problem was compounded as some of the 15 union republics, availing themselves of the more permissive atmosphere in the country, began to carry out revision of their republic constitutions on their own initiative. The Baltic republics led the way, eventually to be followed by the Russian Republic, the country's largest, under Boris Yeltsin's leadership. Other republics followed suit. Some soon came to realize that, in the face of impending systemic change, patching an existing constitution was an exercise in futility. Thus, in addition to the federal constitutional commission, several republics empaneled their own commissions which, in turn, set off in search of constitutional formulas not necessarily consistent with the interests of the center or the integrity of the union itself.

By the end of the 1980s, Soviet law, which just a few years earlier was seen as the key to the long-term durability of restructuring, had itself become part of the problem. The outpouring of conflicting union and republic constitutional proposals was producing a gridlock. A union republic would amend its constitution in a manner at variance with the official Soviet Constitution. Moscow would react by declaring the offending clause unconstitutional and hence null and void. The republic legislature would, in turn, respond that Moscow's writ was not relevant to the matter. Constitutional conflict became the norm rather than the exception as, one by one, republic legislatures began to assert their preemptive right to approve all federal legislation in order for it to have legal force on their territory. This came to be called the "war of laws."

The crisis of the law itself deepened as separatism spread among a number of union republics. Lithuania led the way, and by the end of 1990 virtually all 15 republics had declared their "sovereignty"—as did most of the autonomous republics within their borders. Separatism and the assertion of sovereignty meant insistence that the language of the titular nationality within a republic take precedence over the *lingua franca*, Russian. The new language demands, in turn, caused anxiety among other nationalities living within the various republics, especially among the Russians, some 25 million of whom live outside the Russian Federation. In an extreme case, a group of largely Russian-populated cities in the Moldovan union republic declared themselves a separate republic.

In this heated environment, the "war of laws" meant that republic legislatures began to routinely reject Moscow's new laws and enact their own. Sometimes these laws would be contradictory, but often they were similar, leading to Moscow's criticism that a situation of "parallel power" was being created in many parts of the country. This included dual prosecutors in some places—one appointed by Moscow as in the past, the other locally, and neither recognizing the other's authority. . . .

After decades of Cold War–style Soviet polemics against "bourgeois" ideas, it has been ironic that the underlying principles for contemporary Soviet constitutionalism were drawn from the American constitutional experience. As late as the mid-1980s it would have been unthinkable for a Soviet jurist to speak or write of emulating the American or any other Western constitution. An article with such a suggestion would never have passed the censor. Under Gorbachev, however, this kind of proposal became commonplace, at least among reform-minded lawyers.

The principal themes of this new Soviet realm of constitutional discourse included such familiar Western ideas as the supremacy of law, including a government subordinate to law, the separation of powers (at least of the party from the government), the precedence of the individual over the state, the emphasis on political and civil rights over the erstwhile focus on social and economic rights, and the creation of a civil society encompassing all of the above as well as the right of private ownership of property. In effect, constitutional scholars, following Gorbachev's lead, were in the process of fundamentally redrafting the "social contract" governing relations between the citizen and the party-state.

The first step in reshaping the Soviet constitutional order began with the extensive wave of amendments proposed by Gorbachev and pushed through the old, compliant USSR Supreme Soviet in late 1988. The central features of these changes for further constitutional revision were new election rules and the restructuring of the Soviet legislative process. The main innovations in Soviet electoral law were the introduction of multi-candidate elections (as against the previous practice of one office, one candidate), and incumbency limitation to two consecutive five-year terms. Multiple candidacies—long permitted in some formerly communist East European countries, but a radical move by Soviet standards—gave more substance and significance to the "secret ballot" provision in the existing constitution. Previously, in standard single-candidate voting for government office, Soviet voters had the option of simply dropping the ballot with the candidate's name in the ballot box or, rather conspicuously, going into a curtained booth, crossing out the name, and then casting the ballot.

While the electoral reforms were intended to introduce a degree of popular sovereignty into the operations of the Soviet system, the constitutional reform of the legislative process was intended to provide greater legitimacy to the subsequent constitutional restructuring contemplated by Gorbachev and his reformist advisors. The core of these changes was that the old Supreme Soviet, which had met in *pro forma* proceedings only a few weeks a year, was superseded by a two-tier legislature: the USSR Congress of People's Deputies and the (new) USSR Supreme Soviet.

The new Congress actually rehabilitated a similar institution which had been introduced in the 1924 Constitution, but then subsequently eliminated in the 1936 Constitution. The old Congress of Soviets had been a typical Bolshevik facade institution designed to give the appearance of popular participation in government in a party-controlled system. The new Congress of 1989, however, was set up to be an actual working supra-legislature with real policy-making powers.

But the party was still the dominant player in Soviet politics, and there was a "catch." The 2,250 deputies to the new Congress were divided into three categories, each with 750 seats. One category was to be directly elected from election districts of equal size. Another group of 750 deputies would be elected on a proportional basis corresponding to the administrative status of the unit, i.e., 32 deputies to be elected from each union republic, 11 from each autonomous republic, 5 from each autonomous region, and one from each autonomous district. Because of the complex nominating process built into the new electoral process, it could be assumed that the party would exercise considerable influence over the selection of candidates. This, indeed, proved to be the case in the first elections to the Congress of People's Deputies in 1989. The party's real political insurance, however, was the third block of 750 seats, which were reserved for deputies to be elected by so-called social organizations. In Soviet practice, the Communist Party itself was classified as a social organization—and at that time it still controlled virtually all other economic, social, and political organizations, such as the Young Communist League and the centralized trade union system.

The newly elected Congress of People's Deputies sat for the first time in the spring of 1989. Among its foremost exclusive powers were "the adoption and amendment of the USSR Constitution," decisions on the structure of the Soviet state, and election of the new Supreme Soviet and its chairman. Thus the Congress created a commission headed by Gorbachev to draft a new constitution, and elected from its membership one-fifth of the deputies (542) to convene the first session of the redesigned Supreme Soviet. The latter body was in session twice a year, for months at a time, and served as the USSR's daily, working legislature empowered to enact all necessary subconstitutional and enabling legislation. Gorbachev was, not unexpectedly, elected its first chairman.

A kind of muted Soviet separation-of-powers doctrine began to take shape, including demonopolization of the party and the emergence of new executive and judicial institutions to complete the triad of powers. Regardless of institutional developments, the most ardent reformers felt that no change of consequence could be implemented as long as the party—even if behind the scenes—retained its monopoly of power over the system. Hence, in early 1990 the Constitution was amended to deprive the party of its exclusive control over policy making and implementation (Art. 6), opening the possibility for party pluralism. Shortly thereafter, the Constitution was again amended, this time to create the new office of the executive presidency, modeled after the French and American presidencies.

In the 1988 amendments, modest steps had already been taken toward a more independent judiciary and a limited constitutional judicial review. To free judges of party and local influence, they were no longer directly elected but were appointed at the lowest level by the next highest governing soviet. Again, to try to ensure more independence, their previous terms of five years were extended to 10. . . .

Simultaneously with the grand structural changes in the Soviet constitutional universe, important subconstitutional legislation was being created to grant significant individual, group, and union republic rights. All Soviet constitutions since the 1936 version had included a heavily caveated "bill of rights." In 1936 and 1977 it was generally understood that these clauses were meant merely to give the document some democratic window-dressing for propaganda purposes. Aside from the fact that there was no enabling legislation for most of these rights, no Soviet citizen under Stalin and few in the post-Stalin years attempted seriously to exercise their individual rights of speech, assembly, demonstration, or press. Then, beginning in the 1960s, a relatively small number of bold dissidents began to act on their abstract constitutional liberties as affirmative rights, reconstruing or ignoring altogether the embedded caveats that directed the exercise of rights to the purpose of strengthening and developing the socialist system. These political dissenters and ethnic activists, numbering no more than a few thousand from the mid-1960s to the mid-1980s, invariably suffered for their courage, experiencing bureaucratic deprivations, prison, psychiatric confinement, and, in some cases, expatriation. . . .

Although legal restructuring had been under way for several years, a number of traditional Russian and Soviet methods of governance remained fundamentally unchanged in spirit. This should not be too surprising since many of these familiar habits were (and remain) deeply ingrained in the elite political culture. Thus we found alive and well in the early 1990s such political traditions as the concentration of power at the top, rule from above, heavy reliance on police power, manifestations of elite legal nihilism (or the circumvention of the law by officials), and the persistence of still largely unaccountable bureaucratic control over public life.

What was new, as part of the rhetoric of reform politics, was the "constitutionalization" of these heretofore unabashed expressions of power and unchecked demonstrations of political will. As the former Soviet Union moved into the modern era—into the politics of appearance as well as reality—political fashion demanded that power be draped in constitutional garb. Political power no longer lurked behind the "magic wall" of party secrecy; it has metamorphosed into a form of constitutionalism. The question for the future became, could the new constitutional forms impose reasonable limits and encourage the exercise of restraint, or would these arrangements eventually become merely a more routinized and efficient means of societal domination?

The most conspicuous contemporary example of the transformation of tradition into constitutionalism was the emergence of the office of the executive presidency under Gorbachev. By the end of the 1980s, after this new Soviet institution had been the recipient of several rounds of legislative strengthening, Gorbachev had gathered in his hands formal, legal powers almost equivalent to the autocratic prerogatives of the last tsar, Nicholas II. These included nearly unlimited decree-making powers, the right to prorogue parliament under certain circumstances, and the authority to suspend the Constitution itself and impose various degrees of martial law. . . .

As befit a Soviet leader who sought to maintain or regain order, President Gorbachev began to deploy the enormous police power at his disposal. Since the USSR was still more a police state than the legal state it aspired to become, the state's coercive reserve was one of Gorbachev's most important political resources for holding the union together in the face of the powerful forces pulling it asunder. In effect, with his political capital dwindling along with his personal popularity, Gorbachev was left with few options to try to keep the country afloat and continue at least a semblance of economic reform.

Part of the force structure available to the Soviet president operated within the constitution writ large, but much remained, as it had been throughout the Soviet period, extraconstitutional. In the past, the nominal superior of the military and the police was the USSR Council of Ministers, through its system of ministries and state committees, while the real master of these forces was the Communist Party leadership, through the Central Committee Secretariat, with its network of oversight committees staffed by cadres of party instructors and supervisors. However, as the party's institutional authority and organizational domination gradually declined in the late 1980s, its tutelage and control over the agencies of force weakened, especially at the all-union level. Since these agencies had not yet been depoliticized (i.e., they still contained Communist Party committees before the August coup), linkage had continued, especially at the regional and local levels in many parts of the country where party organizations still exercised considerable power, including influence over the police.

The net result was that the civil–military relationship that operated within the party's national institutions, as well as the civil–police relationship developed after Stalin's death to yoke the secret police to party control, had been weakened. Ideally, the supervisory slack was to be taken up by the new parliamentary committees intended to exercise oversight. These committees, however, were packed with military and KGB officer-deputies who in most cases were not inclined to carry out systematic oversight of their parent organizations. Consequently, the armed forces and the KGB had begun to operate more independently in the more open political environment of recent years, in contrast to the past, when they were confined to playing "crypto-politics" within the closed party system. Hundreds of military and even KGB officers served as elected deputies throughout the hierarchy of legislatures, while the KGB routinely gave interviews, held press conferences, and operated its own public relations offices in the various republics.

To bring both of these powerful organizations fully within the emerging constitutional order, legislation was passed in 1991 defining the rights and duties, powers and obligations, and roles, generally, of the secret police, while a similar statute was being drafted on the defense establishment at the time of the coup. The first public statute governing the KGB, however, did nothing to allay liberal concern that this behemoth organization of the totalitarian era would continue to wield inordinate power in the country, except now in fully legitimate, legally sanctioned form. The process of codification seemed intended to institutionalize the KGB's extensive powers rather than subject to government regulation its myriad internal police and foreign intelligence functions. . . .

The term "constitution" and its variations had become the new codeword of Soviet politics, superseding such standbys of the bygone era of Communist Party rule as *partiinost*, or "party-mindedness." Thus, opponents who in the past were castigated as "anti-Soviet" were now routinely labeled anti-constitutional. In nearly all public discourse, the participants invoked the constitution in one meaning or another. This plurality of usage, sometimes more aptly described as a cacophony, complicated the process of decoding what Soviet politicians were actually saying.

Invoking the constitution came to mean any of at least four things in contemporary Soviet politics, depending on the speaker, the context, and the objective sought. The most familiar usage, carried over from the time of the 1977 Constitution's unchallenged hegemony in the Soviet system, was to regard the constitution as a metapolicy or a framework for subconstitutional policy making. Interpreting the constitution metapolitically had been an easy task: the party secretariat, on behalf of the leadership, would provide an authoritative rendering to guide the policymaker. In conditions of perestroika, the problem was complicated by several factors. There had come into existence multiple sources of putative authoritative constitutional interpretation, and they were frequently divided among themselves in various ways, including a division familiar to American legal scholars—whether to take a narrow or a broad constructionist approach to the constitution. A major difference with the legal history of the United States is the fact of a single, undisputed constitution and a high court endowed with the power to interpret the document authoritatively.

This brings me to a more recent and novel (for the USSR) meaning of the prevailing codeword, the idea of the constitution as "supreme law." This usage came into vogue in 1988, the year of the 19th Party Conference, which formally launched the concept of a "law-based state" as a model for the Soviet future. If the existing authoritarian state were to be transformed into a government subject to law, then it was necessary to accord to the law itself in its consummate constitutional form the status of supremacy. . . .

A final consideration was the question of who, or what body, could authoritatively interpret what the Constitution said and resolve possible conflicts between its clauses and executive edicts, legislative enactments, and competing subnational constitutions. In effect, how could the doctrine of constitutional supremacy be protected in practice? The first effort in this direction was the creation by constitutional amendment in 1988 of the Committee for Constitutional Supervision (Art. 125), nominally a committee of the new USSR Congress of People's Deputies but actually subordinate only to the Constitution itself. The enabling statute setting up the committee was not passed, however, until 1990. Its jurisdiction over union-republic legislation (other than acts concerning human rights) was made contingent upon the negotiation of a new union treaty. Thus, the question of the supremacy of the law would be a moot issue until a new treaty was signed. . . .

In the political theater of the Soviet Union in the early 1990s, constitutional rhetoric had become two-dimensional. Beneath the everyday exchanges in the press, the executive suites, and in the parliaments over tactical political issues, a constitutional convention *writ large*, addressing strategic questions on the future shape of the political system, had been under way for several years. I am not referring to a discrete, organized meeting such as the American Constitutional Convention in Philadelphia; the Soviet convention was quite different, and in fact probably unique in world constitutional annals as it was riven by ambivalences. It was both planned and spontaneous, and occurred over time in multiple venues; the quiet of constitutional deliberation was occasionally punctuated by gunfire and violence; negotiation was both continuous and episodic, operating on several levels simultaneously at different tempos and with varying degrees of intensity;

and essential compromise, so vital to constitution-making, advanced and receded as circumstances constantly changed and inveterate antagonisms welled up to block the prospect of peaceful union and, in the end, the process of an orderly dissolution of the union.

What the world witnessed in the last months of the USSR was an amorphous, transitional constitutional convention not likely to produce durable agreements because that was really not its inchoate purpose. The idea had been to keep the dialogue going, to keep bringing adversaries back to the table, to continuously try new words and formulas for revitalizing old ties, forging new ones, or, if all failed, dissolving relationships amicably. Gorbachev, with his tolerance for ambiguity and reserves of optimism, had been a master of this crucial dialogue of transition. His aim was to avert the alternative, civil war, and its companions, misery and chaos.

The economic crisis: reaching for the last carton of milk. (Liu Heung Shing/M. Photo)

III Democratization and Crisis, 1989–1990

Michael E. Urban

The Democratic Experiment

In keeping with the constitutional amendments that he had pushed through the party and the government, Gorbachev opened the 1989 election campaign for the new Congress of People's Deputies. With the Communist party still legally privileged, the election was far from being perfectly democratic; nevertheless, it was the first multicandidate contest the Soviet Union had seen since the election of the ill-fated Constituent Assembly in 1917. The election and its outcome have been studied in detail by Michael Urban, professor of political

From Michael E. Urban, *More Power to the Soviets: The Democratic Revolution in the USSR*, pp. 89–90, 93–99, 101, 103–107, 109–113, 115–116. Copyright © 1990 by Edward Elgar Publishing Ltd. Reprinted by permission of the publisher.

science at the University of California, Santa Cruz. In this selection, he brings out the many contradictions between the democratic principles proclaimed by the Gorbachev leadership and the continuing attempts at political manipulation on the part of Communist bureaucrats.

National Elections

The period of nationwide assessment brought the wings of Gorbachev's reform coalition into open opposition. During the electoral campaigns that ensued, this opposition spilled over into the streets. As Soviet commentators have remarked, the political clashes that occurred were the more or less predictable outcome of the dynamic contradiction that drove the reform process. The Constitutional amendments and new Law on Elections opened up, on the one hand, an opportunity for the population to organize and to influence via public elections the composition of the government. On the other hand, this legislation also enabled the apparatus to intervene at various stages in the process in order to limit that same opportunity. Struggle in a number of forms—subterfuge, manipulation, public demonstration, intimidation, violence and, ultimately, voting—became the means by which contests between democratic and conservative forces were settled during the electoral phase of the democratization process.

In part, the intensity and scope of the electoral struggle derived from the legislative project that set it in motion. The apparatus, for instance, regularly attempted to utilize the "filters" emplaced in the procedures for nominating candidates in order to keep their opponents off balance and, more importantly, off the ballot. Democratic forces, in turn, often met these attempts with the only resources available to them: publicity, legal appeals and the weight of their (mobilized) numbers. Sometimes they succeeded in clearing away the impediments thrown up by the apparatus and went on to score some impressive victories at the polls. . . .

The immediate encounters that took place between the apparatus and the forces oriented toward democracy were mediated by electoral commissions in each electoral district and within each public organization entitled to name deputies to the Congress. The enforcement of election procedures fell to these commissions, but since they themselves were ordinarily controlled by the apparatus, their role as impartial referee was severely compromised and they often became party to the very conflicts that they were formally charged to regulate. . . .

Nominations and Elections in the Public Organizations

A total of 39 public organizations named deputies to the Congress. The number of seats awarded to each ranged from 100 (the Communist Party and the All-Union Council of Trade Unions) to just one (e.g., the All-Union Volunteer Society for the Struggle for Sobriety, the All-Union Society of Philatelists). By the close of the nominations phase, a total of 880 candidates had been registered by public organizations for the 750 seats earmarked for them in the Congress. In some instances, the nominations process within public organizations was genuinely competitive and generated no small amount of excitement. In most, however, it was thoroughly orchestrated by the executive apparatus of the respective organizations, leading one reporter to note that it is far from the case "that the strictures corresponding to the spirit and even the letter of the Law on Elections have been everywhere observed."

The Communist Party began the selection of its 100 deputies with a summons from its Electoral Commission that called on party members to submit the names of prospective candidates to their respective primary party organizations, whence they would be sent up the organizational ladder, with the possibility of deletions and additions occurring on each rung. Accordingly, the 31,500 candidates proposed by primary party organizations were reduced to 3,500 by party committees at the next level. This number was further whittled to 207 by republic and regional party bodies, reinflated to 312 by the Central Committee and finally fixed at 100 by the Politburo. It would seem fair to conclude, therefore, that the election of deputies (the same 100 "nominated" by the Politburo) that took place on 15 March at the Plenum of the Central Committee (enlarged to 641 members) represented no more than a parody of democracy. Although millions of party members had participated at one stage or another in the process, it was in the Politburo that the actual "election" occurred. Moreover, as Boris Nikol'skii, the Editor of *Neva*, subsequently pointed out, by nominating 100 candidates to fill its allotted 100 seats in the Congress, the Communist Party leadership in fact sent an important signal to lower party bodies that competition in the upcoming elections could, and perhaps should, be avoided. . . .

Among the other public organizations entitled to send sizable blocs of their members to the Congress, the process of nominating and electing deputies transpired much as it did in the Communist Party. While over 1,000 nominations were sent up from the ranks to the All-Union Council of Trade Unions, only three of these names appeared on the final list of nominees adopted by an enlarged Plenum of the Central Committee of the Trade Unions. The 100 deputies elected at the subsequent plenary session were drawn from a list of 114 nominees. In the Komsomol [Communist Youth League] only 207 nominations were introduced from below. The Komsomol's Central Committee reduced this number to 102 and later, at an enlarged Plenum, elected its 75 deputies. . . .

In other cases, however, more democratic practices prevailed. The nominations meeting at a Plenum of the Union of Cinematographers got off to a dreary bureaucratic start with a prepared list of nominees read out from the Presidium and little apparent interest displayed by the audience. As the proceedings progressed, however, the tone of the discussion sharpened and soon the meeting became a rather stormy one that continued for two days, almost around the clock. In the end, 20 candidates, almost all of whom had been nominated from the floor, were registered to compete for the Union's ten seats in the Congress. Similar contests occurred in the Writers' Union and in the lecturers' association, Znanie. The largest and longest display of political fireworks, however, found a somewhat unlikely venue in one of the country's more staid and decorous institutions, the Academy of Sciences.

At its first meeting on 26 December, the Presidium of the Academy decided to broaden the representation of the scientific community in the new legislature by giving five of its 30 seats in the Congress of People's Deputies to the newly-formed Union of Scientific Societies and Associations. It then convened in a enlarged plenary session on 18 January to register its own candidates for the remaining 25 seats. Those attending this meeting, however, rejected 98 of the 121 proposed nominees, leaving the Academy two candidates short of its quota in the Congress. A decision to open nominations from the floor was taken and then reversed when V. N. Kudryavtsev, the Academy's Vice-President, mounted the rostrum and persuaded the hall to close nominations and solve the problem of a deficit of candidates by ceding five more of its seats to the Union of Scientific Societies and Associations.

A number of contextual factors appear to have contributed to the storm of protest that this meeting subsequently provoked. While formally not undemocratic, the voting at the Academy's enlarged Plenum displayed to many small concern for the wishes of the general membership since precisely those who had been nominated by the largest number of the Academy's constituent institutes were knocked out of contention at this meeting. Moreover, the list of these popular but unsuccessful candidates read like an abbreviated roster of the nation's leading progressive figures: Andrei Sakharov, Roald Sagdeev, Tatyana Zaslavskaya, Gavriil Popov, Dmitrii Likhachev and others. Since it was an open secret that these same individuals had long been conducting a struggle within the Academy against its senior and thoroughly conservative officials, it seemed blatantly obvious to many that the conservatives were avenging themselves for the past by attempting to deny the progressives a political future. . . .

Incensed by this turn of events, members of the Academy and others began bombarding the Academy's Presidium, the CEC [Central Electoral Commission] and the press with angry letters and telegrams. The CEC reviewed the case and upheld the actions of the Academy's Presidium and Electoral Commission, arguing, unconvincingly as things turned out, that those reform leaders who had been denied registration by the Academy still had time to find a place on the ballot in some electoral district. This decision precipitated a boisterous protest staged on the steps of the Academy a few days later by over 1,000 supporters of the excluded democrats.

Jolted by the realization that a revolt was brewing in the ranks of the Academy, the authorities began scrambling for a compromise solution. A series of meetings followed that involved, at various times, the CEC, officers of the Academy and its Electoral Commission, the directors and party secretaries of academic institutes as well as leaders of a newly organized inter-institutional initiative group, For Democratic Elections in the Academy of Sciences. In the end, a compromise was arrived at by supplementing the 903 voters in the Academy with another 554 delegates chosen by academic institutions around the country who were expected to reflect a more progressive orientation in the scientific community. The three-day meeting convened in mid-March provided a forum for impassioned speeches and denunciations of the Academy's old guard, said to be oblivious to the democratic transformation sweeping the country and woefully out of step with the requirements of the time. To make the point clearly, the meeting passed a vote of no-confidence in the Academy's Electoral Commission and then proceeded to reject all but eight of the 23 nominees before it. The new election prompted by these actions took place the following month and witnessed victories for many of the reform leaders who had earlier been excluded, among them Andrei Sakharov, Roald Sagdeev, Dmitrii Likhachev and Nikolai Shmelev.

Nominations in the Electoral Districts

Although the new Law on Elections provided for the nomination of an "unlimited number of candidates" to compete in elections to the Congress, the mechanisms that it established for proposing and registering them became the grounds on which innumerable battles were fought on the issue of just who the candidates would be. In general, prospective candidates had to cross one and, often, two thresholds. The first involved obtaining a majority of votes from one of the nominating bodies—labour collectives or meetings of voters in their places of residence with at least 500 in attendance. The second concerned the pre-electoral district meetings that were called by local electoral commissions in 868 of the country's 1,500 constituencies in order to winnow the number of nominees who had crossed the first threshold. . . .

One method by which local elites attempted to shut out challenges to their preferred candidates during the initial stage of the nominations process involved the manipulation of the nominating meetings that were held in labour collectives. One ally in this endeavour was the force of inertia, owing to the fact that local elites had always nominated the candidates of their choice behind the facade of unanimous affirmations from (de-politicized) workers. The passivity induced by this longstanding practice meant that many simply acquiesced in continuing the old ways under the new circumstances. However, when this inertia was overcome by groups of politically active workers, local elites often manipulated the nominations procedures and machinery to ward off unwelcome challengers. . . .

The second battle of the electoral campaign was fought in the trenches of pre-electoral district meetings. Electoral commissions . . . possessed the legal right to hold these meetings in those districts in which more than two nominees had been put forward by the voters during the first round of nominations. In some areas, most notably Estonia where the political leadership regarded pre-electoral district meetings as both undemocratic and unnecessary, such meetings were not called. Instead, the names of all those who had been nominated in the first round, regardless of their number, were simply placed on the election ballots. In a few of the districts in which pre-electoral meetings were held, they produced the same result by registering all the nominees, thus leaving the matter of candidate selection solely to the voters. However, in the overwhelming majority of districts in which pre-electoral meetings were conducted, the attrition rate among nominees was high. About two-thirds of the candidates named in the first round failed to survive the second.

In some districts, and these appear to mark the exception rather than the rule, pre-electoral meetings resulted in lively, policy-oriented debates among nominees and delegates alike. Press accounts describe them as veritable models of democracy wherein the delegates were able to transcend their initial personal or organizational attachments and reach decisions on whom to register primarily, if not exclusively, on the grounds of a shared sense of the common good and the arguments put forth by the candidates. . . .

The Election Campaign

Of the 7,558 candidates initially put forward during the first phase of nominations, 2,895 managed to have their names entered on the ballot by the close of the second. Almost identical numbers of candidates were registered in territorial (1,449) and national-territorial (1,446) districts. . . . Two-candidate races were the norm. . . . However, . . . the idea of electoral competition had not yet caught on in a considerable number (384) of constituencies, especially those located in Central Asia and the Caucasus.

The period of electoral campaigning that stretched from 23 February until 25 March, the day prior to the national elections, represented a critical phase in the transformation of the Soviet political system. What had been discussed in the press and in journals, what had been resolved at the Nineteenth Party Conference, what had been debated in the autumn and initiated in winter would now be acted out on a mass scale by the entire Soviet population. Real elections. Democracy. And more: an open struggle between the old guard and an emergent popular leadership that steadily grew accustomed to speaking in the name of the people and against the ruling apparatus, its unconscionable privileges, its incompetence and its abuse of power.

The contest for office unfolded, of course, differently in different places. . . . But it was in Moscow that the grand drama of the elections unfolded.

Moskovskaya Tribuna, which had come into existence in October, surfaced early in the electoral process as the leading voice among democratically-oriented intellectuals in the Soviet capital. Many of its more prominent members were invited by the weekly, *Moscow News*, to take part in the "social council" that the newspaper was organizing to work out an election platform that reflected the views of its readership. Subsequently, the "radical-democratic" programme adopted by the social council was promulgated by the newspaper as a common platform for a number of Moskovskaya Tribuna members who were campaigning for office. By early February when it was officially chartered, Moskovskaya Tribuna was assuming the character of an opposition party in embryo, complete with an illustrious leadership, a distinct political programme, its own press outlet, and organizational links to opposition movements in the Baltic and Armenia. A new and decisive stage in the development of an opposition was reached when this group unofficially joined forces with a political leader capable of igniting the larger public, Boris Yeltsin. . . .

The elections afforded Yeltsin a new forum in which to continue his assault on the conservatives entrenched in the apparatus. After having been excluded from the list of candidates selected by the Communist Party to fill its 100 seats [in] the Congress of People's Deputies, Yeltsin was reportedly advised by senior party officials to stay out of the elections altogether. He chose, however, to stand for election in the country's most prominent district, Moscow's national-territorial district No. 1, which encompasses the entire capital and includes nearly six million voters. During the campaign, Yeltsin's opponents in the apparatus seemed to spare no effort to make life difficult for him. They disrupted the production of his campaign literature, distributed anonymous pamphlets that viciously attacked his character, placed threatening phone calls to his home and damaged his property, and organized an inquisition in the form of a special subcommission of the party's Central Committee charged with determining whether Yeltsin should be expelled from the party because of the views that he was expressing. All of this backfired splendidly. The more the conservatives attacked Yeltsin, the larger and more enthusiastic became the crowds he drew as he stumped around Moscow.

The ineptitude of the conservatives reached its apogee on 19 March when some 5,000 Yeltsin supporters gathered in Gorky Park [in Moscow] to stage a campaign rally that had received official sanction from the city authorities. No sooner had a crowd assembled when a sizable cohort of police appeared on the scene to inform them that the Moscow City Soviet had changed its mind about the rally, that their demonstration was now illegal and that they must disperse at once. Brilliantly, the rally's organizers turned this apparent setback to their own advantage. They led the crowd on foot to the offices of the Moscow City Soviet in order to demand an explanation from the authorities for the rally's cancellation. As the crowd, waving placards and chanting slogans, marched the two miles through the capital's central districts to the City Soviet, thousands of Muscovites came off the pavements to join them in the street. Their numbers thus swelled to some 10,000 by the time they reached their destination. Emboldened by this spontaneous display of public support and, perhaps equally, by the timidity of the authorities (none of whom would leave the fortress-like confines of the City Soviet to meet with the demonstrators) the crowd decided to continue its rally there on Gorky Street. For Yeltsin's supporters, the symbolism of the ensuing event could scarcely have been more poignant. Traffic was stopped on Gorky Street for the remainder of the day. In front of their City Soviet, through whose windows some of Yeltsin's most bitter foes helplessly looked on in dismay, the people of Moscow staged a celebration of democracy.

The Yeltsin campaign underscored the only aspect of the nationwide elections that appeared to be clear and unmistakable, namely, the breadth and depth of public opposition to the ruling apparatus. In the context of the political reawakening under way in Soviet society, Yeltsin tapped an enormous reservoir of popular discontent simply by repeatedly reminding the voters of one incontrovertible fact: those who are ruling badly are living well. The success that he and other left-democratic candidates enjoyed seemed primarily attributable to a mood among the voters of unqualified opposition to the apparatus and all that it symbolized. . . .

. . . The absence of genuine programmatic competition was not lost on the electorate themselves. A mass survey conducted by the Scientific Research Institute of the Academy of Social Sciences disclosed that 60 per cent of the voters regarded the platforms of the candidates as collections of unrealistic promises that would not be fulfilled were these candidates elected.

Finally, we have the voters themselves, 34 per cent of whom were reported during the campaign to be prepared to vote for whomever the authorities instructed them to support. Among two-thirds of the electorate not voting blindly, the most important criterion relied upon was the personal qualities of the candidates. As far as issues were concerned, local problems, rather than questions of national policy, headed the list. Indeed, faced with the Communist Party's unified but vacuous platform at one end, and the thousands of isolated programmes offered by individual candidates at the other, it is difficult to imagine the electorate behaving in any other way. Hence, the message sent by the voters on election day on the matter of issues and policy represented the complement to the Communist Party's campaign platform. The former was as fractured as the latter was abstruse.

These shortcomings in the electoral campaign would seem to be wholly traceable to the Communist Party's monopoly on political power. In fact, the campaign itself tended to subvert that monopoly and, in the process, reveal something of import with respect to the nature of the Communist Party itself; namely, that it is not at all a political party in any meaningful sense of the term. The campaign platform that it issued was for all intents and purposes simply irrelevant to the actual competition among candidates; in the overwhelming majority of instances, members of same "party" stood in opposition to one another for seats in the legislature; nearly half (44 per cent) of the members of the Communist Party negatively evaluated the activities of their own party committees in the elections. . . .

. . . The primary political function of this organization is a negative one. It prevents the formation of political parties. In the past, simple repression was sufficient to accomplish this purpose. In the period of *perestroika*, however, its method has changed to allow a pluralism of opinion to express itself beneath the expansive umbrella of permitted speech that it has provided. But this change of method is not without consequences. Indeed, the question arises as to how long the Communist Party might retain its monopoly of political power when some of its own members stand for public office and are elected on programmes that advocate the creation of a multi-party system. It is perhaps in the nature of transition periods such as the one under consideration here that that which is in the process of becoming remains unclear and difficult to apprehend, while that which is passing shows itself full-face for the first time.

Election Results

High voter turnout was the first significant result of the national elections. In the past, the authorities had relied upon a combination of persuasion, coercion, illegal practices and outright fraud to post incredibly high rates of participation in excess of the 99 per cent mark. These methods were effectively abandoned in the elections of 26 March, and citizens were at liberty to refrain from voting if they so chose. Yet 89.8 per cent of the electorate turned out to cast their ballots. . . .

. . . Unlike the Constitutional assessment, the elections gave the public a direct voice. They could vote. Even in those constituencies in which only one candidate had been nominated, voters were required by law to mark their ballots in secret and, protected by the privacy of the voting booth, they could strike off that one name with impunity if they so desired. Particularly in those areas where a more developed political culture prevailed, the voters used their new electoral rights to deliver a series of surprising and often crushing defeats to the apparatus and their preferred candidates. In addition to the 76 run-off elections occasioned by the absence of a clear majority for any candidate in fields of three or more, new elections were forced in 199 districts in which a majority of the voters had crossed off either the name of the single candidate standing for the seat or the names of both of the candidates competing in that district.

The most spectacular of the electoral outcomes was Boris Yeltsin's victory over Evgenii Brakov, director of Moscow's ZIL Automotive Plant. Yeltsin, the premier anti-apparatus candidate, captured an astounding 89 per cent of the 5.7 million votes cast in this contest, while his well-financed opponent failed to reach the seven per cent mark. The Yeltsin phenomenon surely contributed to the success of a number of other left-democratic candidates in the capital who spared no effort to associate their candidacies with his, and to the defeat of Moscow's Mayor, Valerii Saikin, who was running in one of the territorial districts. It also became a *cause celebre* in the run-off and repeat elections that ensued, with voters regularly quizzing the candidates about their relation to Boris Yeltsin.

In Leningrad, the apparatus was decimated at the polls. Yu. F. Soloviev, First Secretary of the Leningrad Obkom [province committee], ran unopposed and was favoured by some voting booth irregularities that compromised the secrecy of the ballot. Over 60 per cent of the voters, however, struck off his name. A. N. Gerasimov, First Secretary of the Leningrad Gorkom [city committee], managed to capture only 15 per cent of the vote, losing to Yurii Boldyrev, a shipbuilding engineer and member of the political group, Leningrad Perestroika. The remaining four top officials in the region—the Mayor and Deputy Mayor of Leningrad, the President of the Regional Soviet and the Second Secretary of the Leningrad Obkom—were also all defeated at the polls. The voters in Leningrad seem to have responded readily to the city wide leafleting campaign, conducted by a number of political groups who had joined forces under the name, "Elections '89," that had urged them to strike from their ballots the names of all those in the local elite.

Elsewhere around the country, a number of prominent members of the apparatus also experienced humiliating defeats. All of the party's 166 regional first secretaries stood for election, usually unopposed, and 33 of them were rejected by the voters. Portentously, this latter group included all of the party leaders in the mining regions of the Urals and Western Siberia that would be rocked by a wave of strikes within a few months. In Kiev, both the Mayor and the First Secretary of the Gorkom ran in uncontested races and lost. . . .

. . . Instances of police violence and open struggle within the apparatus indicated how much was at stake in these elections. Not only did high-ranking officials face and, often enough, experience the humiliation of rejection at the hands of the voters, but their positions in the apparatus and, by implication, those of their clients were also at risk. In his address to representatives of the mass media delivered shortly after the balloting in March, Gorbachev spoke of the defeats suffered by party officials as the outcome of "a normal process, a democratic one, that we must not regard as some kind of tragedy." He went on to note that these defeats were "signals to the Central Committee and to [the respective] party committees concerning cadres policy." In short, failure to win a public election might suffice to remove one's name from the *nomenklatura*.[1]

When the Central Committee of the Communist Party convened in plenary session on 25 April, this daunting prospect provoked a sharp reaction from a number of conservatives who spoke

---

[1] *Nomenklatura*, the upper levels of the party or party-controlled officialdom.—Ed.

of the democratization under way in Soviet society as the root cause of all the difficulties, real or imagined, that currently beset the country. . . .

Despite the cascade of protest issuing from Central Committee conservatives, the Plenum represented a moment of triumph for the reform leadership. Against the backdrop of the election debacles experienced by many leading figures in the apparatus, 74 members and 36 candidate-members of the Central Committee who had retired from their full-time posts over the past three years tendered their resignations from that body, thus radically shifting the balance of power in the Central Committee in favour of the progressives. In his concluding remarks, Gorbachev repeatedly referred to the election results as a mandate for *perestroika* and, by implication, as something of a vote of "no confidence" in the ruling apparatus whose conservative elements he likened to military commanders who have remained behind sitting in their bunkers, while the troops whom they are supposed to lead are conducting the offensive on their own. With the elections, he argued, *perestroika*, begun on initiative "from above," has reached "a decisive stage characterized by a powerful movement from below—a movement of the broadest mass of working people."

In retrospect, it would appear that the architects of democratization in the USSR had been wagering on the emergence of this movement all along. Although the compromises that they had struck with conservatives had equipped the apparatus with a formidable protective armour to deflect the challenges of the democratic forces (the "filters" contained in the Constitutional amendments and Law on Elections, the relative absence of safeguards against manipulation of the nominations process and electoral campaigns by the local apparatus), a weapon of even greater consequence had been placed in the hands of the people—the opportunity to vote by secret ballot. In using this weapon, the citizenry for the first time entered the arena in which the struggle for democratization was being fought out. Never mind that their numbers were not proportionately reflected in the composition of the new legislature. The weight of their numbers stood behind those entering the Congress with the avowed aim of extending the process of democratization, in part by removing the antidemocratic features of the initial compromise.

Giulietto Chiesa

The Congress of People's Deputies

The Congress of People's Deputies elected in March 1989 and the new Supreme Soviet, which the congress selected out of its own membership in May, were dominated by Communist party officials. Nevertheless, both bodies displayed their new political freedom by acting like real parliamentary institutions and dividing all across the political spectrum over the question of the country's future. This process has been described close-up by Giulietto Chiesa, the long-time Moscow correspondent of the Italian Communist daily *L'Unità* and now roving East European correspondent for *La Stampa* of Turin.

"It is evident to everyone that the deputies are beginning to lay the foundations for a state of law in a situation where the culture of democracy is still in a preliminary stage of formation." So, at least, wrote V. Nadein in an editorial in *Izvestiya* in March of 1989. External observers watching the Congress on television "from countries where parliamentary procedures have repeated themselves for centuries," Nadein continued, may have been astonished—even bewildered—at what they saw happening in Moscow. During the Congress, tens of millions of people, both in the Soviet Union and abroad, felt themselves to be present at an unprecedented spectacle. The sacredness of the old power networks crumbled in the face of an almost total *glasnost*; political, social, and national tensions revealed themselves with full force and unadorned crudity; and the political struggle, once hidden away from public view in the Kremlin, became visible, explicit, and very public. In Nadein's words, "we are who we are,

From Giulietto Chiesa with Douglas T. Northrup, *Transition to Democracy: Political Change in the Soviet Union, 1987–1991*, pp. 70–76, 81–85, 92–93, 96–98, 202–203, 205. Copyright © 1993 University Press of New England. Reprinted by permission of the publisher.

. . . [even if] we are no longer who we were." His remark neatly sums up the Congress' historic significance, both recognizing the current limits of, and outlining the future possibilities for, Soviet democracy.

However one judges the Congress, whether in terms of its actual proceedings or of its ultimate results, it must be admitted that the novelty of live, near-total television coverage affected the assembly greatly, and increased dramatically its already marked cultural impact. In discussing the Congress, we are not simply considering the convening of a new parliament, even of one completely unprecedented in Soviet history. The USSR was reaching for democracy only after a delay of many decades; citizens' democratic rights had been restored. This restoration, however, can only be understood as the result of an interplay of traditional political forces with the disruptive strength of the modern mass media. The media dimension is crucial because the modern media wield an extraordinarily powerful influence in shaping public opinion. The integral nature of this connection was realized by many observers, both Soviet and foreign, but many (especially of the foreign observers) simply considered it "normal." They did not trouble themselves about the basic questions of how and why it came into being. Allowing a live telecast of the Congress, though, was by no means a foregone conclusion; indeed, until the last moment there were serious attempts to prevent it. Only Gorbachev's personal intervention resolved the dispute in favor of such an ostensibly "normal" state of affairs. . . .

The experiment was a complete success for Gorbachev, who emerged as the country's only credible leader. Even so, the situation was highly volatile. Live television was risky even for Gorbachev, a fact he probably knew only too well. An assembly of 2,250 deputies with real power was dangerous, and replete with unknowns. The elections of 26 March had altered and significantly broadened the Soviet political space. Decision-making became more difficult, requiring compromises between groups that were intractably opposed. Clearly tactics, too, had to change. The Soviet leader held one strong card: the rules and procedures governing the new parliament had not yet been defined. This fact gave Gorbachev considerable latitude of action, especially as most deputies had little, if any, parliamentary experience. Even

Gorbachev lacked parliamentary experience, though, and he often found himself forced to invent on-the-spot solutions to a multitude of procedural, technical, and political problems that the main architect of the Congress, Anatolii Lukianov, neither had foreseen nor could resolve.

In some ways Gorbachev had no real alternative to pressing for the maximum possible publicity at Congress sessions. He faced a conservative majority, and needed to use popular pressure as a counterweight. At the same time, though, favoring media exposure was a strategic choice that fit well with his vision of the Soviet Union's future. In his view, the Congress had rapidly to gain the prestige necessary to become a real alternative power base to the Party. Only by doing so could it eventually become the focus of a new order based on a pan-Soviet compromise of all fifteen Soviet republics. Gorbachev realized that the CPSU by itself could no longer support or sustain the process of rapid reform in the USSR. Hence, he wanted the Congress gradually to assume state power as well as a share of political responsibility, thereby both alleviating pressure on the Party and simultaneously broadening the bases of reform. In short, Gorbachev felt that the USSR needed to pass through a "school of democracy." This sincere pedagogical impulse was an important contributing factor in convincing him to show millions of Soviet citizens the value—and the difficulties—of democratic debate. The Soviet leader was fully aware of the risks inherent in such an exercise, though, and only allowed it to begin after taking a variety of precautions. . . .

. . . Real uncertainty characterized the period leading up to the Congress. Gorbachev had had to deflect direct attacks by conservatives at the plenum held in April 1989, which had revealed a largely panicked *apparat*. Conservatives at the plenum knew that in constitutional terms the Congress would have the power to determine the new government and to define the nature and powers of a wide range of state offices. They further realized that, although the character of this new state power remained undefined, it depended heavily on choices which could easily imply a fundamental redistribution of power within the Party leadership. . . .

. . . In truth, the plenum had also discussed—and, at least in broad outline, approved—Gorbachev's overall program for the Congress, a program which was not debated publicly until two days later, at the republican and regional "Conference of Group Representatives."

This conference, consisting of 446 deputies (many of whom had been participants in the plenum), took place on 24 May—the eve of the Congress—and lasted for nine hours. It showed in a general way the relative strengths of the political forces to be mobilized at the Congress. It had no legal authority, but enabled Gorbachev to gain support for his agenda from a widely based, yet nonparty, body. He was therefore able to present the Congress with a package of procedural and organizational proposals that had been made, at least formally, by deputies from all fifteen Soviet republics. . . .

The radicals' main fear was that conservatives, holding a majority at the Congress, might elect a homogeneous Supreme Soviet in their own image, thereby creating a standing sovereign body impervious to pressures for change. They thus stresed the importance of the Congress as a place of legislative production and of political debate. Gorbachev, for his part, did accept two radical proposals, each further elevating and empowering the Congress. The first, requiring a constitutional change, called for not one, but two sessions of the Congress each year. The second required both that half of the members of Supreme Soviet committees and permanent commissions be members of the Congress *not* elected to the Supreme Soviet and that all committee and commission members have an equal vote.

Even after winning the agenda battle—and thus being relatively sure of his ability to control the Congress—Gorbachev clearly did not want irreversibly to oppose the radical reformers. He evidently shared, at least partially, the radicals' fears, and maneuvered to ensure that the radical minority would retain a certain degree of influence in, and control over, the Supreme Soviet. As it turned out, such worries were perhaps overblown; in the end, the Supreme Soviet—elected by a conservative Congress majority—proved surprisingly autonomous from the apparatus.

Nevertheless, the manner in which Gorbachev proposed his agenda for the Congress revealed exaggerated defensiveness. He was determined to dictate, not to negotiate, the exact rules for the Congress to follow, even though his brutal determination threatened his personal popularity. Deputy Nursultan Nazarbaev was given the job of presenting Gorbachev's platform to the Conference, and elucidated it in ten points. The first four dealt with election procedures: the first with the mandate commission to certify deputies' election, and the next three with the elections of, respectively, the president of the Supreme Soviet, the Supreme Soviet itself, and the vice president of the Supreme Soviet. Only in the agenda's fifth point was provision made for a political report by the president, followed in the sixth by a similar report from the head of government. The seventh concerned the election of the president of the Council of Ministers, and nominations to other state offices followed until the tenth point, which allowed "other business."

Nazarbaev's agenda, however, the best insight we have into the mind of Gorbachev at this critical juncture, was marred by contradictions and inconsistencies. The election of a president, for example, preceded any political discussion whatsoever. Neither did elections to the Supreme Soviet allow time for preliminary debate, discussion, or campaigning. Only after allowing candidates to speak, on the other hand, was the head of government to be elected. Political calculation was clearly aided by widespread confusion in its attempt to craft an agenda to restrict debate. Efforts to curtail or impede discussion, however, only backfired, and an intense political debate sprang up almost immediately after the Congress was called to order on 25 May. Indeed, theatrics characterized the proceedings from the very first, starting with the Latvian deputy Vilen Tolpezhnikov, who marched up to the platform—without being given leave to speak—and abrupty proposed a minute of silence in memory of those killed by government forces in Tbilisi. Tacitly foregoing a vote, the entire hall immediately stood in silence.

Shortly afterwards, Gorbachev's agenda was again challenged by Andrei Sakharov, who called for constitutional changes and whose mere presence in some ways implied an alternative to the official line. Sakharov's was only the first of many demands for constitutional modification at the Congress. Did the deputies, he demanded, wish to transform this assembly into an "electoral

Congress"? It was unacceptable, he continued, simply to delegate legislative power to the Supreme Soviet, which would contain only one-fifth of the Congress' members. Furthermore, the proposed rotation of the Supreme Soviet's members was misleading, since "Only 36 percent of the deputies could take part." Sakharov presented the Congress with the text of a proposed decree to affirm its full sovereignty. The rest of his speech was a direct warning to Gorbachev personally. "We will cover ourselves with shame before the people," Sakharov announced, by dodging the universally accepted practice of allowing candidates and their platforms to be discussed before being elected. The Congress must also consider multiple candidates for high state offices. His support for Gorbachev was, he declared, beyond dispute. But the reason—"I do not see another person of rank to lead the country"—ominously bespoke support that was half-hearted and conditional. . . .

. . . Members of the Supreme Soviet were chosen by their republican and regional delegations, but these delegations in turn were dominated by party oligarchs. Reformers thus found themselves isolated within their delegations, and could not join forces effectively with like-minded men and women from other parts of the country to secure election to the Supreme Soviet. Conservatives could eliminate proponents of democracy from the standing legislature, and, ironically, could do so "democratically."

This technique had no parallel in the history of world consitutional law, and left reformers at a loss. It also precluded a real decision by the Congress on such matters as those alluded to by Popov. In the end, it guaranteed that each delegation had virtually absolute control in selecting members to sit in the Supreme Soviet. . . .

. . . [Deputies] V. Biriukov and G. Burbulis proposed that Yeltsin become a candidate for president. . . . Deputy A. Kraiko then took a pragmatic line, asking Yeltsin to renounce his nascent candidacy, so as not to endanger Gorbachev's political position. "Remember, however," Kraiko continued in a warning to the conservative majority, that such a step by Yeltsin would be anomalous in the extreme. Yeltsin had, after all, been elected with five million popular votes, yet "inside here hostile shouts arise every time his name is mentioned." The Congress was out of step with the country, he concluded.

For essentially tactical reasons, Yeltsin did not at this time wish to undercut Gorbachev. Thus, whatever Gorbachev's fears, Yeltsin posed little real danger to the Soviet leader. Indeed, if such a danger existed, Gorbachev could easily have used the Congress' conservative majority to quash it. In the end, Yeltsin took the floor to remove his name from consideration. Significantly, however, he withdrew only at the end of a long debate. He allowed his name to remain in discussion during successive stages of the debate, and ended his candidacy only after gauging the assembly's mood and recognizing the likely dimensions of a near-certain defeat. With his decision, the vote began. With 2,123 votes in favor, 87 against, and no reported abstentions, Mikhail Sergeevich Gorbachev was elected president of the Supreme Soviet.

As the Congress shifted its sights to the next item on the agenda, that of electing members to the new Supreme Soviet, another legislative fight erupted. Battle lines were quickly drawn on what would prove to be one of the sharpest disagreements to face the Congress. Two distinct chambers, the Soviets of the Union and of Nationalities, had to be elected, each containing 271 deputies. The existing constitution mandated slight differences in the way members were chosen for each chamber, but in practice the composition of both bodies was determined by strictly proportional representation of all republics and autonomous regions. . . . This approach minimized deputies' freedom of maneuver. It also reduced political outlook—or even basic competence—below territorial origin as a criterion in selecting deputies for either chamber. Each of the fifteen republican delegations (plus the Moscow delegation as a separate group) chose its own nominees to these upper houses, and thus the final (secret) ballot contained sixteen lists for each chamber. The agreement among delegations, however, provided that each would present blocked lists, offering only one nominee for each seat. The Congress as a whole could not propose new candidates, but could only approve or reject those candidates put before it. Any nominee obtaining the support of more than fifty percent of the valid votes cast was elected.

A small number of Party powerbrokers who controlled their respective republican delegations, therefore, could tailor the lists to their liking. Independent-minded or meddlesome deputies were easily excluded. Denouncing this practice, the Ukrainian deputy A. Boiko declared that, "In many republics candidates have been proposed by the 'apparatus method.' We all know very well what this system is. We also know what outcome will result. . . ." The Uzbek deputy V. Zolotukhin illustrated the problem as it existed in his own delegation. The slate of candidates from Uzbekistan presented to the Congress included such figures as the Uzbek Party's first secretary and three of its first regional secretaries, the president and first vice president of the Uzbek Supreme Soviet, the president of the Uzbek *Gosplan* agency, and the president of the Uzbek Committee of Popular Control. Zolotukhin's point was clear: Uzbek *apparatchiki* attempted to protect their interests by occupying the maximum number of seats in the new national bodies.

Many radicals and independents on the Left attempted to force a change in this method of deputy selection, but had little success. As already mentioned, therefore, the Moscow delegation, dominated by reformists, decided to set an example by presenting an open list of fifty-five names to fill the twenty-nine spots available to it in the Soviet of the Union. The Congress at large could choose amongst them, and thus had a voice in determining the makeup of the final Moscow contingent in the Soviet of the Union. . . . The Russian Republic, too, nominated four extra candidates to the Soviet of the Union, and put forward twelve names for the eleven posts allocated to it in the Soviet of Nationalities.

This last, apparently small, difference, only involving one too many nominees, might seem almost insignificant. It, however, actually stirred the largest scandal when the Supreme Soviet vote was finally taken. Boris Yeltsin—the Congress' most popular deputy—finished last of the twelve in the Congress vote, with 964 cancellations. Conservatives of all stripes had joined forces to prevent him from entering the Supreme Soviet, and the apparatus had taken its revenge. Indignation swept the country. Conservatives apparently were determined not to relinquish their iron grip on the country, nor to compromise in any way with progressives.

Only the intervention of Aleksei Kazannik, an unknown deputy from Omsk, rescued the Congress from complete disrepute. Kazannik challenged the vote as it stood, offering his seat in the Supreme Soviet to Yeltsin and demanding an eleventh-hour revote to legitimize such a transfer.[1] Despite the procedural irregularity, Gorbachev seized this opportunity to resurrect the Congress' prestige and to restore to it a measure of credibility. Gorbachev brought his personal prestige to bear, pressuring the conservative Congress majority to accept Kazannik's offer. Perhaps not surprisingly, therefore, the second vote righted the perceived wrong of the first, and Yeltsin entered the Supreme Soviet. The conflict, however, left a bitter aftertaste. It showed the depth of the political divisions wracking the Soviet Union, and progressives could only resent the exclusion of almost the entire Muscovite radical intelligentsia from the Supreme Soviet. A Supreme Soviet so composed, with a majority so obviously disdainful of democratic norms, appeared to many as a body fatally flawed. Apparently dominated by the *apparat*, it seemed to offer little promise as an alternative power base to the party. To reformists' surprise, however, this same Supreme Soviet soon displayed an unexpected vitality and a startling degree of autonomy from the apparatus. . . .

Over the course of the Congress the Soviet leader repeatedly demonstrated his capacity to adapt to unforeseen developments and to modify his positions. When radicals protested that certain procedures were too hasty, for example, he sought a compromise. During the debate on his own candidacy for the post of president of the Supreme Soviet, Gorbachev ostentatiously corrected the presiding officer Vorotnikov, calling for all scheduled deputies to be allowed to take the floor, even if only briefly. He also accepted an unsolicited motion of Andrei Sakharov's that called for Gorbachev to present his political program to the Congress before the vote was held. Realizing that it would be a mistake to reject this request, Gorbachev declared—in words echoing Sakharov's—"I have to respond in some way to the questions that have been put

---

[1] Kazannik, a lawyer, was temporarily rewarded for his sacrifice when Yeltsin appointed him prosecutor general of Russia in October 1993.—Ed.

to me." The agenda had been changed substantially, then, at the behest of radicals. . . .

. . . Iurii Afanasev and Gavriil Popov had reacted strongly to the results of the vote on the Supreme Soviet, and radicals had sustained a major defeat with the exclusion of Boris Yeltsin and many of the most intellectually qualified candidates from the Supreme Soviet. The Congress majority was clearly in no mood for compromise, and Afanasev declared the need for a break, to formalize the obvious political division.

Afanasev then launched two main attacks. The first denounced the "aggressive and subordinate" majority that had elected a "Stalinist-Brezhnevite" Supreme Soviet; the second attacked Gorbachev personally, asserting that he "relies judiciously on this majority for support and at the same time is able to use it with great skill." Popov then took the podium and asked, "Why has all this been arranged? Why did anyone want this mechanical voting? There can only be one answer. Because they wanted to create a Supreme Soviet that would take orders from the *apparat* and continue to pressure the progressive wing of the leadership, this time through the Supreme Soviet." Nothing remained for the minority to do but organize an opposition, as it seemed to have been cut completely out of positions of real power. Hence, reformers laid their cards on the table; both speeches, vigorous and decisive, were addressed more to the nationwide television audience than to the Congress itself.

Ironically, much could be said about how mistaken were the radical predictions. In following months the Supreme Soviet showed itself to be far less "Brezhnevite and Stalinist" than it seemed in May. Even at the time, many thought—with some justification—that Afanasev's move would only further isolate the minority before many deputies had even decided their political loyalties. A moment's reflection, however, shows this opinion to be overhasty. Radicals could not silently accept their exclusion from power by an increasingly out-of-touch Congress majority. Had they done so, they themselves would have lost popular credibility. Furthermore, radicals by this point had realized that they had more power, even within the Congress, than originally expected. The first votes, particularly when reformers won 831 votes to oppose the *ukaz* of 28 July (which had substantially limited the right of public demonstration), showed great political fluidity. These votes implied that maintaining a superficial unanimity would only curtail the minority's potential for expanding its support.

The threat of a political break also served as a warning to the apparatus. Its members in effect had been given notice that they could not act with impunity, even if they did control a Congress majority. . . .

. . . No simple picture renders Gorbachev or his motivations accurately. . . . The Soviet president's relationship with Andrei Sakharov, for instance, is itself an entirely different chapter, shedding light on another side of Gorbachev's personality—a side in which humanity transcended the practical exigencies of political struggle.

At the Congress Sakharov was the most vigorous exponent of a political line opposed to Gorbachev's. Thus, two and a half years after Gorbachev released Sakharov from internal exile in Gorkii, the two men found themselves adversaries. Both remembered history, however, and although they recognized their differences of political opinion, neither saw the other as an enemy. Gorbachev remained convinced that the wrong done to Sakharov by the Party and the government could never fully be righted. Sakharov realized that Gorbachev represented the only hope for the Soviet Union to move towards his own political and humanitarian goals. As a result, they continued to struggle, but minimized attacks on each other.

Sakharov was among the first to take the floor at the Congress, although Gorbachev was well aware that his words were likely to be combative. Indeed, Sakharov managed to address the Congress—and with it the nation—eleven times during the First Congress. While his life history testifies to his extraordinary courage, it should be remembered that at the Congress Sakharov was also permitted uniquely generous opportunities to speak. Every time Sakharov took the podium, Gorbachev showed his respect for the elderly academician and former dissident, sometimes even protecting and defending him against the hostility of plebian, intolerant deputies. On the Congress' final day, Sakharov again asked for the floor, and again it was clear that his speech intended to make a break explicit. Gorbachev could easily have denied him the floor, even justifying himself by the majority sentiment—hostile shouts erupted as Sakharov waited by the tribune. Nevertheless, Gorbachev put Sakharov's request to a perfunctory vote, quickly announcing (without a vote-count) that the Congress had approved the academician's request for five minutes of podium time. Even when Sakharov spoke for much longer, Gorbachev interrupted only when the uproar from the audience threatened to become uncontrollable.

Gorbachev achieved all the basic goals he had set out to attain during the Congress, but allowed the Left the privilege of concluding the Congress. Any objective balance sheet of the Congress, in fact, must recognize that Gorbachev actually *guided* the majority of deputies to approve much of the radical political program: creating commissions of inquiry to investigate the Tbilisi massacre,[2] the Molotov-Ribbentrop Pact,[3] and the Uzbek Mafia[4]; modifying the Congress vote that had excluded Boris Yeltsin from the Supreme Soviet; postponing any decision on the Constitutional Control Committee; calling two, rather than one, convocations of the Congress each year; cancelling a section of the decree of 8 April that had mandated criminal penalties for the criticism of public officials and government organs; and creating a special commission at the Congress to study constitutional change.

Seeing the conduct of the First Congress as an example of *enlightened authoritarianism*, or of *astute manipulation* of an assembly that had not yet become a full parliament, is a useful simplification. Such simplifications, however, do not convey the full picture. Through Gorbachev's conscious choice, the First Congress represented the end of an era of *democracy bestowed from above*. It marked the beginning of a new democratic dialectic, of a *democratic chorus* in which all participants had much to learn and in which the *sacredness* of power disappeared forever. The Party's entire leadership faced a merciless, public critical pounding. Millions of Soviet citizens heard deputy L. Sukhov, an unknown chauffeur from Kharkov, compare Gorbachev with Napo-

[2] See pp. 225–226.—Ed.
[3] Reference to the German-Soviet Non-aggression Treaty of 1939.—Ed.
[4] Uzbek Mafia: reference to links between government of Uzbek Republic and organized crime.—Ed.

leon—who, Sukhov argued, had also used "this adulation, and his wife" to transform a republic into an empire. In May the Politburo had been seated at a special tribunal on the president's right. By the start of the Second Congress in December, however, television cameras showed them seated in strict alphabetical order, mixed together with the other deputies. . . .

. . . The elections of spring 1989 represented an extraordinary leap forward in the Soviet Union's ongoing democratization. The parliament that emerged, although by 1991 already a dinosaur, had attempted to do the impossible: namely, to reform Soviet communism. At the same time, this parliament witnessed a complex, largely hidden struggle among at least three opposing forces: Gorbachev, his conservative adversaries, and emerging democratic public opinion. Each of these forces pursued its own objectives at the Congress, allying with others only when it seemed necessary to do so.

In the end, however, conservative bureaucracies suffered the greatest defeat. In much of the USSR they emerged decimated by the electoral campaign, despite—or perhaps because of—their misguided confidence that the dangers of popular political involvement could be limited. At least initially, this confidence did seem justified, as a variety of precautionary laws (for example, those regarding the POSs[5]) secured a solid conservative majority at the Congress. This short-term victory, however, proved ultimately fatal by persuading conservatives that they could withstand mounting popular pressures for reform indefinitely. Hence they failed to grasp the reality that the Communist Party at this time missed its last chance to participate in an inevitable, thoroughgoing social transformation.

Such was Gorbachev's gamble. As president and general secretary, he continually delayed implementing democratic and market reforms in the hope that the Party would catch up with his ideas, thereby rescuing itself. As a result, Gorbachev himself, caught in the middle, paid the unavoidable political price of postponing change in the face of popular pressure. Yet at the same time government and Party bureaucracies remained resistant and slow

[5] "Pre-electoral district meetings"; see pp. 148–149.—Ed.

to change—a ruling class that failed to realize the futility of re-sisting change. Having learned nothing from recent events, these bureaucracies continued to oppose all types of reform, failing even to devise workable tactics to delay or minimize them. Orthodox Communists had become the high priests of a religion they no longer understood, and failed even on their own terms—not recall-ing the most elementary of Marx's lessons, namely that at a certain point developing productive forces irresistibly overwhelm estab-lished productive relationships.

In Marxist terms, this is what transpired in the Soviet Union seventy-four years after the October Revolution. The evolution that Gorbachev had hoped to lead became transformed into a revolution. In one of the many ironies of the Soviet situation, though, Gorbachev—the Louis XVI of the second Soviet revolu-tion—was not yet shunted aside. His role was to sign the death certificate of the first stage of change—the stage which he himself had begun—and to determine the birth date of the next phase, the phase which now has only begun in the former Soviet Union. Only then, in December 1991, did he resign. To many in the West, Gorbachev had appeared a leader of virtually limitless power; yet as the Marquis de Custine wrote one and a half centuries ago, "One must go to Russia to understand what cannot be done by the person who can do anything." Gorbachev realized the need to "restore politics to the people," but those around him failed to share this realization. . . .

Looking back on the Congress after the demise of the Soviet Union itself, however, we can see its importance in an essential transitional stage, the stage in which the formal vestiges of a one-party system faced the realities of a *de facto* multiparty democrary. True democracy cannot be created by fiat, but rests on the weight of accumulated experience and requires the presence of certain psychological and objective conditions characteristic of a rela-tively developed, civilized society. Virtually none of these ele-ments existed in the Soviet Union of 1989; all could develop only gradually, and at greatly differing rates in the different national communities that comprised the Soviet state.

This development of the social preconditions for democracy, however, proceeded much more rapidly than it had in other Western, particularly European, democracies. Despite apparent

backwardness in many areas, Soviet society showed great democratic vitality and promise. The ideological burden of Marxism-
Leninism that had paralyzed intellectual life for a time concealed,
but did not altogether prevent, various characteristics typical of
developed, urbanized, industrial society from emerging. Once
freed to influence public life, these characteristics created a Pan-
dora's box of energies, some creative and some destructive.
The shape of the new society that will emerge from today's
tumult depends on the outcome of the struggle among these
energies.

John Morrison and Boris Yeltsin

The Renaissance of Boris Yeltsin

Yeltsin, previously party first secretary in the province of Sverdlovsk,
was brought to Moscow by Gorbachev in 1985 to clean out corruption
in the city's party organization. However, in 1987 he fell out with
the Soviet leader over the slow pace of reform and the frustration
of his own ambition. Despite his consequent demotion from the
Communist party leadership, Yeltsin took advantage of the new political rules to achieve an unprecedented comeback as the leader of the
most ardent democratic reformers. His fall and recovery are described
by his biographer, the British journalist John Morrison. Yeltsin's role
in the 1989 election of the Congress of People's Deputies is recounted
in the form of diary entries in the autobiography that he published
shortly afterward.

From John Morrison, *Boris Yeltsin: From Bolshevik to Democrat*, pp. 45–46, 48,
51–59, 74–75, 77–78, 80–81, 84–85. Dutton. Copyright © 1991 by E. P. Dutton
Publishing. Reprinted by permission of the publisher; from Boris Yeltsin, *Against
the Grain: An Autobiography*, translated by Michael Glenny, pp. 39–40, 57–60,
84, 104–106, 211, 213–214, 241–250, 261–263. Copyright © 1990 by Summit Books.
Reprinted by permission of the publisher.

Morrison, *Boris Yeltsin*

The Moscow City Party Committee (Gorkom) met on December 24, 1985, to hear an address by Gorbachev, retire Grishin on pension, and install Yeltsin as its new leader. Gorbachev's presence was seen by some Western analysts as a sign of resistance by Grishin to his removal, but there was no hint of this in public.

In 1985, there were still fixed rules and customs in the Soviet political system: Once Yeltsin's appointment had been decided by the Politburo, the Party's inner council, the meeting of the Moscow party committee to elect him was a mere formality. It would have been unthinkable for Grishin or his supporters to have resisted openly. The signal set by Gorbachev's presence was that a wholesale cleanup of the Moscow party structure was on the agenda. The Grishin system, a major unit in the network of mutually supporting clans which had flourished under Brezhnev, was under threat. Yeltsin's mission was to reform the biggest and most influential party organization in the country. It was a tall order.

At this point Gorbachev had been CPSU (Communist Party of the Soviet Union) General Secretary for less than a year, and the scope of his reform policies was still uncertain. Many hoped that behind the fog of new words and the bustle of new academic advisers *perestroika* would turn out to be just another Brezhnev-style campaign which would last a few months, then fade away. Later, one of Gorbachev's conservative critics, the writer Yuri Bondarev, was to compare him to a pilot who takes off without knowing where he is going to land. Bondarev's jibe was close to the mark, but Gorbachev's initial vagueness was also due to tactical caution. His room to maneuver was severely limited by the lack of a decisive majority in the Party's leading organs for anything more than cosmetic change. Under Brezhnev, even the word "reform" had been banned from the official vocabulary because of its echoes of the 1968 Prague Spring in Czechoslovakia, suppressed by Warsaw Pact intervention.

Gorbachev was therefore forced to move ahead step by step, leading his conservative colleagues down a road they would probably have refused to travel, had they been able to imagine the likely destination. In the Politburo, the presence of Ligachev was a mixed blessing for Gorbachev. While he was certainly an ally in cleaning up the corruption and cronyism of the Brezhnev period, he was a conservative ideologue with no real interest in reform.

A more experienced politician than Yeltsin would have been better attuned to the ambiguities of Gorbachev's position and aware of his patron's relative weakness in the Politburo, which was still largely staffed by holdovers from the Brezhnev period. Yeltsin, from Gorbachev's point of view, could be counted on as a counterweight to the veterans and a source of support for his limited reform agenda: to reverse the slowdown of the Soviet economy, to promote a new generation to replace the Brezhnev men, to curb corruption, and to restore vigorous party leadership. In this early stage of Gorbachev's rule, democratization and *glasnost* were not yet fully on the agenda, and reform was envisaged as a process moving in the traditional Soviet direction—from the top down.

Yeltsin's axe fell first on the elderly Vladimir Promyslov, the globe-trotting Chairman of the Moscow Soviet, or mayor of the capital. Out he went, to be replaced by Valery Saikin, manager of the ZIL truck factory. Yeltsin picked Saikin because he wanted a man from outside the ranks of full-time party officials. Out went Grishin's personal staff and his assistants, the other Moscow party secretaries left over from the old regime. Within days of his appointment, Yeltsin was touring suburban shops and factories, waiting in line for buses, and catching the metro. Sometimes he took the television cameras with him, as when he signed on at his local polyclinic, rather than the Kremlin hospital. This was the style he had adopted in Sverdlovsk. For a Western politician, it might be thought routine image-making, but for Moscow it was a radical innovation. . . .

His . . . remarks on the issue of social justice broke a party taboo. "It is particularly painful when people talk bluntly about special benefits for leaders." Citing Lenin to back up his argument, he said such privileges should be abolished at all levels, though he qualified this radical demand by adding "wherever they are unjustified." Yeltsin's call won no support from other Politburo members and it was clear he was going out on a limb. The origin of the split between Gorbachev and Yeltsin can be

The nationalities crisis: the old Soviet Union confronts young Lithuania, Vilnius, January 1991. (ITAR-TASS/SOVFOTO)

seen in the populist tone of this speech and in Yeltsin's abrasive attitude to the party *apparat*, led by Ligachev.

It is hard for outsiders to imagine just how sensitive a subject Yeltsin was raising. The privileges of the party elite were not just a fringe benefit but a vital part of the structure of political control at all levels. Yeltsin describes the system in his autobiography: "The higher one climbs up the professional ladder, the more there are comforts that surround one, and the harder and more painful it is to lose them. One becomes therefore all the more obedient and dependable." As a new Politburo candidate member, Yeltsin found to his horror that he and his wife Naya were allotted three cooks, three waitresses, a housemaid, a gardener, and a whole team of under-gardeners. His new *dacha*, previously occupied by Gorbachev, had marble walls, countless outsize rooms, and its own cinema.

In a shortage economy, where most goods and benefits, such as decent medical care and housing, were in short supply, the right to allocate these benefits was an all-powerful political weapon. . . .

. . . In Moscow, [Yeltsin] was a lonely provincial outsider with no friends or allies. In a world where politics was based on clans and alliances between groups, he did nothing to win himself friends and seems to have made enemies quite quickly of those he promoted. "I did not know the personnel," he admitted afterwards. "I had just arrived in Moscow and had to pick new people." . . .

Meanwhile Gorbachev, far more sophisticated at inner-party politicking, was still trying to avoid any kind of showdown with his opponents, and for many months he would go on denying for tactical reasons that any opposition to *perestroika* even existed. Toward the end of his time in Moscow, Yeltsin began to realize that it was not just the people, but the system. The Party, far from being the main vehicle of change, was in fact the main obstacle to any meaningful reform of Soviet society. But he could not say so publicly. Gorbachev was eventually to come to similar conclusions, but much later. . . .

The friction between Ligachev and Yeltsin was evident from the start. "Yeltsin immediately reacted negatively to Ligachev's style and the way he worked in the Central Committee," Vladimir

Dolgikh[1] recalled. Yeltsin described his relations with Ligachev at Politburo meetings as confrontational: "He was on one side and I was on the other." Ligachev's version is that "Mr. [not Comrade] Yeltsin talked a lot. But he never did anything."

Yeltsin came under fire not just for failing to take the anti-alcohol campaign seriously enough: Ligachev and others objected to the way he began to tolerate political street demonstrations in Moscow and the first glimmers of a cultural free-for-all in the Arbat Street pedestrian zone. . . .

It was evident that the Russian tradition of the Potemkin village, of *pokazukha*,[2] was too ingrained to be swept away. Yeltsin said the Party's window-dressing had deep roots and compared it to coal dust eating into the pores of the skin. "Many leaders have outdone even the clergy in ritualism. They know at what point to clap, when to say what, how to greet the authorities, and what decor to put up for an event." It was no longer a matter of individuals: Yeltsin was in conflict with a whole political culture, whose rules and rituals he had come to detest. Yet he was himself a product of this system and its prisoner. The result was an inner tension.

Instinctively, he felt he was on the side of the people against the party *apparat*, of which he was a leading member. But Yeltsin lacked the political ability to conceptualize his dilemma satisfactorily. The further *perestroika* advanced, the stronger the resistance would be, he told an interviewer, in what may have been an unconscious echo of Stalin's theory of the permanent sharpening of the class struggle. Either way, there was no room for compromise. "The choice is simple. Either throw open the windows so the wind can blow away the cobwebs, or again sweep the dust into the corners and close the heavy bolts." . . .

Yeltsin took his Politburo differences with Ligachev into the open at a Central Committee plenum in June 1987. According to Poltoranin's account, Yeltsin also criticized Ligachev in the summer of 1987, at a meeting of the Moscow party *aktiv*. This would have been a clear violation of the Party's unwritten rules.

[1] Dolgikh, candidate member of the Politburo, 1982–1988.—Ed.
[2] *Pokazukha*: appearances, false front; Potemkin village: from the village streets dressed up by General Grigory Potemkin to impress Empress Catherine the Great.—Ed.

By this time, Yeltsin began to realize he had entered a battle he could not win. Ligachev, as the man who helped bring Yeltsin to Moscow, should by rights have been entitled to Yeltsin's fealty. But Yeltsin was not prepared to play by the patronage rules.

Ligachev managed to wield an effective veto over Yeltsin's ability to carry out further personnel changes in the Moscow party districts. . . .

. . . his [Yeltsin's] increasingly outspoken speeches led to worsening relations with Gorbachev, who was not prepared to tackle the party *apparat* head-on. In January 1987, the Central Committee had blocked his ideas for introducing inner-Party democracy, with several candidates for each post. "You can't ride two horses at once," Yeltsin commented, when he summarized his objections to Gorbachev's style in his autobiography. For Gorbachev, riding two horses at once was the essence of his political style. Given Yeltsin's total contempt for most of the other members of the Politburo, it is hard to see what concessions Gorbachev might have been able to offer him, to avoid the final breach. The two men met for two hours and twenty minutes to discuss their grievances, but without reaching a conclusion.

Before Yeltsin decided to resign, there was one final dispute, when the Politburo met to discuss an early draft of Gorbachev's November speech. Yeltsin volunteered a string of caustic comments. According to Yeltsin's account, Gorbachev exploded and stalked out of the room, reappearing half an hour later to deliver a diatribe that was "almost hysterical." Gorbachev was also under great strain at this time, though Yeltsin was not prepared to take this as an excuse. "There can be no doubt that at that moment Gorbachev simply hated me." After that, their relations cooled rapidly. "I was too obviously a misfit in his otherwise obedient team," Yeltsin wrote.

Yeltsin was pushed over the brink by another big run-in with Ligachev, at a Politburo meeting on September 10, at which Ligachev objected to Yeltsin's tolerance of demonstrations and set up a commission of inquiry into how he was running Moscow. Gorbachev had gone away for six weeks, to work by the shores of the Black Sea on his speech for the seventieth anniversary of the Bolshevik Revolution, leaving Ligachev in charge at the Kremlin.

Yeltsin wrote to Gorbachev, still on his Black Sea vacation, on September 12, to tell him of his decision to resign from the Politburo. "My style, my frankness, and my past history reveal me as being untrained for work as a member of the Politburo," he confessed. He appealed to Gorbachev to do something about Ligachev's way of running the party apparatus; *perestroika* had been reduced to a crawl by the party bureaucrats, half of whom should be fired. There were too many members of the Politburo whose apparent support for reform was insincere, he told Gorbachev.

> I am an awkward person and I know it. I realize, too, that it is difficult for you to decide what to do about me. But it is better to admit one's mistakes now. Later, given my present relations with my colleagues, the number of problems I am likely to cause you will increase and will start to hamper you in your work. . . .

It is virtually certain that Gorbachev, knowing since early September that Yeltsin wanted to resign, wanted to preserve the facade of party unity and postpone the whole issue of Yeltsin's future until after the November 7 anniversary. This was not just the usual annual Red Square parade, but a big international jamboree to celebrate seven decades of Soviet power and to show that the Kremlin was under new and united management. The sudden ouster of a candidate member of the Politburo, just before the ceremonies, would hardly have served Gorbachev's interests.

Besides, Yeltsin's presence in the leadership enabled Gorbachev to hold the center ground between radicalism and conservatism, a tactical advantage which he would lose if Yeltsin were removed. Gorbachev was later to accuse Yeltsin of breaking an agreement with him to postpone the issue of his future until after November 7. Yeltsin's version is that Gorbachev, on his return from vacation, said ambiguously, "Let's meet later." When no invitation to discuss his resignation arrived before the plenum, Yeltsin concluded Gorbachev had changed his mind about a meeting and decided to make his own plans. Later he was to admit: "The mistake was not in the content of what I said but in the timing."

Yeltsin's resignation speech to the Central Committee was planned in advance, rather than being a spontaneous outburst.

But it was what Poltoranin later called the "gesture of despair" of a man under severe mental and physical strain. He had been working eighteen-hour days almost nonstop. Some nights when his chauffeur drove him home, he was too tired to climb out of the car.

Although it was not until November 9, nearly three weeks later, that Yeltsin collapsed and was taken to the hospital with a heart attack, it is likely that he was already psychologically and physically near the end of his tether, by the time of the showdown, on October 21. . . .

Altogether, it cannot be said that Yeltsin handled his resignation well. Not only did he misread Gorbachev's intentions and pick the wrong moment, but his inability to present a coherent political case and his humiliating climbdown gave plenty of ammunition to his enemies. It was a setback for reform in the short term, though in the long term, Kremlin politics would never be quite the same again. . . .

Politically, Yeltsin became a nonperson, expelled into the outer darkness. Even though he remained in the Central Committee, he was in a kind of quarantine, isolated by the taboo, imposed by Lenin, against forming inner-Party factions. Yeltsin was punished under the old rules, but his action helped to destroy them for the benefit of those who would follow. Three years later, when Foreign Minister Eduard Shevardnadze resigned, the rules of Soviet politics had become more fluid, thanks in part to Yeltsin's willingness to be a pioneer. In December 1990, Shevardnadze, like a Western politician, delivered a coherent statement of his political motives for resigning and skillfully positioned himself as a democratic opponent of dictatorship. As French political analysts say, when a socialist minister resigns on a left-wing issue of principle, "He fell to the left."

Yeltsin's second major error was to personalize his dispute with Ligachev and thus strengthen his opponent's position. Gorbachev was forced to rally publicly to the defense of Ligachev, making his conservative number two untouchable for the next few months. Throughout the winter of 1987–1988, the reformers were on the defensive. In March 1988 came the most serious attempt yet to reverse Gorbachev's reforms, through what became known as the Nina Andreyeva affair.[3] . . .

It certainly looked as though Yeltsin's political career was finished. As one Western commentator wrote, "Yeltsin will probably be remembered as a transitional figure." In this view, Yeltsin's authoritarian style was suited only to the first phase of the post-Brezhnev reform, and he would be out of his depth in the second phase. This judgment was to prove incorrect—Yeltsin was to bounce back, still recognizably himself, but in many ways a changed character. His earthy, populist style was unchanged, but the new Yeltsin would owe his loyalty more to the people than to the Party. He was also to develop a sense of political guile and timing that he had not shown before.

After his resignation Yeltsin had to fight not only heart problems but deep depression. Stories circulated that he tried to take his own life, and most of his colleagues and friends shunned him. "It was as though a circle had been traced round me, which no one could enter for fear of contamination." Unable to seek relief either in God or in the bottle, according to his autobiography, Yeltsin began an obsessive analysis of himself, his career, and his beliefs. "All that was left where my heart had been was a burnt-out cinder." Tormented by headaches and insomnia, he finally survived thanks only to his family and to old close friends from his student days in Sverdlovsk. . . .

Yeltsin seems to have realized only belatedly, in his political isolation, that he risked not being elected a delegate to the Nineteenth Party Conference, despite his position as a minister and his membership in the Central Committee. Grass-roots party groups in Sverdlovsk, Moscow, and elsewhere tried to nominate him, but each time, the party *apparat* intervened to prevent his name going forward. Finally, Yeltsin squeaked home just in time, managing to get elected as a delegate from the small autonomous republic of Karelia, between Leningrad and the Finnish border.[4] Other reformers and Gorbachev supporters had similar problems

---

[3] See pp. 121–128.—Ed.

[4] The author appears to confuse the large Karelian Republic, between the Finnish border and the White Sea, with the Karelian Isthmus (which is not part of the republic).—Ed.

getting elected as delegates, a sure sign that the conservatives were beginning to organize. . . .

The Nineteenth Party Conference was the first gathering since the 1920s to break the pattern of well-scripted unanimity at the top of Soviet politics. For the first time, there would be spontaneity and disagreements; not everything would be pre-ordained from above. And the political balance had shifted from the moment, eight months earlier, when Yeltsin had been shot down in flames. Unlike a closed-door Central Committee meet-ing, the conference was a public and televised occasion. . . .

. . . By the fifth and final day, Yeltsin realized that nobody planned to rock the boat by inviting him to speak. So he left the balcony for the main hall and strode to the front, challenging Gorbachev to allow him to the rostrum. "All eyes were on Yeltsin and no one was listening to the speaker," Klimov recalled. This characteristically bold maneuver succeeded and Yeltsin was fi-nally allowed to have his say.

After setting the record straight about his television interview and repeating his call for Ligachev to resign, Yeltsin made his speech. It was a far more coherent performance than his resigna-tion speech. Yeltsin said the idea of applying *perestroika* to the Communist Party itself had come far too late. All elections, inside and outside the Party, should be universal, direct, and secret, with office-holders limited to two terms and an age limit of sixty-five. This alone would provide guarantees against a return to "leaders and leaderism" [*vozhdi i vozhdism*]—in other words, to Stalinism. Yeltsin's call went further than anything Gorbachev was proposing, though not as far as Gorbachev himself was to go later on. At this stage only those outside the Party were posing the daring demand for a multiparty system, and Yeltsin was not prepared to go this far. He demanded that Politburo members who shared responsibility for the sins of the Brezhnev era should be dismissed and the system changed to enable a new leader to assemble his own team. Re-turning to a theme he had raised at the time of his resignation, he said the party leadership was still effectively beyond criticism. Yeltsin urged the creation of a Central Committee commission to set long-term policy guidelines and oversee policy implementation, a proposal which would balance the power of the secretariat and the Party's permanent executive organ.

Next Yeltsin renewed his criticism of *perestroika*'s failure to solve any real problems and the Party's failure to confront its past mistakes. He followed this up with a powerful plea for greater inner-Party openness and democratization and an attack on the privileges of the *apparat*. "In my opinion, the principle should be as follows: If there is a lack of anything in our socialist society, then that shortage should be felt in equal degree by everyone, without exception," he declared to applause. The *apparat* should be drastically trimmed, he said.

So much for politics. Yeltsin next raised a personal issue—his own rehabilitation. Noise erupted in the hall, and Yeltsin offered to leave the rostrum, but Gorbachev intervened to tell him to continue. "I think we should stop treating the Yeltsin affair as a secret," he said.

"Comrade delegates! Rehabilitation fifty years after a person's death has now become the rule, and this has had a healthy effect on society. But I am asking for my personal political rehabilitation, while I am still alive." Yeltsin pointed out that, while his speech at the October 1987 plenum had been condemned as politically erroneous, many of the issues he had raised had since been voiced by others, including Gorbachev himself. "I consider that the only error in my speech was that I delivered it at the wrong time." Yeltsin asked the conference to withdraw its condemnation of his views, which he said would help the cause of *perestroika* by boosting popular confidence in the Party. . . .

. . . It was clear that Yeltsin's views were evolving toward a more radical critique of the lack of democracy in the Soviet system. "We have stifled man spiritually. He has been under the pressure of exaggerated authorities, orders, unceasing instructions, an infinite number of decrees, and so forth. We have accustomed others not to unanimity but rather to unanimous stifling. Is this socially just? If we are voting, then inevitably it is almost all one hundred percent; if we are raising our hands, everyone to a man is 'for.' It is a shame that the word pluralism has reached us from our ideological enemies." . . .

[An] Austrian interviewer described Yeltsin as humorous, but also as unbroken and militant. Yeltsin's changed mood reflected not only his recovery from depression but a new atmosphere in the country at large. Soon the balance of Soviet politics was to shift even further toward reform, as the country lurched through a worsening economic crisis and the disaster of the Armenian earthquake.

Less than a year after Yeltsin's disgrace, his criticism of the conservatives in the Politburo was to be spectacularly vindicated. In September 1988, Gorbachev mounted a sudden coup against his conservative opponents and did exactly what he had promised the Central Committee he would never do—he reorganized the central party apparatus from top to bottom. Former foreign minister Andrei Gromyko retired as Chairman of the Presidium of the Supreme Soviet, effectively head of state, and Gorbachev took his place. Solomentsev and other conservatives were dropped from the Politburo, and Ligachev lost his key job in charge of ideology. The way was clear for the Supreme Soviet to approve Gorbachev's constitutional plans for a new Congress of People's Deputies, to be elected in multicandidate elections on March 26, 1989.

Gorbachev was creating an opportunity for Yeltsin's political resurrection. The Party clearly had no intention of rehabilitating him, but the people might.

Yeltsin, *Against the Grain*

February 19, 1989

A start has been made. I have gotten past the nominating meeting. Now my election depends on the people. I was proposed as a candidate in nearly two hundred constituencies, and this support for me has come largely from big factories and other organizations that are thousands strong.

But such constituent support still counts for nothing. The nominating meetings, which are organized, conducted, and controlled by the *apparat*, allow it to eliminate any unsuitable candidates. A majority of these meetings, made up of so-called workers' representatives, were packed with party secretaries, their deputies, and members of workers groups, who have been "instructed" to the point of intimidation. Naturally it is no problem to manipulate such an audience, and from all corners of the country protests have come pouring in to the central electoral commission, declaring that the meetings usurped the people's right to hold real, meaningful elections. The authors of this charade, called the Election of People's Deputies, USSR, rubbed their hands together and delighted that their carefully laid plans had been put into effect so successfully.

Even so, they have miscalculated. Their plan has not been successful everywhere. They somehow failed to realize that even the secretary of a party committee might defect and vote as his conscience dictated; that even an obedient member of a workers collective might mark his ballot with the name of a candidate who was not the one he had been told to vote for. . . .

February 21, 1989

It's strange, and I still can't believe it: I have been accepted as a candidate for Moscow deputy. What the *apparat* didn't want to happen and what they opposed so desperately has happened after all.

But to tell the story as it happened, I was supposed to have been blackballed at the nominating meeting. Of the one thousand people in the hall, only two hundred represented the ten candidates, while eight hundred had been carefully chosen—obedient, brainwashed selectors. . . .

I knew that the hall was filled with people who had been given provocative questions to ask me, and they were only waiting for the signal from the organizers to stir up controversy. I decided to use an unexpected method. Candidates usually choose to answer the most potentially favorable questions; I decided to do the reverse. Of the written questions put to me, I picked those that were most unfair, unpleasant, or insulting.

I began answering such questions as "Why did you let down the Moscow party organization with your cowardly failure to face up to difficulties?" and "Why was your daughter able to move into a new flat?" and so on, all in the same spirit, except that no one asked why I had been questioned by the police or whether I had any discreditable links with dubious figures. The answers that I gave ruined completely the plans of the people who had instigated these moves. Nearly all the hostile questions that they had expected from the floor had already been answered. I could sense the audience starting to thaw. It began to look as if the meeting might not end the way the organizers had planned it. . . . I collected more than half the votes, and the plans of my enemies failed.

I believe my enemies have often been frustrated because for some reason they think they are dealing with people who are bilious and ill-natured. They always base their tactics on an appeal to the rotten apples in the barrel, and there are too few of them. That is why they fail. If they had managed to fill the meeting with people like that, then there is no doubt I would have lost. But in all Moscow they could not find eight hundred people of their own ilk. What bad luck for them!

A new stage in the election campaign had now begun. I had cleared the first hurdle and my chances of winning had increased, but the resistance of those who saw my election as a catastrophe increased. I represented to them a collapse of faith in the unshakability of the established order. The fact that the established order had long since turned rotten did not worry them. The main thing for them was to keep Yeltsin out.

It seemed, though, that it was too late for that. . . .

February 22, 1989 . . .

I estimated my chances in Moscow as being about fifty-fifty. My election campaign was like a continuation of the speech I made at the October 1987 meeting of the Central Committee. Then, I was alone, however, with the upper echelon of the party bureaucracy infuriated with me. The situation was quite different in my campaign: My opponents were the same bunch as before, only this time I was not on my own. The people of Moscow were on my side—and not only Muscovites. The majority of the country also detested the self-righteousness, hypocrisy, mendacity, condescending smugness, and conceit that riddle the entire structure of government. . . .

March 6, 1989 . . .

. . . Everything that has been done has given me a martyr's halo, which gets brighter every day. The official press has kept silent about me, and the only interviews with me are those broadcast by Western radio stations. Every new move against me only makes the Moscow voters more and more indignant; and since there have been a lot of such moves, the result is that my enemies have sabotaged their own efforts and ensured that Yeltsin be elected deputy for the Moscow number 1 constituency. . . .

. . . Simpleminded though it may sound, I have had only one tactical weapon in the campaign—common sense. In practice, this means never doing or saying anything that might insult or denigrate my opponent, Brakov. On campaign swings and at meetings, I only tell the truth, however uncomfortable or detrimental it may be; I strive to be utterly frank and, most important of all, always to sense people's thoughts and feelings.

Almost every day I held meetings with huge groups of people, and during the last month before the election I attended two such meetings daily. This was exhausting, but they filled me with confidence. Though winning was my personal objective, I was beginning to feel sure that with people like these, who had such a genuine hunger to see justice and good done, we were bound, in spite of everything, to haul ourselves out of the situation in which we found ourselves. . . .

Mass meetings can be dangerous weapons in a political battle. People don't restrain their emotions, and they don't use parliamentary language. Consequently, a speech made at such a meeting must be precisely worded and all the more carefully calculated in advance. It is hard for me to be exact, but I have probably taken part in as many as twenty large meetings, each one attended by several thousand people. Complex feelings are aroused when a huge mass of people catch sight of you and rhythmically chant, "Yeltsin, Yeltsin!" Men, women, young, old. . . . To be honest, I feel no pleasure or elation at such moments. One has to go up to the rostrum as quickly as possible, take the microphone, and start to speak, in order to calm that wave of excitement and euphoria. When people start listening, the atmosphere changes. I regard such enthusiasm with a certain inner caution, because we all know only too well how easily people can be thrilled and, equally, can easily lose faith in you. For that reason it is better not to fall prey to any false illusions. After these meetings I would get into arguments with my trusted supporters, who believed that the louder people chanted my name, the greater the success of the meeting. That is nonsense. . . .

March 26, 1989

Sunday. The last day. . . .

. . . When all those film, television, and camera lenses were aimed at me, I couldn't help feeling how stupid it must look to an onlooker. Muttering "This doesn't make any sense. It's like a flashback to the Brezhnev era," I quickly deposited my ballot in the slot and made a dash for the exit. . . .

For about half an hour I could not force my way out of the solid encircling ring, while I answered questions about the election, about my own chances of being elected, about the past, and so on. Finally I struggled free and together with my family almost ran from the pursuing journalists to the home of my elder daughter, who lived closer to the polling place. Taking refuge there, we were able to get our breath back in peace and reflect on the events of that day. For the day was a decisive one; it would decide the outcome of my election battle—not against my opponent but against the party *apparat*.

My campaign workers were stationed at practically every polling place in the capital. Their first job was to watch carefully for any dirty tricks or rigging of the electoral process (although I didn't believe that anyone would stoop to that), and second, they were to pass on to me the results of the voting when the initial returns came in.

We had every reason to worry about the figures, about every single vote. We had heard of an unexpected decision made by the authorities, according to which all the Soviet officials working abroad in twenty-nine different countries were to be registered as voters in the Moscow number 1 constituency. Without doubt this was one final attempt to influence the result of the election. Everyone realized that our figures for these overseas votes would be dismal. It was most likely that in every Soviet embassy the officials and employees would vote obediently in line with the ambassador's preference. They were, after all, abroad. Precisely for that reason the number of votes in Moscow had to be overwhelmingly in my favor, to counteract any votes from citizens abroad. . . .

That evening I was told the preliminary results. I was far ahead in every polling district. Now practically nothing could prevent me from winning the seat.

March 27, 1989

It is all over. The months-long marathon is finished. I don't know which is the stronger feeling—exhaustion or relief.

I have been told the precise results of the election: 89.6 percent of the electorate voted for me. This is not quite a normal figure—in a more civilized election, the number of votes for me should have been lower; but here people had been brought to such a state and such efforts had been made to discredit me, tell lies about me, and prevent my election that I might well have collected even more votes. . . .

[1990] I sometimes feel that I have lived three different lives. The first, although not without its difficulties and tensions, was much like other people's lives—study, work, family, a career as an industrial manager and then as a party official. It ended on the day of the October 1987 plenum of the Central Committee. Then began my second life—as a political outcast, surrounded by a void, a vacuum. I found myself cut off from people and had to struggle to survive, both as a human being and as a politician. Then, on the day I won the election as a people's deputy, my third life began—my third birth, so to speak. . . .

. . . I was . . . aware that my presence in the Congress would worry Gorbachev and that he would want to know my intentions.

About a week before the opening session, he phoned me and suggested that we meet for a talk. The meeting lasted about an hour. For the first time in a long while we sat face-to-face. The conversation was tense and nervous, and I revealed to him much of the anxiety that had built up inside me over the past months. My own problems worried me least of all; what horrified me was that the country was falling apart. The bureaucracy was playing the same old games, keeping all power within its own hands and not allowing a scrap of it to pass to the Congress of People's Deputies. I kept on trying to probe for the heart of his position: Was he with the people—or with the system that had brought the country to the brink of disaster?

His answers were brusque and harsh, and the longer we talked, the thicker grew the wall between us. When it became obvious that no human contact was going to be made, that no relationship of mutual trust could be built up, Gorbachev modified the tone and intensity of his remarks and asked about my plans for the future. What was I going to do, what sort of work did I see myself taking up? I replied straight away that the Congress would decide everything. Gorbachev did not like that answer. He wanted me to give him some kind of guarantee. . . .

Soon after that the Congress opened. . . . Gorbachev made the important decision that the entire session should be broadcast, live, on national television. Those ten days, in which almost the whole country watched the desperate debates of the Congress, unable to tear themselves away from their television sets, gave the people more of a political education than seventy years of stereotyped Marxist-Leninist lectures multiplied a millionfold and flung at the Soviet people in order to turn them into dummies. On the day the Congress opened, they were one sort of people; on the day that it closed, they were different people. However negatively we may assess the results of the Congress of People's Deputies, however much pain and regret we may have felt at the missed opportunities, the political and economic measures that were *not* taken in the right direction—nonetheless, the most important thing was achieved: Almost the entire population was awakened from its state of lethargy.

As usual, it did not pass off without some tense moments for me. During the discussions on the method of choosing the members of the new Supreme Soviet from among the people's deputies, I insisted categorically that this process should be a contested election. I honestly admit to hoping with all my heart that I would be elected to the Supreme Soviet, although I also realized quite soberly that this particular body of people's deputies might well decide otherwise. The silent and obedient majority, which we had inherited from the recent past, would squash any proposal that displeased the leadership. And so it was. The first few votes cast showed how successfully Gorbachev was managing to manipulate the Congress, and the elections to the Supreme Soviet only confirmed the fact that the cast-iron majority would block the path of anyone who was likely to step out of line. Sakharov[5], Chernichenko, Popov, Shmelyov, Zaslavskaya—all

---

[5] Yeltsin misspeaks here—Sakharov *was* elected to the Supreme Soviet.—Ed.

of them excellent, respected, and highly competent deputies—failed to be elected to the Supreme Soviet. There were
indeed so many who were *not* elected that it would be impossible
to list them all. And I was among them. . . .

It was, of course, a scandal. Everyone realized that because
of me this state of affairs might ultimately become explosive. The
voters of Moscow regarded the outcome of the elections to the
Supreme Soviet as a crass disregard of the wishes of several million
people. That evening there began a series of spontaneous meetings, and here and there calls were heard for a political strike.

As always in Soviet conditions, an individual emerged who
had the sense to find a way out of this impasse. On this occasion
the person who saved the situation was Yuri Kazannik, a deputy
from Siberia. He was elected to the Supreme Soviet but withdrew
his candidacy in my favor. The Congress was obliged to approve
this "castling" move; when hands were raised in the Congress hall
and Gorbachev saw that the substitution would be approved, his
face showed a look of unconcealed relief.

Thus I became a member of the Supreme Soviet of the USSR,
and the question of my future employment became redundant.
A few days later I was elected chairman of the Supreme Soviet's
Committee on Construction and Architecture, and thus, ex offi-
cio, I also became a member of the Presidium of the Supreme
Soviet of the USSR. . . .

Generally speaking, the nearly two months' work of the session of the Supreme Soviet, which included organizing the Committee on Construction and Architecture from zero, was marked
by our traditional chaotic disorder—no offices for us to work in,
no rooms in which to receive our constituents, incomprehensible
instructions concerning a deputy's secretary or assistant, the dictatorship of the Supreme Soviet's permanent staff over the deputies.
We will learn; at the moment we are still in the infants' class of
the great parliamentary school, and I think it will take a long time
before we reach university level. . . .

Another very important event, in which I took an active part,
was the formation of the Inter-Regional Group of Deputies.

I believe that July 29–30, 1989, will go down in the history
of Soviet society. It was then, in the House of the Cinema in
Moscow, that the IRGD first met. The epoch of monolithic unity

was brought to an end. In spite of unprecedented pressure put on the deputies to convince them that there was no place in the numerous halls of the Kremlin for such a meeting to be held, in spite of the attempt to label us schismatics, splitters, dictators, and so on—the words of abuse were unending—we nevertheless gathered.

Why did we have to do it? Because what is happening to our country borders on catastrophe. The situation cannot be saved by half-measures and timid steps. Only decisive, radical measures can drag us back from the abyss. Everything that progressive deputies had announced in their electoral platforms, all the best ideas for getting us out of the blind alley, were combined in the program and platform of the IRGD. Elections were held to choose five cochairmen of the group; Sakharov and I were among them.

I don't want to theorize in this book, but perhaps the time has come to indicate, even if only in a few words, the program for which I stand and which is shared by many of the deputies who have joined the IRGD.

There are not many points of principle that divide the so-called rightists and leftists of the group. No doubt the main one is the question of property. If one accepts the private ownership of property, then this means the collapse of the main buttress that supports the state's monopoly of property ownership and everything that stems from it: the power of the state, the alienation of the state from the individual and his labor, and so on. The second point in our program is probably less important: the land question. The slogan "Land to the Peasants" is now even more relevant than it was seventy-odd years ago. Only when the land is worked by the people who own it will the country be fed. Next is the decentralization of power, the economic independence of the republics and their genuine sovereignty—this will go far toward solving the country's ethnic problems. We also call for the elimination of all structural and financial limitations to the economic independence of enterprises and labor collectives. There must be a reform of the country's financial situation, which is directly linked to the measures referred to above (e.g., the proposals concerning property, land, and regional independence), although special financial measures must also be taken to prevent the complete collapse of the ruble. . . .

I remember Yuri Afanasiev, at the first session of the Congress of People's Deputies, graphically describing the newly elected Supreme Soviet as being "Stalinist-Brezhnevite" in makeup. For all my respect for the coiner of this phrase, I cannot agree with his assessment. Our Supreme Soviet is not "Stalinist-Brezhnevite"—that is if anything too high, or perhaps too low, an evaluation of it. It is "Gorbachevian," faithfully reflecting our chairman's inconsistency and timidity, his love of half-measures and semidecisions. Everything the Supreme Soviet does is undertaken too late. Like our chairman, it is constantly lagging behind the march of events. And that is why so many urgently needed measures have not been passed into law. . . .

I am very glad that . . . changes have taken place in the neighboring socialist countries—glad for their sakes. But I also think that these changes will force us to think again and reassess what we so proudly call *perestroika*, and that we shall soon realize that we are practically the only country left on earth which is trying to enter the twenty-first century with an obsolete nineteenth-century ideology; that we are the last inhabitants of a country defeated by socialism, as one clever man put it.

The latest news: Rumors are going around Moscow that a coup is being planned for the next plenum of the Central Committee, with the aim of dismissing Gorbachev from his post of general secretary of the Central Committee of the Communist Party of the Soviet Union but leaving him as chairman of the Congress of People's Deputies. I don't believe these rumors, but even if they come true I shall fight for Gorbachev at the plenum. Yes, I shall fight for him—my perpetual opponent, the lover of half-measures and half-steps. These tactics he prefers will eventually be his downfall; unless, of course, he realizes his chief failing in time. But for the present, at least until the next Party Congress, at which new leaders may emerge, he is the only man who can stop the ultimate collapse of the party.

Our right-wingers, unfortunately, fail to understand this. They believe that by the old mechanical method of voting by a show of hands they will succeed in turning back the clock of history.

The fact that these rumors circulate is, of course, symptomatic. Our huge country is balanced on a razor's edge, and nobody knows what will happen to it tomorrow.

Anders Åslund

The Economic Impasse

The challenge of economic stagnation gave the initial impetus to perestroika, yet in the end the Soviet economy proved much more resistant to reform than the government. The attempts under Gorbachev to reform and modernize the economy have been closely tracked and critiqued by the Swedish economist Anders Åslund, who has since been an adviser to the Yeltsin government.

In 1989 and 1990, a vibrant discussion raged in the Soviet Union on how to amend the economic reform in face of a fast aggravation of the economic crisis. Increasingly, the realisation dawned upon the Soviets that the only viable option was a transition to a full-fledged market. It was a staggering revelation to many. Soon, the market as such was broadly accepted, but its nascent nature with high prices and "speculation" was objectionable to a broad public. In particular, private enterprise aroused old communist animosity and deep-rooted egalitarianism.

From the summer of 1989, the USSR faced an avalanche of reform programmes. . . .

It is perhaps most surprising how long it took before the Soviet leadership became aware of the economic crisis. In hindsight, we can see that it was in 1988 that the economic crisis turned serious. In June–July 1988, the 19th Party Conference of the CPSU was held. Academician Leonid Abalkin spoke as senior economist.

From Anders Åslund, *Gorbachev's Struggle for Economic Reform*, updated edition, pp. 203–211, 221–222, 225–228, 231–232. Copyright © 1989, 1991 by John Spiers Publishing, Ltd. Reprinted by permission of the publisher.

He pointed out that "a radical breakthrough in the economy has not occurred and [the economy] has not departed from its state of stagnation." For this rather understated assessment, Abalkin was scolded by a score of speakers and eventually by the General Secretary himself. Gorbachev's party was not prepared to listen to such pessimism yet. Instead, the resolution of the Party Conference proudly stated: "The country's slide toward economic and sociopolitical crisis has been halted."

Radical economists such as Nikolai Shmelev and Vasili Selyunin had long blown the whistle. In October 1988, the Minister of Finance finally admitted that there was a sizeable budget deficit. Still, this was not perceived as a matter of great public concern. A package of austerity measures designed to cut the budget deficit by 30 billion rubles was put together and adopted in March 1989. As Yegor Gaidar has pointed out, this was the last time a traditional fiscal approach was possible. "The technocratic period in economic policy" was replaced by "the economic practices of populism." A new severe restriction on Soviet economic policy had been introduced through the first partly democratic elections on 26 March 1989. The positive effect was that the Soviet leaders at long last started becoming aware of the existence of a severe economic crisis.

According to senior Soviet economists, Gorbachev did not delve deeply into economic reform issues from the summer of 1987 until September 1989, and little could happen in the USSR without the involvement of the General Secretary himself. The signal that something positive was about to happen was the formation of the "State Commission on Economic Reform" at the Council of Ministers of the USSR on 5 July 1989. The Reform Commission was to be headed by a senior academic reform economist, Leonid Abalkin, who was appointed Deputy Prime Minister for this very task. The Commission got its own apparat and considerable powers.

The most positive interpretation one can make of Gorbachev's attitude to economic affairs is that he reckoned that it was impossible to achieve a breakthrough for economic reform before substantial political changes had been made. One outcome of the 19th Party Conference in the summer of 1988 and the ensuing

CC [Central Committee] Plenum was that the CPSU lost most of its influence on economic policy. In particular, most branch departments of the CC apparatus were merged into one socio-economic department, still supervised by CC Secretary Nikolai Slyunkov but with ever less power.

Instead, the power over economic policy was concentrated in the Council of Ministers, initially, Gosplan. However, with the emergence of the government's Reform Commission, the fall of 1989 was characterised by a competition between Gosplan and the Reform Commission, and their chairmen Yuri Maslyukov and Leonid Abalkin, respectively, over economic reform. Gradually, Abalkin joined hands with his new colleagues in the Presidium of the Council of Ministers and parted company with his old academic friends. By August 1990, Abalkin had completed his switch of allegiance, but even so he was ousted in January 1991.

In 1990, a new centre of power emerged around the President's office. In January 1990, Nikolai Petrakov, corresponding member of the Academy of Sciences and an outspoken marketeer of long standing, was appointed Gorbachev's personal economic adviser. In March 1990, Gorbachev was elected President by the Congress of People's Deputies. He appointed a Presidential Council, which included academician Stanislav Shatalin, another prominent marketeer. In the presidential apparatus, a socio-economic department [was] headed by Anatoli Milyukov, who had previously been one of the closest collaborators of both Nikolai Ryzhkov and Nikolai Slyunkov. . . .

. . . The best young, radical market economists assembled around Boris Yeltsin, since May 1990 the Chairman of the Supreme Soviet of the RSFSR. "Mr. Yeltsin is collecting a highly competent team, not so much by attraction as by gathering the bright, innovative people Mr. Gorbachev keeps pushing away" (Flora Lewis). The most prominent representatives were the RSFSR Deputy Prime Minister for economic reform, Grigori Yavlinski (38), and RSFSR Minister of Finance Boris Fedorov (32).

The policy-making centres in Moscow thus turned out to be the Council of Ministers, sometimes divided into Gosplan, versus the Reform Commission, the presidential advisers, and Yeltsin's Russian team. The CPSU was strangely absent. The same was true of the other republics, which focused on their own reforms, mostly with a striking lack of competence and imagination.

A multitude of think tanks are beneficial for the generation of proposals on economic reform. However, it was a serious drawback for policy-making that the central decisive body, the presidential apparatus, was far too weak to be invested with such great powers. The inevitable result would be that the many decrees that the President churned out were uncoordinated. Too many forces drew it too much in too many directions. The policy-making system guaranteed in itself that most decisions would be arbitrary and was a recipe for disaster. This was entirely the fault of the President, who appeared unable to hire a sufficient number of competent people.

The issue of economic reform had gained new life after the formation of the government's Reform Commission under Abalkin in July 1989 and Gorbachev's active interest. As early as October 1989, the commission presented an outline of a programme headlined "Radical Economic Reform: Immediate and Long-Term Measures." This "Abalkin programme" stood out as extraordinarily radical. It contained an explicit preference for the market to central planning in a turn of phrase typical of Abalkin: "From our own experience, we have been able to convince ourselves, that there is no worthy alternative to the market mechanism for coordinating actions and interests of economic subjects." Moreover, the market had to be characterised by "free prices and economic competition" in order to function efficiently.

The Abalkin programme also made great advances on ownership. The presence of many forms of ownership was supposed to be "a normal state of a socialist economy." Such forms were leaseholds, cooperatives, peasant farms, joint stock companies and "other economic partnerships," but the programme stopped short of accepting private ownership. It outlined a system of ordinary financial institutions, such as a stock exchange, and broke with Soviet traditions of import substitution by advocating import competition. The programmes envisaged a convertible ruble with an exchange rate established through currency auctions. It offered three alternative speeds of transition, but the whole transitionary period was supposed to last for six years. The sequencing was neither clear, nor convincing. The lasting value of this programme was that it opted for a full-fledged market economy, broke with a whole range of communist taboos, and it offered a reasonably comprehensive programme of transition.

This programme was promoted by Gorbachev at three big meetings in October and November 1989. In particular, a three-day conference in mid-November produced a substantial documentation for the further work on reform. But there was a considerable backlash from party conservatives.

In parallel with the Abalkin Programme, Gosplan under the leadership of the two First Deputy Prime Ministers Yuri Maslyukov and Lev Voronin had worked out its own programme that focused on stabilisation but also ventured into reform. On 13 December 1989, Prime Minister Nikolai Ryzhkov presented his programme under the headline "Efficiency, Consolidation, Reform—the Road to a Sound Economy." Ryzhkov presented it as a continuation of the Abalkin Programme, and reportedly it was a compromise between the Gosplan and Abalkin programmes, but it represented a substantial retreat. Its essence was that three years of preparations were needed before any marketisation could be introduced. Meanwhile, the economy would become more centralised. Ryzhkov took exception to private ownership and denationalisation on a large scale. Retail prices should not be touched at least until 1992.

The government continued its double-track approach. The young radical economist Grigori Yavlinski had become the head of one of the departments in the Abalkin Commission. In February 1990, he and two young collaborators, Mikhail Zadornov and Aleksei Mikhailov, composed the so-called 400-day programme, which exists in various forms. Its salient features were rapid privatisation in order to stabilise the economy and swift marketisation. Its most radical element was the massive privatisation. It was presented to the government as a more radical version of the Abalkin Programme much inspired by the "shock therapy" in Poland.[1] The authors presented it with the words: "The time for gradual transformations has turned out to have been missed, and

---

[1] "Shock therapy": Sudden decontrol of prices, balanced budget, and tight credit.—Ed.

the ineffectiveness of partial reforms has been proved by the experiences of Hungary, Yugoslavia, Poland and China." The authors humbly stated that their programme was to be seen as an outline, requiring considerable elaboration.

Surprisingly, the 400-day programme was preliminarily accepted, first by Abalkin, then by Maslyukov and Voronin, and finally by Ryzhkov. This discussion was reflected in Gorbachev's first programmatic speech as President to the Presidential Council, when he spoke of the need for "radicalisation of economic reform," "a normal full-blooded market," and "a land reform." However, in April 1990 the Presidential Council turned it down and the government switched to its prior stand.

Instead of going for any further radicalisation, the government returned to elaborating its own programme from December 1989, which had been adopted by the Congress of People's Deputies. On 24 May 1990, Ryzkhov presented a programme to the Supreme Soviet that was merely a concretisation of his December programme. It contained little new apart from details on higher retail prices (almost 50 per cent) and compensation for two thirds of that amount. This was no vote-winning programme. The popular reaction was a massive run on all shops and extraordinary hoarding. For two months, bank saving was negative. The face of the government was saved in the Supreme Soviet by a decision in mid-June that it should be given respite until 1 September to further improve its programme.

The newly elected Chairman of the Supreme Soviet of the RSFSR, Boris Yeltsin, was favoured by the collapse of confidence in the central government. In June, the RSFSR Congress of People's Deputies adopted a declaration of "State Sovereignty" of the RSFSR. The 400-day programme—that was only known to insiders—was transformed into a 500-day programme (because it sounded better) by Mikhail Bocharov, when he stood as a radical candidate for the premiership of the RSFSR in mid-June. Bocharov lost with a slim margin, but the compromise candidate Ivan Silaev embraced the 500-day programme and Grigori Yavlinski became Deputy Prime Minister of the RSFSR for economic reform.

At the 28th Party Congress, 2–13 July 1990, President Gorbachev undermined the last vestiges of power of the Communist party and seemed to be free to move in a direction of his own liking. On 27 July, he stunned the intelligentsia by inviting the most prominent really radical economists and economic journalists for a prolonged meeting. Next he met with Yeltsin, and they swiftly agreed to set up a joint working group "On the preparation of a concept of a union treaty for the transition to a market economy as a foundation of a Union treaty," which was formalised through a presidential decree.

This working group was to be called the Shatalin group after its chairman. It included Gorbachev's top economists (Shatalin and Petrakov), the original authors of the 400-day programme (Yavlinski, Zadornov and Mikhailov) as well as Boris Fedorov from Yeltsin's team, and a number of radical reform economists from the Academy of Sciences. It was also supposed to incorporate two leading government economists, Leonid Abalkin and his collaborator Yevgeni Yasin, but Abalkin refused to join the group, since he did not share such radical views. In addition, representatives of the governments of all republics apart from Estonia participated in the group.

The Shatalin group had the mandate to produce a "concept of a programme" by 1 September. It did so after three weeks of perpetual work. The result was published in two volumes. One contained the actual programme and was simply called "Transition to the Market: Conception and Programme." A second part contained 21 drafts of legal acts covering the most important aspects of the transition. The essence of the Shatalin programme was a rapid stabilisation and a fast transition to a market economy coupled with large-scale privatisations and a general delegation of powers to the union republics. It was very concrete with a detailed schedule for the transition during 500 days. The authors seem to have been most anxious to put forward a sufficient number of concrete proposed measures. Because of the haste a large number of inconsistencies were inevitable, and frequently no reasoning behind the proposals is offered. Still, the USSR had never seen a reform programme that was as concrete, comprehensive or radical. The word *socialism* was not even used. It may be seen as the breakthrough for nonsocialist economic thinking in the USSR.

In parallel, the government's top economic experts sat working in another dacha outside Moscow, and their programme was ready a few days after the Shatalin programme. . . .

The two programmes were presented to the Supreme Soviet in September 1990, and there was a general expectation that the issue would be resolved that very month, and that the Shatalin programme would be adopted, because the economic crisis and the national tensions were so severe and the mood was radical. Even Abalkin called the Shatalin group "the President's group."

Instead Gorbachev organised a veritable circus. First, he criticised the government programme and stated that if only a proper stabilisation plan existed, "it is necessary to adopt the idea of the Shatalin group." Still, Gorbachev hoped for a compromise between the two programmes, although both sides stated that their approaches were contradictory. Gorbachev asked academician Abel Aganbegyan to produce it swiftly. Aganbegyan did so, but there was broad agreement that his new programme virtually coincided with the Shatalin programme. It was co-signed by Aganbegyan and Shatalin, while Abalkin submitted a written reservation. Gorbachev turned more critical, stating that Aganbegyan's "draft is still far from being perfect and irreproachable. It also contains controversial clauses." The outcome was that the Supreme Soviet did not decide upon any programme. Gorbachev managed to have a decision adopted on 24 September, giving him three weeks' respite to produce a new programme himself on the basis of the Shatalin, government and Aganbegyan programmes.

In October 1990, the political situation was altered. The radicals had run out of steam. The eminent political analyst Igor Klyamkin has credibly argued that October marked a turning point for Gorbachev. He effectively broke his alliance with Yeltsin and the left and embraced the right instead. Instead of a comprehensive programme, Aganbegyan presented on behalf of the President "Basic guidelines on economic stabilisation and transition to a market economy." . . .

On most of the crucial differences between the government and Shatalin programmes, the basic guidelines took a clear stand for the government position. Their contents verged on pure platitudes. The republics were to enter the union "voluntarily," but no other option was conceived. While free prices were recognised as an indivisible element of a market economy, administrative means should be used in order to stop uncontrollable inflation. Privatisation should occur, but it could be very drawn out. One of the few numbers limited the budget deficit to 2.5–3 per cent of GNP or 25–30 billion rubles in 1991 (which implied no inflation or a sharp fall in GNP in 1991). These dim directions went through the Supreme Soviet with surprising ease and were adopted on 19 October. A few days later, Gorbachev stated with reference to the Shatalin programme: "We have refuted a programme that was like a timetable for passenger trains. . . ."

Since the guidelines contained so little substance, there was no public reform programme. Instead, the President churned out one decree more surprising than the other with little or no coordination. Without any pronounced programme, no sequencing was possible. Senior Soviet economists tend to concord that this actual programme has turned out to be worse than both the competing programmes, but in the process the President managed to concentrate most formal powers in his own hands. . . .

Boris Yeltsin took a clear stand as soon as the Presidential guidelines were published. He noted that the "central organs endeavour to preserve control over material supplies and food-stuffs at any price" and warned of hyperinflation. Soon, a protest ensued from the whole Shatalin group against both the central and Russian authorities. Its tenet was that a great opportunity had been missed, as the 500-day programme could no longer be carried out. The programme actually implemented was based on the logic of the USSR government programme. The Shatalin group also warned of hyperinflation and sharply falling standards of living. . . .

When the time arrives for a final assessment of Mikhail Gorbachev, it is likely that September–October 1990 will stand out as a turning point from both a political and economic point of view. The Shatalin programme was far from perfect as has been pointed out above. There were other serious flaws, falling outside the discussion: notably it insisted on import substitution and appeared excessively protectionist. Still, as far as principles and basic intentions are concerned, it is difficult for a western market economist not to side with the Shatalin programme on all the major points of dispute, although this does not mean that the programme would have functioned. Whatever its faults, the Shatalin programme signified an understanding of the necessity of a quick change of economic system and the forging of a new kind of relationship between the constituent republics of the Soviet Union. If the economy is in steep decline, gradualism equals a prolongation of economic suffering. Therefore, a swift change of system is necessary for the population's welfare, which can only be boosted by future capitalism.

In September 1990, President Gorbachev could have possibly opted for a tentative resolution of the national crisis together with an initial cure of the economic crisis. However, he failed on both accounts, because he was not prepared to accept a diminution in his own power, a far-reaching weakening of the union, and large-scale privatisation. The window of hope was closed by October. Then, both the economic and political preconditions for any resolution had been swept away, though they might never have been strong enough.

After such a spectacular failure even to try to salvage his people, Gorbachev can expect little mercy in his country or in history. His popularity is dwindling ever more with an approval ratio of 21 per cent in October 1990. It no longer seems possible to control the budgets or national tensions by peaceful means. Hyperinflation is plausible and it will bring about a sizeable decline in the national income.

In most ways, the USSR in the winter 1990/91 resembled Poland during the winter of 1981/82, though the problems are far worse in the USSR, especially because of the national complications. Still, in the same way as that Polish crisis broke communism for good in that country, the current Soviet crisis is likely to bring an end to the system created by Lenin and Stalin in their native land. . . .

Looking back at Soviet economic policy during the second half of the 1980s, it is difficult to avoid the impression that virtually every possible mistake has been made. Perestroika has proved to be an utter economic failure. The most appropriate analogy appears to be Poland in the late 1970s under the rule of Edward Gierek. Recent Soviet economic policies and dilemmas resemble a tragic review of the unfortunate second part of the Gierek era and the Solidarity period.

The Soviet government has fallen into a similar trap of rising wages and rigid prices: the government lost control over wages, which rose more than production; it was politically impossible to raise prices accordingly; as a result, subsidies as well as shortages grew, eventually causing a decline in the national income. To a considerable extent also, the causes were the same as in Poland. While playing on democratic moods, neither Gierek nor Gorbachev was prepared to accept full democratisation. In the same vein, both toyed with economic reform, but stopped short of a proper market economy with predominant private ownership. Instead, both indulged in the populist game of trying to satisfy the population with more commodities, first through monetary benefits, then through excessive imports of consumer goods, forcing their countries into severe foreign indebtedness. . . .

As a member of the Presidential Council, academician Stanislav Shatalin made a telling statement:

> . . . I understand that even [Gorbachev and Ryzhkov], who started perestroika, are not able to, if you wish, do not have the biological facilities to, change their philosophy instantly, to move from the existing way of thinking to the new realities. As everyone, they have been fed for decades with the ideas of a strict plan and a technocratic approach to the solution of economic questions.

At the same time, Soviet society has undergone a fundamental qualitative change. The "command-administrative system" created by Stalin remains in place, but it functions ever worse. It can no longer catch the imagination of anyone but eccentrics. The same is true of Marxism-Leninism. Literally, perestroika means reconstruction, but in reality it has signified the destruction of Soviet-type communism. Considering how strongly entrenched this system was when Mikhail Gorbachev became General Secretary of the CPSU, it is truly remarkable that Gorbachev managed to destroy it in only six years. Given the totalitarian nature of Soviet communism, it is not surprising that its destruction opened a void that brought severe suffering to Soviet society. It would be to set expectations too high to hope that the man who fatally wounded communism also would be sufficiently imaginative and skilful to construct a new viable system. The problem is that when Gorbachev had exhausted his destructive programme, there was no mechanism to eject him.

It might appear disappointing that six years of attempts at economic amelioration have caused a drastic deterioration, but this period might prove both inevitable and valuable. It will teach the Soviet leadership, their advisers and the Soviet people a number of important lessons. Influential groups have already learnt five lessons.

First, the lingering conservative Brezhnevian model has become thoroughly discredited. Too many shortcomings of the Soviet economy have been exposed, and at long last been contrasted with other economies. Domestic Soviet criticism has also taken on a systemic nature. In particular, the excellent articles by Nikolai Shmelev and Vasili Selyunin have presented a liberal view of the Soviet economic system to broad segments of the population. Phrases frequently spoken are: "This system does not go any further." "We are in a dead end." There is a common yearning for a "normal" society, essentially a euphemism for a modern, democratic, western society—a far cry from traditional Soviet claims to originality and superiority.

Secondly, several measures that we may call neo-Stalinist (campaigns against alcoholism and unearned income, massive personnel changes) have been implemented with such frenzy and poor results, that they have been discredited among a large number of Soviet citizens. At the same time, the economic history of Stalinism is being revised into a moderate achievement at extraordinary cost. The neo-Stalinist view, that the system is good but poorly run, must have become less convincing to people outside the circle of fanatic neo-Stalinists.

Thirdly, a streamlining of the Soviet system on GDR [German Democratic Republic, i.e., East German] lines has also been discredited. Most of this programme of technocratic modernisation (production associations, a new investment policy, new wage tariffs, more shiftwork, and quality control) was attempted under Lev Zaikov's aegis, but it made little headway. Some measures could be implemented in Leningrad or Belorussia, but they appeared to be rejected by the system in other parts of the country. The Soviet leadership largely failed to impose efficiency from above. The apparent reason was that the Soviet administration is much more difficult to steer than the GDR administration. Soviet officials fend much more for their own vested interest with less concern for the national interest. GDR measures simply do not appear applicable, and they were not very effective in their original form.

Fourthly, the experiments with enterprise management (like the experiences of the reforms of 1965) led influential Soviet economists to conclude that it is not feasible to reform enterprises alone. They have resolved that it is necessary to undertake a comprehensive reform, involving all superior bodies, the economic system ("the economic mechanism"), and the political system.

A fifth lesson could be drawn from an abortive event. Numerous observers have deduced from the Chinese and Hungarian reforms that a reform would be most effective in agriculture, services, small-scale production and trade—that is, in small-scale, consumer-oriented activities. One frequent suggestion is that Gorbachev has made a mistake by not promoting family agriculture. However, Gorbachev repeatedly pushed for agricultural reform with family farms—at the 27th Party Congress in February 1986, in a speech in August 1987, and at big CC meetings on leasehold in agriculture in May and October 1988. The principal problems were first that he failed to win sufficient support from the rest of the leadership, and later on that the farm managers joined hands against him. The political resistance has been overwhelming. Fundamental agricultural reform would deprive a large share of the party apparatus of the reason for its existence. The conclusion is that not even agricultural reform seems to be possible in the USSR without political reform. Unlike China and Hungary, the Soviet Union appears unable to reform any branch of its economy without both ideological revision and political reform.

All these experiences have influenced Soviet policy-makers' thinking on economic reform. Another source of inspiration has been previous Soviet reforms. From the New Economic Policy in the 1920s, reformers have drawn a range of permissible socialist alternatives blessed by Lenin. The economic reforms of 1965 were rarely mentioned in the early 1980s. In 1985, they became a positive reference for reformists, while conservatives tended to

criticise them as inflationary. By 1987, however, the reforms
of 1965 were turned by reformers into examples of failed half-
measures, illustrating the necessity of going further. . . .

. . . *Public ownership* as such seems one of the greatest impediments to a successful transition to a market economy. All of a
sudden, the realisation has dawned upon a majority in formerly
socialist countries that the predomination of private enterprise is
a necessary condition of a well-functioning market economy.
As early as 1920 Ludwig von Mises wrote: "Exchange relations
between production-goods can only be established on the basis
of private ownership of the means of production." Now, the problem is how to move as fast as possible from an economy with
predominant public ownership to predominant private ownership. Massive privatisation is required for many reasons: true
independence of enterprises, a division between politics and economics, Schumpeterian creative destruction, innovations, and
the rational allocation of capital through a functioning capital
market. . . .

Finally, there is a general *danger that a switch to a market
economy is not sufficiently clean and consistent.* It must be remembered that there is an abyss between a command economy
and a market economy. There is no theoretical or practical ground
for looking upon the transition as a continuous process. Convergence between the two systems has never taken place. On the
contrary, first the old system must be destroyed—what Gorbachev
has largely accomplished in the USSR—then the foundations of
the new market economic house must be built on the other side
of the abyss, presupposing that society as a whole has dared to
leap across the chasm.

Stanislav Shatalin

The Radical Alternative

By 1990 the Soviet economy was not only failing to respond to treatment; output and living standards had actually begun to fall. Drastic
"shock therapy" was proposed by a number of radical economists to
dismantle the system of centralized state control and introduce the

market and private property as rapidly as possible. Led by Stanislav Shatalin, deputy director of the Institute of Forecasting and Scientific-Technical Progress, the critics published their "Five-Hundred-Days Plan" of rapid desocialization, resisted by Gorbachev but embraced by Yeltsin.

This program could appear only under the conditions of restructuring, and it lies entirely within the channel of the policy begun in 1985. M. S. Gorbachev and B. N. Yeltsin were the initiators of its preparation. It can be carried out only with their joint support.

As a result of many years of domination by a totalitarian social and political system, our society has ended up in a state of deep crisis. The indecisiveness of the government and the miscalculations it has made in economic policy have brought the country to the brink of catastrophe. People's lives are becoming more and more difficult, and hopes for a better future are being lost. The situation can be overcome only by well-thought-out and energetic actions, supported by the people and grounded in their solidarity and patriotism.

Our society has accumulated a great deal of negative experience with economic reforms, which people now link only with changes for the worse in their lives. Unfortunately, life has taught us to believe more readily in the bad than in the good. Implementation of the proposed program should disprove this sad experience.

The program's main distinguishing feature is that it is grounded in a fundamentally new economic doctrine. Movement toward a market will be above all at the expense of the state, not at the expense of ordinary people.

An essentially antipopular policy was pursued for a long period: a rich state with a poor people. The state concentrated in its hands enormous resources, virtually the entire ownership of

From S. Shatalin et al., "Man, Freedom, and the Market (Outline of the program for changing over to the market)," *Izvestiya*, September 4, 1990. English translation in *The Current Digest of the Soviet Press*, vol 42, no. 35. Copyright © 1990 by *The Current Digest of the Soviet Press*, published weekly at Columbus, Ohio. Reprinted by permission of Digest.

means of production. Resources were spent thoughtlessly on gigantic and inefficient projects, on building up military might and on foreign-policy adventures with an ideological underpinning, although all this has long been beyond our means.

The program sets the task of taking everything possible away from the state and giving it to people. There is serious reason to believe that the return to the people of a significant share of property and resources on various terms will ensure much more efficient and thrifty use of this property and these resources and will make it possible to avoid many negative phenomena in the process of changing over to a market. It is necessary to resolutely reduce all state spending, including spending on items concealed from society.

Only when all the possibilities and resources that are being devoured today by the gigantic state machine are turned to the needs of people and when people learn that this is being done, only then will the country's leadership have the right to appeal to the people to show patience, to bear the greatest possible burdens in the name of the homeland, in the name of their own future and that of their children.

We also should appeal to other countries for assistance. They will support us if they consider our program to be sufficiently resolute and well-crafted, if they are confident that the assistance they provide will be used sensibly and effectively for the good of people. . . .

No one is imposing a kind or type of activity on anyone; everyone is free to choose for himself, gearing his choice to his desires and possibilities: whether to become an entrepreneur, a hired employee in state structures or a manager in a joint-stock enterprise, engage in individual enterprise, or become a member of a cooperative. The reform grants citizens the right of economic self-determination, establishing rules the observance of which will prevent certain entities (people, groups of people, enterprises or geographic areas) from securing their own interests by infringing on the economic rights of others. It is freedom of choice that is the basis of people's personal freedom, the foundation for disclosing the individual's creative potential. These are still not the rules of the future market economy—they will emerge in the course of the formation and development of this society. The economic content of the proposed program is the changeover to a market, the creation of the foundations of a society with a new economic system.

The system of economic relations and management of the national-economic complex that currently exists in our country is to blame for the fact that in a very rich country industrious people live at a level that does not at all correspond to the wealth of the area or to their talents and efforts. People live worse than they work, because they either are not producing what they themselves need or what they do produce is lost or not used.

The proposed program outlines ways of changing over to an economic system that is capable of eliminating this situation and providing all citizens with a real opportunity to make their lives significantly better. Thus, the program can be regarded as a program for realizing citizens' rights to a better, more adequate life.

A Person's Right to Property.—The right to property is realized through destatization and privatization, through the transfer of state property to citizens. It is in the return of property to the people, first and foremost, that the social orientation of the economy is manifested. This is not an act of revenge but the restoration of social justice, a form of codifying a person's right to his share of the country's accumulated national wealth and of the wealth that will be created in the future. Privatization—and special emphasis should be placed on this—is a form of distributing responsibility for the condition and level of the development of society among all of its members who desire to take on this responsibility. Privatization should be absolutely voluntary and should not resemble collectivization in reverse.

Property in the hands of everyone—this is a guarantee of the stability of society, an important condition for preventing social and national upheavals. A person who has his own home and plot of land, which he can always transfer or leave to his children, a person who owns stocks or other financial assets, has an objective stake in the stability of society, in social and national concord. On the other hand, our sad experience shows how dangerous for society, for its normal life and development, is a person who has nothing to lose.

The program gives equal chances to everyone. However, this equality of chances should not be perceived as a mirror image of wage-leveling. In order to prevent privatization from turning into a means for the legal and excessive enrichment of the few, the procedure itself should ensure participation in privatization by very broad strata of the population: Virtually everyone, even if he has no substantial initial capital, should be able, if he so desires, to obtain his share of the national wealth. Equality of opportunity will be ensured by a diversity of forms of privatization, which will make it possible to lease property, to buy it on credit, to acquire it on a joint-stock basis, etc.

It is a point of fundamental importance that the state cannot and should not give out its property free of charge. Property must be earned, since a person has little faith in or appreciation of property that he has received as a gift. At the same time, some state property should be considered as having already been earned by people, and it may be given to them free of charge or for a symbolic payment. What is involved here, above all, are long-occupied apartments with minimal living space per person, small garden plots, and many other things.

Immediately after this, work is to begin on the creation before the end of the year of 50 to 60 joint-stock companies based on large state enterprises, as well as the transfer or sale for a symbolic payment of certain (to all intents and purposes, already earned) categories of housing and plots of land. . . .

The right of citizens to economic activity is to be ensured by the redistribution of property between the state and citizens in the course of destatization, and also by the adoption of a Law on Entrepreneurial Activity. The state will create an economic environment that will facilitate the development of initiative and enterprise, will simplify as much as possible the procedure for opening one's own business, will help to organize it properly, and will support it with tax benefits and credits in competition with large enterprises. The program proceeds from the premise that small businesses are necessary to society in order to turn production toward satisfying the requirements of each specific person, to combat the diktat of monopolists in the consumer and producer markets, and to create the necessary conditions for the rapid putting to use of new scientific and technical ideas, to which small and medium-sized businesses are the most receptive.

The Right of Citizens to Economic Activity.—How, technically speaking, will people's right to property be realized?

On the very first day of the beginning of the program's implementation, equal rights for all physical and juristic persons to carry on economic activity will be officially proclaimed. A program of privatization, the transformation of large state enterprises into joint-stock companies, and the sale of small trade, public-catering, consumer-service and other enterprises will be announced. This same statement will talk about granting guarantees of ownership rights to any type of property, except that which belongs exclusively to the state. An amnesty will be announced for those convicted under articles dealing with entrepreneurial activity, and these articles themselves will be removed from criminal and administrative legislation. At the same time, the struggle against crimes against citizens' property will be stepped up.

By legislative means, a favorable atmosphere will be provided for withdrawing enterprises from state ownership at the initiative of labor collectives that apply to the State Property Fund or republic Committees for the Management of State Property.

The state will provide incentives for the development of international economic ties and travel abroad for work or study. Attempts to construct a system fenced off from the outside world have virtually consigned most branches of our economy to degradation and stagnation. The opening up of the domestic market will make our country's entrepreneurs compete with inexpensive imported goods both within the country and abroad, which will give our economy dynamism and flexibility in satisfying the requirements of the market, and hence of the consumer.

The Right of Citizens to Freedom of Consumer Choice and Fair Prices.—Freedom of consumer choice holds a rather important place among the rights and liberties in the new economic system. The country's consumer market today has been destroyed virtually completely, and our consumers—that is, all of us—are, accordingly, without rights. The citizens of a great power have turned out to be hostages of empty stores, having, for all practical purposes, fallen under the power of goods-producing monopolists and goods-distributing monopolists.

Among the many reasons for this situation, in the front rank is the inflationary sums of money, not backed by goods, that have been paid to the population, mainly in the past few years. The constantly heard reproaches to the effect that people supposedly have a great deal of "surplus" money and that it must be taken away somehow are essentially immoral. Can we really consider as "surplus" savings that come to a little more than 1,500 rubles per capita? If we take into account citizens' personal property, which is meager for the most part, it is clear that the overwhelming majority of the possessors of "surplus" money are not far from the brink of poverty. Even the total sum of all the money that consumers are ready today to invest immediately in various goods is extremely small. But our consumer market cannot stand up to even this monetary confrontation.

The reform is aimed at normalizing the condition of the consumer market through liberalizing price formation. But during the transitional period this will be done by forming commodity reserves, including through import deliveries, taking into account the forthcoming stage-by-stage changeover to unrestricted prices for many types of goods. An unrestricted exchange rate for buying and selling foreign currency will be introduced, and a foreign-currency market will be developed. A number of large banks will receive the right to trade in foreign currency at market prices, and Soviet citizens will be permitted to keep foreign currency freely in banks. . . .

The Right of Citizens to Income Growth and Social Guarantees.—One serious shortcoming in the system of the state regulation of incomes and the population's standard of living that has been in operation up to now is its inefficiency and inflexibility. For decades, many payments from public consumption funds have remained unchanged, and minimum wage levels have not been revised. In the intervals of many years between revisions, these levels totally lose their ability to meet their original purpose. Moreover, the low income levels of large groups of the population reinforce their underdeveloped, beggarly perception of their needs. The negative processes that arise in this sphere are concealed by uncoordinated measures the point of which comes down to smoothing over already existing contradictions. This sluggishness and inability to react promptly to changes in real life is a characteristic feature of the system now in operation.

The market, as a very mobile system, not only liberalizes economic processes but also creates mechanisms making it possible to regulate changes that take place in the standard of living.

These include the indexing of cash incomes, regular revisions of income levels in accordance with the dynamics of a minimum consumer budget, and a system of social assistance for individuals living below the poverty line. . . .

. . . Without . . . structural reorganization it will be impossible in principle to achieve any kind of significant growth in the standard of living. Of course, the shutdown and reconfiguration of many production facilities will require temporary layoffs and retraining for a large number of people. In this way, a new, more efficient employment structure will be formed, and arduous and hazardous production sectors and manual labor will be cut back. And the more highly skilled employees at new, high-efficiency production facilities will earn more money.

It is planned to reorganize job-placement services and introduce the payment of benefits to those who for some reason are looking for new jobs. When people are looking for jobs, with the active participation of state services, they may take part in public works projects: in the building of roads or homes, first of all homes for themselves. Those who so wish will be able to obtain a plot of land and till it.

There are plans to organize courses and programs for the retraining and refresher training of workers and office employees and to form a system of volunteer-manned public works projects. The critical nature of the employment problem will be eased considerably by the creation of additional job slots at new production facilities, in trade and in the service sphere, and by providing incentives for the development of entrepreneurship and small enterprises.

The regulation of employment should ensure not the permanent assignment of a worker to a specific job but the creation of conditions for continuous growth in qualifications and occupational skills. It is the development of such a continuously operating mechanism and its improvement in accordance with emerging problems that will become the core of state employment policy.

The Right of Enterprises to Freedom of Economic Activity.—The economic freedom of enterprises consists in granting them the opportunity to operate in the interests of their employees, stockholder-owners and the state and in accordance with market conditions, to independently determine the volume and structure of their production, the volume of sales and prices for their output, and to choose their partners.

From virtually the very beginning of the program's implementation, enterprises will have the opportunity to change their owners: either through privatization (mainly for small and medium-sized enterprises) or through transformation into joint-stock companies (primarily for medium-sized and large enterprises). Hence, right after the program is announced enterprise collectives can begin preparations and go through this process as painlessly as possible, a process that differs fundamentally from our practice of sending down such decisions like bolts from the blue. They will be able to resolve as they see fit the question of hiring highly qualified managers on contract.

With a view to maintaining economic stability, established economic ties will evidently be frozen until July 1991. However, after that enterprises will receive the right on their own to determine their product mix and production volume and their customers and suppliers, and to organize the unrestricted marketing of output throughout the country.

Enterprises will withdraw from the system of branch monopolies and will have to establish horizontal ties with their partners. They will also be able to acquire material resources on the wholesale market, including unfinished construction, etc., to freely sell surplus equipment, stocks of materials and other property, and to lease out their fixed assets. They will be granted the right of direct participation in foreign-economic activity. Enterprises will be able to buy and sell foreign currency on a domestic currency market.

In acquiring new rights and expanding the sphere of their economic freedom, enterprises should take into consideration that the program proposes harsh restrictions for them: an increase in charges for credits, the reduction of budget subsidies to zero, a sharp decrease in state capital investments, a reduction in state purchases, and foreign competition. An awareness of these realities will help enterprises do a better job of dealing with their newly acquired freedom.

The Republics' Rights to Economic Sovereignty.—These rights are to be ensured, in accordance with this program, on the basis of a Treaty of Economic Union Between Sovereign States and a number of agreements supplementing it. The conclusion of agreements on interrepublic deliveries and on deliveries for all-Union needs, as well as on mechanisms of maintaining economic ties during the transitional period, is also proposed.

The main thesis in relations between the republics and the center is that no one is to direct or give orders to anyone else. The entire program is based on respect for the declarations of sovereignty adopted by the republics. It is impossible to conduct the economic reform on the basis of directives from the center, no matter how right they may be. The peoples will no longer put up with a situation in which fundamental questions of their lives are resolved at the center, without their participation. The program takes into account the rapid growth of national self-awareness, and therefore the principal role in implementing the transformations is assigned to the republic governments and local bodies of power. Power should be brought closer to people.

In exercising their rights to economic sovereignty, the peoples will receive an opportunity to dispose of the national wealth of their republics on their own, to prevent the senseless wasting of resources, and to preserve the environment and mineral wealth for coming generations. The republic governments now bear responsibility for the development of the territories under their jurisdiction and, accordingly, they are taking on a large part of the powers related to managing the economy.

The republics will determine the level of the basic taxes and the forms and methods of privatization, and they will regulate prices for most goods. Each republic will itself find ways to carry out land and housing reforms, and the republic governments will work out their own systems of social guarantees and form the republic budgets on their own. Money will be transferred to the Union to finance only those programs in which the peoples have a real stake. . . .

Participation in the economic union should be advantageous to the sovereign republics, and therefore the voluntary nature of entry into the union and the right of free withdrawal therefrom must be stipulated. At the same time, a member of the economic union is to take on certain obligations agreed upon by all its participants. If a republic refuses to fulfill these obligations but wishes to participate in certain social and economic programs the union, it receives the status of an associate member (observer), which constricts its rights within the framework of the union.

The Economic Rights of the Center.—These rights constitute the sum total of the rights delegated by the sovereign republics. Within the framework of these agreed-upon rights, the center exercises its powers with respect to the management of all-Union property and funds and all-Union economic programs, and it also ensures the maximum possible coordination in the implementation of the reform.

The Right of Society.—Our society has the unconditional right to live better right now, not in the distant future, and the proposed program for the changeover to a market economy is aimed at the fullest possible realization of this right.

Stephen White

The Minorities' Struggle for Sovereignty

The new elective political forums that Gorbachev created in 1989 and 1990 gave the restive Soviet population an opportunity to vent their frustrations as never before. Above all, many national minorities took control of their respective local governments and pressed for full self-determination as well as rectification of old grievances among themselves. This stage in the process of national awakening, leading inexorably to both interethnic strife and the breakup of the Soviet Union, is treated by the political scientist Stephen White of the University of Glasgow.

The first significant expression of nationalist discontent after Gorbachev's accession was in the Central Asian republic of Kazakh-

From *Gorbachev and After* by Stephen White, pp. 157–158, 160–172, 175–178. Copyright © 1993 by Stephen White. Reprinted by permission of the author and Cambridge University Press.

stan, following the nomination of an ethnic Russian, Gennadii Kolbin, to replace the Brezhnevite incumbent Dinmukhamed Kunaev as party first secretary. Kazakhstan had a very substantial Russian population—37.8 per cent of the total according to the 1989 census, almost as many as the Kazakhs themselves—but it was the home of the great majority of the Soviet Union's Kazakhs and it had become accepted that the republic's party and state leadership should be drawn from the national group after whom the republic was named. Not less important, Kunaev was at the centre of an elaborate network of patronage and corruption which was clearly threatened by the imposition of an ethnic and political outsider. The demonstrations that followed Kolbin's appointment may have been covertly encouraged by Kunaev's clients; there was certainly no doubt that, as *Literaturnaya gazeta* reported in early 1987, the news provoked "inexperienced and politically illiterate youths" to take to the streets, later to be joined by "hooligans, drunks and other anti-social types." Nationalist slogans, "pulled out of the murkiest depths of history," were chanted, and the crowd, armed with metal posts, sticks and stones, then proceeded to beat up local citizens, overturn cars and set them on fire, and smash the windows of shops and other public buildings. Government sources subsequently acknowledged that up to 3,000 people had been involved in the demonstrations, and that 200 had been injured; unofficial sources suggested that as many as 280 students had lost their lives, together with twenty-nine policemen and soldiers.

The next national issue to take the form of open public discontent was in the summer of 1987 when a group of about 700 Crimean Tatars staged an unprecedented demonstration in Red Square. . . . The Tatars, remarkably and unexpectedly, were allowed to hold their demonstration without police harassment, and following discussions with government representatives a commission headed by then President Gromyko was established to "study the merits of their case." In June 1988 it reported, recommending the removal of any improper restrictions upon the right of individual Tatars to return to their native land and calling for more attention to be paid to their cultural needs, but also rejecting the Tatars' call for the reestablishment of their autonomous republic. Substantial numbers of Tatars returned to live in their traditional homelands and, following a referendum in which the idea had received overwhelming support, a Crimean autonomous republic was finally restored by a vote of the Ukrainian parliament in February 1991. . . .

More important, perhaps, was the emergence in the Baltic republics themselves of an open, widely supported and coordinated nationalist movement taking the form of "popular fronts" (or in Lithuania, Sajudis). Ostensibly "in favour of *perestroika*" and incorporating many party members within their ranks, the new movements were nonetheless associated with a policy stance which went very much further than the party conference resolution. Their founding congresses in October 1988, for instance, called (in the case of Sajudis) for "sovereignty" in all areas of Lithuanian life, the formation of a "pluralist society" with no organisation "usurping" political power, a partly privatised economy, and the demilitarisation of the republican territory (in effect, withdrawal from the Warsaw Treaty Organisation). The Latvian Popular Front, similarly, called for the "economic sovereignty" of the republic, and for the ending of immigration and the abolition of special privileges for all high-ranking officials. In a series of related developments the old flags of the independent Baltic states between the wars were legalised, in Lithuania the pre-war national anthem was restored, and legislation was initiated with a view to establishing Lithuanian and Estonian as official languages in their respective republics. In Lithuania the Roman Catholic cathedral, used as an art gallery for forty years, was restored to the faithful in October 1988. Estonia left the Soviet [Moscow] time zone and aligned itself chronologically with Finland; Christmas became a public holiday; and the republican capital, Tallinn, was given its Estonian name (with two *n*s rather than one) for all-union purposes.

The publication of draft constitutional amendments in October 1988 led to widespread public protests. Baltic opinion, in particular, objected that the changes proposed were centralising in character and that the republics' (admittedly nominal) right of secession had been prejudiced. The Estonian parliament, influenced by these concerns, adopted a constitutional amendment on 16 November providing for the right of veto over all legislation that was intended to apply to the USSR as a whole. The decision was held to be unconstitutional by the Supreme Soviet Presidium on 20 November and the Baltic republics came in for severe criticism from other delegates at the Supreme Soviet session on 1 December which passed the constitutional amendments into law. . . .

Relations between the Baltic republics and the central authorities, in the event, became still more strained over the period that followed. A form of economic decentralisation, already approved by the Baltic legislatures, was given a cautious welcome by the USSR Supreme Soviet in July 1989 and was formally adopted at the winter parliamentary session. The legislation applied to the three Baltic republics and (under a separate provision) Belorussia in the first instance; some regions of the Russian Republic indicated that they too would seek to place their relations with the central government on this new basis. Legislation on the position of the local languages in early 1989 aroused more controversy: according to the views of some commentators in *Izvestiya*, the new directives, at least in Estonia, placed non-native speakers at a considerable disadvantage and probably infringed their civil rights. Lithuania and Latvia, in May and June 1989 respectively, established a form of republican citizenship. A set of constitutional amendments adopted by the Estonian Supreme Soviet proved most controversial of all. The amendments (which were later rescinded) restricted the right to vote to those who had lived in the constituency for at least two years, or elsewhere in Estonia for five years or more; deputies themselves had to have lived in Estonia for at least ten years. The change provoked an extended strike on the part of the largely Russian speaking blue-collar labour force, and the Supreme Soviet Presidium in Moscow declared the legislation unconstitutional on the grounds that it violated the principle of equal electoral rights (some 80,000, it was estimated, would be deprived of the franchise under the new regulations). The interests of the non-indigenous population were articulated by bodies such as "Interfront" in Latvia, set up in January 1989, and its counterparts in the other republics; the concerns of the substantial Russian-speaking minority in these republics were also expressed in letters to the central press, and found some reflection in the speeches of members of the party leadership.

The central party leadership, in fact, went so far as to issue a formal statement on the Baltic situation in late August 1989, warning against the activities of "extremist" and "anti-socialist" forces that were pursuing a separatist line with "growing persistence and aggressiveness." Declarations of this kind, however, no longer had much effect. The stance that local leaderships had taken had enormous public support, expressed both in the number prepared to take part in public meetings and in opinion polls, and openly nationalist pressures became if anything still stronger. On 23 August 1989, the 50th anniversary of the Nazi–Soviet pact, an estimated two million Balts formed a human chain across the three republics in the biggest demonstration that had yet been seen. The popular fronts themselves became still more intransigent in their demands: both the Latvian and the Lithuanian fronts, in late 1989, were openly contemplating the possibility of formal secession from the USSR, not simply a greater measure of autonomy, and the three fronts jointly organised a Baltic Assembly which called for political independence for the republics within a "neutral and demilitarised Balto–Scandia." Perhaps most disturbing from the point of view of the central authorities, the party organisations in the three republics, particularly in Lithuania, began to press for a greater degree of independence, establishing direct links with outside ruling parties and adopting their own programme and statute, within or if necessary outside the framework of the CPSU as a whole.

Inter-republican relations in the USSR entered an entirely new stage when in February 1990 supporters of Sajudis won a majority of seats in the republican parliament and then, on 11 March, formally declared Lithuania independent on the basis of its prewar constitution. Gorbachev, addressing the Congress of People's Deputies, described the Lithuanian action as "illegitimate and invalid" and refused to open negotiations with what remained, in his view, an integral part of the USSR. The central authorities issued an ultimatum demanding the withdrawal of the declaration of independence; when the Lithuanians refused to comply with this an economic blockade was imposed on 18 April. These pressures notwithstanding, the neighbouring republics of Estonia and Latvia adopted more cautiously worded declarations of independence on 30 March and 4 May respectively. The situation eased, at least temporarily, when the Lithuanian declaration of independence was suspended by parliamentary vote on 29 June, allowing the blockade to be lifted and a negotiation process to begin. Gorbachev, visiting Lithuania in January 1990, had unexpectedly promised that legislation would be introduced allowing republics to become fully independent; but the law on secession, approved on 3 April 1990, specified a two-thirds majority in a referendum on the issue and then a transitional period of up to five years in which territorial, property and other issues would be resolved. Only the Lithuanians accounted for so large a proportion of the population of their own republic, and the measure was widely seen as blocking rather than facilitating a transition to fully independent status.

The resolution of differences in this or any other way became still more unlikely when in January 1991 military force was used to restore central authority in Latvia and Lithuania on the pretext that the Soviet Constitution was being violated (in particular, that the civil rights of the non-indigenous population were being infringed and that the call-up of recruits into the armed forces was being impeded). In Lithuania, 13 died and 112 were injured when troops stormed the television centre in Vilnius; in Latvia, four died in a battle for government buildings in Riga. The Soviet defence minister, seeking to justify the action, claimed that organised attempts were being made to establish a "dictatorship of the bourgeois type" in the area; the Lithuanian president, Vytautas Landsbergis, saw the conflict as a result of the "fifty-one year confrontation between Lithuania and the USSR," and the Russian president, Boris Yeltsin, more forthrightly described it as an "offensive against democracy." At least to some observers the action in the Baltic represented an attempt by hard-line party and military officials, organised in a shadowy "Committee of National Salvation," to seize power and overthrow the nationalist administrations. Whether they had taken such action with the explicit authorisation of President Gorbachev remained unclear, although it was widely agreed that he had failed to respond adequately to the loss of life that had occurred. . . .

. . . Of all the Soviet nationalities, the Baltic nations looked the most likely to establish (or as they saw it, resume) their independent statehood in the 1990s; their opportunity to do so came soon after the attempted coup when (in September 1991) the USSR Council of State formally approved their independent status and they were admitted into the United Nations and other international organisations.

The pressures for independence or at least a greater measure of autonomy that emerged in the Baltic republics were the most serious of their kind that the Soviet leadership had to confront in the early Gorbachev years. In all three republics, with minor local variations, a largely united people with a distinct cultural identity and a previous history of self-rule were seeking to renegotiate the nature of their relationship with the Soviet state and its economic and political system. The ethnic differences that emerged elsewhere in the USSR in the late 1980s were for the most part more traditional, almost "tribal" in character, in that they sprang from antipathies between ethnic groups with different religious, linguistic and historical backgrounds and expressed themselves in the form of communal clashes rather than pressures for formal independence. The first of these disputes to emerge was in the Caucasus, where the most serious civil disturbances in Soviet post-war history took place between Armenians and Azerbaijanis over the disputed territorial enclave of Nagorno-Karabakh. There were comparable difficulties elsewhere, particularly in Georgia and Uzbekistan, and indeed there were few parts of Soviet territory that did not experience some form of nationalist self-consciousness combined with pressure for a greater degree of cultural and economic autonomy.

Nationalist tensions took a particularly violent and intractable form in the case of Nagorno-Karabakh, an autonomous region which had since 1923 formed a part of the Azerbaijan republic. A mountainous enclave of about 4,400 square kilometres, Nagorno-Karabakh had originally been assigned to Armenia but had then been transferred to the jurisdiction of its traditionally Muslim neighbour. Its 1979 census population of about 162,000 was 75.9 per cent Armenian and only 22.9 per cent Azerbaijani, and there had been pressure for some years for its transfer back to Armenia and for a greater degree of autonomy for its predominantly Christian people. The open conflict of early 1988 was precipitated, it appears, by the rejection by the central party authorities of an appeal for Nagorno-Karabakh to be returned to Armenia which had been signed by 75,000 Karabakh Armenians. Demonstrations began on 11 February in Stepanakert, the regional capital, and led to the adoption of a resolution by the regional soviet on 20 February which called for Nagorno-Karabakh to be transferred back to Armenia. Further demonstrations took place in the Armenian capital, Yerevan, to support the call for Nagorno-Karabakh's reincorporation into the republic. Up to a million Armenians, by late February, were reported to be demonstrating daily in the city's Opera Square. The demonstrations came temporarily to an end after a personal appeal by Gorbachev on 26 February, but a report that two Azerbaijanis had been killed the previous week led to an anti-Armenian riot on 28–29 February in the oil town of Sumgait in which 32 people were killed and 197 were injured, including more than 100 police officers. The party first secretaries of Armenia, Azerbaijan and Nagorno-Karabakh were all replaced in May 1988; the Central Committee meanwhile promised that steps would be taken to improve housing, schools and hospitals in the region, and to extend broadcasts in both Armenian and Azerbaijani. . . .

. . . In January 1990 the dispute extended into intercommunal violence across both republics, precipitated by an Armenian decision to extend the provisions of their republican budget and electoral law to the disputed enclave. Tens of thousands took to the streets in Baku alone, up to sixty people (mostly Armenians) lost their lives in pogroms, and there were further fatalities when a state of emergency was declared by the USSR Presidium and troops were used to restore order on 19–20 January. At least ninety-three people lost their lives in the first days of fighting. There was a further, still more violent outbreak of hostilities in early 1992; for Volsky [Gorbachev's representative], interviewed in the press, the whole area was in danger of becoming the Soviet Union's "home-grown Lebanon."

Two further ethnic disputes reached the point of violence and bloodshed during 1989 and 1990: a dispute between Meskhetian Turks and the native population in the Ferghana valley in eastern Uzbekistan, and a complex dispute in Georgia involving both a strong separatist movement and communal tensions between Georgians and Abkhazians, a national minority within Georgia itself. The violence in Uzbekistan, which erupted suddenly in early June 1989, swiftly became the bloodiest in Soviet peacetime history. . . .

Long-standing tensions also emerged in Soviet Georgia during 1988 and 1989, inspired in part by nationalist pressures for a greater degree of autonomy within (if not total separation from) the USSR, and in part by differences of a social and ethnic character within Georgia itself. Georgians were not simply distinctive in their cultural and historical background; they were also the most "patriotic" of the major Soviet nationalities, as measured by the proportion that lived in their own republic, and their share of the republican population had been steadily increasing, unlike the position (for instance) in the Baltic republics. . . .

Further demonstrations in support of independence took place in early 1989 on the anniversary of the republic's incorporation into the USSR (February 1921). Some 15,000 protesters were involved, according to Western press reports, 200 of whom were detained. Still more substantial demonstrations were organised in April 1989. Reports indicated that more than 100,000 demonstrators had gathered in front of Georgian party and government headquarters; many factories were on strike as well as the local television, and troops and armoured personnel carriers were on duty. The demonstrators held banners demanding both the secession of Georgia from the Soviet Union and the full integration of the Abkhazian republic, which had itself been seeking to secede from Georgia and to resume the union republican status it had enjoyed from 1921 until 1931. An Abkhaz nationalist grouping, Ayglara (Unity), had been formed, and the Abkhaz party secretary (dismissed in early April) was reported to have favoured the idea of secession. The leader of another informal nationalist grouping, the Forum for the Peoples of Abkhazia, was elected to the Congress of People's Deputies and to the new-style Supreme Soviet, where he expressed some reservations about the idea of strengthening the fifteen union republics at the expense, almost certainly, of the smaller national-territorial units that were subordinate to them. Georgians, however, accounted for by far the largest share of the population of the Abkhaz republic (Abkhazians themselves were a small minority), and they were resolutely opposed to any diminution of their links with their own republic, holding rival demonstrations within Abkhazia and within Georgia to make their position clear.

Matters reached a critical stage when the demonstrators in central Tbilisi were attacked by interior ministry troops on the evening of 9 April 1989. At least sixteen people were killed, according to official sources, and a curfew had to be introduced. The demonstration followed a hunger strike and a wave of industrial disturbances, and was led by the National Democratic Party of Georgia, the Party of National Independence and two other nationalist groupings broadly similar in character to the popular fronts established in the Baltic. Some of the demonstrators, Tass reported, had put forward "nationalist, anti-socialist slogans" and had called for strikes, civil disobedience and the liquidation of Soviet power in Georgia; some "extremists" had been armed with sticks, stones and metal objects. Local sources insisted that all the dead had been unarmed and that they had been attacked with sharpened spades and a noxious gas, which had itself been responsible for the death of two women. No such brutal suppression of a peaceful demonstration had been seen in the Soviet Union since at least the early 1960s, strengthening rumours that the action, directed by the Ministry of Internal Affairs rather than by Georgian officials, might have been covertly encouraged by Kremlin conservatives intent on discrediting Gorbachev and the policy of *perestroika*. The foreign minister and former Georgian party leader, Eduard Shevardnadze, cancelled his plans to attend a Warsaw Pact meeting and flew to Tbilisi to appeal for calm while tanks patrolled the city streets. Gorbachev added a personal appeal on 13 April. At a plenum of the Georgian central committee the following day the party first secretary, Dzumber Patiashvili, resigned and was replaced by the former head of the Georgian KGB, Givi Gumbaridze; the Georgian prime minister and head of state also tendered their resignations. A Georgian parliamentary commission which was established to investigate the incident later concluded that the interior troops had carried out a "punitive action—a planned mass massacre, committed with especial cruelty." . . .

There were strong pressures from still further national minorities for a greater degree of control over their own affairs. A popular front came into existence in the Ukraine in late 1988, influenced by concerns about the environment (and the further development of nuclear power in particular) as well as by enduring linguistic and other cultural issues. The Front, known as "Rukh" ("Movement"), held its founding congress in September 1989; the local authorities, meanwhile, began to address one of its central concerns by making Ukrainian the official state language in the republic. A declaration of sovereignty, adopted in July 1990, asserted the republic's right to its own armed forces and security as well as natural resources. A Belorussian popular front was formed in June 1989, although its founding congress had to take place in Lithuania because of the hostility of the republican leadership. Soviet Germans, about two million strong, established a new All-Union Society of Germans in early 1989 and called for the restoration of their autonomous republic, which had been abolished at the outbreak of the war in 1941. There were demonstrations in Moldavia (renamed Moldova) calling for greater control over local affairs, and in particular for official status for the Moldavian language; there were counter-demonstrations by the republic's non-Moldavian population, more than a third of the total, against what they saw as a form of reverse discrimination (Russian, in the event, was retained as a means of inter-nationality communication). Both Tatars and Bashkirs claimed full union republican status, in the autumn of 1990, and complained of the management of up to 97 per cent of their oil-rich economy by outside agencies. There were further calls from many of the Soviet Union's "little peoples"—minority nationalities of relatively modest numbers which generally lacked their own national-territorial areas—about falling populations and the use of their area for unrestricted industrial activity. The most serious problems were in Siberia, where press reports spoke of the "unregulated and uncontrolled destruction of the very conditions of existence of the indigenous population." . . .

Gorbachev's speech to the Central Committee in Janaury 1987, made shortly after the riots in Kazakhstan, marked a new stage in his awareness of the complexity of national issues. The events in Alma-Ata,[1] in the General Secretary's view, required a "serious analysis and a principled assessment." There were "negative phenomena and deformations" in relations between the nationalities, as there were in other spheres of Soviet life; and there had been incidents elsewhere not very different from those in the Kazakh capital. Gorbachev still identified internationalism as the

[1] See pp. 217–218.

policy which could deal most effectively with problems of this kind. But he also mentioned the need to ensure that the various nationalities were properly represented in political and economic life, and he acknowledged that party officials had sometimes handled nationality issues without the degree of sensitivity that they required. . . .

. . . At the 19th Party Conference in the summer of 1988, Gorbachev, in his address, still felt able to claim that the establishment of a union of nations and nationalities enjoying equal rights was "one of the greatest accomplishments of socialism." At the same time there were "omissions and difficulties" and "occasional failures to reconcile the interests of individual nations with those of the USSR as a whole." The way forward, in his view, lay in developing economic links of all kinds among the republics, and deepening the domestic division of labour. The economic and constitutional rights of the republics, at the same time, should be increased and defined more precisely; but any changes of this kind must take account of the fact that each of the republics was itself a multinational state in which the interests of all national groups must be properly respected. Any other policy would "lead to disaster." The resolution on nationality relations adopted at the conference reflected very similar concerns. A "new historical community—the Soviet people" had come into existence, based upon a common destiny and an interdependent economy. The various nations and nationalities of the USSR, at the same time, had their specific concerns, and the neglect of these during the Stalin and Brezhnev years had led them to take the form of "public disaffection, which now and then escalated into conflicts." To deal with these problems there should be a further development of the democratic principles of the Soviet federation, extending the rights of the union republics and lower levels of government. Local languages and cultures should be fostered, as well as Russian; and a national research centre should be established to examine these and other issues in more detail. . . .

. . . In March 1989 a set of directives on economic relations between the USSR and its constituent republics was published, which called for the transfer of up to 36 per cent of industrial production to local control (the existing figure was only 5 per cent), with much higher levels—up to 72 per cent—in Georgia and the Baltic republics. The somewhat opaque slogan of a "strong centre and strong republics" began to appear in official speeches from early 1989. And a working group on constitutional reform, established by the Supreme Soviet in late 1988, began—at least in its reported meetings—to develop the notion of "republican precedence," by which the union republics should have full authority over all matters that had not been specifically transferred to the USSR government.

Finally, and most important of all, the Central Committee published a draft "Platform" on the national question in August 1989 setting out the basis on which it proposed to conduct the long-promised plenum, which was now to be held in September. The Platform began by acknowledging the damage that had been done to national relations by the repression of the Stalinist years and by later attempts to accelerate convergence on the basis of an allegedly full and final resolution of the national question. Russians, as well as other nations, had suffered from these policies. In the future, the Central Committee suggested, there should be radical changes in state structure leading to a "renewed federation" with greater devolved powers for the union republics, including their transfer to a cost-accounting basis within what would continue to be a single domestic market. The Russian Republic, in particular, should enjoy greater rights, including its own party organisation. The CPSU as a whole, however, should remain a united, "consolidating and directing force of social development," based on a democratic centralism, and with a single statute and programme. National languages should be encouraged, but Russian remained the language of inter-ethnic communication and all languages must have equality of status. There could not, however, be prescriptions that were valid for all cases; national policy was a "continuous creation," and what was necessary above all was a realistic and undogmatic approach, free of national chauvinism but receptive to legitimate expressions of national self-consciousness. . . .

. . . By the early 1990s it was clear that only a reconsideration of the very bases of Soviet statehood would be likely to satisfy the aspirations of the various republics and nationalities. Not simply would the future USSR be a "renewed federation"; it would also, necessarily, be a voluntary association of republics based upon a new union treaty, whose features became increasingly distinct as the Central Committee plenum faded into obscurity. Gorbachev, speaking after his election as President, called for the conclusion of a "new union treaty" of this kind; and the Federation Council, when it met later in the year, agreed that a union treaty was necessary which would "guarantee real economic and political sovereignty for the republics." A working group, with representatives of all the republics concerned, was established to prepare a first draft. Interethnic relations, Gorbachev conceded in his speech to the 28th Party Congress in July 1990, had deteriorated since the congress before it, and especially over the previous few months. There had been considerable loss of life, and thousands had been forced to leave their homelands. What was needed in these circumstances was an updated union in the form of a "real union of sovereign states," enshrined in a new union treaty which would replace the treaty of 1922 on which the USSR had originally been founded.

Demonstration for democracy, Moscow, January 1991. (AP/Wide World Photos, Boris Yurchenko)

PART

IV Disintegration, 1991

Patching Up the Union

Documents from *Pravda* and *Izvestiya*

By the beginning of 1991, Gorbachev's most pressing problem was
the separatist movements in the minority republics, colliding with
the centralist instincts of Russian nationalists and communists. This
dilemma was an inevitable consequence of democratization in the
Soviet Union, though Gorbachev did not fully appreciate it until too
late. During his last few months in power, he endeavored to rescue
the union by a series of concessions, expressed in the Novo-Ogaryovo

From "Joint Statement on Urgent Measures to Stabilize the Situation in the
Country and Overcome the Crisis" [Novo-Ogaryovo Agreement], *Pravda* and
Izvestiya, April 24, 1991; and "Draft Treaty on the Union of Sovereign Republics,"
Pravda and *Izvestiya*, March 9, 1991. English translation in *The Current Digest
of the Soviet Press*, vol. 43, no. 17, pp. 10–13. Copyright © 1991 by *The Current
Digest of the Soviet Press*, published weekly at Columbus, Ohio. Reprinted by
permission of the Digest.

Agreement concluded at the president's country retreat near Moscow in April 1991. This arrangement, endorsed by Gorbachev, Yeltsin, and the heads of eight other union republics—the "nine plus one"—called for a new union treaty to replace the bogus document of 1922 and preserve the union on the basis of a loose confederation. The treaty was supposed to be signed August 20, but the coup attempt of August 19 left it a dead letter.

The Novo-Ogaryovo Agreement

The crisis in our society continues to deepen. Society is torn by social conflicts and strife between nationalities. The production slump is getting worse. The living standard is falling, and a threat is being created to the provision of prime necessities to people. Law and order and discipline in the country have been seriously disrupted. Very acute problems that have built up over decades, the painful difficulties of the transitional period and the mistakes that have been made during perestroika have come together in a single focus.

Having discussed the situation in the country at their meeting on April 23, 1991, the President of the USSR and the leaders of the supreme state bodies of the following Union republics—the Russian SFSR, the Ukraine, Belorussia, Uzbekistan, Kazakhstan, Azerbaijan, Tadzhikistan, Kyrgyzstan and Turkmenistan—have deemed it necessary to carry out coordinated actions without delay.

First. The participants in the meeting believe that the adoption of resolute measures for the restoration of constitutional order everywhere and for unswerving observance of existing laws, pending the adoption of a new Union Treaty and Union Constitution, is an indispensable condition for stabilizing the situation in the country. Union and republic bodies of power, local Soviets and executive committees, officials of all organizations and enterprises, and citizens should proceed from this premise in their activity.

Second. A top-priority task in overcoming the crisis is the conclusion of a new treaty among sovereign states, taking into account the results of the all-Union referendum that has been held. In this connection, the meeting's participants consider it necessary:

—to complete work on the draft of the new Union Treaty in the near future, so that an agreed-upon document can be signed by delegations of the aforementioned republics;

—no later than six months after the treaty is signed, to prepare and adopt, at a Congress of USSR People's Deputies, a new Union Constitution, to be based on the provisions of the treaty on a Union of sovereign states;

—after the new Constitution is adopted, to prepare for and hold elections to the Union bodies of power provided for by the treaty and the Constitution;

—to ensure the normal activity of Union and republic bodies of power and Soviets of People's Deputies at all levels throughout the transitional period;

—while acknowledging the right of Latvia, Lithuania, Estonia, Moldova, Georgia and Armenia to decide for themselves the question of acceding to the Union Treaty, the top leaders of the Union republics participating in the meeting at the same time consider it necessary to establish most-favored-nation status for the republics signing the Union Treaty, in the framework of the single economic space formed by them;

—to regard discrimination on the basis of nationality, the incitement of conflicts between nationalities and violations of the rights of USSR citizens, no matter where they live, as impermissible. Law-enforcement agencies are to resolutely stop all instances of this sort.

Third. To reaffirm the commitments of Union bodies and republics as codified in the economic agreement for 1991 and the need for the unconditional fulfillment of these commitments, first of all with respect to budgets and the formation of off-budget funds.

In this regard, there was unanimous support for conducting joint anticrisis measures that take the aggravated social and economic situation into account.

The further strengthening and development of economic ties among enterprises, regions and republics are to be ensured, and the USSR Cabinet of Ministers and the Union-republic governments are to bear increased responsibility for this.

With a view to stabilizing the situation in the national economy, the meeting's participants called for the introduction of special work rules in the basic branches of industry, at enterprises that produce consumer goods and in railroad transport.

When necessary, republic bodies of power will take additional measures to ensure the normal work of the national economy.

The meeting's participants consider providing the population with food products to be a top-priority task. Central and republic agencies will carry out coordinated actions to fulfill scheduled deliveries of material resources to agriculture and enterprises of the agro-industrial complex. During the second quarter, the USSR Cabinet of Ministers and the Union-republic governments are to work out and adopt decisions on maintaining equivalent relations between agriculture and enterprises of the agro-industrial complex, on the one hand, and other branches of the national economy, on the other.

Fourth. Recognizing that not all the factors having a negative effect on the population's living standard were taken into account when the retail price reform was conducted, the meeting's participants consider it necessary to adopt a number of additional measures in the interests of providing social protection for citizens, especially the needy. . . .

. . . The leaders of the Union and the republics appeal to miners and all working people to stop economically and politically motivated strikes and to exert themselves to make up for lost time in the near future.

Fifth. In view of the exceptionally acute crisis situation in the country, the leaders of the Union and the republics regard as intolerable any attempts to achieve political goals through incitement to civil disobedience and strikes and any calls to overthrow existing, legitimately elected bodies of state power.

They called for cooperation and interaction, within the framework of the law, between all public and political forces, using the opportunities provided by the development of democracy, the activity of representative bodies of power, and glasnost.

In doing so, special emphasis was put on the point that, at the present critical time, the interests of the people and practical work to extricate the country from crisis, continue the democratic transformations in society and further radicalize the economic reform while simultaneously carrying out measures of social support for the population are to be placed above all else.

The meeting's participants realize that all these measures to stabilize the situation and overcome the crisis are inconceivable without a fundamental enhancement of the role of the Union republics.

Draft of the Union Treaty

The sovereign states that are parties to the treaty,

expressing the will of their peoples for the renewal of the Union;

recognizing the right of nations and peoples to self-determination;

proceeding from the declarations of state sovereignty proclaimed by the republics;

taking into account the closeness of their historical fates, striving to live in friendship and concord, and ensuring equal cooperation;

wishing to create conditions for the all-round development of every individual and the provision of reliable guarantees of his or her rights and liberties;

showing concern for the material well-being and spiritual development of the peoples, the mutual enrichment of national cultures, and the ensuring of general security;

drawing lessons from the past and taking into consideration the changes in the life of the country and throughout the world;

have decided to construct their relations in the USSR on new principles.

Basic Principles

First. Each republic that is a party to the treaty is a sovereign state.

The USSR is a sovereign federal democratic state formed as a result of the voluntary association of equal republics and exercising state power within the bounds of the powers it is endowed with by the parties to the treaty.

Second. The republics forming the Union retain the right to the independent resolution of all questions of their development, and they guarantee to all peoples living on their territories political rights and opportunities for social, economic and cultural development. The republics will resolutely oppose racism, chauvinism, nationalism and all attempts to limit the rights of peoples. The parties to the treaty will proceed from a combination of universal human and national values.

Third. The republics recognize the priority of human rights, in accordance with generally recognized norms of international law, as a highly important principle. All citizens are guaranteed the possibility of the study and use of their native language, unhindered access to information, freedom of religion, and other political, social, economic and personal rights and liberties.

Fourth. The republics see the formation and development of a civil society as a highly important condition for freedom and well-being. They will strive to satisfy people's requirements on the basis of a free choice of the forms of ownership and the methods of economic management and implementation of the principles of social justice and safeguards.

Fifth. The republics forming the Union possess full state power and will independently determine their national-state and administrative-territorial structure and system of bodies of power and administration. They recognize democracy based on popular representation and direct expression of the peoples' will as a common fundamental principle, and they are striving to create a state based on the rule of law that will serve as a guarantee against any tendencies toward authoritarianism and high-handedness.

Sixth. The republics consider the preservation and development of national traditions and state support for education, science and culture to be one of their most important tasks. They will promote intensive exchanges and the mutual enrichment of the peoples of the country and the whole world with humanistic spiritual values.

Seventh. The parties to the treaty declare that the main goals of the Union in the international arena are lasting peace, the elimination of nuclear and other weapons of mass destruction, cooperation among states and the solidarity of peoples in solving mankind's global problems.

The republics are full-fledged members of the international community. They have a right to establish direct diplomatic, consular, trade and other ties with foreign states, to exchange authorized representatives with them, to conclude international treaties, and to participate directly in the activity of international organizations that does not infringe on the interests of the parties to this treaty or their common interests and does not violate the USSR's international commitments.

The Structure of the Union

Art. 1. Membership in the USSR. The republics' membership in the USSR is voluntary. The republics that are parties to the treaty possess equal rights and have equal duties. . . .

The republics that are parties to the treaty have the right to freely secede from the Union in accordance with procedures established by the parties to the treaty.

Art. 2. Citizenship. A citizen of a republic that is part of the USSR is at the same time a citizen of the USSR.

Citizens of the USSR have equal rights, freedoms and duties that are codified in the Constitution, laws and international treaties of the USSR.

Art. 3. Territory. The territory of the USSR consists of the territories of all the republics that are parties to the treaty.

The republics that are parts of the USSR recognize the boundaries between them that existed at the time the treaty was signed.

Boundaries between republics may be changed only by agreement between them.

Art. 4. Relations Between Republics. Relations between the republics are regulated by this treaty and by other treaties and agreements that are not at variance with it.

The republics that are parties to the treaty construct their relations within the Union on the basis of equality, respect for sovereignty, territorial integrity, noninterference in internal affairs, the resolution of disputes through peaceful means, cooperation, mutual assistance, and the conscientious fulfillment of commitments under the Union Treaty and interrepublic agreements.

The republics that are parties to the treaty pledge not to use force or the threat of force against one another, not to carry out any forcible actions, and not to infringe on the territorial integrity of other republics.

The republics pledge not to allow the stationing of armed formations of foreign states on their territory or the siting of foreign military bases there, and not to conclude agreements that are at variance with the goals of the Union or that are aimed against the interests of republics that are parts of the Union.

Art. 5. The Demarcation of Powers in the USSR. The parties to the treaty endow the USSR with the following powers:

—protecting the sovereignty and territorial integrity of the Union and of the republics that are parts of the Union;

—ensuring the state security of the USSR; fixing and guarding the USSR State Border; changing the USSR State Border, with the consent of the relevant republic;

—organizing defense and the leadership of the USSR Armed Forces and the USSR border, internal and railroad troops; declaring war and concluding peace;

—managing defense enterprises and organizations involved in the creation and production of arms and military equipment;

—implementing all-Union foreign policy; representing the USSR in relations with foreign states and international organizations; concluding international treaties of the USSR; coordinating the foreign-policy activity of the Union and the republics;

—implementing foreign-economic activity within the bounds of the powers of the USSR;

—confirming and fulfilling the Union budget;

—managing space research, all-Union communications and information systems, geodesy, cartography, meteorology and standardization;

—monitoring observance of the USSR Constitution and laws; adopting legislation on questions falling under Union jurisdiction; establishing principles of legislation on questions agreed upon with the republics;

—coordinating activity to safeguard public order and combat crime.

The USSR exercises the following powers in conjunction with the republics:

—adopting the USSR Constitution, and making changes in and additions to it; ensuring the rights and liberties of citizens of the USSR;

—determining the USSR's foreign-policy course and monitoring its implementation through the system of the Union's supreme bodies of state power; protecting the rights and interests of citizens of the USSR and the republics in international relations; establishing the principles of foreign-economic activity; unified customs operations; exercising the sovereign rights of the Union and the republics to the natural resources of the USSR's economic zone and continental shelf;

—determining the strategy of state security for the USSR and the republics that are parts of it; ensuring the state security of the members of the Union; establishing the conditions governing the USSR State Border and the USSR's waters and airspace;

—determining the military policy of the USSR; carrying out measures to organize and ensure the defense of the USSR; resolving questions associated with the stationing and activity of troops and military installations on the territory of the republics; establishing uniform procedures for call-up to and the performance of military service; organizing the mobilization of the national economy;

—determining the strategy for the country's social and economic development, and creating conditions for the development of an all-Union market; conducting a uniform financial, credit, monetary, tax and price policy based on a common currency; drawing up the Union budget and monitoring its fulfillment; using the USSR's gold reserves and its diamond and foreign-currency stocks; developing and carrying out all-Union programs; creating all-Union funds for regional development and for eliminating the consequences of natural disasters and catastrophes, as well as other funds agreed upon with the republics, and managing these funds; providing assistance to foreign states, and concluding agreements on international loans and credits; regulating the external and internal state debts;

—managing defense enterprises and organizations involved in the creation and production of civilian output;

—managing the country's unified fuel and power system and railroad, air, maritime and trunk-pipeline transportation;

—establishing principles for the use of natural resources and environmental protection, and conducting a coordinated ecological policy;

—establishing the principles of social policy, including questions of employment and migration, working conditions and job safety, social security and insurance, public education, public health, and protection of the family, mother and child; providing a guaranteed minimum subsistence level; promoting cultural development;

—ensuring the preservation of the primeval habitat for numerically small peoples, and providing the necessary conditions for their economic and cultural development;

—organizing and conducting basic scientific research and encouraging scientific and technical progress; determining policy and the basic principles of its implementation in the development of higher schools and in the training and certification of highly skilled research-and-teaching personnel.

The powers defined in this article may be changed only with the consent of all the republics that are parties to the Union Treaty.

Disputes over questions of exercising the USSR's powers or implementing rights and fulfilling duties in the field of the joint powers of the USSR and the republics are resolved through conciliatory procedures. When an accord is not reached, disputes are submitted to the USSR Constitutional Court for consideration.

Art. 6. The Republics' Participation in the Exercise of the Union's Powers. The republics participate in the exercise of the USSR's powers through the joint formation of Union bodies and the creation of other mechanisms and procedures for coordinating interests and actions.

Each republic may, by concluding an agreement with the USSR, additionally delegate to the latter the exercise of certain of the republic's powers, and the Union, with the consent of all the republics, may turn over the exercise of certain of its powers to one or several republics on their territory.

Art. 7. Property. The USSR and the republics ensure the unrestricted development and protection of all forms of property provided for by USSR and republic legislation, and promote the functioning of a single all-Union market.

The republics are the owners of the land, its mineral wealth and other natural resources on their territory, as well as of state property, with the exception of that part which, on the basis of treaties, is assigned to Union ownership for the exercise of the powers entrusted to the Union.

Union property is used and augmented exclusively in the common interests of the republics, including evening out the levels of their social and economic development.

The republics have the right to a share of the USSR's gold, diamond and foreign-currency stocks and participate in their utilization.

The use of land, its mineral wealth and other natural resources for implementing the Union's powers is carried out within the framework of legislation of the republics, which are to create the necessary conditions for the USSR's activity.

Art. 8. Taxes and Fees. The republics independently establish taxes and fees and determine their budgets.

Union taxes and fees are established for the exercise of the USSR's powers, in amounts determined by agreement with the republics; pro rata payments for all-Union programs are also established, with the amounts and destinations of these payments regulated by an annual agreement between the Union and the republics, taking into account the indices of their social and economic development.

Art. 9. The USSR Constitution. The Union Treaty is the foundation of the USSR Constitution.

The USSR Constitution is adopted by a Congress of representatives of the states that are parties to the treaty.

The USSR Constitution must not be at variance with the Union Treaty.

Art. 10. Laws. USSR laws and republic Constitutions and laws must not be at variance with the provisions of the Union Treaty.

USSR laws on questions within USSR jurisdiction have supremacy and are binding on the territory of all republics.

On republic territory, republic laws have supremacy on all questions, with the exception of those falling within the Union's jurisdiction.

USSR laws on questions falling within the joint jurisdiction of the USSR and the republics take effect if the republic whose interests are affected by the given laws does not object.

A republic has the right to protest a USSR law if it violates the Union Treaty or is at variance with the republic's Constitution, or with republic laws adopted within the bounds of the republic's powers. The USSR has the right to protest republic laws if they violate the Union Treaty or are at variance with the USSR Constitution, or with USSR laws adopted within the bounds of the USSR's powers. In both cases, disputes are resolved through conciliatory procedures or turned over to the USSR Constitutional Court.

Union Bodies

Art. 11. The Formation of Union Bodies. Union bodies of power and administration are formed on the basis of the representation of the republics and operate in strict accordance with the provisions of this treaty.

Art. 12. The USSR Supreme Soviet. The Union's legislative power is exercised by the USSR Supreme Soviet, which consists of two chambers. . . .

Art. 13. The President of the USSR. The President of the USSR is the head of the Union state and wields supreme administrative and executive power.

The President of the USSR acts as the guarantor of observance of the Union Treaty and the Constitution and laws of the USSR; he is Commander in Chief of the USSR Armed Forces; he represents the Union in relations with foreign countries; and he monitors the fulfillment of the USSR's international commitments.

The President is elected by the citizens of the USSR on the basis of universal, equal and direct suffrage and by secret ballot for a term of five years, and may serve no more than two consecutive terms. A candidate who receives more than half of the votes of the voters taking part in the election, in the Union as a whole and in a majority of the republics, is considered elected. . . .

Concluding Provisions

Art. 20. The Official Language of the USSR. The parties to the treaty recognize Russian as the official language of the USSR.

Art. 21. The Capital of the USSR. The city of Moscow is the capital of the USSR.

Art. 22. The State Symbols of the USSR. The USSR has a state emblem, a state flag and a national anthem.

Art. 23. The Entry Into Effect of the Union Treaty. The Union Treaty is adopted by the republics' supreme bodies of state power and enters into effect as of the moment it is signed by authorized delegations of the republics. The Union Treaty is opened for signing by decision of the USSR Council of the Federation.

For the republics that sign the Union Treaty, the 1922 Treaty on the Formation of the USSR is considered null and void as of the same date.

Relations between the Union and republics that do not sign the Union Treaty are subject to regulation on the basis of existing USSR legislation and mutual commitments and agreements.

Art. 24. Changes in the Union Treaty. The Union Treaty or individual provisions thereof may be rescinded, changed or supplemented, on representations by the republics, only with the consent of all member-states of the USSR.

The Party Tries to Change

Draft Program of the CPSU

From 1988 to 1990 Gorbachev progressively shifted political power away from the Communist party and into the civil government with himself as president. He was forced to fight a running battle with the conservatives in the party apparatus but prevailed over them at each critical moment. Finally, in July 1991 he persuaded the Central Committee (at the last meeting it ever held) to approve a new party program embodying the principles of perestroika and the new role

From *Draft Program of the Communist Party of the Soviet Union,* "Socialism, Democracy, Progress," *Pravda,* August 8, 1991. Translated by Robert V. Daniels.

of the party under democratic pluralism—just before the Old Guard attempted to undo his reforms in the coup of August 1991.

Our country has entered the 1990s under the sign of deep changes. Perestroika has opened up the space for a long-ripening democratic reformation of all aspects of life. This process is developing in a contradictory and complex way. Establishment of the new is accompanied by social-political and nationality tension, economic crisis, and great shifts in social consciousness. The Communist party as well is going through a critical phase of its development.

Under these conditions we need an objective evaluation of the past and the present, a deep comprehension of the realities of our society and of the whole course of world civilization, a perspective of socialist development. We need a clear and realistic program of action, of steady advance toward a humane, just, democratic society.

The purpose of the present program is to give an answer to the questions of our time, to serve as the basic ideas for communists and all supporters of the socialist choice to consolidate around. With this program the party presents itself to everyone for whom the fate of the Fatherland, civil peace, and welfare of the peoples of the Soviet Union are dear.

I. Our Principles

Placing the interests of working people first of all, the CPSU [Communist Party of the Soviet Union] today comes forward as a party of social progress and democratic reforms, a party of social justice and human values, a party of economic, political, and spiritual freedom.

. . . In its political activity the CPSU will be guided by:

—the interests of comprehensive social progress, which is assured by way of reforms. . . .

—The principles of humanism and universal values. . . .

—The principles of democracy and freedom in all their various manifestations. . . .

—The principles of social justice. . . .
—The principles of patriotism and internationalism. . . .
—The interests of integrating the country into the world community. . . .

II. The Lessons of History . . .

The October socialist revolution was one of the great events of world history. It was a people's revolution, in keeping with the interests and social impatience of the masses. The people supported the program proposed by the party to save the country from a nationwide catastrophe. In its program were the termination of the world war, the free transfer of land to the peasants and of the mills and factories to the workers, the liquidation of the class system with its privileges, the introduction of measures of social protection never before seen at that time, the proclamation of the equality of nationalities.

The toilers sincerely believed in the possibility of the rapid creation of a complete and just socialist society, and for its sake endured sacrifice and deprivation. . . .

. . . The tragedy of our society was that the initial work of building socialism was distorted and burdened down to the extreme by mistakes, despotism, and crude perversions of the principles of socialism and popular rule.

Lenin's New Economic Policy (NEP), which opened up the possibility of progress toward socialism through multiple forms, bringing together the interests of various social strata, mastering the achievements of the most developed countries, was overthrown and rejected by the Stalinist leadership.

The place of multiple forms and market relations was taken by the monopoly of state property and the administrative-allocational system. The principle of material stimulation was replaced by leveling and impersonality. The policy of civil peace and cooperation was replaced by reliance on the sharpening of the class struggle. Instead of the development of democratic institutions, methods of compulsion and repression were used more and more widely.

The creative energy of the people was shackled by the political omnipotence of the party-state bureaucracy, intolerance of democracy and glasnost, ideological dictation, and vulgarized Marxism. Thus, in fact, the choice was made in favor of the totalitarian system and "barracks" socialism.

The CPSU unreservedly condemns the crimes of Stalinism, which cut lives short and warped the fates of millions of people, of whole nations. For this there is not and cannot be any justification. Even in those years many communists raised a voice of protest against the policy of the leaders who had usurped power in the party and the state. But they were disposed of as "enemies of the people." A significant part of the party was physically liquidated. The tragedy of the communists of that epoch was that they were unable to block the totalitarian dictatorship, which led to grave consequences for the country and to the discrediting of the idea of socialism. . . .

A major event in the history of the country and party was the Twentieth Congress of the CPSU [1956]. It gave birth to great hopes. The mass repressions were condemned, many elements of the totalitarian regime were rejected, and a search was begun for new forms of economic life to fulfill social needs.

However, the reforms that were begun were not developed. The causes and character of the deformations in the social system were not understood, and this led to serious miscalculations in defining the prospects that were formulated in the third program [1961] of the CPSU. Authoritarian-bureaucratic methods prevailed in the system of power and administration. In the last analysis this prevented deep democratic reforms in society. A tendency prevailed to allow only partial changes in the economy and in the legal and political spheres.

The situation was further complicated because the Cold War and rivalry with the leading Western powers in the arms race exhausted our economy and did not allow us to develop the social sphere. This went on against the background of rapid progress by the industrially developed countries, which were able to enter the technological revolution sooner than us and ensure a notable growth in the living standards of their populations. Our society lost the historic initiative and was burdened down in a protracted crisis. . . .

The whole course of our history has made perestroika vitally necessary. Glasnost has opened the way to the variety of opinions and spiritual freedom. The political system is being reformed on democratic foundations. A process is going on of transition from the supercentralized state to a union that is based on self-determination and the voluntary association of nations. . . .

The CPSU will strive for further development of the positive tendencies that perestroika has given birth to.

The process of reform has turned out to be much more difficult than was expected beforehand. This is due not only to the weighty heritage of the past, but also to miscalculations and delay in resolving problems that have come up. Vacillation and compromises stemming from the tendency to put off harsh, unpopular measures or avoid them altogether, have only worsened the situation. The force of inertia and resistance to reform was underestimated. Under circumstances when the old mechanisms of administration and planning no longer worked but the formation of new ones was unacceptably delayed, many processes acquired a spontaneous character. A rupture of economic-production connections took place, shady arrangements in the economy gained strength, inflation grew, and the living standards of many strata of the population declined. Trust in the organs of power fell, and centrifugal tendencies increased. Serious conflicts arose among nationalities. No quick way out of the crisis appeared. All this drove part of the working people away from the party and forced them to seek support in other political movements. The development of the country was complicated under the influence of relationships of conflict among various political forces, which exacerbated the manifestations of crisis. . . .

III. Our Immediate Goals

. . . The CPSU stands for the achievement of the following goals:

In the political system. Development of the Soviet multinational state as a genuine democratic federation of sovereign republics;

setting up a state under the rule of law, and development of democratic institutions; the system of soviets as foundations of the state structure, as organs of popular rule and self-administration and of political representation of the interest of all strata of society; separation of powers—legislative, executive, and judicial;

guaranteeing the rights and freedoms of citizens of the USSR over the entire territory of the country, and instituting legislation on the rights of man corresponding to international norms; respect and defense of the rights of citizens to participate in professional associations and different political parties and social movements, and rejection of interference by government organs in the activity of social organizations that are acting in accordance with the requirements of the Constitution and the laws;

strict observance of the laws and legal order; extirpation of criminality, a struggle with the shadow economy, defense of the security of citizens and their possessions and of the constitutional foundations of government and social life; overcoming legal nihilism.

In the area of nationality relations. Equal rights for all people independent of their nationality and place of residence; equal rights and free development of all nationalities under the unconditional priority of the rights of man;

the right of nations to self-determination, affirmation of the dignity of nationalities, and development of the native language and culture and national customs and traditions. . . .

In the economy. Structural rebuilding [*perestroika*] of the national economy, reorienting it toward the consumer;

modernization of industry, construction, transport, and communications on the basis of high technology, overcoming our lag behind the world scientific-technical level, and thinking through the conversion of military production;

transition to a mixed economy based on the variety and legal equality of different forms of property—state, collective and private, joint-stock and cooperative. Active cooperation in establishing the property of labor collectives and the priority development of this form of social property;

formation of a regulated market economy as a means to stimulate the growth of economic efficiency, the expansion of social wealth, and the raising of the living standards of the people. This assumes free price formation with state grants to needy groups of the population, the introduction of an active antimonopoly policy, restoring the financial system to health, overcoming inflation, and achieving the convertibility of the ruble;

working out and introducing a modern agrarian policy; free development of the state, collective, and private forms of farming, ruling out any violence in regard to the peasantry; allotment of land (including leaseholds with the right of inheritance) to all who are willing and able to work it effectively; state support of the agro-industrial sector, of the social development of the village, and of equivalency and price parity in the exchange of the products of industry and agriculture;

comprehensive integration of the country in the world economy, and broad participation in world economic relations in the interest of the economic and social progress of Soviet society.

In the social sphere. Carrying out a state policy that allows us to reduce to a minimum the unavoidable difficulties and expenses connected with overcoming the crisis in the economy and making the transition to the market; . . .

realization of anticipatory measures against unemployment, creation of new jobs, organization of the retraining of the work force and training in new lines of work;

averting the slide toward ecological catastrophe, solving the problems of [Lake] Baikal, the Aral Sea, and other zones of ecological impoverishment, and continuing the liquidation of the consequences of the Chernobyl disaster.

In education, science, and culture. Spiritual development of the people, improving the education and culture of each person, and strengthening morality, the sense of civic duty and responsibility, and patriotism. . . .

IV. Whose Interests the Party Expresses

Our party was founded as the political organization of the working class. It linked together the struggle of the proletariat in alliance with the peasantry and the possibility of the revolutionary reform of society in the interest of all working people.

The progress of the forces of production and the scientific-technical revolution has introduced radical changes in the social structure of society. The proportion of people employed in science and culture, technology and the organization of production, education and health care, in the sphere of administration and services, has risen sharply. We see a close interweaving of the interests of various strata of the working people.

Not to recognize these fundamental changes means condemning the party to political isolation and defeat. It can count on the realization of its programmatic goals only by consistently reflecting and defending the interests of all working people. . . .

. . . In cooperation with the labor movement and the trade unions we will defend the interests of the workers, to secure: due representation of the working class in the organs of power at all levels, real rights of labor collectives to run enterprises and dispose of the results of their labor, a reliable system of social protection—especially at the stage of transition to the market, structural changes and modernization of production, and conversion of the defense industry; improvement of working conditions, freeing women from work harmful to their health, taking account of the specific needs of miners, petroleum workers, metal workers, construction workers, other workers in the basic branches of industry, people in heavy physical labor, of all who work in complicated conditions to win new territories [e.g., settlement in Siberia], far removed from home and family.

Together with the organizations of rural toilers we will defend the interests of peasants, while respecting their free choice of forms of property and farming. . . .

In cooperation with the unions of creative people and scientific-technical societies we will defend the interests of the intelligentsia, and strive for a heightening of the social status and appreciation of intellectual work; we will promote, free from ideological and administrative dictation, the creative inquiries of scholars, engineers and designers, and people in literature and the arts; we will strive for fitting pay and high social recognition for the work of teachers and doctors, of people employed in government service and in the sphere of social administration, servicemen, and staff in law-enforcement organs.

We are for the affirmation of real equal rights for women in all spheres of life, including the sphere of administration. Together with women's organizations we will assist in the creation of conditions that will guarantee women freedom of choice, and allow them to realize themselves in the family, career, and social activity. The CPSU stands for the orientation of government policy toward raising the status of the family in society. . . .

. . . Defending the interests of the broad strata of working people, we reject any form of discrimination on the basis of social or occupational membership. The party views positively the useful work and business activity of private entrepreneurs.

We categorically reject any form of discrimination on the basis of nationality, while firmly defending internationalism and friendship and cooperation among the peoples of this country.

We stand for freedom of conscience for all citizens. The party takes a respectful position toward the feelings of believers. . . .

. . . We are against militant anticommunism as a form of political extremism and negation of democracy that is extremely dangerous for the fate of society. . . .

V. For a Party of Political Action

Communists are clearly aware that only a radically renewed party—a party of political action—can successfully solve new tasks. . . .

The most important direction of renewal for the party is its profound democratization. This assumes the independence of the parties of the republics that belong to the CPSU, and space for the initiative of local and primary organizations. . . .

. . . Guarantees must be worked out in the party so that its cadres never utilize their posts for mercenary interests, never speak contrary to conscience, and do not fear a hard struggle to achieve noble ends.

The renewal of the party presupposes a new approach to the understanding of its place in society and its relations with the state, and in the choice of means for the achievement of its political goals. The party acts exclusively by legal political methods. It will fight for deputies' seats in democratic elections, winning the support of voters for its electoral platform and its basic directions of policy and practical action. Taking part in the formation of the organs of state power and administration, it will conduct its policy through them. It is ready to enter into broad collaboration wherever this is dictated by circumstances, and to conclude alliances and coalitions with other parties and organizations in the interest of carrying out a program of democratic reform. In those organs of power where the communist deputies are in the minority, they will assume the place of a constructive opposition, standing up against any attempt at infringing on the interests of the working people and the rights and freedoms of citizens. Collaborating with other parliamentary groups, communist deputies will manifest cooperation toward positive undertakings that come from other parties and movements. . . .

The CPSU is built on the adherence of its members to the ideas of certain values. For us the main one of these is the idea of humane, democratic socialism. Reviving and developing the initial humanitarian principles of Marx, Engels, and Lenin, we include in our arsenal of ideas the entire richness of national and world socialist and democratic thought. We consider communism as a historic perspective, a social idea, based on universal human values, on the harmonious union of progress and justice, of the free self-realization of the individual.

The industrially developed countries, where the chief centers of capitalism were historically formed, entered into the technological revolution earlier than others, and have already completed the transition to predominantly intensive production, which allows them to resolve many social problems. Nevertheless, contemporary capitalism does not guarantee the harmonious development of society or of the human being. The individualist ideas of Western civilization do not provide the key for resolving many acute contradictions. Sharp social contrasts, the tendency to solve one's problems at the expense of other nations, authoritarian and militaristic tendencies, the crisis in morality and culture, the practical exclusion of broad groups of the population from participation in political life, remain realities. This is why the prospects for social progress cannot be based only on the "Western" view of social problems, without taking account of the particularities of culture, tradition, and situation of every country in the world.

The changes now going on in the world allow us to take a new look at the historic fate of socialism. The socialist movement arose in the industrial era and basically took advantage of the confrontational political culture that reflected the sharp class antagonisms of the society of that time. The new civilization that is forming in the process of contemporary world development does not fit the usual pictures of industrial class society, of its harsh division into opposed classes, of the polar opposition of labor and capital and the confrontation of social systems.

The entire experience of the twentieth century testifies that socialist tendencies are not localized in selected countries, but represent a global process of the development of the world community, which rests on the highest achievements of the labor and culture of all peoples and reflects the striving of people for social justice, freedom, and democracy. Broader and broader flourishing of socialist practices in a worldwide process of the development of civilization—such is already a clearly visible prospect.

Socialism, democracy, progress—such are the goals of the Communist Party of the Soviet Union. We are convinced that these goals answer to the interests of the people. The future lies with a society in which the free development of each is the condition for the free development of all.

Martin Sixsmith

The August Coup

Faced with the dissolution of the party's power and the virtual breakup of the USSR, the Old Guard, led by people Gorbachev himself had appointed, attempted forcibly to turn the clock back in the famous failed coup attempt of August 1991. Martin Sixsmith, a British correspondent in Moscow, recounts in the book *Moscow Coup* his personal observation and explanation of the events of those crucial days.

Monday, 19 August

The first indication that things were badly wrong that Monday morning was the solemn music that Soviet TV was putting out in place of its usual early morning news and chat show. A quick check on the radio revealed all channels broadcasting the same composers—Tchaikovsky and Chopin: the classical harbingers of grave news in the Soviet Union. A growing sense of panic was briefly relieved by a glance through the curtains to the street below: there, people were still going about their business, the usual militiaman was on guard duty outside the front entrance of the flats opposite and cars were heading down the main road into the city centre. But the relief was only momentary. The strains of "Swan Lake" were unceremoniously interrupted, and a funereal sounding announcer made the proclamation that was to chill the hearts of millions:

> *In connection with Mikhail Gorbachev's inability to carry out his duties of President due to reasons of ill health and in accordance with article 127 of the Soviet Constitution, all presidential powers have been transferred to the Vice-President of the USSR, Gennady Yanayev.*

For any Russian listening, the situation was already clear: retirement for health reasons was the cynical old formula that had been used for decades to remove public officials unwillingly from their posts. But in case there was any doubt left that a coup was in progress, the announcement went on to spell it out:

> *With the aim of overcoming the deep crisis, political, inter-ethnic and civil confrontation, chaos and anarchy which are threatening the life and safety of citizens of the Soviet Union, as well as the sovereignty, integrity, freedom and independence of our fatherland, we the undersigned hereby announce . . . the introduction of a state of emergency in parts of the USSR for a period of six months beginning on 19 August at 4 A.M. Moscow time . . . and the setting up of a State Emergency Committee to run the country and effectively administer the emergency regime.*

The list of signatories left little doubt about the nature of the new regime. It was headed by Yanayev, and included all the hardliners from the top Kremlin leadership—Vladimir Kryuchkov, head of the KGB; Valentin Pavlov, the conservative Prime Minister; Boris Pugo, the Interior Minister who controlled the militia and forces of special troops; and Defence Minister, Marshal Dmitri Yazov. These were the men who for months had been expressing growing irritation with the way things were going in the Soviet Union, not overtly criticizing Mikhail Gorbachev, but making plain their belief that reform had gone far enough and that it was time to reintroduce a little law and order. . . . By 10 A.M. on that Monday morning it was clear that this was a hardline putsch by men who would be doing their utmost to return the USSR to its old, orthodox-Communist past. . . .

In mid-afternoon a phalanx of the heaviest tanks drew up outside the Russian parliament on the banks of the Moskva River. This was the headquarters of Boris Yeltsin, the Russian President whose outspoken support of radical reform had made him the natural rallying point for resistance to the coup. As soon as the takeover was announced in the early hours of Monday morning, Yeltsin had gathered his trusted aides and taken refuge in the parliament, a soaring white marble building whose nickname of Belyi Dom—the White House—quickly made it a nationally and internationally recognized symbol of democracy. It was here that the fight for the democratic ideal in the Soviet Union was to be fought out over the next two days and nights.

When the tanks arrived, belching acrid fumes and smoke, thundering noisily along the embankment and leaving the deep imprint of their tracks in the tarmac, Yeltsin was inside the building trying to formulate a response to the coup. The parliament was undefended, there were no crowds present and the building was seemingly ripe for the taking. I watched the line of armour draw up at the base of the parliament steps and was convinced they had come to seize the parliament, Boris Yeltsin and all who opposed their masters in the Kremlin.

For twenty minutes the tanks stayed in place, revving their engines and filling the air with a blue haze. But the order to attack did not come, and at the crucial moment it was Yeltsin himself who seized the initiative. Instead of waiting for the troops to come for him, Yeltsin went to the troops. Emerging dramatically from the parliament's main entrance, Yeltsin descended the steps and strode confidently towards the leading tank in the column. . . .

In a master stroke of public image-making, he heaved his burly frame firmly onto the back of the tank he had selected, and then squarely onto the turret itself. Panting from the effort, he leaned down, shook hands with two startled tank crew who were peering from inside the vehicle, and then rose to his full height. Staring defiantly at the soldiers and militia around him, he declared to all within earshot that the army was with the people, that the troops would not attack the defenders of democracy and that the plotters in the Kremlin were doomed to failure. Right across Russia, said Yeltsin, workers were heeding his appeals for protest strikes and were walking out to show their opposition to the coup. . . .

The plotters were obsessed with shutting down the domestic media. It was the old Soviet reaction to seize control of sources of information, and it looked like signalling a definitive end to the brief flowering of glasnost. In the circumstances it was a policy which seemed well founded: under Gorbachev, newspapers and broadcasters had begun to speak with an independent voice, even though Gorbachev himself had recently begun the process of reining back the media freedoms he had earlier initiated. (His appointment of the lugubrious Leonid Kravchuk as Head of State Broadcasting several months previously had resulted in the banning of the most outspoken news and current affairs programmes, an incursion into glasnost which was only partially made good by the development of television's Second Programme run by Yeltsin's Russian Federation and largely reflecting his views.)

The result of the media clamp-down was that the overwhelming majority of Soviets had no access to unbiased information about events in Moscow and the other major cities. They simply did not know that tanks were on the streets; they did not know that resistance was building around the Russian parliament; and if the coup had succeeded, they would probably have never known the truth of what occurred in the capital. It would have been the victors who wrote the history of the times, and past experience of Bolshevik manipulations suggested that the coup leaders would have written it in a way which reflected only their point of view.

A new decree by the State Emergency Committee, made public in mid-afternoon, also banned all newspapers and magazines except for nine specified publications. . . .

In the early evening of Monday, the battle lines for an impending showdown had been drawn on the streets and were about to be drawn in the corridors of power too. From the Russian parliament, Boris Yeltsin issued a final challenge to the men in the Kremlin: the Yanayev regime, said Yeltsin, was illegal and its decrees must be disobeyed. All the orders of the State Emergency Committee were hereby revoked on the territory of the Russian Federation and any official carrying out such orders would himself be subject to prosecution.

But all Yeltsin's threats—and he himself was aware of this—carried little real weight. He was a prisoner in his own parliament, unable to act or to enforce his own rulings, and the officials he was threatening were the last people he could have expected to obey his demands: they were the middle-ranking bureaucrats, formed and nurtured by the Communist system, owing their livelihood to the apparat, and the very people who would most welcome the return to the old ways of Communist orthodoxy that the coup seemed to promise. So in his statement Yeltsin tempered his threats with appeals: he appealed to the army not to shoot on the people; he appealed to the people to stage massive protest strikes and demonstrations; and he appealed to foreign heads of state and government to come to his aid, saying the Yanayev regime was determined to return the world to the era of the cold war. Hurried phone calls to George Bush and [British prime minister] John Major appealing to them not to recognize the new regime added to the impression that Yeltsin was surrounded and staging a last stand for democracy, just as the Czechoslovak and Hungarian patriots had done decades earlier.

While Yeltsin was stating his position in the Russian parliament, his foes were doing the same on the other side of town. In the conference hall of the Soviet Foreign Ministry, Gennady Yanayev and four of his co-conspirators took to the stage before the world's press: the atmosphere was electric, tenser than any press conference ever held in the building. The vast majority of the journalists present had nothing but contempt for the men who appeared before them—all wanted the answers to a series of vital questions: were the coup leaders preparing to use force to maintain their grip on power? What had they done with Mikhail Gorbachev, and could they refute persistent rumours that the President had been executed? How did they explain their lip-service support of democracy when they had just ridden rough-shod over every democratic norm? What were their intentions regarding international politics, and were they about to initiate a new era of East–West confrontation?

At first the men on stage appeared confident, relaxed, even jovial. Yanayev corrected one questioner who referred to him as a member of the politburo, but added genially, "Those sort of distinctions are not important now." Next to him, Boris Pugo, the hardline Interior Minister, tried hard to smile, but succeeded only in appearing more wild-eyed and unhinged than ever, his mad-professor hair shooting out around the sides of his bald pate. Absent from the press conference were KGB chief Vladimir Kryuchkov and Defence Minister Dmitri Yazov: it was assumed they had more important things to do despatching tanks around the country. Also missing was the boorish Prime Minister Valentin Pavlov, nicknamed hedgehog-bum because of his peasant-style crew cut; we learned later that he had been hitting the bottle a little too hard.

With hindsight it is easy to see the eight conspirators as bumbling no-hopers destined to fail, but on that Monday afternoon they were the men who held ultimate power in the Soviet Union, and the questioning from the floor was hostile. Yanayev's first tactic was to suggest the takeover was designed to protect the reforms which [had] been taking place in the country but which had run into the sand. "At a crucial moment for the Soviet Union and for the whole world," he said, "the crisis we have come up against must not be allowed to continue. This would threaten the whole of our reform programme and lead to a serious cataclysm in international life." But it did not take long for the double talk to be replaced with something more straightforward. Yanayev warned:

> *The country is beginning to disintegrate and we are determined to take the most serious measures to prevent this . . . to reimpose law and order, and to clean the criminals from our streets. . . .*

*In international politics, we wish to live in peace, but we state
firmly that we will not allow any outside forces to infringe our
national sovereignty, independence and territorial integrity. . . . We are not afraid of expressing our pride and patriotism,
and we are determined to bring up our coming generations in
this same spirit . . . it is the duty of every citizen of the Soviet
Union to give support to the State Emergency Committee as it
carries out its programme. . . .*

The next line of questioning . . . was enough to remove all
traces of Yanayev's previous cockiness. What, he was asked, do
you think about Boris Yeltsin's statement this afternoon in which
he describes your accession to power as a right-wing, reactionary,
anti-constitutional coup? Yeltsin's words—and the implied threat
of concerted opposition to the new regime—seemed to throw
Yanayev into a panic. His face began to twitch and his fingers
twisted nervously on the desk in front of him. "We of course are
ready to cooperate with Mr. Yeltsin to develop democracy, the
economy, culture and human rights. But . . . "—and here he
paused to swallow hard—"if Yeltsin is calling for general strikes,
then he's acting very irresponsibly and that's something we can't
allow. The country is in crisis. . . . the Russian leadership are
now playing a very dangerous political game. This could lead
to excesses and armed provocations. It is the duty of the State
Emergency Committee to warn all Soviet people about this. We
trust that calm and order will be maintained in all areas."

When pressed about the way he had come to power, Yanayev
looked grim. "I will permit myself to disagree with your contention
that a state coup has taken place," he said. "We are acting according to the norms of the constitution. . . . "

At the end of Yanayev's news conference, there was little
doubt left that the junta was tough, ruthless and determined to
crush any opposition to its authority; and even though estimates
of the regime's efficiency were revised over the next three days,
the first signs were that the repression had already begun. . . .

Wednesday, 21 August

. . . At two o'clock in the afternoon, startling reports began to
arrive of tank movements on Leningradsky Prospekt (the continuation of Gorky Street where it leaves the Moscow boundary), and

this time the tanks were heading not into the city but out of it. . . .

Moscow Radio now confirmed that a withdrawal had indeed been ordered: the announcement read over the airwaves was signed by Dmitri Yazov, not in his capacity as a member of the plotters' State Emergency Committee, but under his old title of Defence Minister. It was confirmation that the reports of Yazov's resignation by the Russian parliament were indeed premature; but at the same time it was an indication that the Emergency Committee was no longer running the show. Nursultan Nazar-bayev, the liberal president of Kazakhstan and an old acquain-tance of Yazov, said later that he had repeatedly telephoned the Defence Minister during the coup and had found him worried and uncertain. After the killings on the barricades, Yazov had been hesitating between throwing in the towel and facing criminal prosecution, or gambling on a last desperate attack on the Russian parliament, which would almost certainly bring more casualties without guaranteeing the triumph of the coup leaders. It was the ferocity of the resistance offered by Yeltsin and the democrats which seems to have surprised the plotters and caused them to argue among themselves (although they could hardly have been serious in expecting Yeltsin to cooperate with them, as they had at one point proposed). . . .

Thursday, 22 August

Mikhail Gorbachev had been scheduled to come back to Moscow from his summer vacation in the Crimea on Monday, 19 August. His return was delayed until the early hours of Thursday, 22 August, just three days late. But he had missed the most important 72 hours in modern Soviet history and it was clear from the moment he stepped off the plane that he was going to find it hard to catch up.

Looking dishevelled and unsteady as he descended the steps of the aeroplane, the President gave the impression of being con-siderably shaken by his ordeal. He was dressed in an open-necked shirt and a white, unzipped anorak; behind him, blinking in the camera lights as they walked onto the tarmac, were Raisa Gorba-chev and their young granddaughter Anastasia who had shared the President's captivity. Gorbachev's first words bore all the hall-marks of a man who was expecting to step back into his old role as leader of the Soviet Union. He immediately tried to claim for himself some of the credit for defeating the coup:

> The main thing is that all we have been doing since 1985 has borne fruit. People and society have changed, and it was this which provided the main obstacle to the adventurists. . . . I congratulate the Soviet people, who have shown responsibility and honour, because they proved the respect they have for those to whom they entrusted power. . . . It is the great victory of perestroika.

While it was true that the long-term factors which prompted people to resist the tanks were indeed the disdain for totalitarian-ism and the encouragement to independent thought which Gorba-chev had initiated, it was only in his later remarks that the Presi-dent identified the true reason for his salvation from the clutches of the plotters: "I express my gratitude to the Soviet people; for the principled position adopted by Russia, and to the President of Russia, Boris Nikolaevich Yeltsin."

Gorbachev, though, was clearly anxious to portray himself in a heroic light, perhaps feeling already that he had been badly upstaged by Yeltsin. He stressed the pressure he had been put under by the conspirators, talking of his isolation from the world, and the blockade from land and sea which had been thrown round his seaside holiday villa. But this was producing little impression compared to the blockade Yeltsin had had to endure. He talked of the coup leaders' attempts to "break" him and his family, and said he had resisted them at every step. But for Russians, the resistance they identified as defeating the coup was that of Boris Yeltsin.

The putsch, Gorbachev said, must be a lesson to everyone, including the President, politicians and journalists, and he cor-rectly identified the causes of popular unrest which the plotters had tried to play on: "the problems with food supplies, fuel for the winter, finances, the market situation . . . and the concern over what tomorrow may bring." But there was a certain compla-cency in his simply saying that he was "dealing with these prob-lems." Even at this early stage it was clear that Gorbachev had not in fact learned the lesson to which he himself had referred.

In his press conference later that day and in a prepared speech on Soviet television, Gorbachev filled in the details of how his arrest had been engineered, and how he had reacted. At the press conference, there was unprecedented applause from the journalists as Gorbachev walked in: he himself was visibly very emotional, halting in his speech and seemingly choking back tears on more than one occasion. He called the coup the greatest test perestroika had had to face in all the years of reform, and he foreshadowed a criticism he would repeatedly have to face in the coming days: "The organizers of this anti-constitutional coup, those reactionary forces, turned out to be men in the very centre of the leadership, close to the President himself. These were men whom I had personally promoted, believed and trusted." He seemed genuinely surprised and dismayed that such close colleagues could have led the plot against him: he admitted that he had particularly trusted Yazov and Kryuchkov.

In his account of the drama in the Crimea, Gorbachev described how he had been in his study at his holiday villa on Sunday, 18 August when there was a knock at the door. It was the head of his personal bodyguards, who told him that a delegation had arrived to see him. Gorbachev was suspicious and decided to make inquiries by telephone before receiving the delegation. "I had a whole series of telephones, a government phone, an ordinary phone, a strategic phone, a satellite phone and so on. I picked up one of them and found it wasn't working. I picked up a second, a third, a fourth, a fifth—they were all the same. Even the internal phone was disconnected. I was isolated."

Realizing the full seriousness of the situation, Gorbachev called in his wife, daughter and son-in-law. "I knew there was going to be some sort of attempt at blackmail, or an attempt to arrest me and take me away somewhere. Anything could happen . . . they could have tried all sorts of things, even with my family." He said his family gave their full backing to his decision not to capitulate to the conspirators.

The delegation turned out to be four envoys sent by Gennady Yanayev's State Emergency Committee with an ultimatum: Gorbachev must either sign a decree introducing a state of emergency in the country, in which case he could stay on as President, but would have to remain in the Crimea; or he must sign over his powers to the Vice President, Gennady Yanayev.

The terms of the ultimatum suggest that the plotters felt they had some grounds for hoping Gorbachev would go along with the state of emergency (in other words, that he would agree to at least a figurehead role in a hardline putsch). Whether he had hinted at this in conversations with them in the past is impossible to tell; but his behaviour over the Baltic crack-down and his previous cooperation with conservative forces certainly led many to believe that Gorbachev might not be averse to the introduction of tough measures designed to restore discipline, law and order.

We have only Gorbachev's word for how he reacted to the plotters' demands, but the President was absolutely adamant in stressing that he refused point blank to have anything to do with them:

> I told them that they and the men who had sent them were nothing but adventurists. I told them that the course they had decided on would mean their own doom and the doom of our country . . . only someone bent on suicide could propose the introduction of such a totalitarian regime in our country. . . . [I said:] you are trying to play on the problems people are facing today; you are counting on people being tired and being ready to submit to any sort of dictator. . . . But I will only support the politics of agreement, the deepening of reform, and cooperation with the West.

It was a declaration of fundamental importance by Gorbachev: after all the years of his political balancing act, of trying to reconcile hardliners and liberals, he had finally summed up the two sides of the political choice he had long been unwilling to make, and—before the world's press—he had publicly made that choice. Unfortunately for Gorbachev, it had come too late: now it hardly mattered which side he came down on, because power had slipped from him and all the really important decisions would soon be taken by others, chief among them Boris Yeltsin. Gorbachev at this stage was continuing to talk about the need to press ahead with the Union Treaty he had worked out with nine of the republics, not seeming to realize that few of them would now accept any form of subjugation to the centre, even the looser ties the

Treaty was proposing. In talking as if the negotiations could simply be picked up from where they were left before the putsch, Gorbachev was again showing that he had not adapted to the new realities of the post-coup era. . . .

Eventually, when the coup was on the point of failing, Gorbachev said that a desperate group of plotters turned up on his doorstep . . . , but he had refused to speak to them. He did, however, agree to receive Lukyanov, and he initially seems to have had difficulty in believing that his old university friend could have been behind the plot against him. When the Russian parliamentary delegation arrived, Gorbachev said he welcomed them with open arms, expressing his gratitude to them for their conduct during the coup and saying he never again wanted to see a split between himself and the "other democratic forces."

But at the same press conference, just a few minutes later, Gorbachev was still defending the Communist party, seemingly unable to accept that it was the party itself which was the coup's organizing force:

> *I will do everything possible to drive the reactionary forces out of the party. I believe that on the basis of the party's new programme, it is possible to unite all the progressive and best elements. Therefore, when people speak of the party as a whole being a reactionary force, I cannot agree with that. I know thousands of people in the party's ranks who are true democrats, devoted to perestroika and our struggle. . . . I do not think after all we've been through that we should start organizing witch hunts like they did in the past.*

He defended the Central Committee, which later turned out to have sent instructions to party branches in many areas of the country to support the coup; and he defended men like Moscow party boss Yuri Prokofyev who also took an active role in the coup. Even when pressed, the closest Gorbachev came to criticizing the Communist ideal was to say that it had in the past been distorted by Stalinism; and as for his personal position as head of the party, he prevaricated but quoted Lenin and said he would remain firmly devoted to the ideals of socialism. It was hardly a performance which corresponded with the mood of society; and that mood was being seized on and exploited with relish by the country's other leading politician.

In contrast to Gorbachev's low-key return to Moscow, Boris Yeltsin was about to be swept up in a tidal wave of gratitude and adulation. His first public appearance that Thursday morning was to oversee the departure of the tanks which had helped defend him during the siege of the Russian parliament. The troops were sent off with the cheers of the people ringing in their ears, and with their vehicles draped in home-made banners and daubed in slogans by the crowd: one said simply "Thank you lads," another read "The pride of Russia." The celebrations marked the end of the coup, but also the elevation of Yeltsin to a new position of pre-eminence in the Soviet Union. His decisiveness and quick witted determination over the next few days of political manoeuvring were to ensure that Gorbachev would be given little chance to redress the balance.

The Thursday session of the Russian parliament brought further praise and applause for Yeltsin. A standing ovation from the MPs greeted him as soon as he walked onto the stage, and he responded by calling the parliament to its feet to listen with pride to the Russian national anthem. Yeltsin's speech began by celebrating the victory of democracy: he said he had received congratulations from every republic of the Union for the stand Russia had taken, and he himself was unstinting in his praise of those who had defended him and the parliament over the past four days. But he quickly moved on to the theme of retribution for the coup, clearly sensing that decisions taken now would influence the whole balance of political power in the country.

In contrast to Gorbachev's warning against "witch hunts" in the aftermath of the putsch, Yeltsin seemed ruthless and unmerciful: . . . "All those involved in the coup will be brought to justice and will face the appropriate charges." He added that there would be no mercy for any official who actively supported the putsch or failed to oppose it. . . .

. . . Yeltsin was clearly relishing the moment, and he drew wave after wave of applause with a highly charged, emotional speech. The square outside the parliament was being renamed Victory Square, he said, in recognition of the victory that had been won by the people of Russia; 22 August was being declared a national holiday; and, most important of all, Russia's old Soviet flag with its hammer and sickle was being replaced by the pre-Communist tricolour which had become a symbol of freedom.

Again Yeltsin showed his determination to press home his political advantage against Gorbachev and the Communists. It was the party, he said, or at least its Stalinist core, which was to blame for the coup; therefore he had decided to ban all Communist cells in the army and the KGB. He was also determined to win greater freedom from the rule of the central Soviet authorities; he would insist that Gorbachev accept a national government appointed by the republics. . . .

Friday, 23 August

The end of the week brought the political showdown which was to determine the country's future. Gorbachev's efforts to defend the Communist party and the old structure of power had had the predictable effect of hardening the stubborn Yeltsin in his resolve to sweep away the whole edifice. He had invited Gorbachev to appear before the Russian parliament on the Friday afternoon, a meeting which he had clearly planned as a trap for the Soviet President, and which he proceeded to use as a public sanctification of his own ascendancy. The televised confrontation between the two men who held the Soviet Union's future in their hands was to become a moment of the highest political theatre. From being a long-time rival and enemy of Gorbachev, Yeltsin had been turned into the President's saviour; and now his unforgiving character and thirst for self-vindication were to drive him to humiliate the man he had saved from the plotters. Gorbachev appeared remarkably naive and remarkably unprepared for his rival's ferocious assault. . . .

The occasion, though, began encouragingly, with both men talking of the areas of agreement between them. Yeltsin said that at their private meeting that morning, there had been complete accord on matters of personnel and appointments to public positions vacated by sympathizers of the coup, including those in the KGB and the army. (In many cases it later transpired that the "agreement" was, in fact, the result of Yeltsin's imposing his candidate on a reluctant Gorbachev. In the case of the Defence Minister, Gorbachev had initially appointed General Mikhail

Moiseyev, only to be told by Yeltsin that Moiseyev had been a collaborator who should be removed. Yeltsin then proceeded to nominate Yevgeny Shaposhnikov, the former air force commander, whose appointment Gorbachev rubber-stamped.)

Gorbachev then took the floor and drew loud applause when he thanked Yeltsin and the Russian deputies for their part in defeating the putsch. But the Soviet President clearly thought he could spend the rest of the meeting recounting his own adventures during the coup. . . . This drew heckling and jeers from the radical deputies, who wanted to turn the encounter into an occasion to grill Gorbachev and win concessions from him. After repeated booing, Gorbachev turned to the hall and asked: "What do you want from me? I am telling you what I think; what more do you want?"

The radicals, essentially, wanted blood; and when Gorbachev began to defend some of the ministers whom he had promoted to positions of power before the coup, Yeltsin staged a dramatic piece of theatre. Strolling across the podium, he produced a sheaf of papers and thrust them under Gorbachev's nose, demanding that he read the contents of the documents to the hall. A nonplussed Gorbachev looked at the papers and realized that they were the minutes of a cabinet meeting held on the first day of the coup. They contained incriminating evidence about nearly every member of the government and the way they had welcomed the putsch. All were men Gorbachev had supported, and it was clearly going to be very embarrassing for him to read the minutes out in public. But that is exactly what Yeltsin forced him to do. . . .

Sensing the mood of the chamber, Yeltsin's hawk-like instincts told him it was time to move in for the kill. In a second piece of theatre, he fixed Gorbachev in his sights and asked him to confirm publicly that he had agreed to endorse retroactively all decrees issued by Yeltsin during the coup. Gorbachev mumbled something about an understanding they had reached "not to give away all our secrets." But Yeltsin was already one step ahead, demanding to know if the agreement included the transfer of all property rights and resources previously controlled by the Kremlin to the jurisdiction of Russia. "You won't catch me in that trap," responded Gorbachev, "there will have to be a decision after the Union Treaty is signed."

And then Yeltsin made the gesture which may well have sealed the fate of Communism. "On a lighter note," he said quietly, looking down at a piece of paper lying on the table in front of him, "I will now sign a decree banning the functioning of the Communist party of the Russian Republic." There was immediate and prolonged applause. Yeltsin held aloft the decree, showing his signature on it, while Gorbachev struggled to make himself heard. When he did so, it was a bumbling answer, reflecting how taken aback he had been by Yeltsin's thunderbolt: "I am sure the Supreme Soviet will not agree to that," he stammered. "If the Russian Communist party backed the plotters, I would agree with your decree . . . but to ban the RCP would be a major mistake."

By now, though, it was too late. The idea of banning the Communist party (albeit just the Russian branch of it, not the CPSU) had been uttered in public. What is more, it had received a tumultuous welcome from the Russian deputies; and, most important of all, it had been heard on television by millions of ordinary people, most of whom welcomed the proposal with joy.

John Miller and J. L. Black

The Breakup of the Communist Party

As Gorbachev steadily whittled down the functions of the Communist party apparatus and forced it to democratize (at least in principle), resistance rose, and, as Professor John Miller of La Trobe University in Melbourne, Australia, shows, factions of reformers and conservatives split irreconcilably. Deeply implicated in the August coup and

From John Miller, *Mikhail Gorbachev and the End of Soviet Power*, pp. 127–128, 134–144. Copyright © 1993 by St. Martin's Press. Reprinted by permission of the publisher; J. L. Black, *Into the Dustbin of History: The USSR from Coup to Commonwealth, August–December 1991*, pp. 20–22, 25–26, 36–40, Copyright © 1993 by Academic International Press. Reprinted by permission of the publisher.

repudiated by Gorbachev himself, the apparatus offered little resistance when Yeltsin and the presidents of the other Soviet republics moved to suppress its activities. The collapse of the party, as recounted by Professor J. L. Black of Carleton University in Ottawa, Canada, left only a few implacable splinter groups, hoping for a future opportunity to recover some of their old influence.

Miller, *Mikhail Gorbachev and the End of Soviet Power*

Was Gorbachev a cuckoo in the nest? Could he have been aiming all along to bring the Communist Party down? One can be forgiven for entertaining this question: Gorbachev's relations with the CPSU require a chapter to themselves.

Gorbachev was made by the Party, and rose to head it. Without the CPSU he would have had no means of realising his political vision; to embark on *perestroika* he made full use of the wide discretionary powers vested in a General Secretary. And yet the *prima facie* evidence is compelling that he deliberately made trouble for the Party: that he criticised it, encouraged outside opposition to it, weakened it, and then cast it aside.

In 1987 he began saying that *perestroika* was a social movement, and that the Party either risked lagging behind, or was lagging behind a more dynamic society. Few people hearing this will have missed the suggestion that the Party, far from being the vehicle of political reform, stood in its way. Nor will the departure from Leninism have been missed: Lenin had always stressed the dangers of social spontaneity, and the need for the working class to be led from outside.

From August 1988 he began cutting down the size, scope and activity of Party institutions. The number of Central Committee departments was reduced from twenty to nine, principally by pulling officials out of intervention in economic management, and the same cuts were extended to provincial committees. The latter no longer received a steady stream of central directives but were told to appraise and resolve their problems for themselves. For years the Politburo had met at least once a week; but during

1989—to judge by press announcements—its sessions were held more like once every three weeks, and occasionally five weeks elapsed between meetings. It is hard not to connect these changes with the departure of nine politicians from the Politburo in September 1988 and September 1989, and with the "resignations" in April 1989 of 110 Central Committee figures. Some of these may have been ordinary retirements, but for the outsider the central message was one of struggle at the top and hence of divided councils, wasted energy and weakness.

Still more damage (Party officials thought) was caused by the external pressure Gorbachev unleashed against them. By tolerating or encouraging the *neformally* [informal organizations] he had an instrument for mobilising society that bypassed the Party. Give them *glasnost'* and they were able to create a climate in which every Party worker became "a bureaucrat who stops people living well." Officials could scarcely oppose free choice in public, so they blamed this climate for their defeat in the 1989 elections. . . .

By late 1989 Gorbachev was clearly disappointed in the Party's response to his calls for internal reform. The circumstantial evidence pointed to two more things. His approach to the election results, the attempted distinction between "leading" and "avant-garde" roles, the waiving of Party Rules in respect of deputies, the preparations to withdraw from Party control of non-Party editors and appointments all suggested that he meant to undermine the practical effects of Article six [on the Communist Party monopoly]. Second, the contrast between his behaviour in Party and in legislative fora, [and] his failure to convene Politburo meetings, suggest that he was distancing himself from the Party, preparing a public image of himself as above party politics.

Article six stated: "The leading and guiding force of Soviet society and the nucleus of its political system, of all state organisations and public organisations is the Communist Party of the Soviet Union." It had been introduced in 1977 (from the Party Rules) and had had no equivalent in earlier constitutions. Gorbachev's position was a complex one. He was determined to inaugurate competitive politics and must have foreseen that they would lead to a challenge to the Party monopoly. He had to safeguard his own position and dare not appear hostile to the Party, nor let the leadership get into hostile hands. Yet the Party's inflexibility put a serious fight on behalf of Article six out of the question. His public tactics were to resist formal constitutional change, which, he argued, should properly be made only on the basis of substantial popular demand; the implication was that he should not give a lead and should leave it to others to work out what they wanted and to make the running. He continued to defend Article six until the end of the year, though his defence was often unconvincing and cost him popularity, especially when he clashed with Academician Sakharov over it.

By mid-January 1990 he was ready to move in formal terms against the CPSU monopoly. Yet every effort was made over the ensuing months to save the Party's face and let its exit be smooth and dignified. Suggestions of a defeat for the CPSU and of a triumph for democracy were played down. The measure was presented as a free and considered decision for which the Party thought the time was ripe. Party disestablishment turned out to be exactly that and no more: political appointees were not sacked, legally elected authorities were not dislodged, property was not confiscated, there was no new governing party nor positive discrimination; voices urging reprisals were met with studied unresponsiveness. Especially controversial issues—like the political organs in the armed forces or CPSU media ownership—were smothered. Everything was done to minimise disruption, confrontation and humiliation, and at the same time to counter any impression that he was the Party's hostage.

Why did the CPSU fall in with disestablishment? We have seen how difficult it would have been to retreat to a politically neutral monopoly, and the competitive option had its supporters, especially among professionals and the assertive, "troubleshooting" type of official. Nevertheless it seems that the Party as a whole drifted, or let itself be pressured, into the decision. Gorbachev had made up his mind, and the logic of *perestroika* pointed to competitive politics. These were already a reality in the legislatures and in the Baltics, and all over the country anything smacking of centralisation or monopoly had become the object of strong hostility. Against this tide of events the docile, unimaginative and exhausted Party workers . . . could offer little resistance; it was characteristic that, after much resentful invective, their

Central Committee representatives voted overwhelmingly for the change on 7 February 1990; only Yeltsin voted against!

After the February Plenum A. N. Yakovlev communicated the news to the press with the bland statement that the CPSU "would fight for an avant-garde role in society in equal competition with any sociopolitical movement." The understatement could not hide the end of an epoch. After seventy-two years the CPSU had lost its direction of policy and had to face the loss of its administrative privileges and the probable collapse of its morale, prestige, membership and resources.

So drastic was the change that many of its details had not been worked out a year later. Millions, inside and outside the CPSU, did not immediately absorb its full impact, and . . . it never filtered through to remote provinces. . . .

How well did the CPSU equip itself for its new incarnation in competitive politics? The question directs attention to two processes: democratisation, and disengagement from the functions and privileges of a state-party. Neither process was ever fully completed, but their main thrust and scope was determined at the XXVIII CPSU Congress in July 1990, a Congress which rewrote the Party Rules.

If Party members were to stay in the CPSU rather than resign or join the opposition, the Party needed to be able to show them that they could make an effective contribution through membership. This meant a new balance of power between centre and local branches, and between members and *apparat*, and the new Rules sought to enshrine this. Entry into the Party now became the business of primary organisations alone; the requirement of references, probation and confirmation by higher organs served little purpose now that the Party had no perquisites to offer, and was dropped. The principle of secret competitive election was established for the selection of all delegates, committees and officials, and as if to underline the point it was specified that candidates might nominate themselves. After July appointments of provincial Party officials were no longer submitted to the Central Committee for "confirmation." Office-bearers might not serve more than two terms at the same office, nor sit on more than two committees simultaneously. . . .

The main measure against appointed and paid *apparatchiki* was to deprive them of automatic tenure: elected bodies must now appoint an *apparat* for the same term of office as their own, and have access to the meetings and the documents of their paid staff. Coupled with the fact that there was now less business for paid functionaries, these provisions might have been successful in making appointed staff the servants rather than the masters of elected bodies. But it would have taken time to bring this about, and the problem of an experienced, angry and underemployed *apparat* was an immediate one. It was pressure from such elements that led to the foundation in June 1990 of a distinct Communist Party of the RSFSR [Russian Soviet Federated Socialist Republic] and the election of the conservative I. K. Polozkov as its first secretary. Many reform-minded Russian communists were furious at being transferred automatically to Polozkov's organisation; part of the intention must surely have been to subject Party members in the central institutions to another discipline than Gorbachev's.

The new Rules kept the phrase "democratic centralism" and the formal ban on factions, but their substance was reduced to a rudiment of what it had been. Majority decisions must still be carried out by people who disagreed with them, but minorities might now "defend their positions at meetings," "have them entered into the record," "demand that questions be reopened" and insist that controversial items be subjected to a two-thirds majority. They were also permitted to communicate with like-minded minorities elsewhere, by setting up "platforms" on the basis of common views, problems or interests; two such platforms, the Democratic and the Marxist, had been formed early in 1990 and their spokesmen were identified as such at the Congress. The creation, however, of "factions with their own internal organisation and discipline" remained forbidden. How a "platform" differs from a "faction" was not clarified but is plainly central here. . . .

. . . The dilemma was very real. The Democratic Platform had flourished because of support from the Moscow Higher Party School; in July many of its members resigned from the CPSU and in November founded the Republican Party of the RSFSR. The following year Gorbachev was to speak of the "two, three or four parties" struggling within the CPSU framework. Hundreds of thousands of members must have been tempted to leave, or work for a split, so as to organise effective common action with like-minded people; they held back in part because new parties would lose any claim to the CPSU's assets and infrastructure. But this was no dilemma for the *apparat:* their interest in preserving existing structures, and hence in preventing members' finding their natural alignments was unambiguous.

Intra-Party democracy evidently included decentralisation, but marrying Party unity with the new recognition of diversity was especially difficult in the ethnic field. In the three Baltic republics communists prepared to work with local nationalists who had broken with the CPSU in the first half of 1990, and in Lithuania and Latvia these factions were more popular than those that maintained the central connection. Congress's response was to move the fifteen first secretaries of the republican Party organisations into the Politburo *ex officio* and to introduce quasi-federal elements into the Central Committee also. Republican CPSU organisations were now to work out "their own programmes and normative documents" and decide for themselves "political, organisational, staffing, publishing [and] financial" questions on the basis of the All-Union Rules and Programme. But this was not legal language and it did not, as federal arrangements should, demarcate the spheres of competence of the republican parties in relation to the CPSU. Failure to solve this issue made the CPSU increasingly irrelevant in the Baltics and Transcaucasia.

Democratisation might succeed in holding the membership together, but what counted for a major part of the electorate was to see CPSU influence expunged from state institutions—whose senior staff, it will be remembered, were almost entirely Party members. This process could take two forms, each labelled, rather confusingly, "depoliticisation." There was no doubt that policy-making, for example, had to be "departisanised"—freed from the influence of one Party so that others might have access—and for Gorbachev such "departisanisation" was a sufficient remedy for the problem of CPSU influence in the army and bureaucracy. For others, notably Yeltsin, nothing short of the removal of all party-political influence—"depoliticisation" in a strict sense—would produce a trustworthy public service. It will be apparent that the former was a cautious and conciliatory line which required no more than administrative action, whilst "depoliticisation" was a political issue affecting the employment of several million persons.

At the highest level of policy-making the President and Presidential Council effectively replaced the Politburo, which after July 1990 contained no ministers or members of the Presidential Council apart from Gorbachev. . . .

The Party had enjoyed a number of "administrative privileges" the more easily to dominate political life, privileges which in principle had been ended by the amendment of Article six. But legal curtailment left significant problems in practice. Take the example of *nomenklatura* [jobs controlled by the party]. After March 1990 the CPSU had no right to approve any appointments other than its own; but it was still in possession of personnel files on millions of people, and tens of thousands of communist employers will have had little idea how to conduct a fair and competitive job search (and probably less inclination). . . .

Party organisations had always been set up at the workplace rather than at places of residence, and CPSU business had been conducted on factory (office, etc.) premises, in factory time and in other respects at cost to factories—privileges that cost-conscious managers would scarcely want to extend to a variety of political parties. Even before the Law on Public Associations prohibited political activities in working time, there were signs of management (sometimes with workers' support) seeking to depoliticise the workplace. But to ban party activity in working time was not the same as to ban work-based party organisation, and in government offices, for example, one can well imagine that the continued existence of a Party organisation of senior staff made a difference to the way people did their jobs. The issue was fought hard until Yeltsin's decree of July 1991 prohibited political organisation at workplaces under RSFSR jurisdiction; that was still before the Committee of Constitutional Supervision when the August coup settled the question.

The workplace controversy was linked to that of CPSU property. The Party had assets that it valued (perhaps conservatively) between 4.9 and 7.7 billion roubles, much of it administrative buildings in city centres, or hotels and sanatoria. It was also a substantial entrepreneur: of its annual income of 2.7 billion (more than the budget of the smaller Union-Republics) forty per cent derived from economic activity, principally publishing. Party leaders insisted that its assets were protected by law and Constitution, but many were none too scrupulous about clinging to material perquisites; members of *obkomy* [regional committees] and Central Committees, it emerged in November 1990, were still exempt from customs inspection. Pressure mounted for [the party] to divest itself of property, with or without compensation. A case could be made that it had acquired much of its property not by purchase but by simple transfer from the state. And Party media holdings, and still more its ownership of printing presses, came so close to monopoly, it was argued, as to constitute a threat to democracy. This is the background to the fighting around communications premises in Lithuania and Latvia in early 1991; the Riga Press Building was the only publishing facility in Latvia.

For the CPSU the "jewel in the crown" had always been its organisations in the armed forces, KGB and MVD [Ministry of Internal Affairs]. These "political organs" were not set up and run by their members (as was formally the case with civilian Party organisations) but by a distinct corps of political officers, who were in turn appointed by a Main Political Administration (MPA) of the Central Committee. It was characteristic of the state-party amalgam that political officers were paid by the state but answerable to the Party. However managed, the severance of this nexus was bound to threaten Party power and at the same time abolish a discipline that had kept the Army out of public politics. Gorbachev's solution, decided in March 1990 but not completed until a year later, was the compromise one of "departisanisation": command of the political officers was transferred from Party to state so that they became a body of morale, education and welfare officers with duties not unlike those of padres [chaplains] and the education corps in a western army. . . .

Together these were the Party reforms that Gorbachev engineered at the XXVIII Congress. It was probably his most brilliant campaign and characteristically it was conducted in the Party's familiar ordered environment. More than forty per cent of the delegates were paid Party workers and many were determined to get him overthrown; many too had had the chance to coordinate their tactics at the Congress of the RSFSR Communist Party a fortnight earlier. In the event Gorbachev managed to stay General Secretary, to avoid a major split and to turn the CPSU into a party which for most of its members was still a tolerable framework for the pursuit of their political interests. What he failed to achieve was a party equipped to pursue electoral and constitutional politics in the Soviet Union of the 1990s. In that sense it was a hollow victory and his energies would have been better spent elsewhere.

The problem he failed to solve was that of the *apparat*. The paid Party functionaries continued to immobilise the energies of ordinary members whilst deterring non-communists from trusting the Party. They had major financial and organisational resources, and powerful allies especially in the armed forces. And they knew their future was at stake. Dislodging or neutralising them could not have been done by rules or legislation; they were a social and political problem. This was the key to Gorbachev's relations with the CPSU in 1990–1, and in particular to his decision to combine the posts of General Secretary and President. Attempts to confront the *apparat* (he seems to have thought) would succeed only in driving them underground into a subversive and armed subculture; but enough of them might still be won round to the service of a reformed Party and this process would serve to blunt the efforts of the rest; and he was the only senior Party figure with the commitment, experience and authority to bring it off. The approach entailed trying to hold the Party together—something that was in any case dear to his heart. But in the event he failed to avert reaction and the costs of the failed policy were enormous: energies were diverted, options foreclosed, urgent agenda postponed and precious support dissipated.

At disestablishment the CPSU had 19.2 million members. Some 6.8 million were blue-collar workers in industry and agriculture, while 6.4 million were white-collar employees in production and services apart from administration; the latter absorbed 1.4 million—including somewhat less than 200,000 Party *apparatchiki*—and 1.2 million were in the armed or security forces, mainly as officers; the remaining 3.4 million was made up of pensioners, housewives, students and others outside employment. Between January 1990 and July 1991 the Party lost 4.2

million or about a fifth of these members. Losses were slightly higher in the non-Russian Union-Republics than in the RSFSR—the Party had virtually collapsed in the Baltics and Trans-caucasia—but even in Russia losses approached two out of 10.4 million. Falling membership meant loss of income from Party dues, and many members stopped paying their dues without re-signing; in 1990 Party income from its members fell by almost half. This was not all. The Law on the Press had crippled the Party's publishing income: prestigious journals rejected Party own-ership, more orthodox ones like *Pravda* suffered a massive fall in sales and the Party was under pressure to hand over its publishing facilities. Long before the August coup it was clear that the CPSU was running a deficit and drawing on its assets.

Black, *Into the Dustbin of History*

By 1991 divisive trends within communist ranks had split the party even further. A neo-Bolshevik movement was founded by Nina Andreeva, famous for her 1988 open essay "I Cannot Forego Principles" in support of Stalin, and a Communist Initiative Move-ment was established by Central Committee member Alexei Ser-geev. A professor of political economy who claimed to have over three million supporters inside the party, Sergeev and other oppo-nents of the new CPSU program said that Gorbachev's platform was not even a new form of social democracy; rather, it repre-sented a type of bourgeois liberalism. Thus were lines drawn clearly in the sand within the CPSU itself.

Along with the CPSU opposition to various liberal actions, Soyuz [Union] and the Liberal Democratic Party, headed by rabid right-winger Vladimir Zhirinovskii, were still out there to make Gorbachev's political life miserable. Zhirinovskii, who placed a distant third in the RSFSR presidential race, . . . on 30 July insisted that a military coup would be a final step "to save the state."

In the heat of victory after the 26 July plenum Gorbachev lost another of his key advisers. The very next day Yakovlev resigned his post on the general secretary's staff and told journal-ists that he believed the CPSU to be beyond reform. He made a point of supporting Yeltsin's ban on the Communist Party's privileged position in Russian enterprises and collectives. Yakovlev then joined Shevardnadze and others who now hoped to turn the party-based Democratic Reform Movement into a genuine national opposition party, to be called the United Democratic Party, at the September Congress. When the Congress met a month after the coup more than 1000 people showed up. But by that time the situation was much changed. The reformers then decided to choose delegates from their own ranks to attend yet another congress in October for the purpose of establishing several democratic parties to compete against the communists, whom they assumed would undergo a revival. In the meantime Yakovlev, who resigned from the CPSU itself on 16 August, issued public admonitions about the likelihood of a coup, only to be met with apparent indifference. . . .

Prepared the conservatives may have been; competent they were not. The panacea they offered for the ills of Soviet society proved to be worse than the disease for the CPSU and the USSR. Dictatorship failed in the very country in which it had been perfected. On the other hand, the fact that the leading institutions of the USSR's newly developed democracy remained passive during the three-day coup was very discouraging to those who preferred parliamentary to either presidential rule or dictatorships. Yeltsin's quickness to close down the CPSU press and lay claim to the party's assets by presidential decree might have satisfied widespread feelings of hostility towards the CPSU, but could hardly be called a sign of resurgent democracy. Mixed perceptions of how "democrats" might behave apparently also confused the coup leaders. The Russian deputy chief procurator, Ye. Lisov, said on 21 January 1992 that because Gorbachev had moved to the right early in 1991 the plotters assumed they would have the Soviet president's support after his government was overthrown. They were wrong but, as several observers have remarked, their biggest mistake in this regard may have been in the ham-handed manner in which they treated Gorbachev and his immediate family.

Political support for the coup did come from the Soyuz group of deputies and the small Liberal Democratic Party of the Soviet Union, founded in March 1990 by V. Zhirinovskii and V. Bogachev to support a "law-government state with a presidential form of government and a market economy," and strong "Soviet" citizenship as opposed to a splintered society based on ethnic divisions. Representatives of Russian and other minorities in the Baltic states, Moldova and Georgia, backed the coup verbally but could offer nothing of substance to help maintain the junta in power. Leading agencies of even the CPSU, such as the Politburo and the Central Committee, said nothing. In fact, Gorbachev had emasculated the Central Committee and the Politburo was dominated by republican party leaders since July 1990. Thus the CPSU, which later took the full brunt of blame for the event, stood mostly on the sidelines while the coup was underway; the coup leaders had no real political base from which to generate powerful support. More critical was the degree to which important national sectors openly defied the junta. A surprising number of provincial city and oblast soviets joined Moscow and Leningrad in speaking out against the coup from the beginning. . . .

A crucial part of the structural changes in the USSR was the general assault on CPSU institutions. Yeltsin acted first against the CPSU, decreeing on 23 August that all CPSU publications temporarily were suspended from publishing in the RSFSR. Thus, *Pravda, Sovetskaia Rossiia, Glasnost, Rabochaia tribuna, Moskovskaia pravda*, and *Leninskoe znamia* ceased publication for a short time. Although this action was strongly protested by several major papers with more democratic reputations, among them *Komsomolskaia pravda* and *Izvestiia*, as undemocratic and was criticized bitterly by Gennadii Seleznev, *Pravda*'s deputy editor-in-chief, the CPSU press clearly was vulnerable. Some of the papers that protested Yeltsin's decree had been suspended by the coup leadership. An *Izvestiia* writer, V. Nadein, warned Yeltsin in a 24 August article that he had made a mistake and that he must not behave like Yanaev. Nadein reminded his readers of a Bolshevik decree of 1918 that had "temporarily" closed opposition papers—for 73 years!

When *Pravda* (after one day) and *Rabochaia tribuna* (five days) reappeared they both had eliminated the Communist Manifesto's call to revolution ("Proletarians of all Countries, Unite!") from their masthead, and *Sovetskaia Rossiia* (12 days) pronounced itself an "Independent People's Paper" rather than the "Newspaper of the Communists of the Russian Federation." Although the CPSU's monopoly on the dissemination of information was challenged openly since 1986, and broken officially upon adoption in June 1990 of the USSR Law on the Press and Other Means of Mass Information, it took the events of August 1991 to end forever the inestimably important grip the Communist Party had over all forms of information in the USSR.

On 22 August the CPSU Central Committee Secretariat issued a statement to the effect that it strongly supported perestroika and the exclusive use of constitutional means to extricate the USSR from its "deep crisis." It said that the "anticonstitutional" regime established by the GKChP[1] had been "inadmissable." The Russian Communist Party issued a similar, if somewhat less repentant message. The Ukrainian CP unambiguously condemned the coup on 22 August, and Kravchuk resigned from the party. But it was too late for most CPs to rally. Nazarbaev resigned from the CPSU Politburo and its Central Committee on the 22nd. Kyrgyzstan's Akaev and his vice president left the CPSU on the 26th. The Estonian and Lithuanian governments outlawed communist parties in their republics the same day. Latvia and Georgia followed suit on the 27th. Ironically, the Latvian government arrested Alfreds Rubiks, first secretary of the Latvian CP, shortly thereafter for supporting the August coup d'état in a country of which Latvia was no longer a part.

The example set by Nazarbaev and Akaev soon was emulated by President Karimov of Uzbekistan and Moldova's party leader, G. Yeremei. A clear sign of the public anger against the CPSU and the KGB was the removal of the huge statue of Felix Dzerzhinskii, founder of the Cheka, predecessor to the KGB, from its place in front of the infamous KGB building in Moscow.

Yeltsin suspended all other activities of the Communist Party of Russia on August 24th, saying that it had "grossly" violated his decree of 20 July banning the activity of organized political parties in RSFSR state agencies. He further prohibited all political groups from operating within the armed forces, KGB and MVD on Russian territory, and nationalized the property of both TASS and Novosti [the official news services]. A USSR presidential decree "About the Property of the Communist Party of the Soviet Union" (24 Aug.) placed all CPSU properties in the hands of the soviets

---

[1] The "State Committee on the Emergency Situation"; see p. 254.—Ed.

The August Coup: Boris Yeltsin atop an armored personnel carrier at the Russian White House, defies the plotters on August 19, 1991. (AP/Wide World Photos)

of people's deputies. The next day Gosbank (USSR State Bank) suspended all CPSU accounts to prevent funds from being secreted away. On the 29th the USSR Supreme Soviet voted (283–29–59) to suspend all "activity of the CPSU throughout the territory of the Soviet Union." Even though he defended the CPSU in his televised press conference on the 22nd, Gorbachev resigned as general secretary two days later. All CPSU properties were seized by the state for the purpose of redistribution. Political departments in the army, KGB, MVD, Railroad Troops and state agencies were abolished by presidential decree on 24 August. Hundreds of thousands of Communist Party members lost their jobs and privileges, which included cars and housing, and access to special stores, health care and resort spas.

On 26 August the Komsomol Central Committee Secretariat proposed to its members that the organization give up its role as a communist political body and become an independent youth organization. This proposal was accepted by a Komsomol plenum in early September.

Other factions of the Communist Party went their own way. On 29 August the Democratic Party of Communists of Russia (DPCR), which still counted Rutskoi as a member, registered at the RSFSR Ministry of Justice as a distinct Russian political entity for both "honorable communists" and non-communists. Headed by Vasilii Lipitskii, the DPCR condemned the coup and supported Gorbachev. At a congress in October it renamed itself the Party of Free Russia. In an interview given to *Pravda* on 25 October USSR people's deputy A. A. Denisov, who helped organize a congress on 26–27 October to draw together Russia's left-wing socialists, including members of the suspended CPSU, said that Gorbachev "supports" the new party and wished it success. Roy Medvedev was another active organizer of the congress.

A more orthodox communist organization met on 4 September to oppose Gorbachev and to savor a brief moment of revenge. The organizational committee of the Bolshevik Platform in the CPSU, still chaired by Nina Andreeva, expelled him from the party for "betraying the cause of Lenin and the October Revolution, betraying the international working class and Communist movement, for disrupting Socialist power, for destroying the Leninist party, for desertion and playing a double game, for deceiving working people, and for demagogy." It is unlikely that Gorbachev took these accusations very seriously, but they are interestingly anachronistic because they sound so much like the charges levelled against Tito by Stalin in the late 1940s and early 1950s.

Andreeva's group, which met again on 8 November to form an All-Union Communist Party of Bolsheviks, called both Gorbachev and Yeltsin "traitors." In settling its platform in November the new party said that it would restore the "supremacy of socialist ownership," a planned economy, and a Soviet state guided by the "dictatorship of the proletariat." Andreeva was elected general secretary and promised to re-establish the Soviet Union as a great power on the basis of return to Leninism. Because of increasing pressure on individual communists, a group calling itself "In Defense of Communists' Rights" was formed in October, specifically to provide aid to families of Communists (such as Rubiks) whom they believed were being persecuted for their convictions. The organization was registered with the Moscow city Administration of Justice as an official public organization on 29 December 1991, under the leadership of Professor V. S. Martemianov, an academic jurist.

Peter Rutland and Marek Dabrowski

The Collapse of the Planned Economy

In 1990 and 1991 the Soviet economy went into a general decline. Production and living standards fell at an accelerating rate, and shortages intensified. As is shown by Peter Rutland, an economist at

From Peter Rutland, "Economic Crisis and Reform," in Stephen White, Alex Pravda, and Zvi Gitelman, eds., *Developments in Soviet and Post-Soviet Politics*, pp. 200, 214–216, 219, 226. Duke University Press, quoted material copyright © 1992 by Peter Rutland, reprinted by permission of the publisher; and Marek Dabrowski, "The First Half-Year of Russian Transformation," in Anders Åslund and Richard Layard, eds., *Changing the Economic System*, pp. 1–4, 7–9, St. Martin's Press, Copyright © by Anders Åslund and Richard Layard, reprinted by permission of the publisher.

Wesleyan University in Connecticut, the Gorbachev government was fatally weakened by its inability to find an effective and consistent answer to the economic crisis. Marek Dabrowski, a Polish economist who has served as deputy minister of finance, faults the economic efforts of Gorbachev's successors.

Rutland, "Economic Crisis and Reform"

Six years after Gorbachev took office, his programme of economic reform had clearly been overtaken by political and economic disintegration. On 18 December 1990, shortly before his resignation, Prime Minister Nikolai Ryzhkov bluntly stated that "In the form originally conceived, *perestroika* has failed." The attempted coup of August 1991 was a reaction to this political and economic collapse, and to the failure of Gorbachev's policies. The coup itself accelerated these centrifugal forces, and it is too early to judge what sort of new political and economic order will emerge from the wreckage.

What is clear, however, is the magnitude of the task facing the new leadership. The system of central planning which Stalin imposed in the 1930s, at tremendous human cost, ground on for five decades and totally reshaped the economy of the USSR in all its aspects: geography, institutions, social structure and psychology. After 1985, the old system started to break down. The power of central planners steadily eroded, with enterprises and republics behaving in an increasingly independent manner. From 1988, the previous macroeconomic and foreign trade balance of the Soviet economy also broke down. These processes have left the post-Soviet economy in an institutional vacuum: it is neither a market nor a planned economy, but a curious hybrid whose laws of operation are as yet unclear. . . .

As *perestroika* unfolded, clear contradictions emerged between the political elements of the programme—*glasnost'* and democratisation—and the economic reforms. It was *not* a good idea to try to democratise a political system, while simultaneously launching a reform programme, in the middle of an economic crisis.

Glasnost' increased the opportunities for people to express their discontent with the economic situation. Investigative journalists filled the papers with articles showing people just how badly off they really were. They even turned up problems, such as infant mortality, which the public had not been aware of because of the suppression of official data. Gorbachev's own "meet the people" tours, beginning with a visit to Krasnoyarsk in September 1988, brought him face to face with some very dissatisfied consumers, and presumably convinced him of the explosive situation in Soviet society. . . .

Thus, by pursuing *glasnost'* and democratisation, Gorbachev sowed a field of dragon's teeth for his *perestroika* programme. His political manoeuvrings were perhaps necessary for the consolidation of his own personal power, but they sharply reduced the leadership's ability to modify its economic policy. Political liberalisation made it far more difficult to take tough decisions that would hurt the interests of certain industrial sectors or social groups.

Gorbachev's vision of *perestroika* was of a carefully managed, step-by-step process, with himself playing a pivotal role, balancing the conflicting demands of the democratic left and the conservative right. As time wore on, Gorbachev found it increasingly difficult to maintain this balance, and his policy started to lurch violently from one side to the other. . . .

On 1 October 1990, the Russian parliament decided to press ahead on its own with the Shatalin plan. Meanwhile most of the other republics were unhappy with the Gorbachev *and* Shatalin plans,[1] since both seemed to them to leave too much central control in Moscow. In the case of the Shatalin plan, for example, they objected to reliance on a single currency issued by a federal reserve bank in Moscow.

On 16 October Gorbachev countered with his own programme, "For the stabilisation of the economy and the transition to a market economy," which emphasised the urgency of stabilisation and offered no specific timetable for the dismantling of central planning. Gorbachev's own former economic advisers, Shatalin and Petrakov, denounced his plan on 4 November, as did most of the republics. Throughout the autumn Yeltsin played a

[1] See pp. 199, 207–216.—Ed.

game of bluff and counter-bluff with Gorbachev. Many of Yeltsin's economic advisers resigned, among them Yavlinsky, unsure whether Yeltsin was really prepared to break with Gorbachev.

Amid a growing sense of panic and open talk of an authoritarian "Jaruzelski variant"[2] among party officials, Gorbachev won additional powers from the Supreme Soviet to rule by decree. Yeltsinites were convinced that Gorbachev had abandoned his commitment to reform and turned to the right, and the public seemed to agree. Polls showed that Gorbachev's popularity "rating" had collapsed from 52 per cent in December 1989 to 21 per cent in October 1990.

In November, Gorbachev used his presidential powers to raise the price of luxury goods and impose a 40 per cent tax on the dollar earnings of Soviet enterprises. (This merely served to accelerate the collapse of Soviet exports in 1991.) On 14 December he issued a decree imposing the same output targets on enterprises for 1991 as for 1990.

On 18 December Ryzhkov suffered a heart attack; he was replaced as USSR Prime Minister, in January 1991, by Valentin Pavlov, formerly Finance Minister. According to reports, there was at this time a stormy meeting between Gorbachev and several hundred leading industrial directors, many from defence plants, who warned him of impending economic catastrophe unless strong steps were taken.

In January 1991, key industrial input prices were raised by 50 per cent, and all 50- and 100-ruble notes were abruptly withdrawn from circulation in a bid to cut back on the monetary overhang. (In fact the withdrawn notes amounted to less than 3 per cent of the total.) There was a new crackdown on "economic crime," with an enhanced role for the KGB in the struggle against "speculation." In March retail prices were raised by 60 per cent, while consumers were compensated for 85 per cent of the increase. Apart from a brief general strike in Minsk, the Belorussian capital, the public response to the price increases was surprisingly muted.

The economic system of the former Soviet Union is currently in turmoil. The familiar structure of the CPE [centrally planned

---

[2] Reference to the imposition of martial law by President Jaruzelski in Poland in December 1981.—Ed.

economy] has been destroyed, but the transition process is not following anyone's blueprint for reform. Rather it is a product of complex political and economic struggles, with an unknown outcome.

The future economy will almost certainly be one in which market forces play a major role. Equally it could well be an economy whose factories and farms remain under the control of local political officials. However, rather than being locked into a vertical chain of command obeying Moscow's orders, the regions and republics will be interacting independently, through a mixture of political dealing and market trading. Four major themes have emerged during the first stages of this transition process.

The Breakdown of Central Planning

From 1988 on, the central ministries progressively lost control and the economy fragmented into a confusing crazy quilt of autonomous enterprises and regional authorities. Firms changed themselves into new types of organisation, often of a type not covered by existing laws. By January 1991, there were 1,420 "associations," 126 "concerns," 156 "intersectoral associations," 102 "consortiums" and 1,200 joint-stock companies. These firms felt, as one director put it, "like a dog who has lost his master" and began grouping together into new voluntary associations, such as the Scientific-Production Union (founded in June 1990).

The emergence of joint-stock companies was perhaps the most interesting development. In June 1990, a new law was passed allowing state enterprises to convert themselves into joint-stock companies. The giant Kama truck plant, with 120,000 workers, became the first such company. Most of the new joint-stock companies are in fact controlled by their managers and amount to "*nomenklatura* privatisation" of the sort witnessed in Hungary. Most shares are held by other firms, usually the suppliers and customers of the firm in question. Share trading is usually forbidden and shareholder rights are limited.

The other side to destatisation was the continued growth of the non-state sector. By mid-1991, out of a 135 million strong labour force, roughly 15.3 million were employed outside the state sector; 4.5 million were self-employed, 6.5 million were in cooperatives and 4.2 million in leased industrial units. It is not clear to what extent the shadow economy was able to expand to make up for the slump in state sector output. According to official data on the black market, now being gathered for the first time, it amounted to 100 billion rubles in 1991, or about 8 per cent of GNP. Most of this sum was accounted for by [moonlighting], resale of state goods and bribes to state shop assistants.

Leasing was much slower to develop in agriculture. The number of independent farmers was a mere 47,000 by mid-1991, mostly to be found in the Baltic and Caucasus. At that time there were only 9,000 in Russia and 218 in Ukraine. On the other hand a Russian republic programme gave one million hectares of land to individuals for allotments or housebuilding. Thus plans were well advanced before the coup to carry out a radical "destatisation" of the Soviet economy. Under USSR legislation introduced in February 1991, the state sector was expected to shrink from 90 to 30 per cent in five years. These laws have now been superseded by republican privatisation legislation. For example, Russia and Kazakhstan passed such laws in July and August 1991, and local State Property Committees started valuing state assets. Auctioning of shops and apartments began during the summer on an experimental basis in cities in several republics, including Russia.

Popular savings are only 700 billion rubles, while the total asset value is three to four trillion rubles, so privatisation will have to proceed through some sort of free distribution, probably using a variant of the Czechoslovak voucher method. Workers are to be given the opportunity to buy shares in their own firm at a discount, and it is likely that most privatisations will take the form of worker/manager buy-outs.

This decentralisation coincided with a massive slump in output in virtually all sectors. In the first nine months of 1991, GNP fell 12 per cent, consumption fell 17 per cent and investment 20 per cent. Food output fell 8 per cent and the procurement of food items through the state and cooperative sector fell by 16 per cent for meat, 19 per cent for cheese and 12 per cent for sugar. Industrial output fell 6.4 per cent, with falls of 20 per cent in soap, 11 per cent in clothing and shoes, 10 per cent in oil and 11 per cent in coal.

Ironically many firms saw increased profits in 1991, as they took advantage of greater laxity in price setting. By mid-1991, 45 per cent of industrial products and 60 per cent of consumer goods manufactures were sold at "free" prices (set by the producer) or "contract" prices (agreed between producer and customer enterprises). In the first nine months of 1991 the prices of industrial goods rose at an annual rate of 164 per cent, while retail prices rose by 103 per cent and agricultural procurement prices rose 56 per cent.

The one sector of the economy where producers were not enjoying significantly increased autonomy was agriculture, where farmers found themselves caught in a price scissors—between rising industrial prices and fixed state procurement prices. In 1990, fruit and vegetables were taken off the state procurement system, with the worrying result that output fell while prices rose 40 per cent. Farms responded to the 1991 price scissors by refusing to sell grain to the state, instead storing it in the hope that they would be allowed to get a better price as the winter of 1991 progressed.

As industrial firms struck out for independence from the central planning system, they moved quickly to set up banking and trading networks to start to take over the coordination functions abandoned by the centre. In 1990, the old sectoral state banks were abolished and more than 2,000 aggressive new "commercial" banks sprang up, mostly controlled by industrial enterprises and specialising in interfirm lending. As a result credit issues rose 36 per cent, to 496 billion rubles, in 1991. Before long "bank wars" broke out as the USSR State Bank and Russian Central Bank struggled to rein in the commercial banks.

The same year saw the emergence of over a hundred commodity exchanges, where everything from oil to passenger cars to dollars was traded, at free prices. Large state enterprises also dominate the trading exchanges, although a new breed of aggressive entrepreneurs have emerged as brokers in these exchanges.

Monetary and Fiscal Crisis

In 1991 there was further deterioration in the country's financial balances. Retail spending was down 24 per cent in physical volume but up 66 per cent in money terms. By mid-1991, the population held 422 billion rubles in savings accounts and 150 billion rubles in cash, and unsatisfied demand was estimated to be up 44 per cent on 1990.

In the first nine months of 1991 federal spending was 150 billion rubles, only 69 per cent of the planned level. This had catastrophic implications for the funding of federal services, from the armed forces to health services. (Some 62 billion rubles were reportedly spent on the military.) Worse still, federal receipts totalled only 74 billion rubles—40 per cent of the expected level—owing to the withholding of funds by republican governments. Yawning budget deficits also opened up at republican and local levels, and by July 1991 the combined union and republican deficit was running at an annual rate of 200 billion rubles (compared to a projected total personal income of 710 billion rubles). Hyperinflation will almost certainly result. The churning printing presses led to a collapse of faith in the ruble. By the end of 1991, while the "official" commercial rate was 1.6 rubles to the dollar, the tourist rate was 42 rubles and the rate on dollar auctions was reaching 90 rubles. In December 1991, the State Bank was forced to abandon the official rates altogether.

In retrospect one can see that the budget imbalance was exacerbated by the 1987 Law on the State Enterprise, since after the measure was introduced budget remittances fell while retained profits and wages jumped sharply. Sheer economic incompetence by government leaders also played a part. However the 1991 inflation was also a product of years of suppressed inflation. The old price structure became increasingly unrealistic, with black market prices rising 100 per cent in 1991 and standing at three to five times official prices for the same goods (not that they are available in state stores).

Measures introduced in 1990 and 1991 with a view to strengthening the social safety net were an additional burden on the federal budget. A set of measures in August 1990 increased transfer payments for pensioners and low-income families, and 1991 saw a 49 billion ruble compensation package accompanying the retail price increases. Another 160 billion rubles were allocated to compensate savings account holders, payable in installments. These were very large sums for a government facing a yawning budget deficit. There were also other selective wage increases: for example, the coalminers' strike won them a 25 per cent wage increase in April 1991. Food subsidies continued to be a crushing burden, amounting to 160 billion rubles in 1991 (more than half the production cost). . . .

The International Debt Crisis

By the end of 1991, the USSR was close to defaulting on its $58 billion hard currency debt (not to mention its $17 billion debt with former CMEA[3] members and other soft currency partners). By the end of 1992, $22 billion was due in interest and capital repayments and there was little chance that the former members of the USSR could find such a sum. It even turned out that Soviet gold reserves had been run down, with 1,100 million tonnes sold since 1989 and only 240 million tonnes (worth three to four billion dollars) left in the vaults.

Foreign trade in the first half of 1991 was 37 per cent lower than in the same period in 1990. The collapse of CMEA and the shift to hard currency payments from January 1991 (at Moscow's insistence) caused a catastrophic 50 per cent drop in trade with East Europe. Trade with capitalist countries also fell 33 per cent, largely because of the disruptive reorganisation of foreign trade and a 10 per cent contraction in domestic oil production in both 1990 and 1991. In 1991, food imports rose; they could reach 49 million tonnes of grain (one-quarter of consumption needs) over 1991–2. Imports of all other types of goods, from industrial spare parts to consumer electronics, were radically cut back, by 30–60 per cent. These ruthless economies enabled the USSR to post a $3 billion surplus for the first half of 1991, but this was still far short of the sums needed to avoid a default on its foreign debt.

The looming crisis stimulated urgent calls for emergency assistance from the West, the most celebrated being the economic programme written by Graham Allison and Grigorii Yavlinsky, entitled "Window of Opportunity." This proposed a new Marshall Plan to finance the transition to capitalism in the USSR, with Soviet officials requesting $14 billion aid and Allison talking of

---

[3] Council of Mutual Economic Assistance, linking the former Communist countries of Eastern Europe with the USSR.—Ed.

Russia as "possibly the Klondike of the late twentieth century." However, in July 1991, the G7[4] meeting in London turned down such proposals on the grounds that the political chaos in the USSR meant it was unrealistic to expect *any* transition plan to be implemented. Germany, responsible for two-thirds of all the lending to the USSR, was understandably the most reluctant to contemplate writing off some of the Soviet debts.

The Break-up of the Union

In 1991, the political cohesion of the USSR collapsed, and with it what was left of the old structures of central planning. . . . In 1991, a "war of laws" broke out between republican and all-Union authorities, wreaking havoc in the economy. More and more firms withdrew from participation in the Union economy, ignoring output plans and refusing to pay taxes. Most enterprises in Russia chose to pay their turnover tax to the republican government and not to the Union authorities (Yeltsin set the Russian tax at 38 per cent, below the 45 per cent Union rate). Within Russia and Ukraine, regional soviets emulated the Baltics by banning the "export" of food and consumer goods to other regions. In December 1990, the Russian Republic passed a law allowing private ownership of land—something not permitted in the Union Law on Land of February 1990.

Gorbachev struggled to find a consensus among republic leaders for a new Union. On 23 April the "nine-plus-one" agreement was concluded, committing the signatories to approve a new Union Treaty by the end of the year. In July 1991, a joint anti-crisis stabilisation programme was adopted by Moscow and ten republics. A series of meetings over the summer resulted in a new draft Union Treaty, due for signature on 20 August. The central theme of all these negotiations was the preservation of a common "economic space," while recognising the right of the republics to sovereign control over property, natural resources and taxation. The same ideas were carried forward into the new Economic Treaty, signed in Alma Ata in October 1991 by eight republics (with Ukraine an awkward absentee).

[4] G7: The United States, Japan, Canada, Great Britain, France, Germany, and Italy.—Ed.

All sides recognised that after 70 years of joint development the abrupt severing of economic links between factories in different republics would have a catastrophic impact. (An estimated 20 per cent of Soviet GNP in 1990 consisted of interrepublican flows.) An equally pressing constraint was the fact that the republics were saddled with the foreign debt accumulated by the old regime and the West would not offer any further assistance until there were guarantees that the republics would collectively strive to meet these obligations. The republics were aware that only Russia, with its vast natural resources, was capable of running a positive foreign trade balance in the immediate future. They were fearful of Russian threats to raise the price of oil from its current level of 70 rubles per tonne (two dollars) to the world market price of 140 dollars.

Despite these powerful arguments in favour of cooperation, there are many obstacles to the emergence of a viable economic union. Will all the former Union enterprises become the property of the republics, without compensation for past investment? How much will the republics contribute to the budget of the central institutions that are left? Can the ruble be salvaged as a currency and a reliable central emission bank be created?

The post-coup events left no authoritative central political institutions which could find a consensus on these questions. In fact economic problems have been manipulated by republican politicians as part of an internal and external struggle for political power. Commitment to a separate national currency became a symbolic test of one's commitment to sovereignty. This was most blatant in Ukraine, where former communist leader Leonid Kravchuk seized upon the independence issue in response to the electoral challenge from the nationalists. More worrying still, there are doubts whether any of the republican governments have the ability to enforce their own decisions within their own borders: the "war of laws" has been replaced by a legal vacuum. It will fall upon Russia, as the largest state, to take the lead and cajole the other republics into line. Unfortunately the Russian government itself is deeply divided over economic and political issues, and until it gets its own house in order will be unable to play a leading role. . . .

. . . In October 1991, Yeltsin began to adopt independent policies, in an apparent attempt to outflank the Silaev "government" and bypass Gorbachev's protracted negotiations over a new Union Treaty. Yeltsin took over as Russian Prime Minister in addition to his position as President, and announced his intention to abolish all price controls and move rapidly towards a market economy. At an historic meeting in Brest on 7–8 December, Yeltsin's independent line received support from presidents Kravchuk of Ukraine and Shushkevich of Belorussia, when they joined together to announce a new Commonwealth of Independent States based upon a "common economic space" as well as other forms of coordination. It was in turn these new republican leaders, with their counterparts from other Commonwealth states, who began to carry out the transition to a full-fledged market system in the early 1990s; the first results of their endeavours, with rising prices and a continued fall in production, made it clear why Gorbachev had been reluctant to take this step although (like him) the republican leaders insisted there was "no alternative."

Dabrowski, "The First Half-Year of Russian Transformation"

In the beginning of November 1991, the new Russian government started its policy of radical economic reforms. Its declared aims were the transformation from planned to a market economy and macroeconomic stabilization. . . .

The economic conditions in which the Russian transformation was to begin in the autumn of 1991 were extremely difficult. The economy of the former USSR and of the Russian Federation was in the deep disintegration typical of most post-communist countries in Central and Eastern Europe. In such an economy the central planning system has already ceased to work as a mechanism of microeconomic discipline and macroeconomic coordination. Nor has a new market mechanism yet assumed this role. We have the typical syndrome of a non-planned, non-market economy, without sufficient microeconomic motivation or the means to achieve elementary macroeconomic equilibrium. Moreover, the government is weak in the sense that it does not have political support, and it is prepared to buy temporary social peace in exchange for inflationary money. . . .

. . . Declining oil export revenues and oil profits, resulting from a steady decrease in oil production, also contributed to fiscal difficulties since oil exports had been a significant source of budget revenue.

The level of repressed inflation continued to increase because of monetary expansion, increasing money in circulation, and the continuing price controls. . . .

After 1 April 1991, and the price reform of [Prime Minister] Valentin Pavlov, inflation started to have a more open form. The average price level in state retail trade was 89.5 per cent higher in 1991 than in 1990, and the state retail price index rose by 146.1 per cent from December 1990 to December 1991. The consolidated retail price index rose by 152.1 per cent, and the kolkhoz market price index by 281.2 per cent. Inflation (and later hyperinflation) in the second half of 1991 showed up partly in the form of open price increases, partly in the form of rising market shortages.

The rising budget deficit, financed exclusively by credit from the USSR State Bank (Gosbank), was a key cause of hyperinflation in 1991. According to IMF [International Monetary Fund] estimates, the total budget deficit of the Russian Federation in 1991 (including the consequences of taking responsibility for the former all-union budget) reached a level of 31 per cent of GDP [gross domestic product]. The sources of this huge fiscal deficit were ever-increasing state subsidies to support administratively controlled prices, the decrease of output, and poor tax discipline.

This weakening of the financial discipline at the micro level brought about the fast growth of nominal and "real" wages in the second half of 1991. In the last quarter of 1991 the "real" wage in industry was 33 per cent higher than its average level in 1990. This contributed to the significant decrease in the real profits of enterprises.

In the years of perestroika, the economic growth of the USSR and the Russian Federation was lower than in the preceding decades and was gradually decreasing. The net material product (NMP) of Russia increased only by 2.4 per cent in 1986, 0.7 per cent in 1987, 4.5 per cent in 1988, and 1.9 per cent in 1989. In 1990 the NMP started to decrease: by 3.6 per cent in 1990 and by 11.0 per cent in 1991 (preliminary estimates). In the same period, gross industrial output grew by 4.5 per cent in 1986, 3.5 per cent in 1987, 3.8 per cent in 1988, 1.4 per cent in 1989, and fell by 0.1 per cent in 1990 and 8.0 per cent in 1991.

The main reasons for the 1990–1991 recession were the crisis of the central planning system, the motivational crisis in state-owned enterprises, the disintegration of trade relations between Eastern European countries after the collapse of CMEA, as well as the gradual weakening of trade links between former USSR republics. After the political dictatorship and terror were gradually dismantled under perestroika, the system of central planning lost its capacity to mobilise resources for economic growth. For example, the rate of investment decreased in the second half of the 1980s. Also lost was the ability to guarantee elementary macroeconomic balance and microeconomic discipline. The deep recession in the former USSR supports the hypothesis that a deep fall in output is unavoidable in post-communist economies even before the start of a real stabilization and liberalisation. . . .

. . . The Yeltsin-Gaidar cabinet never published any clear formulation of the government programme. President Boris Yeltsin and Vice-Prime Minister Yegor Gaidar had only made general statements in their public presentations. But this is not to say that the new government had no comprehensive concept for economic reform at the onset. Indeed, the concept was drafted by Gaidar's "team" just before its nomination to government. In October and early November 1991, a special working group, appointed by President Yeltsin and headed by Gaidar, gathered in a government dacha in Arkhangelskoe (near Moscow) to perform this task.

Stabilisation and Reforms, the name of the unofficial working document prepared by this special group, proposed a gradual stabilization and liberalisation package to be implemented over the course of one year. In the first stage, most prices were to be deregulated and foreign economic relations were to be partially liberalised: foreign exchange auctions were to be introduced, and export and import transactions were to be partially liberalised. However, this was to be done without convertibility for the ruble and without a unified exchange rate. After 8–9 months, the next stage of reform was to be implemented, namely, currency reform. A new Russian ruble convertible to Western currencies was to be introduced.

The group's proposal was widely criticised by foreign experts, including this author, on the following counts:

First, the proposal aimed to transform hidden (repressed) hyperinflation into open hyperinflation for a period of at least half a year, risking that inflation would get out of control altogether.

Second, under hyperinflation, the indexation of wages and other incomes creates a very strong inflationary thrust making it difficult to break the hyperinflationary spiral.

Third, a longer transition period means that undesirable compromises must be made, such as maintaining the system of administrative allocation of resources.

Fourth, the continuing macroeconomic crisis, combined with plans to introduce the new currency, will contribute to the disintegration of the ruble area, which can run counter to the economic and political interests of Russia.

Fifth, currency reform is a very complicated operation technically, and very risky politically. Reducing effective nominal money balances through currency reform, while it is a frequently used means of monetary adjustment in countries with hyperinflation, seems difficult, given the current Russian circumstances.

Sixth, political and social support for a new government will not be long-lived. Therefore it is better to apply one big shock than a series of shocks over an extended period. Otherwise, the government may lose political support before embarking on the decisive phase of monetary reform. Moreover, gradual implementation of reform can provide the traditional bureaucracy with a better opportunity to consolidate antireform forces. . . .

Starting at the end of November 1991 the Yeltsin-Gaidar cabinet began to implement measures for liberalisation and stabilization. But despite the warnings of foreign experts, the scenario of gradual changes proposed in the *Stabilisation and Reforms* document was chosen. The one important deviation from this proposal was the abandonment of the currency reform idea. Instead, they intended to tackle monetary adjustment through a corrective inflation.

The results of this policy seem to confirm my reservations regarding the two-stage scenario. By mid-June 1992 Russia had accomplished only a partial domestic liberalisation, and neither monetary stabilization nor the elimination of the shortage economy had taken place.

Hélène Carrère D'Encausse

The Triumph of Self-Determination

By the beginning of 1991 the independence of the former Soviet republics had become virtually inevitable, thanks in part to the endorsement of republic rights by Boris Yeltsin and the government of the Russian Republic. Nonetheless, Gorbachev continued to wage a losing rearguard action both before and after the August coup to salvage some semblance of the union. His failure, and the triumph of nationalism in the republics up to the moment of the final liquidation of the USSR, are recounted by a noted French historian of the Soviet nationalities, Hélène Carrère D'Encausse of the Ecole des hautes études en sciences sociales in Paris.

Within one year—November 1990 to November 1991—the fragmenting USSR unequivocally came to an end. Finishing off Lenin's political system, the mighty Communist party, and the patiently assembled empire of the Bolsheviks required a coup d'è-tat—failed, of course—but also and mainly the unremitting hunger of the people belonging to the Soviet Union to determine their own fate. By November 1991, the signs of their victory were unmistakable. After more than seventy years, the traditional celebrations of the revolution were given up and replaced in

From Hélène Carrère D'Encausse, *The End of the Soviet Empire: The Triumph of the Nations*, translated by Franklin Philip, pp. 239–251, 253–255, 259, 270. Copyright © 1993 by HarperCollins. Reprinted by permission of the publisher.

Leningrad (now St. Petersburg) by ceremonies to mark the shedding of the name carried by the city since 1924, the year of Lenin's death. Elsewhere, ceremonies commemorating the triumph of the Bolsheviks gave way to demonstrations commemorating the victims of the Soviet regime. Still elsewhere, some nostalgic communists, with the red flag in front of them, maintained that the whole experience of 1917 had not failed. Nearly everywhere else, however, the red flag was replaced by the national flags that were reintroduced in 1989. And even over the Kremlin itself, the symbolic center of what remained of Soviet power, the red flag of the revolution flew in close proximity to the tricolored flag of Russia. In this competition of national emblems the red of communism increasingly capitulated to the brilliant, varied colors of the national traditions, a metaphor for the events in the huge area that is no longer Soviet land. The Soviet Union evaporated, and the search for a new bond between the republics continued to feature the retreat of a central government that no one knew what to call. . . .

. . . In the fall of 1990, the upheavals in the USSR were affecting life in the multiethnic republics. The growing anarchy clearly called for some minimum organization.

The debate over organization divided those in power. Three conceptions of the USSR's future then emerged and dominated all attempts to devise a union treaty. Still thinking he was in control, Gorbachev wanted to impose a union that was a federation. For him, this meant not only the preservation of a central power but a strong center working with strong republics. He accepted the sovereignty of the republics within the framework of the sovereignty of the federation, which was an integrative structure. Confronting Gorbachev was Boris Yeltsin, who argued for a confederation—even though he avoided the term—based on the sovereignty of the republics, direct agreements among the republics, and a center that was of course retained but deprived of any means for interfering in relations between the republics. Although Gorbachev conceived of the whole system from the center, Yeltsin organized it from the periphery, sidestepping as much as possible the center's involvement. The logic of Yeltsin's plans was strong republics, weak center. The third variant was the one proposed by the Baltic states: pure and simple separation, thus depleting the union of its components.

Added to this first debate on the future union was another one on the limits of the right to sovereignty. Could any national group assembled on some determinate territory claim sovereignty, or only the constituted republics that could generally claim to descend from older governing structures? Here, too, positions diverged. Gorbachev favored recognizing sovereignty in anyone who requested it. We can see the advantages of this idea. The minorities of nearly every republic in the USSR demanded sovereignty. By supporting the right of the Abkhazians to form a sovereign state or that of the Lithuanian Poles or the Estonian Russians, Gorbachev may have been hoping to squelch the desires for independence in Georgia and the Baltic countries by showing them that independence would inevitably lead to the disintegration of their territories. Confronting Gorbachev, Yeltsin and the leaders of all the independent republics were agreed in defending the idea of sovereignty limited to the constituted states. It was then up to them to find conditions of life together acceptable to their minorities. But Yeltsin said that the status of minorities within the republics was part of their sovereignty and could not be interfered with by the future union. After all, a sovereign republic must be master of its territory and population.

The profound differences between the various parties to this debate made it hardly surprising that the union treaty was the occasion for interminable negotiations punctuated with sudden electrifying developments and failures, and—in the last analysis—the first cause of the collapse of the whole Soviet system.

The first stage in this pursuit of an impossible union was the treaty plan prepared and presented by Gorbachev on November 23, 1990, and then submitted for public discussion. Worked out at the Council of the Federation in consultation with all the republics (except for the three Baltic countries and Georgia, which abstained), this text initially had a rather favorable reception, mainly because of its nonideological nature. The word *socialism* did not appear in it, while the condition of rights, the choice of forms of property, and the modern management of the state and the economy all written into it by the plan's drafters suggested that it expressed a new vision of the relations between the nations of the future union.

Nevertheless, when the plan was presented to the parliaments, it provoked considerable opposition. The Congress of People's Deputies, meeting for its fourth session in December 1990, witnessed a clash between Gorbachev and Yeltsin, a clash not dramatic in its form but serious in its substance. Although Gorbachev praised the plan—"We are through with the unitary state and have developed a multiethnic state"; "We have found equilibrium and coherence between the sovereignty of the USSR and of the republics"—Yeltsin counterargued that "the center is trying to hold onto its unlimited power over the republics"; "The center is ignoring the declarations of sovereignty and trying to preserve its bureaucratic control over them." The two men were no less opposed on secession and sovereignty than they were on the plan's basic orientation. For Gorbachev, existing Soviet law applied as long as the treaty and new law had not been worked out, and, of course, this referred to the whole legal system that made the center paramount. For Yeltsin, this was already an outmoded conception; the republics should decide what laws and principles applied to them, and the center was obliged to defer to these manifestations of sovereignty. . . .

. . . Gorbachev's position was to argue every inch of the way for the urgency of the union treaty, for its priority over any institutional construction, for establishing beforehand the mode of functioning of a sovereign state, and then and only then, for working out plans for the common life of its constituent states. The plan of December 1990 merely intensified an already heated debate over whether to build the union from the center or from the republics.

In the attempt to find a way out of this dilemma, a second version of the plan was presented in March 1991. The two versions differed little; opposition to it was nearly as strong and the treaty remained stalled.

One feature of the two versions made them unacceptable to all the republics—the one concerning the right to secede. For the first time in Soviet constitutional history, the amendments of November 1990 did not mention the right to secede. On the other hand, they did describe the conditions under which the member states of the union could be expelled from it. They also defined a bifurcated union—one made up of states that were signatories to the treaty; the other, of those who had refused to sign it but could not withdraw from the union and who remained subject to the Soviet laws in effect. These restrictive arrangements, in complete opposition to the country's real development—the Baltics had already proclaimed their independence—immediately condemned the sovereign federal state, the end product of these two successive plans, to being a mere idle fancy.

A new attempt to advance the debate was the referendum of March 17. Consulted about its desire to preserve a union, the people came out broadly in favor of union, thus giving Gorbachev the necessary support for working on a treaty. No doubt the reference to public support had some weak points. Several republics, beginning with the Baltics and Georgia, had banned the referendum from being held on their territory. The results also were tainted by irregularities in Georgia, for example, where the army had "protected" the voting in minority areas and the electoral lists and the verification of the voters' identity were questionable. More seriously yet, various republics had added their own questions or modified the ones submitted for referendum. Thus, although the vote was in favor of the union in the Ukraine, the western part of the republic came out for secession, pure and simple.

Despite these results, negotiations about the treaty were reopened. . . . [They] ended on April 23 with the signing of the Novo-Ogaryovo Accord reuniting nine republics (Armenia and Moldavia had joined the three Baltic republics and Georgia in dissenting). This accord, concluded not on the basis of the (amended) plan of March 1991 but simply on the idea of the treaty's urgency, clearly posited that only the republics of the union would be signatories to the treaty. Decisive on this point, Yeltsin and his colleagues had beaten Gorbachev, who henceforth would at each stage of the debate have to make further concessions that even more greatly weakened the central government. . . .

On June 12, despite the efforts of the entire Soviet leadership, including Gorbachev, to forestall this event, Boris Yeltsin was elected by universal suffrage to the presidency of Russia. This suddenly jeopardized the future institutions of the union, particularly the presidency. The president-elect of Russia was less inclined than ever to put up with central structures that would hamper his activities. The problem of the center was even more drastically presented by Ukraine, where Leonid Kravchuk, chairman of the presidium of the Ukrainian legislature, refused to sign a treaty that put the union and the republics on the same level. He said that the only union possible was not "nine plus one" but a union agreed to by the new signatory republics. The union, a flexible alliance, had no need of an additional partner who must in no way be a sovereign state. Russia was determined to downgrade the status of the union, and the Ukraine very much wanted a union, but without a state as such. In these circumstances, the agreement of the seven other republics, which after all, were not absolutely unanimous, carried little weight.

Until March 11, 1990 (the date of Lithuania's independence), the Soviet Union was made up of fifteen republics. . . . The negotiations on the union treaty ended in a statement of the "nine plus one" type, and then in a group of seven republics more or less resigned to signing some sort of accord.

In August [1991], these interminable debates and the permanent revision of the plan seemed to have borne some fruit. A significantly modified plan making many concessions to the republics was about to be adopted, although not by everyone. The Ukraine would not announce its decision before the end of the year, when elections would be held, and Russia intended to get many more amendments. On the eve of the signing, Yeltsin did not hesitate to declare at a press conference that he and Nursultan Nazarbayev, the president of Kazakhstan, wanted substantial changes in the plan that would even further reduce the center's authority. In fact, besides Russia and Kazakhstan, whose accord was conditional, only three other republics were ready to take part in the signing on August 20—Uzbekistan, Tadzhikistan, and Kirghizia. The others (minus Ukraine) promised to sign in September, but the number of potential partners in the union was constantly diminishing.

Gorbachev's main goal, however, was the adoption of the treaty and the survival of even a badly injured union. This hope was dashed by the coup of August 19, which destroyed what remained of the USSR.

Considerable numbers of books about the coup have appeared in the USSR, and all suggest that one of the conspirators' main objectives was to act before the signing of the union treaty. In their minds, any attempt to check the erosion of the system and its structures had a preliminary condition—to maintain the general framework, that is, the USSR. On August 19 (the plan was to be signed on August 20), a compromise whose inadequacies the parties agreed to underscore was violently attacked by Lukyanov, president of the Supreme Soviet. The person later said to be the "ideologist of the coup" then strongly emphasized that the plan took no account of the critical remarks of the Supreme Soviet of the USSR, that it gave the republics untold opportunities to suspend the laws of the union on their territory, and that it was in the last analysis a bonfire fueling the "war of laws" and heating up the conflicts.

Meeting in a smaller group two days earlier, the USSR's ministerial cabinet expressed the same reservations. The central government's problems and constant postponements in signing a treaty and Russia's rise in power (which since Boris Yeltsin's election appeared to be the union's rival state, a rivalry symbolized by the installation of Yeltsin's offices in the Kremlin and the coexistence of two flags on the spot that since 1918 had been the center of Soviet power) were signs that henceforth the union's continued existence was questionable.

The coup's failure triggered a development that Gorbachev had long been trying to avoid. First, the coup prompted those who had already abandoned the USSR to consolidate their independence. On August 21, Latvia, which had adopted a plan for the restoration of de facto independence, voted for a declaration of total independence. Moldavia affirmed that it would proceed with its secession. In Estonia and Lithuania, the banning of the Communist party indicated the desire for the prompt elimination of all agencies that allowed the Soviet government to interfere in the life of the independent republics. Zviad Gamsakhurdia, the president of Georgia, appealed to the international community, emphasizing the urgency of recognizing the independence of the new state in order to avoid their overthrow by a successful coup. For the same reason, the government of Ukraine aggressively reverted to its favorite proposal—to set up national units and put Soviet troops stationed in the republic under Ukrainian control. In Armenia, the referendum of September 21, in which 94.3 percent of the electorate voted, resulted in 99.31 percent of the votes being in favor of immediate independence. Once the coup was over, it was important for all the republics to strengthen all means for resisting the central government and the union that would not quite expire. The idea was gaining ground that the union was dangerous and hence must cease to be.

Could a common plan be reactivated after the coup? On his return from his confinement in his vacation home in Foros, Gorbachev at first thought so. But reality—a legitimacy weakened by a coup whose perpetrators had been his closest collaborators, the suspicion of softness or complicity that dogged him, and the growth in prestige of those who mounted the resistance to the coup, with Yeltsin at their head—forced him to reconcile.

The new Soviet parliament organized after the coup met for the first time and grappled with the still-pending problem of the union. It was an odd parliament in which the governing structures were undefined. On September 2, 1991, the Congress of People's Deputies, meeting in special session, analyzed the failed coup and admitted that the whole organization of the hitherto existing state had vanished. Nursultan Nazarbayev, the president of Kazakhstan and now one of the country's leading players, then became the spokesperson for a radical political revolution. Noting that the constitution no longer existed, he proposed the setting up of transitional political structures in expectation of the much-discussed union treaty that would provide a definite spatial framework for the future system. Meanwhile, the congress, which did not want to commit total suicide, organized a remodeled assembly for concluding the union treaty as quickly as possible and, above all, setting up interim power structures in the State Council. This constitutional revolution led to a decisive role for the republics—made their presidents become equal to the president of the USSR in the State Council—and to the quasi-nullification of the central government.

In this context in which the republics' authority continued to be affirmed, an agreement was worked out for an economic community that Gorbachev still hoped would be the first stage of a union treaty. For many of the republics, however, it was the hoped-for end product of all the negotiations.

The agreement signed on October 18 was primarily the result of the efforts of Nazarbayev, president of Kazakhstan, and for several days, Alma-Ata, its capital, was the actual political center of the country. He endeavored to persuade his partners that because of a lack of agreement on a political future, first things came first and they had to find modes of a common economic organization. He finally managed to obtain agreement on a plan drafted by a team of specialists headed by Yavlinsky, the source of most of the plans proposed since the coup and whom the West considered an authority on economics.

Debated in Alma-Ata, the plan was finally signed in Moscow on October 18 by nine heads of state: eight for the republics and Gorbachev for the USSR. A close reading of this plan and comparison of it with the plan accepted on October 1 at Alma-Ata make clear the retreat of the center and the dynamism of the republics. Certainly, the signatories agreed, for want of a political union, to set up an economic community of "independent states, members or former members of the USSR." Nevertheless, with the exception of Armenia, the former members were careful not to take part in the preparation and not to sign the final document. In addition, Ukraine withdrew: "It has nothing to sign with the center," said the vice president of the national parliament, and at the last moment, Azerbaijan decided to stay outside the community. A few hours before the signing, Mikhail Gorbachev let it be understood that even the most independent states could join a community limited to economic matters, but he was soon disabused of this illusion. . . .

The economic community that succeeded the USSR on October 18 thus appeared to be a demonstration of good will, quite unlike a serious framework for organizing an economy based on lasting commitments. At this time, one could glimpse that beyond the plan, from which all concrete problems had been omitted or deferred to the signing of later "special agreements," the good will of the signatories had been primarily directed toward the industrialized countries and probably represented a wish to convince them that the former USSR remained an economic partner with which they could do business.

As watered down as this treaty of economic union was, it soon appeared too constrictive for the states concerned. Those who had not agreed to sign it issued declarations underscoring their refusal to join the community. And by adopting, on November 16, a plan of its own for immediate economic transformation, Russia, whose support would have given meaning to this last attempt to save the appearance of a common plan, dealt it a fatal blow.

On October 21, the first session of the postcoup variant of the remodeled Supreme Soviet was to assess the Soviet breakup. Despite the signing of the economic treaty three days before, only seven republics attended the session (there had been eight seventy-two hours earlier). As in Agatha Christie's well-known mystery *Ten Little Indians*, the former family of Soviet peoples lost a member with each passing day. And this handful even had to put off a number of discussions in the hope of seeing some representatives of Ukraine show up. But none did, except as observers, and this much-reduced assembly of republics listened with a certain skepticism to Gorbachev's announcement that the debate on the union treaty would be resumed on the basis of a new plan. The latest plan—containing twenty-three articles—represented an odd compromise between Gorbachev's still-present unionist hopes and the dismantlement of the center by the authorities of the Republic of Russia. Despite this plan's very general clauses and principles—adherence to democracy, human rights, the UN charter, and so forth—articles one to eight defined the basis of the union by largely restoring the federation on the earlier model—with a common constitution, a president elected by universal suffrage, a large area of common interest. The Union of Sovereign States (with unchanged initials) wished to be a sovereign state, subject to international law, and the successor to the old USSR. These claims did not satisfy most of the states called on to join it. . . .

The question of the union, which continues to agitate what was the center, has for the most part been overtaken by two partially connected problems: first, that of the parallel emancipation of *both* Russia and Ukraine, and next, that of the relations between them and, more generally, Russia's relations to the other republics.

Ukraine, long cautious in its aspirations for independence, suddenly and quickly stated some extreme demands. For a long time, the Soviet government counted on the soothing certitude that the complexity of this republic, its links to the union's authority—the Ukrainians had provided it with a considerable proportion of its bureaucrats and officers, and they also have a seat at the UN, a privilege shared with Belarus but not with Russia—and the presence of a large Slavic community would neutralize many of the temptations of independence. Certainly, its division into three distinct regions—western Ukraine, belatedly Sovietized and fervently Catholic even though it was forcibly annexed to Soviet orthodoxy after 1945; eastern Ukraine, widely subject to the pressures of Russification; and the industrial Ukraine, populated by Russians—was long a source of weakness for the nationalist movements. But recent events had somewhat modified these divisions. Western Ukraine spearheaded the nationalist movement. The referendum of March 17, 1991, and even more, the coup, encouraged the rapprochement between two Ukraines, eastern and western, and the radicalization of their demands. To avoid being overwhelmed, Leonid Kravchuk, the president of the Ukrainian Supreme Soviet—a product of the Communist party who refused to leave it—made the nationalist demands his own: the setting up of a totally responsible state with complete economic and military independence. . . .

Although the coup stepped up a widespread demand for Ukraine's independence, it is noteworthy that even before August 19, Leonid Kravchuk gave all his political positions a virulent nationalist twist. Addressing the Ukrainians in celebration of the first anniversary of the declaration of sovereignty, described by the Ukrainian press as the "day of independence" (*Pravda Ukrainy*, July 14, 1991), Kravchuk painted a dramatic picture of the price Ukraine had paid for its attachment to Russia. Concerning the prerevolutionary past he said, "For us, as for other people, moreover, the time [that of union with Russia] was not a time for developing our national culture, material and spiritual." Condemning this period and the tragic consequences for Ukraine of its inclusion in the USSR, Kravchuk in passing hailed the memory of all the Ukrainians who had attempted to advance the cause of a national state. Thus the communist Kravchuk found himself in the same camp as the fiercest anticommunists in Ukraine.

This psychological evolution was confirmed by the referendum on Ukraine's independence on December 1, 1991, which accompanied the election by universal suffrage of the republic's president. Nearly 80 percent of the electorate turned out, which meant that all or nearly all the Ukrainian and Russian voters massively supported independence. . . .

Ukraine was not the only republic worried about the rise of Russia. Kazakhstan, where nearly 7 million Russians lived, also heard Boris Yeltsin's warning to the aspirants for independence and his insistence on the frontiers and Russian-populated areas that he could claim. If all the former components of the union could be separated, Russia could incorporate the prosperous northern part of Kazakhstan, with its concentration of Russians. This implicit threat helps explain why Nursultan Nazarbayev, the president of Kazakhstan, advocated that the union be maintained in any form whatever and worked so energetically to save some elements of the former USSR. . . .

In less than two years, communism collapsed everywhere, without the conquerors being tempted to spill blood. They are to be lauded for their maturity and level-headedness. For all that, within the borders of what used to be the USSR, blood is being shed and flashpoints are multiplying. The causes of this trend are the national communities, not social groups or individuals. The heirs of Marx, who so disputed the importance of the national problem, suddenly discovered, after rejecting Marxism, that this is the most serious obstacle they face. They now know that the future of democracy depends on their responses to the aspirations or rebellions of the national groups. No issue is more urgent and decisive in what was the USSR and the mythical "historical community of a new type, the Soviet people, fruit of the friendship of peoples" than the one posed by these same people. The nation, which Lenin thought he had exorcised, has returned; it is wreaking vengeance for being ignored. It has proved this by destroying communism, for its collapse came about through the rebellion of the nations.

The End of the USSR

As the various Soviet republics, including the Russian Federation, asserted their independence following the August coup, the government of the Soviet Union under Gorbachev was reduced to a mere shadow. Early in December 1991, President Yeltsin met with presidents Leonid Kravchuk of Ukraine and Stanislas Shushkevich of Belarus, near the latter's capital of Minsk, and formally liquidated the USSR in favor of an amorphous "Commonwealth of Independent States." Gorbachev had no choice but to resign his presidency and allow the union to pass into history.

Statement by the Heads of State of the Republic of Belarus, the Russian SFSR, and Ukraine

We, the leaders of the Republic of Belarus, the RSFSR and Ukraine,

—noting that the talks on the drafting of a new Union Treaty have reached an impasse and that the objective process of the secession of republics from the USSR and the formation of independent states has become a real fact;

From "Statements and Agreements of the Heads of State of the Republic of Belarus, the Russian Federation, and Ukraine," *Izvestiya*, Dec. 9, 1991; Gorbachev, Speech on Central Television, December 25, 1991, *Rossiiskaya Gazeta*, December 26, 1991. English translations in *The Current Digest of the Soviet Press*, vol. 43, no. 49, pp. 10–11, and no. 52, pp. 1, 3. Translation Copyright © 1992 by *The Current Digest of the Soviet Press*, published weekly at Columbus, Ohio. Reprinted by permission of *The Current Digest of the Soviet Press*.

—stating that the shortsighted policy of the center has led to a profound economic and political crisis, the collapse of production and a catastrophic decline in the living standard for virtually all strata of society;

—taking into consideration the increase in social tension in many regions of the former USSR, which has led to conflicts between nationalities with numerous human casualties;

—aware of our responsibility to our peoples and the world community and of the urgent need for the practical implementation of political and economic reforms, hereby declare the formation of a Commonwealth of Independent States, on which the parties signed an Agreement on Dec. 8, 1991.

The Commonwealth of Independent States, consisting of the Republic of Belarus, the RSFSR and Ukraine, is open for accession by all member-states of the former USSR, as well as for other states that share the goals and principles of this Agreement.

The member-states of the Commonwealth intend to pursue a course aimed at strengthening international peace and security. They guarantee the fulfillment of international obligations stemming from the treaties and agreements of the former USSR and ensure unified control over nuclear weapons and their nonproliferation.

Agreement on the Creation of a Commonwealth of Independent States

We, the Republic of Belarus, the Russian Federation (RSFSR) and Ukraine, as founder-states of the USSR and signatories to the Union Treaty of 1922, hereinafter called the High Contracting Parties, state that the USSR as a subject of international law and geopolitical reality is terminating its existence.

Based on the historic community of our peoples and the ties that have developed among them, and considering the bilateral treaties concluded between the High Contracting Parties,

seeking to build democratic states based on the rule of law,

intending to develop our relations on the basis of mutual recognition of and respect for state sovereignty, the inalienable right of self-determination, the principles of equality and noninterference in internal affairs, the renunciation of the use of force and economic or any other means of pressure, the settlement of disputed problems through conciliation, and other generally recognized principles and norms of international law,

considering that the further development and strengthening of relations of friendship, good-neighborliness and mutually advantageous cooperation among our states corresponds to the fundamental national interests of their peoples and serves the cause of peace and security,

confirming our commitment to the goals and principles of the United Nations Charter, the Helsinki Final Act and other documents of the Conference on Security and Cooperation in Europe,

pledging to observe generally recognized international norms on human rights and the rights of peoples,

have agreed on the following:

Art. 1. The High Contracting Parties are founding a Commonwealth of Independent States.

Art. 2. The High Contracting Parties guarantee equal rights and liberties to their citizens, regardless of nationality or other differences. Each of the High Contracting Parties guarantees to the citizens of other Parties, as well as to stateless individuals living on its territory, regardless of nationality or other differences, civil, political, social, economic and cultural rights and liberties in accordance with generally recognized norms of human rights.

Art. 3. The High Contracting Parties, wishing to promote the expression, preservation and development of the distinctive ethnic, cultural, linguistic and religious features of the national minorities living on their territories and of existing unique ethnocultural regions, take them under their protection.

Art. 4. The High Contracting Parties will develop equal and mutually advantageous cooperation among their peoples and states in the fields of politics, economics, culture, education, public health, environmental protection, science and trade and in humanitarian and other fields, will further the broad exchange of information, and will observe mutual obligations conscientiously and unswervingly.

The Parties consider it necessary to conclude agreements on cooperation in the indicated fields.

Art. 5. The High Contracting Parties recognize and respect one another's territorial integrity and the inviolability of existing borders in the framework of the Commonwealth.

They guarantee open borders and freedom of movement for citizens and freedom for the transfer of information within the framework of the Commonwealth.

Art. 6. The member-states of the Commonwealth will cooperate in ensuring international peace and security and in implementing effective measures for reducing weapons and military spending. They are striving for the elimination of all nuclear weapons and general and complete disarmament under strict international control.

The Parties will respect one another's endeavors to achieve the status of nuclear-weapon-free zones and neutral states.

The member-states of the Commonwealth will preserve and support a common military-strategic space under a joint command, including unified control over nuclear weapons, the procedure for which will be regulated by a special agreement.

They also jointly guarantee the necessary conditions for the stationing, functioning, and material and social support of the strategic armed forces. The Parties pledge to conduct a coordinated policy on questions of the social protection of and pensions for servicemen and their families.

Art. 7. The High Contracting Parties recognize that the sphere of their joint activity, conducted on an equal basis through the common coordinating institutions of the Commonwealth, includes:

—the coordination of foreign-policy activity;

—cooperation in the formation and development of a common economic space and of all-European and Eurasian markets, and in the field of customs policy;

—cooperation in the development of transportation and communications systems;

—cooperation in the field of environmental protection, and participation in the creation of an all-encompassing international system of ecological security;

—questions of migration policy;

—the struggle against organized crime.

Art. 8. The Parties recognize the planetary nature of the Chernobyl catastrophe and pledge to unite and coordinate their efforts to minimize and overcome its consequences.

They have agreed to conclude a special agreement for this purpose, one that takes into consideration the gravity of the consequences of the catastrophe.

Art. 9. Disputes concerning the interpretation and application of the norms of this Agreement are to be resolved through negotiations between the appropriate agencies, and if necessary at the level of heads of state and government.

Art. 10. Each of the High Contracting Parties reserves the right to suspend this Agreement or individual articles of it after notifying the signatories to the Agreement one year in advance.

The provisions of this Agreement may be added to or changed by mutual agreement of the High Contracting Parties.

Art. 11. From the moment this Agreement is signed, the norms of third states, including the former USSR, may not be applied on the territory of the states signing the Agreement.

Art. 12. The High Contracting Parties guarantee the fulfillment of their international obligations stemming from the treaties and agreements of the former USSR.

Art. 13. This Agreement does not affect the obligations of the High Contracting Parties with respect to third states.

This Agreement is open for accession by all member-states of the former USSR, as well as for other states that share the goals and principles of this Agreement.

Art. 14. The official location of the Commonwealth's coordinating agencies is the city of Minsk.

The activity of agencies of the former USSR on the territory of the member-states of the Commonwealth is terminated.

Gorbachev's Speech on Central Television

Dear compatriots! Fellow citizens! Due to the situation that has taken shape as a result of the formation of the Commonwealth of Independent States, I am ceasing my activity in the post of President of the USSR. I am making this decision out of considerations of principle.

I have firmly advocated the independence of peoples and the sovereignty of republics. But at the same time I have favored the preservation of the Union state and the integrity of the country.

Events have taken a different path. A policy line aimed at dismembering the country and disuniting the state has prevailed, something that I cannot agree with.

Even after the Alma-Ata meeting and the decisions adopted there, my position on this score has not changed.

Moreover, I am convinced that decisions of such scope should have been adopted on the basis of the free expression of the people's will.

Nevertheless, I will do everything in my power to ensure that the agreements signed there lead to real concord in society, make it easier to get out of the crisis and facilitate the process of reform.

Speaking to you for the last time as President of the USSR, I consider it necessary to express my assessment of the path traversed since 1985. Especially since there are a good many contradictory, superficial and unobjective opinions on this score.

Fate ordained that when I became head of state it was already clear that things were not going well in the country. We have a great deal of everything—land, petroleum, gas and other natural resources—and God has endowed us with intelligence and talent, too, but we live much worse than people in the developed countries do, and we are lagging further and further behind them.

The reason was evident—society was suffocating in the grip of the command-bureaucratic system. Doomed to serve ideology and to bear the terrible burden of the arms race, it had been pushed to the limit of what was possible.

All attempts at partial reforms—and there were a good many of them—failed, one after the other. The country had lost direction. It was impossible to go on living that way. Everything had to be changed fundamentally.

That is why I have never once regretted that I did not take advantage of the position of General Secretary just to "reign" for a few years. I would have considered that irresponsible and immoral.

I realized that to begin reforms on such a scale and in such a society as ours was an extremely difficult and even risky endeavor.

But even today I am convinced of the historical correctness of the democratic reforms that were begun in the spring of 1985.

The process of renewing the country and of fundamental changes in the world community proved to be much more complex than could have been surmised. However, what has been accomplished should be appraised on its merits.

Society has received freedom and has been emancipated politically and spiritually. This is the most important gain, one that we have not yet become fully aware of, and for this reason we have not yet learned to make use of freedom.

Nevertheless, work of historic significance has been done:

—The totalitarian system, which for a long time deprived the country of the opportunity to become prosperous and flourishing, has been eliminated.

—A breakthrough has been achieved in the area of democratic transformations. Free elections, freedom of the press, religious freedoms, representative bodies of power and a multiparty system have become a reality. Human rights have been recognized as the highest principle.

—Movement toward a mixed economy has begun, and the equality of all forms of ownership is being established. Within the framework of a land reform, the peasantry has begun to revive, private farming has appeared, and millions of hectares of land are being given to rural and urban people. The economic freedom of the producer has been legalized, and entrepreneurship, the formation of joint-stock companies and privatization have begun to gather momentum.

—In turning the economy toward a market, it is important to remember that this is being done for the sake of human beings. In this difficult time, everything possible must be done for their social protection, and this applies especially to old people and children.

We are living in a new world:

—An end has been put to the cold war, and the arms race and the insane militarization of the country, which disfigured our economy and the public consciousness and morals, have been halted. The threat of a world war has been removed.

I want to emphasize once again that, for my part, during the transitional period I did everything I could to preserve reliable control over nuclear weapons.

—We opened up to the world and renounced interference in the affairs of others and the use of troops outside the country's borders. And in response we received trust, solidarity and respect.

—We have become one of the main bulwarks in the reorganization of present-day civilization on peaceful, democratic principles.

—Peoples and nations have received real freedom in choosing the path of their self-determination. Searches for democratic reforms in the multinational state led us to the threshold of concluding a new Union Treaty.

All these changes required enormous effort and took place in an acute struggle, with mounting resistance from old, obsolete and reactionary forces—both the former Party-state structures and the economic apparatus—and also from our habits, ideological prejudices, and a leveling and parasitic mentality. The changes ran up against our intolerance, low level of political sophistication and fear of change.

For this reason, we lost a great deal of time. The old system collapsed before a new one had time to start working. And the crisis in society became even more exacerbated.

I know about the dissatisfaction with the present grave situation and about the sharp criticism that is being made of the authorities at all levels, and of my personal activity. But I would like to emphasize once again: Fundamental changes in such an enormous country, and one with such a legacy, could not proceed painlessly or without difficulties and upheavals.

The August putsch brought the general crisis to the breaking point. The most disastrous aspect of this crisis was the disintegration of the state system. Today I am alarmed by our people's losing their citizenship in a great country—the consequences may prove to be very grave for everyone.

It seems vitally important to me to preserve the democratic gains of the past few years. They were achieved through suffering throughout our history and our tragic experience. Under no circumstances and on no pretext can they be given up. Otherwise, all hopes for something better will be buried.

I am saying all this honestly and straightforwardly. This is my moral duty.

Today I want to express my gratitude to all citizens who supported the policy of renewing the country and joined in the implementation of democratic reforms.

I am grateful to the state, political and public figures and the millions of people abroad who understood our plans, supported them, met us halfway, and embarked on sincere cooperation with us.

I am leaving my post with a feeling of anxiety. But also with hope and with faith in you, in your wisdom and strength of spirit. We are the heirs to a great civilization, and its rebirth into a new, up-to-date and fitting life now depends on each and every one of us.

I want to thank from the bottom of my heart those who during these years stood with me for a right and good cause. Certainly some mistakes could have been avoided, and many things could have been done better. But I am sure that sooner or later our common efforts will bear fruit and our peoples will live in a prosperous and democratic society.

I wish all of you the very best.

After the August Coup: Gorbachev returns from house arrest in the Crimea, August 21, 1991. (AP/Wide World Photos)

V Reflections

Charles H. Fairbanks

Revolutionary
Self-Destruction

Setting himself off from most other commentators on perestroika, Charles Fairbanks of the Johns Hopkins University School of Advanced International Studies in Washington, D.C., argues that the Gorbachev revolution began as an attempt to revive the theoretical idealism of communism, against the stagnation and corruption of the Brezhnev era. In his view, the reformers gradually became more radical and ended by destroying the system they were trying to reform.

From Charles H. Fairbanks, Jr., "The Nature of the Beast," *The National Interest*, spring 1993, pp. 46–56. Copyright © 1993 by *The National Interest*. Reprinted by permission of *The National Interest*.

In the last eight years Mikhail Gorbachev. . . . launched a thrilling project of human renewal; but the empire he destroyed was his own. In these years we saw Bolshevism collect the last remnants of its once titanic energies to make itself young again, only to achieve its final extinction.

We saw perestroika as reform, reform by Westernization. But Gorbachev said with utter sincerity, "perestroika is a revolution." In the Soviet Union, revolutionary change could only come from above. In fact, Gorbachev's was, at a minimum, the fourth imposed revolution in Soviet history: first, the October revolution, then Stalin's "Second Revolution," then Khrushchev's de-Stalinization, and finally perestroika. Outside the Soviet Union, the most obvious case of a revolution within the revolution is, of course, Mao Tse-tung's Great Proletarian Cultural Revolution in China, and that provides the best analogy for what Gorbachev did.

The former Politburo member and architect of perestroika, Aleksandr Yakovlev, has eloquently portrayed the constant transformations characteristic of Soviet history before Gorbachev:

> . . . *Marxism was not anything other than a pseudoscientific neo-religion . . . subordinated to the interests and caprices of a monopolistic, absolutist power, and by it frequently and arbitrarily reshaped. Tens of times it raised up, and then trampled in the mud its own gods, prophets and apostles. . . .*

Looking back, one is led to ask: What connection is there between the original Bolshevik revolutionary project and the instability of Soviet politics? . . . And was perestroika directly linked in any way to the earlier extremist phases of Soviet politics? . . .

The evolution of Gorbachev's goals—from the perfection of the regime by "acceleration" in 1985, to the final destruction of the regime in 1991—gives some support to the notion of a revolutionary spirit whose content is mainly negation. What Gorbachev seems to have wanted, more than any particular social or economic order, was a display of energy, of enthusiasm, a change in people.

But to change people is to negate the way people now are. The energy Gorbachev wanted was energy against the past and the present. With the decay of formal ideology, Gorbachev's revolutionary drive, still strong, expressed itself in essentially negative terms, without a fixed content or goal. . . .

. . . One of the elements that produced the collapse of communism in the eighties was the return, in Gorbachev, of the enduring revolutionary desire to re-structure society. Operating in conditions of ideological exhaustion and economic stagnation, the resulting upheaval destroyed the system rather than reformed it. In this sense, the system, sick for many other reasons, finally died by suicide—from an overdose of "revolutionary spirit." And, in retrospect, the original Bolshevik project contained within it the causes of its own destruction, which helps to explain the system's lifespan of only seventy-four years, almost without precedent in history.

Is there, however, any concrete historical link between perestroika and the revolutionary Soviet past? For us, perestroika was a surprise, entirely new. Those in the West who sought its roots looked to Bukharin and to NEP [New Economic Policy]. But the slogans of perestroika do not come from NEP but from a later and less benign episode in Soviet history. . . . It is an ordinary Russian word, but as a common political slogan it was born of Stalin's Second Revolution; the very concept of re-structuring belongs with the communist desire to transform and reorder society. The term *perestroika* is a particular marker of the rhetoric of A. A. Zhdanov,[1] the standard-bearer of ideologically rigorous, mobilizational, "left" Stalinism. . . .

I now wish to raise the possibility that there may indeed be a link between Zhdanov and the perestroika period, in the shape of three men: Otto Kuusinen, Yuri Andropov, Aleksei Rumyantsev. To begin with the most important of these figures, Andropov owed his career to the extremism of the Great Terror, which had heaved him up, in 1938, to the position of First Secretary of the Yaroslavl Komsomol, at the ripe age of twenty-four. He and Kuusinen clearly belonged to the group around Zhdanov, and advocated Zhdanovite or left-Stalinist positions.

In 1949–50 the followers of Zhdanov were purged, often killed, in the "Leningrad Case." It may not be accidental, as the

[1] Andrei Zhdanov, Politburo member and ideological chief under Stalin, died in 1948.—Ed.

old Soviet phrase has it, that one of the provincial Komsomol leaders dismissed in the Leningrad case because of their Zhdanovite patrons was Yegor Ligachev, later to become best known in the West as Gorbachev's rival and opponent, though in the early stage he was, with Gorbachev and Ryzhkov, one of the three principal creators of perestroika. . . .

Under Khrushchev during the fifties and sixties, Kuusinen organized first a "collective" for writing a textbook, then, with Andropov, an editorial staff for the international communist journal *Problems of Peace and Socialism* in Prague, with [Alexei] Rumyantsev as the editor, and finally a Group of Consultants in the Central Committee staff. These groups were organized from intellectuals who turned out to be very influential in the course of perestroika: Burlatsky, Arbatov, Shakhnazarov, Chernyayev, Gerasimov, Brutents, Bovin, Bogomolov, and others. Georgi Arbatov has spoken of the way in which his friends were "indebted to these people [Kuusinen and Andropov] as *teachers*" [emphasis added]. As the legitimacy of the Soviet system sagged, these intellectuals began to mix the Zhdanovite or left-communist ideas inbibed from Andropov and Kuusinen with other ideas which were fundamentally Western. The staff of *Problems of Peace and Socialism*, under the aegis of Rumyantsev, was an important crucible for this potentially explosive mixture, because these intellectuals were living in Prague and talking to Czech intellectuals during the gestation of the Prague Spring. As time went on, the intellectuals, who continued to be linked with Andropov (Kuusinen having died in 1964), became far more radical than he was. At the end of Brezhnev's life, Andropov challenged him and followed him as general secretary. Andropov, himself dying, possessed police power and a group of intellectual reformers of ideology. He needed a political leader of stature to head the reformist group after him; he chose Gorbachev.

When Andropov died in 1984, this entire heritage came into the hands of Gorbachev and those who influenced him as he rapidly changed his views: Yakovlev and the intellectuals who had been affected by the Prague Spring. Many of these intellectuals now became key advisers and speechwriters to Gorbachev, and propagandists of perestroika after 1985. Thus there may have been a historical link between radical Stalinism and perestroika. . . .

The outcome of this long, complex evolution was, in the eighties, a dwindling group of reformers led by Gorbachev who were pursuing more and more extreme changes as time went on. Or, to put it in a way that brings out the paradox, they were pursuing a less and less communist agenda in a more and more communist way. This evolution is well illustrated by Gorbachev's change of view about the market. During the summer of 1990 Gorbachev apparently began to see in the market not the loathsome face of alienation, as Marx did, but a magic that could transfigure life, creating a new man. . . .

We had thought that the path to reform in the Soviet system lay in the leaders' abandonment of the Utopian hope for a New Man. We believed they had abandoned it. But here we see a Gorbachev who, after all the disappointments since 1985, still believed in the imminent arrival of the New Man. The differences between him and Soviet leaders of the movement's earlier and most Utopian phase are these: not communism, but the market, will create the New Man. And the prophet of the new man is not Marx, but Milton Friedman.[2]

It is impossible to understand the collapse of Soviet communism without appreciating the role of ideas and convictions in history. One of the mistakes we made about the Soviet Union was our facile confidence that the more and more far-reaching compromise of its most public claims by the Communist regime would never have any practical consequences, either in loss of popular support or in any Communist attempt to reclaim their principles. In fact, it was the contradiction between the regime's ostensible principles and the sordid reality of its performance that eroded most of its popular support. Late in the day, a small but powerful part of the Communist elite embarked upon a desperate attempt to reverse things by making the system live up to what they understood to be its ideals. But this attempt only had the effect of making the contradiction between ideals and reality more apparent, particularly after glasnost began revealing the atrocious crimes of the Communist past. Before long, the Communist system was irretrievably shattered. It had been destroyed, in large part because of the contradiction between ideals and reality, and almost without a shot being fired. . . .

[2] Friedman is the leader of the "Chicago school" of free-market economics.—Ed.

. . . The collapse of the Soviet experiment after seventy years shows that the Soviet state was exceptional. The attempted restoration of Communist principles in the Soviet Union ended in the final overthrow of those principles. Such is the irony of history. Communism's death can be understood, in large part, as an accidental overdose of its own medicine. . . .

. . . It was . . . a surprise to find the "secret police" intimately involved in the origins of perestroika. The campaign against the "era of stagnation" was opened by Yuri Andropov, chairman of the KGB, who used the organization to blackmail and weaken the Brezhnevite faction in the leadership, and to secure the most powerful position in the country first for himself and then (after the brief Chernenko period) for his chosen heir, Mikhail Gorbachev. As Raisa Gorbachev told Jeane Kirkpatrick, "We owe everything to Yuri Vladimirovich." The subsequent chiefs of the KGB, Chebrikov and Kriuchkov (who had served with Andropov in Hungary), were important allies of Gorbachev during key periods in the radicalization of perestroika, although both broke with him subsequently. Gorbachev's last chairman of the KGB, Vadim Bakatin, has testified that "Gorbachev . . . saw in the KGB not so much a danger to his transformations, as a support for them." Many other supporters of reformism had served in the KGB/ MVD (Shevardnadze as Minister in Georgia) or had close KGB/ MVD connections (e.g., Vlasov, Pugo, Bakatin, Primakov).

It was also a surprise to find militant reformers within the ideological specialization of the Party apparatus and the closely connected part of the central apparat that dealt with the international communist movement. . . .

It is also interesting to take a brief, impressionistic glance at the social origins of the people who made perestroika. In any informal survey of this group's biographies, one is struck by the extent of their connections with the regime's aristocracy. The economists Shmelyov (who married Khrushchev's daughter) and Shatalin (son of a Central Committee inspector and nephew of a Central Committee Secretary, who sat in Malenkov's ample lap as a child) are only extreme cases. There are many children of Old Bolsheviks—Burlatsky, Yegor Yakovlev, Len Karpinsky are examples. There are a number of children of high officials in the security police: Yegor Yakovlev, the son of an NKVD[3] general, Deputy Chairman of the Ukrainian Cheka; Yavlinsky, son of the head of the Moscow KGB; Arbatov, son of a high NKVD operative in Germany and Japan.

In this company, Boris Yeltsin seems unusual in being the child of peasants. In fact, even the supporters of radical reformism who do come from relatively modest origins seem to come disproportionately from the Soviet system's equivalent of the rural gentry: from the families of the strong supporters of communism in the 1920s and 1930s countryside (a definite minority at the time), including collective farm chairmen, the officials of machine tractor stations, editors of rural newspapers, school teachers, etc. . . .

Thus perestroika was in an important sense a movement of an elite, an aristocratic revolution. In this respect it contrasts with most revolutions, like the French, which tend to have been led by members of disadvantaged classes and groups that had been kept out of political power and often isolated from the national tradition, though given enough education and status to contend for power. The USSR after Stalin was full of people of this latter kind: the upwardly mobile sons of peasants or workers who had received educations in engineering, agronomy, or veterinary medicine before moving into full-time party work. It is reasonable to suspect that the majority of these people were technicians or careerists rather than idealist communists. By the reign of Brezhnev they were ruling the country, and Brezhnev himself is a perfect example of them. They provided the environment for the truly fantastic corruption that gripped the country in the seventies.

The key point is that, although by a strange paradox they ruled it, these people were rather isolated from the "high" tradition of their own regime, which was highly theoretical and very Westernizing. A wonderful vignette in Fedor Burlatsky's memoirs conveys the relationship of this social group to "high" Marxism-Leninism. Burlatsky was expounding to Brezhnev the theoretical flaws of a re-Stalinizing memorandum from Brezhnev's enemy Shelepin.

[3] NKVD: People's Commissariat of Internal Affairs, predecessor of the KGB.—Ed.

I began to expound our position to Brezhnev point by point. The more I explained, the more his face changed. It began to look tense and drawn until we realized, to our horror, that Leonid Ilyich had hardly understood a word. I brought my fountain of eloquence to a halt and he said with winning sincerity, "It's hard for me to grasp all this. On the whole, to be honest, this isn't my area. My strong point is organization and psychology," and he made vague circular motions with his fingers spread wide open.

We can now refine our thesis. The perestroika revolution was a revolution begun not by the deprived but by the owners and operators of the Soviet system and their children. It was also, on the whole, a revolution of those who in their youth still cherished the "high" Soviet tradition (Marxist-Leninist ideals) in some sense, against those who actually held political power during the 1970s but represented Marxist-Leninist principles only in a vastly simplified and debased way. In a certain sense, perestroika began as an attempt to take back the revolution from the bumpkins who had stolen it.

The nature of Bolshevik political culture—in particular, the fact that the Soviet tradition was one of periodic revolution from above—goes a long way toward explaining why the Soviet elite was willing to gamble on perestroika. Soviet "aristocrats" were particularly attracted, as we have seen, to a change that promised to somehow bring back their ideals and their power. But why did the Brezhnev-style careerists give up power? After all, the events of 1990–91, culminating in the abortive coup, showed that this category comprised the bulk of the ruling elite.

The ruling elite of the Soviet Union—widely thought before the event to be single-mindedly and ruthlessly power oriented—voted to give up its power. To begin with, the Politburo and Central Committee elected the reformers Andropov and Gorbachev as leaders. Then, at the Twenty-seventh Congress in March 1986, the Party approved Gorbachev's program of moderate reforms. The following year, at its January 1987 meeting, the Central Committee voted unanimously for Gorbachev's startling turn to democratization. At the Nineteenth Conference in the summer of 1988 and following meetings, the Party voted to create an essentially new structure of elected assemblies that would take over much of the party's governing responsibilities, and to elect those assemblies in multi-candidate elections, which when held in 1989 and 1990 fatally wounded the Party's legitimacy. The most decisive step of all was taken in February 1990, when the CC voted for Gorbachev's proposal to end its monopoly of power, agreeing in principle to a multi-party system, and to end its opposition to private property, thus abolishing the core of Leninism and the core of Marxism in one three-day meeting. Having undermined its own legitimacy at the February Plenum, the Party voted at its Twenty-eighth (and last) Congress in July 1990 to destroy itself organizationally by giving up the Party's supervision of the government, by removing all government officials (except Gorbachev) from the Politburo, and by filling that body with nonentities. Well before this, the glasnost' campaign had already substantially relinquished Party control over ideas, a crucial form of power in Bolshevik eyes.

The Bolshevik tradition of democratic centralism explains the suicide of the quintessential Bolshevik institution, the Party. The Communist Party of the Soviet Union was an organization that attained and maintained its power through the doctrine of democratic centralism, that is, by lower organizations' disciplined execution of decisions from real decision-making bodies at the top, the CC Secretariat, CC departments, and the Politburo. Democratic centralism still operated, at the crucial February 1990 meeting, to make the CC accept the Politburo's policy handed down from above. As one CC member, Boris Yeltsin, reported: ". . . there is still some kind of fear, which does not permit them to raise their hands when the members of the Politburo are sitting there on stage." . . .

In a sense, the Politburo was less an institution that conferred on its officeholders certain specified powers, than a name, like that of the Japanese emperor, that was used to legitimize the exercise of power on different issues by different very small groups within the Politburo. This arrangement was ideally suited to facilitate the application of controlled pressures from outside the "legitimate" authority, such as the pressures from certain provincial party secretaries and from the KGB that seemed to have played a role in Gorbachev's election, pressures from holders of *power*, legitimate or illegitimate. The most powerful had ready-made an institution that was used every week to give "constitutional" sanction to decisions made elsewhere. . . .

The enormous power of Gorbachev goes far to explain why the elite gave up power, contrary to our expectations. They gave up power because of their own reformism and because of fear of the public, but most of all because Gorbachev forced them to, by applying and appealing to the doctrine and practice of democratic centralism.

The dramatic changes in the Soviet Union were not only or mainly the result of Westernization or modernization. They were even more the product of communism's own traditions and habits. It was democratic centralism that ultimately enabled Gorbachev to sway the Politburo, enabled the Politburo to control the Central Committee, finally enabled the Central Committee to control the vote of the Twenty-eighth Congress of the Party. Democratic centralism was the lever by which one man toppled the towering edifice of Soviet power. Gorbachev, the leader of the country's Communists, forced his own movement to commit suicide, as Jim Jones forced the other members of the People's Temple to drink poisoned Kool-Aid. The Communist Party lost its power in a Soviet Jonestown.

The Bolshevik tradition inspired Gorbachev. The institutions and customs of democratic centralism empowered him. With that inspiration, and that power, he destroyed the state that he commanded.

Thomas F. Remington

Reform or Revolution?

Was the collapse of communism a reform or a revolution? And was it driven from the top by political leadership or from below by forces

From Thomas F. Remington, "Reform, Revolution, and Regime Transition," in *Dismantling Communism: Common Causes and Regional Variations*, Gilbert Rozman, ed., pp. 121–124, 126–128, 133–136, 138–140, 148–149. Copyright © 1992 by the Woodrow Wilson International Center for Scholars. Reprinted by permission of the publisher.

of social change? Thomas Remington, professor of political science at Emory University in Atlanta, examines various theories and concludes that politics and society interact, and that the prospects for democratic reform rather than destructive revolution depend on the maturity of different societies.

How do regimes cross the threshold from communism to democracy? The extraordinary transformation of world politics in the late 1980s and early 1990s poses major questions about the circumstances under which some communist systems collapse and give way to successor regimes, while others persist in stubborn isolation. Why do some regimes undergo crisis only to emerge under a new dictatorship and others yield to democratic institutions? Are there any centripetal forces short of force majeur that can check the powerful urge of ethno-national communities to secede under conditions of freedom? The Soviet case—or rather, cases—may shed light on these questions. Although the region continues to change profoundly and rapidly, the botched coup d'état of August 1991 and its revolutionary aftermath served as a catalyst for events that had been waiting to happen: the dissolution of the former union and its replacement by fifteen independent nation-states groping for new forms of relationships among themselves.

In this [essay] I shall discuss the relationship of reform to revolution in communist systems, with particular reference to the transformation of Soviet politics. By "reform" I mean changes in policy and authority relations that leave the two essential features of communist rule intact: the leading role of the single party and state ownership of the major means of production. "Revolution," on the other hand, is so sweeping a change in the structure of power and property that the communist regime itself surrenders. It is, therefore, equivalent to the notion of regime transition.

My argument, briefly, is as follows. Under Mikhail Gorbachev the communist leadership in the Soviet Union initiated reforms that liberalized political life. The government tolerated the expression of demands and grievances that had been generated by the long-term processes of social and economic change. These include a peculiar and explosive combination of modernization and system decay. In turn, liberalization—specifically glasnost and demokratizatsiia—led to a moblization of popular demands for deeper change. The outcome of the challenge to the ruling elite depended on the interaction of three factors: whether leaders were willing to share power with the opposition, the organization of popular social movements, and the referent national community. Since associational life outside the state is a good deal stronger at subcentral levels than across the union as a whole, the most intense confrontation between state and society has occurred at the level of the union republics and subrepublican jurisdictions, where the outcomes have been very diverse in their regime character, but alike in their aspiration for national independence. In turn, the struggle over republican rights prompted a search for a new framework for the union. Agreement on a radically decentralizing union treaty was followed by a counterreaction (a brief and unsuccessful putsch), which was followed by the rapid dissolution of nearly all political bonds uniting the republics in a union. Agreement between Yeltsin and President Kravchuk of Ukraine in December 1991 produced a framework for a new form of association falling well short of statehood but preserving unified control of the Soviet strategic arsenal.

The extraordinary events in the communist world in the late 1980s and early 1990s can be understood, in a Hegelian spirit, as the transformation of quantity into quality. That is, the consequences of deep reform spilled out into political change that could not be contained within the existing Communist party-state system. In China the regime had not tolerated a sufficient political liberalization to allow the forces of popular opposition to raise the "costs of repression" so high that they outweighed the "costs of tolerance." . . . Elsewhere in the communist sphere, however, the weakening and division of the ruling elite, coupled with the pressure of organized popular opposition movements, resulted in revolutionary overthrows of communist power. How, then, did reform lead to revolution?

In the 1980s, several communist regimes initiated deep reform programs. Some emphasized economic reform over political reform; others coupled the two. Hungary's government resumed the push for implementation of the New Economic Mechanism (NEM) first adopted in 1968, and it combined this with modest steps toward democratization in the political system. In China, beginning with the December plenum in 1978, the regime actively encouraged commercial enterprise in agriculture, trade and services, and to some extent in industry. Then it fought to contain popular demands for political reform. Yugoslavia adopted a new campaign for market reform in 1982. Poland's government sought popular approval for a program of radical economic reform through a national referendum in 1987, but popular mistrust for the authorities (Solidarity was not legalized until early in 1989) prevented the issue from receiving the two-thirds vote required to carry it. In 1985, following the successive deaths of three ailing leaders, an exceptionally young and energetic leader was elected general secretary of the party in the Soviet Union. Initially Gorbachev was dedicated to a broad-gauged program of "acceleration" of economic progress through fairly traditional measures (stepped-up investment, more foreign trade, improved labor incentives, more reliance on "economic" levers, and technical innovation). In time he embraced more radical positions, and by 1990 he had eliminated the Communist Party's monopoly on power. By shifting the government to a presidential system, he tried to preserve a measure of central control over policy amid a worsening breakdown of the system.

These reforms and their outcomes strongly influenced one another. The member states of the former communist sphere were closely connected not only through organizations such as the Warsaw Pact and Council for Mutual Economic Assistance, but also because of the traditionally powerful forces of mutual awareness and diffusion of ideological influences among them. For this reason, we cannot treat these reform initiatives as entirely independent events. Above all, the radicalization of perestroika in the Soviet Union created ultimately irresistible pressures for democratization in Eastern Europe. One reason was external: the removal of "Brezhnev-doctrine" constraints on Eastern Europe through Gorbachev's new effort at partnership with the West. The other reason was internal: the demonstration effect of democratization in the Sovit Union on populations in the region. By 1989 efforts by communist regimes to reach negotiated compromises on power-sharing with opposition forces had proved futile in every case. By the end of the decade, the wave of economic and political reform in the communist world had been overtaken by a revolution: the collapse of the communist system itself, both as a bloc of states and as a regime type. To be sure, the outcome of the changes occurring in the Soviet regime remained cloudy. China's regime clung to a repressive and orthodox position. Bulgaria was governed by a renamed version of the Communist Party and Romania by a group of ex-communists. Peripheral members of the system such as Cuba, North Korea, and Vietnam had not yet followed the example of the regimes in the core. Nonetheless, the pressure for regime transition from communist rule brought about a full collapse of the communist model throughout Europe. . . .

Scholars differ over the degree to which communist institutional arrangements can adapt to demands for change arising from the domestic and international environments. Because of the complementarity of their political and economic structures, reform in communist regimes, some argue, tends to be either too feeble to achieve the desired breakthrough to a self-sustaining condition of rising productivity and living standards, or else it allows the burden of accumulated frustrations and resentments in society to turn a limited opening in the political system into a general mobilization and radicalization of society. This school of thought therefore argues that communist regimes cannot be reformed, but only destroyed. Another school asserts that long-term processes of social change—rising levels of educational attainment, urbanization, communications, and diffusion of professional qualifications—have created irresistible pressures for democratization of the political regime. . . .

Many scholars have argued that, in the long run, democratization is implicit in the logic of modernization. Usually they view change in political institutions as a function of long-term processes in the social and international environments of the political system. Political elites have little direct control over these processes and in the end must accept them. Although there may be a temporal lag before political structures catch up with qualitative social changes, and some resistance to the inevitable loss of control which they entail, regimes must bow to the impersonal forces of history. For the Soviet Union, these include urbanization, education, professionalization, and communications. . . .

Analysts have identified the qualitative changes generated by modernization. Above all, they stress the profound change in popular expectations and in the capacity for organized collective action. Where once society could be ruled through great hierarchies of state power, the differentiation of identities brought about by social development required the state to establish a less unequal relationship with society. The revolution built a state that commanded society as if it were permanently at war, calling forth sacrifice and faith from the populace and enforcing its power with ruthless force. But the postwar decades of peace and slowly accumulating fruits of modernization subverted this model and demanded the political accommodation of new interests and loyalties. An urban, educated, and increasingly self-directed society was capable of forming autonomous social structures with distinct interests that sought outlets on the political plane. Demands for political expression and for a standard of living resembling that of the developed societies in the West created a constituency for democratic and market-oriented reform larger than many in the West imagined. . . . Simplifying slightly, we can describe interpretations in this vein as a theory of political change emphasizing the consolidation of a civil society that was brought about through modernization. Gilbert Rozman observes that "economic modernization normally brings with it a civil society." . . .

. . . The obstacles to communication between the two vessels of polity and society constrained the leaders' ability to reverse deeply entrenched processes of social change. The leaders found that the structures protecting them from popular opposition left them helpless to carry out meaningful reform. The pressure for new policies needed to become very strong before it spilled over and affected social behavior. For example, a change of slogans or one more ideological campaign was patently inadequate to rally the populace to new banners. Yet it is difficult to imagine Gorbachev or any leader in his place beginning with anything other than a rather conventional reform program. The political system's well-established structures of political recruitment and advancement selected out truly radical leaders long before they reached the pinnacle of power. Moreover, even a reform-minded new leader was obliged to deal with the collective opinion of the senior party leadership. . . .

The Chernobyl disaster in April 1986 illustrates many of the systemic features of Soviet society under the ancien régime. The failure of the nuclear reactor at the Chernobyl plant can be blamed on a host of factors: negligence concerning safety standards in industry, the siting of dangerous facilities close to densely populated regions, and the instinct to conceal unwelcome information; but more important for our purposes are the effects of Chernobyl on the political system. The accident occurred at a point when glasnost was identified as one of the desiderata of Gorbachev-era policy, but was very weakly rooted in the practice of the mass media or official bodies, and shortly before the "democratization" campaign officially encouraged a certain amount of grass-roots political mobilization. Chernobyl thus became one of the most powerful stimuli for popular environmental and national movements in the Ukraine and Belorussia. . . .

Labor protests also fit the pattern of local environmental grievances becoming larger and more radical programmatic movements. Before their summer 1989 strikes, coal miners in the Donets Basin had been alarmed at the buildup of toxic wastes in the groundwaters of the region. Their demands had gone unheeded by the authorities. Environmental degradation in addition to anger over housing conditions, food shortages, and appalling work conditions sparked the massive strike of July 1989. By March 1991, when a new wave of miners' strikes swept the coal mining regions of the Donbass, Kuzbass, Vorkuta, and Karaganda, labor's demands included the resignation of President Gorbachev, the dissolution of the Cabinet and Supreme Soviet, and transfer of power to the Soviet of the Federation. Therefore, it is hard to distinguish labor from environmental or ethno-national causes of opposition in Communist societies. A system in which economic and political powers are fused in a single political elite produces a general sense of alienation from and resentment toward power. Environmental, labor, national, and other streams of protest converge. . . .

. . . To understand the dynamics of change in a communist system, we must examine the interaction between the "communicating vessels" of society and polity in the course of the system's development through time. Modernization in communist societies is accompanied by decay in many spheres, creating severe social tensions as grievances accumulate and are focused on the political realm, where power over the distribution of material and intangible values is concentrated. Communist society, moreover, has a distinctive structure. Its principal elements are the de-differentiation of occupational stratification and the lack of classes defined by opposing property interests, and the superimposition of the political cleavage over other social divisions. As a result, opposition movements have a populist rather than class-specific character, expressing a broad antagonism to those representing "power." Lacking more specific interests to unite it, opposition often rallies to the most general of ideological causes, ethnic nationalism. . . .

Why did Gorbachev move beyond the conventional limits of Soviet reform policies? Historians will be searching for answers to this puzzle for generations. Was he always a radical, or did he become one in the course of his struggle to push through his reform politics over the opposition of the vast and faceless bureaucracy? It is enough for our purposes to examine what, in fact, he did, and what the consequences were. . . .

. . . It is not enough to concentrate on the political or the social domain to the neglect of the other, since what is crucial is an understanding of their interaction *as they evolve.* A state-centered account can illuminate the consequences of the fact that, in a communist regime, economic and political structures are bundled together in complementary, overlapping, and mutually reinforcing administrative structures. Reform programs typically have attempted to relax certain controls, often by giving enterprises greater autonomy vis-à-vis central planners and ministers, to stimulate productivity. In those cases when real liberties are granted to subcentral governments, opposition parties, producers, and parliaments, the Communist Party's monopoly on power breaks down. Points intermediate between a loosened, softened version of the Stalinist institutional framework and a polyarchical, market-driven society are unstable states of the system and soon yield either to a conservative consolidation or to a revolutionary rising against the regime.

The social modernization perspective, on the other hand, underlines the enormous impact of education, urbanization, professionalization, and communications in breaking down traditional structures of political control, facilitating independent and alternative forms of opinion and behavior, and unintentionally producing a shift in consciousness toward individuation and autonomy. Without this analysis we could not explain the successes of the democratic movement in the Soviet Union since 1989. It fails, however, to take sufficient note of the accumulation of antisystem resentment induced by the system, its inequalities of power and privilege, the calamitous decline in the quality of life, the vast carelessness and wastefulness with which it deploys human and material resources. Nor does this view pay sufficient attention to the group identities that fill the void left by the breakdown of a sterile doctrine of proletarian collectivism and that form the basis of new political movements. Given the amorphousness of class identities and the strength of primordial attachments, the very structure of the Soviet state, with its ethnically defined territorial jurisdictions, nurtures ethno-national counterideologies and territorial sovereignty claims. Political transition . . . should be analyzed as the mobilization of discontent into an opposition movement against the system. Its outcome is determined by the degree to which existing channels of social cooperation can sustain cohesive and autonomous aggregative capacities that mediate between the state and society. In the Soviet case these capacities formed first at the republican level, following the national-territorial administrative lines set up by the federal state. Once the claims by these republican national movements were largely accepted by the union center, processes in the direction of the consolidation of social interests at the union level were reinforced.

The reciprocal feedback effects between social and political change are indirect because they are affected by changing definitions of collective interest and by changing levels of freedom for the expression and resolution of grievances. A society where social interests are not well organized and autonomous—a low level of social pluralism—and simultaneously possessing a high degree of regime repressiveness is likely to witness a long buildup of popular frustration followed eventually by anomic rage. There is little reason to expect a democratic outcome in such a case. If social pluralism at the national community level is high, there can be a peaceful negotiated transfer of power to an organized opposition even if there is only a short transition period.

Alexander Rubtsov

The Transition to Capitalism

What kind of system has Russia emerged from? What is it changing into? The philosopher Alexander Rubtsov of the Russian Academy of Sciences argues—in a typically Russian, abstract manner but nevertheless with passion and insight—that neither pure socialism nor pure capitalism can exist; rather, the question of transition concerns how elements of socialism and capitalism are recombined.

At the very beginning of the present thaw the voice of a sort of healthy pragmatism sounded: enough of ideas, enough of fooling people with the dubious charms of socialism and the bogey of the capitalist choice. We need to live "normally," at last, without unnecessary theorizing, as the very "nature" of social and economic life demands.

However, by itself the laudable wish to get rid of the words and give oneself up to an untroubled ideology of life has remained a wish—and not so much out of the resistance of the old ideological machine as out of the naive utopianism of the intention itself. . . .

From Aleksandr Rubtsov, "Mezhdu kapital'nym sotsializmom i sotsial'nym kapitalizmom" (Between capitalist socialism and socialist capitalism), *Svobodnaya Mysl* (Free Thought), no. 8, 1992, pp. 34–43. Translated by Robert V. Daniels. Original copyright © 1992 by *Svobodnaya Mysl*.

. . . It is not necessary to depict the contemporary civilized world as a sort of "socioeconomic organism": a society that often appears on the basis of our everyday experience to be something totally normal, existing quite organically and naturally, outside any ideology whatever, is indeed only one of many no less "natural" ones. It is unthinkable without specific orientations of consciousness, values, visions of the absolute and the obligatory. Without all this, without well-grounded ideological preparation, this "ideal" and—as it seems to some—self-propelled socioeconomic machine would not last one day. And it will not work for us—even if a program like the "500 days" could in a purely technical sense be implemented in one week. "To free ourselves from our dogmas" does not mean to acquire and understand and learn and build anything at all.

And finally, behind these terms that were central yesterday and now are fully discredited, a number of now important and not insignificant problems are hidden. They lie in the question of how in today's world we could relate their "capitalism" to our "socialism" and in the question of whether it is possible for us to escape from capitalist socialism without bringing on a catastrophe, now that this system has completely lost its attraction for us. There is also the question whether tomorrow things will be the same with this capitalism, which we are now espousing with such ardor. Besides, it would be elementary neglect simply to bury our familiar ideology, which could then crawl out of the trenches (with a battle cry). Tired of his own poverty and even more of envy toward the excessive prosperity of his neighbor, contemporary man does not immediately reject every ideal of what capitalist socialism might be, for the sake of building a more suitable socialist capitalism.

In post-Soviet consciousness there still prevails the naturalist, or you might say even geographic, idea about the relationship of socialism and capitalism as a boundary between states or "camps." But international boundaries do not at all coincide with natural frontiers even on the plane of ordinary geography. Nature, as a rule, is indifferent toward those artificial lines by which people mark off their own existence—not to say that "the fences that divide people don't reach to God." . . .

. . . It would be more sensible to look at the socialism and capitalism that are familiar to us, not as something that extends along one or another side of a border dividing the world, but as elements of a highly complicated assemblage that is rarely tied together by one single thought—in other words, to try to draw this boundary not across our view from the East toward the West but rather along it. And not along a single direct line, but taking account of the very complicated configurations that are appearing here, strange combinations, including breaks and unexpected jumps.

If we do not bewitch ourselves with labels that we ourselves have produced, we will discover that we are inclined to exaggerate greatly the socialist or even communist quality of our former socioeconomic setup that has just now slipped into the past. And along with this, we are likely to underestimate or even to overlook altogether many vital elements of openly capitalist arrangements that have always existed here: unregulated redistribution, semilegal barter on a nationwide level, the market for informal services, the intangible capital of "status" in the hierarchy of the nomenklatura, etc. Harsh administration by command, leadership that plans everything, the exceptional formalism of the bureaucracy—all these are myths that mainly satisfy ideology and are abstracted from reality, as though commands were almost always executed by the book, as if plans were carried out in a spontaneously flowing process; and when bureaucrats exercised their powers and grew fat, it was primarily on the basis of the option of using their own discretion whether to submit to formal instructions.

What we call the command-administrative system, in the pure sense, without unspoken prejudgments and extra-ideological motives, could not exist at any time or anywhere, not even as applied in the army—and all the more under post-totalitarian realities. Considering only the now-fallen regime of classical socialism or even "communism" according to A. Zinoviev [the novelist], we have simply forgotten that such "comparatively pure socialism" was Stalin's type.

An equally ambiguous picture is seen in the West, on that side of the socialist choice. The question is not even the fascination of individual Swedish socialists, who perhaps dreamed about real developed socialism, but the fact that strictly socialist arrangements to one degree and form or another exist everywhere there—and not in the form of attractive decorations but as organic, inalienable elements of the whole system of socioeconomic organization of life. And just as our quasi-socialism would not last a day without its own sort of permanent reanimation by black markets and illegal freedoms, Western capitalism without strong socialist components would long ago have been blown up by those whose best representatives over here really became everything while remaining nothing.

Thus, the difference of principle here is not in the presence or absence of capitalistic or socialistic arrangements but in how they are related to each other. You can regulate the market as harshly as you want, but for this to be done at least the market has to exist. You can give the appearance of regulating everything, hiding "in the shadow" of emerging market relations, which under these conditions inevitably take on distorted forms. And even if you put the main emphasis on creating the social state, the question still remains: on what "material" base is this program to be realized?

Socialism is a good thing—if we do not identify this concept with everything whatsoever in our rather unique system. But it is expensive. Even for concrete social programs, one way or another we have to earn the means—and all the more so if in formulating such a program the building of a society of universal guarantees is announced.

The idea that socialism is not simply "fair" distribution but also a breakthrough to new potentials of efficiency in social production is not at all as hopeless as it seems to certain critics of Marx who rejected the doctrine on the basis of their own views of the models and logic of pseudoscientific communism. However, this idea [of socialism as a breakthrough], like any other theoretical hypothesis, works only if you observe certain conditions that are only beginning to be formed in the contemporary world and beginning to open up the moral and creative potential of people who are not absorbed by the struggle for existence.

Meanwhile, under new systems of values and technologies of utilizing "the human material," elements of socialism soften the harshness of social interrelationships, of course, running contrary to society's productive, economic efficiency. In developed countries, socialism, with all the nobility and loftiness of its motives, steps necessarily into the role of a parasite, limiting the efficiency of ongoing capitalist arrangements. Not by accident, even in the West all "leftists" are literally carried away by the issue of distribution, leaving it to their political opponents to worry about the framework of vital ethics and the social and economic mechanisms and motives under which society will create what they [the leftists] are getting ready to divide "according to fairness." Not by chance the West has been living for some time in a delicate thin, dynamic balance: now tightening social protections and lessening somewhat the tension in society to the detriment of the intensity of economic development, and then, in the opposite direction, prodding the economic dynamic of production by way of lowering the level of minimum guarantees and heightening differentiation in social status and wealth. A society that is protected too much clearly weakens some people and inhibits the entrepreneurial initiative of others. This is like electricity: without a high enough voltage there will be no significant current, although along with this one must consider the natural resistance of the conductor and the possibility that the circuit breakers may go off.

It is asked, What were we working for, or more exactly, how much did we pay for our old socialism with its distinct advantages: a style of life not overly intensive, no need to participate in the rat race of naked competition, the luxury of having no responsibilities, the curbing of large-group conflicts, etc.? What we gave up for the "paradise," in the negative sense, what expenses we bore for the familiar and perhaps doubtful pleasure of living in this quasi-idyll—now you can read about all this on any street corner. But how did we pay for this in the positive sense? Where did we get the resources that allowed us to endure in misery under the most inefficient system, absurd leadership, wild allocations to defense, while supporting numerous and usually ungrateful "friends"?

First of all we have to get rid of the illusion of unity and continuity in our socialist history, over the course of which we supposedly lived under one regime or system, even given that it had evolved quite capriciously. This unity in society's consciousness was basically established through the rejection of other out-looks—by contrasting our present system with our own autocratic past and with the parallel past that existed in the history of Western capitalism. The arbitrarily drawn sharpness of these contrasts quite obscures the qualitative character of the differences between successive periods in the establishment of our socialism.

Moreover, we should not absolutize the regime that was destroyed in 1917 (as is done from different standpoints but with the same stubbornness both by the communists and by the romanticists of a shining prerevolutionary past). Similarly, our differences from the West, whatever they were, in many ways were less than the gap between the mass social and physical terror of Stalinism and the selective, basically sociopsychological terror of the post-Stalin period. In the last analysis we return to the level of the individual fate of the simple human body, with its suffering and death. And from this point of view all differences between us and our prerevolutionary or Western antipodes may seem like mere furrows in comparison with the chasm separating people in the gulag from people on the outside, people who are being shot from people who have "merely" been left alive. This is the real chasm right here, separating a regime under which the megamachine of annihilation was the main connection between society and technology, from the corrupt and drunken socialism of the Brezhnev type. These people were virtually of different epochs, of different civilizations: the person who is simply unfree—and the person around whom nighttime arrests methodically beat out an unfillable emptiness; the one is simply frightened—and the other is killed. How could one possibly label all this with one squeamishly offhand term, "homo sovieticus"?

Along with this distinction there are two essentially different ways to "pay" for the socialist choice. In the first case, expenses for the catching-up kind of modernization, magnified by the inefficiency of the system and the vast outlays for governmental display, are covered by the superintensive exploitation of the population, when people work themselves to the bone, the great majority of them out of fear—plain animal fear of the prospect of being torn away from this not-too-sweet everyday life. You cannot leave the renowned enthusiasm of that period out of account, but you must see its extremely specific nature. It is directly connected with fear and in a certain sense is the opposite side, the contrasting outcome of mass terror. It is known that in the war it was simply blind faith that enabled people to close their eyes to the crying failures of the system and the leadership and keep up their morale for the struggle. During that time they often covered up the frank sacrifice of whole units with the images of mass heroism. In peacetime the image of mass enthusiasm was also called upon to cover up all the exhausting work and fear to which and without any enthusiasm the terrorized population was condemned. In this way we paid for the miracle of technical projects pushed ahead to achieve one breakthrough after another in industry. The country was turned into a hungry invalid, who at the end of life has secured for himself a late-model sports car and does not know what to do with it. Not accidentally, our attitude toward fundamental science, industrial conversion, yesterday's pride in the cosmos, and much else bears a character that is not rational and practical but rather emotional, in its own way like vandals.

Post-Stalinist socialism cut off the flame of the productive spirit that had arisen in the course of enthusiastic repressions and repressive enthusiasms and for the first time made it possible to work for the [socialist] idea under conditions whereby it was possible not to work at all without any special risk. It demonstrated the relative economic efficiency of just that freedom that had been won, but at the same time showed the limits of this efficiency and the dangerous inclination of the system to fall into a condition of more and more enervating degradation, which is what happened. "From above" they gave the people the holiday of stagnation, lasting for more decades than one, in the course of which an incompetent and steadily degenerating government with knowing goodwill allowed the working population to vegetate in semiwork and quietly go on stealing working time, if not more. And now the population is much less willing than we imagine to give up this "historic vacation"—even in the name of free self-realization—while we contemplate living in perhaps the most depressing period of Russian history.

Saying farewell to socialism, in spite of our hopes, cannot fail to turn into a funeral feast. We really had something to lose, and what we are getting (for example, emancipation in the sphere of the spirit and verbal self-expression) loses its value rather quickly as soon as it begins to seem that everything has always been this way. So the question must be put pragmatically: Who subsidized this unique vacation that we had under the beloved slogans of communal consciousness, "Everything is free"?

To begin with, we must not underestimate the well-known deceptiveness of this good fortune: strictly speaking, the magnificent long banquet with bad port wine did not cost the authorities too much; in any case it was much cheaper than the everyday menu of the developed countries. And this was accordingly reflected in the moral and physical health of the nation.

Here we need to refer to a subject of our unflagging concern and love: our country's environment. Nowhere else in the world could an ideology like ours drag on for years without a geology like ours. The hypertrophied military machine swallowing up billions, with obvious indigestion; and decades of blowing up the bubble of the socialist camp; and the rot of every kind of liberation movement—all these extravagances were paid for to a vast degree by exploiting our richest natural resources. The same applies to the idleness of the degraded masses, in which practically every wino who had drunk himself penniless could consider himself a rentier, sitting back with the dividends from our national patrimony. In this connection the strategic grab by the governing nomenklatura aiming to privatize regional resources is strikingly similar to the life strategies of the masses down below (that have still not been overcome). It reveals not only the moral and psychological but also "material" causes of the nationalism and regionalism that now flourish.

There is no need to linger over the question [of] how short-term and near exhaustion all these resources were.

In spite of the anxieties of the fans of the socialist choice and the population they have frightened, we are not threatened by the building of capitalism in the near future, if only because the construction site is filled with unfinished framework and mountains of rubbish that have not been cleaned up in all the years of perestroika. So we have to search further for the means to utilize sites that are known to be unprofitable. Further, burying totalitarian socialism will likewise cost even more than supporting it in its semiconscious and finally comatose condition.

Above all, we have to recognize the logical inevitability of the crisis in the economy, if one can call it that. A crisis strictly of the economy is possible in a market system when the economy really has its own priorities and is to a significant degree emancipated from the structure of political power, ideology, etc. Here, in the most direct sense of the word, the economy became knit together with the political and ideological powers, and consequently a change in the type of rule is impossible without a crisis in the whole economy. The crisis in the economy, frankly, is a crisis of the departing government, and that is exactly what does not allow us to create a new economy. So it is naive, to say the least, to dislike the past, to thirst for change, and at the same time to blame the present situation for the untimely breakdown of the old structures. The revolutionary character of a given course of events is almost always aggravated not just by innovators but by the bearers of inertia who singlemindedly and systematically pose the stark alternatives: either back to state socialism or collapse. And to the extent that the way back, to put it gently, is unrealistic, we really have to be cured in every sense—and pay dearly for the treatment.

Further, real socialism still has to show its genuine human face. In particular, it shows itself to be less attractive among us than, for example, among the comparatively civilized East Germans, who have not broken with the old way and clearly are still doing nothing but now demand for themselves a life no worse than that of the population of the former Federal Republic of Germany. They do this in a very socialistic way. And you may not like it. But it is better to understand this without too much obvious moralizing and to take account of one more delayed action mine among those planted along the way out from the socialism that was won in blood and sweat but not yet paid for.

At a certain time, and at a corresponding cost, it will be necessary to emphasize that the elements of our newborn capitalism have themselves taken on a face resembling a human one. It would be naive to hope that everything here can turn out smoothly and without the wildness of the period of primary accumulation.[1] Among our entrepreneurs we will see some of them sprouting the donkey ears of [the folk-tale character] "sovka" with the mania to grab and discard, but not to give. Today only the lazy man will deny that the market is not a mechanism but a culture. We have seen this—over there [in the West]. It is more important for us to understand what flows from the wellspring of the market without the corresponding culture, in a culture that is largely antimarket as a matter of principle—and beforehand, to get ready even in the best case to accept from our half-abandoned regime not an angelic child but a cruel freak, burdened with multiple hereditary diseases, including some of purely socialist origin. The "grimaces of the market" in the streets are largely the grimaces of socialism itself that have splashed out in the form of speculation, which until recently existed basically in the underground and was the prerogative of the few. So far only the democratization of the speculative process is taking place. Today's unorganized mass bazaar is only our capitalist socialism turned inside out.

These unhappy pictures are painted here not with the aim of scaring the common man one more time. We simply have to become aware once again: from socialism "at any price" to a socialism based on market wealth, there is not any "normal," straight, and safe road. Rather it recalls a blind alley, from which the way back is prohibited, and you can try to break through the wall with your own body only at the risk of seriously crippling yourself. On this path you simultaneously have to decide tasks not simply of different levels and content that in practice are sometimes incompatible, but tasks virtually of different epochs: to finish the work of the past century, brutally interrupted at the beginning of the present century, and to dismantle the existing system completely while overcoming furious resistance, but without causing it to collapse. Even perestroika, which at first represented a process of consistent treatment and convalescence, in practice turned into an agony complicated by severe family fights.

But there have been no blind alleys in history that could not be broken out of; catastrophe is only a question of degree. In contrast to an individual person, a "hopelessly sick" society cannot

---

[1] Reference to Marx's theory of early, predatory capitalism.—Ed.

die but can only be reborn while its own suffering is deepened or alleviated, which would not be asserted in the poetics of the contemporary apocalypse, "the path to the abyss," etc. Even when it seems that nothing at all remains, unexpected possibilities open up on a fundamentally new level, in the framework of a qualitative transition. This is like protozoa in the process of subdividing: in a sufficiently nutritious environment, they do not perish, but unexpectedly, "in spite of" their own biology, they gather into a single organism with higher organization, capable of living on in search of a favorable environment.

From this point of view, special interest is evoked by the prospects of mutual relations between the West and the East, between the countries of developed capitalism and the burned-out countries of the former socialist camp. It is gradually becoming more and more obvious: Western aid to the countries that are rebuilding is not a casual act but a structural element of worldwide rebuilding, not the result of exclusively personal agreeableness but a natural and, in its own way, indispensable link in the logic of the global process of civilization. Until we learn to think in other, broader categories, until we understand that this is not a localized episode but the contours of a basically new historical reality, people will still be led into meaningless delusions and will scarcely relate to the essence of the thing: petty political calculations, sick and deformed feelings of national pride, a readiness to rob their own children tomorrow but not to take anything today from yesterday's enemy. All this is Soviet, much too Soviet.

. . . After the worldwide revolutionary conflicts of the beginning of this century, capitalism began to evolve sharply toward its better side. We [in Russia] showed the world not only how not to build a new society but also what will happen if you do not disturb the old one at all. And Western capitalism, relatively soft, with socialistic features, took shape not without our indirect participation, with its foundation mixed up in that sense with the blood of the victims of the construction of capitalist socialism.

At first you could say that capitalism plants elements of socialism on its own territory, which leads us to the conclusion that giving to the indigent is not simply moral but also practical. In any case, it is cheaper than reaping the consequences of social instability. But gradually this becomes a space for a more and more equalized social life. The culture acquires a more and more openly antibourgeois character than before, rooted in the presumption that earning a great deal does not make you a person of full worth but rather closes all possibilities of full self-realization. Riches cease to be of value in themselves—at least that is the tendency. . . .

. . . Realization that you have to pay for wealth is being radically globalized. Aiding developing countries is not the same as taking care of one's own unemployed, but the aim here is one logic and one understanding of the world.

The factor of "peaceful" or rather mutually complementary existence of capitalist and socialist systems similarly breaks through national boundaries and begins to approach the status of a new world order, including the countries of the old capitalist socialism. Even on the basis of the most primitive, vaguely practical considerations, world capital is simply compelled to a significant degree to cover the expenses of de-Communizing the former socialist countries and their gradual movement into the orbit of the world economy and world civilization. Capital has to choose: either to pay for our relative stability or sit together with us on one powder keg. This would be like blackmail, if the situation had not taken shape independently of anybody's wishes.

I can imagine the reaction of the adherents of national dignity, assuming their favorite pose: with proud face, head held high, and—naked backside. And with a readiness to go once more over the virtues of their "own" nature, already pushed to the limit with songs about the inexhaustible riches of the Motherland. Only a person who never was the least bit well off and cannot imagine what this means can desist out of pride from taking from his rich neighbor. This is the logic of those who have never paid their debts, have no hope for their own future, or are not preparing at all to get out of their situation of being lulled to sleep by hopelessness.

I could continue this theme endlessly, but there is another basic level of argumentation relating not to money but to culture, and directed more to the distant but even now significant future. So far, everything really looks like a gift from the munificence of a successful and rich uncle; the developed countries that have pushed ahead distribute aid only out of their own kindness and vision, that is to say, from the higher to the lower. As you gain one thing, you inevitably lose another, and the guarantee of future survival lies only in preserving as much as possible of the totality of global culture. Besides, the Western type of civilization has long been considered not as one called upon to squeeze out all the other, less efficient cultures but rather as one in a blind alley, without prospects precisely because of its simple orientation toward limitless efficiency in reshaping the world. While we are preparing the jump into contemporary Western civilization, the latter is busy instead in reevaluating its fundamental values; while we stare with the rapture of aborigines at their trinkets, they hopefully and calculatingly scrutinize cultures that have avoided the experience of wealth, the industrial explosion, and potentially unlimited consumption. Therefore what looks now like a donation will gradually be reinterpreted as an equivalent exchange in the framework of global cultural interaction. The values granted by technology presuppose the presence of values that defend us from the prospect of being enslaved or completely ruined by this same technology. And no one knows what cultural orientations and skills will be decisive tomorrow.

In our own passion for a very natural glossiness, it does not even occur to us that during his decades of tortuous experiments and mutations, Soviet Man could accumulate qualities that are extremely scarce in the present world, and even more so for the future, qualities that in another situation could evoke new and even greater efficiency. One must not see in "sovka" only the bad: something in him could be worth very much. Strictly speaking, in our beloved West, people who are correct by their own standards are often rather stingy and narrowly specialized, and outside the limits of their strict professionalism are not capable of unexpectedly productive eccentricities.

In any case the reform of socialism can be noncatastrophic only if it takes into account our existing inertia and proceeds from the real possibilities of society. But this gradualness also costs a great deal, in any case no less than the financing of the actual reforms.

The question is only whether the actual resources exist for any such painless reformism. It seems that the country now must not so much enter the market as fall into it, if not crash into it.

And this happens in practice independent of the desire of the reformers who are acting in forced situations. Naturally, there is nothing especially good in this. Nevertheless, even in such an extremely tough situation, one is not prevented from trying to see its pluses.

Crashing into the market does not in itself mean choosing our own path. It only creates the conditions for choice. And the tougher and more decisive this transition will be right now, at the crucial, culminating point of reform, the greater will be the chances that further along, the possibility will arise to ensure the truly evolutionary reform of the system, so that the choice ahead will be truly free and original. The market infrastructure presupposes various arrangements. In the absence of the market, only one arrangement is possible, the "worth" of which is known to everyone.

Elizabeth Teague

The Fate of the Working Class

Most analyses of perestroika and the Soviet collapse, taking the standpoint of high politics or macroeconomics, have relatively little to say about the impact of these events on ordinary people. David Lane of Cambridge University addresses this lack in a collection of articles he has edited by a number of experts who focus not on government but on various social groups and the fortunes of civil society. The largest single element of Soviet society, industrial workers, is tracked through the changes of the 1980s and 1990s by Elizabeth Teague, a political researcher on the staff of the Radio Free Europe/Radio Liberty Research Institute in Munich, Germany.

From Elizabeth Teague, "Manual Workers and the Workplace," in *Russia in Flux: the Political and Social Consequences of Reform*, David Lane, ed., pp. 114–130. Copyright © 1992 by Ashgate Publishing Co. Reprinted by permission of the publisher.

Reform of the Soviet economic and political system promises ultimately to leave every member of society freer and better off. But, as Boris Yeltsin warned the Russian Federation parliament when he announced his economic reform programme on 28 October 1991, the short- to medium-term costs of reform will be high and will be borne by the general population.

Since radical reform will by definition require drastic changes in the pattern of national economic activity, Soviet workers will play, willy-nilly, a key role in the reform process. At present, there is not much evidence either of a worker "push" for change or, conversely, of a "pull" by the leadership to bring the workers in as active constituents. Blue-collar workers—a social stratum not deprived of the ability to defend itself, but one that is nonetheless at present poorly organized and ill-prepared for the major readjustments economic reform will demand—seem to have been very much on the sidelines of the reform constituency so far. They are, however, likely to be among those most affected; only pensioners and others on fixed incomes are likely to be harder hit in the initial phases.

According to the orthodox Soviet definition, blue-collar workers (*rabochie*) make up by far the largest group in the Soviet labour force. In 1989 they were estimated to number 78.7 million people, or 62 per cent of the entire working population in the state and kolkhoz sectors. White-collar workers (*sluzhashchie*) were estimated to form 28.9 per cent of the working population in the state and kolkhoz sectors, with collective farm peasants making up 9.1 per cent. . . .

. . . The workforce is taken initially to be those people who are neither part of the old *nomenklatura* nor amongst the emerging non-*nomenklatura* business class: in short, the unprivileged. This is a group that includes white-collar as well as blue-collar workers. It does not follow, however, that the workforce in this sense, even within specific republics, shares similar interests, let alone that its members are conscious of common interests and feel themselves united by a sense of class solidarity. There are divisions amongst the unprivileged (in addition to nationality divisions) as well as amongst the privileged. This is true within the category of blue-collar workers as well as more widely.

In a landmark study published a decade ago, Alex Pravda asserted that the existence of a homogeneous Soviet "working class" was a myth cultivated by Soviet ideologists as a means of legitimizing the rule of the Communist Party and the Soviet state. Drawing on the research of Soviet social scientists, Pravda argued that the Soviet "working class" was in reality composed of widely differing strata, each with its own interests, and that it was, moreover, growing increasingly heterogeneous. Rather than marking blue-collar workers off from other social groups, Pravda went on, the major divisions in Soviet society cut so deeply through the manual workforce as to cast doubt on the usefulness of the concept of the "working class" as a tool for analysis. For example, differences between blue-collar workers' educational and skill levels showed as much a generational as a class dimension. Pravda suggested that Soviet workers might be more appropriately divided into "old" and "new" segments, with younger, more highly-skilled workers in relatively high-technology production tending to display a different set of interests from older, less highly-skilled ones in traditional "smokestack" industries. . . .

Following the shift of population to the towns, the 1970s and 1980s saw a slow but steady tendency for blue-collar workers to move into white-collar employment and from less skilled to more highly-skilled jobs. By Western standards, to be sure, the proportion of manual workers remained high. . . . Nonetheless the trend was clear: older workers were tending to become concentrated in lower- and semi-skilled professions, while younger workers were tending to enter more skilled ones.

The result of all these factors was that Gorbachev's USSR was a far more complex society than that over which either Stalin or Khrushchev had ruled. Education and skill differentials had stratified the society that had been, only a generation before, relatively homogeneous. National elites had emerged within the more than one hundred ethnic groups inhabiting the Soviet Union. As Soviet society became more differentiated, so the interests of its various strata began to diverge and the potential for social conflict became more acute. And, as the demands placed on the state by society grew more insistent, so too did the need for institutions that could represent those demands.

However, the Soviet economic and political systems remained as if fossilized. Soviet society was changing, yet the institutions by which it was governed hardly changed at all from those created by Stalin. Claiming that capitalist society was riven by conflicting class interests, Marxist-Leninist (that is, Stalinist) ideology closed its eyes to Soviet society's increasing diversity and continued to insist that socialism was characterized by a single "social interest" and would, moreover, become increasingly homogeneous the more "mature" it grew. Supposedly the interests of blue-collar workers did not differ in any fundamental way from those of any other social stratum. The Communist Party based its monopoly of state power on its claim to be uniquely qualified to determine and administer the "general interest."

In the pre-Gorbachev period, blue-collar workers had little influence on state policy. Lip-service was paid throughout the Soviet period to the advantages allegedly bestowed on the working class in what Stalin's *Short Course* called "the first Socialist State of Workers and Peasants in the world," but, in reality, Soviet workers were without political or economic clout. . . .

. . . The fact that in 1984 (the last time the USSR Supreme Soviet was elected by the old quota method) 32.5 per cent of the deputies to the Soviet parliament were classified as blue-collar workers did not . . . mean that these deputies saw it as their duty to defend the interests of ordinary members of the working population. They knew they owed their allegiance to the apparatus. It was to be 1988 before any Supreme Soviet deputy dared to vote against a proposal put forward by the Party leadership in the Soviet parliament.

Second, manual workers had no autonomous organizations to defend their interests *vis-à-vis* the state and the rest of society. The CPSU presented itself as a party representing the interests of the whole of society and embracing within its ranks a wide cross-section of the Soviet population. In reality, the CPSU was never a normal political party in the generally accepted sense of the word, that is, it never competed for power in elections on an equal footing with other parties, and it represented the interests of no one other than the bureaucracy. According to Ivan Laptev, former chief editor of *Izvestiya*, there were always "at least three parties" within the CPSU. The first was made up of the rank-and-file members who, "although they constituted the majority of the Party, never determined its real identity or its policies." The second consisted of a small group of Party leaders who "personified the Party in the eyes of the population and of the world." The third and most important group, according to Laptev, was the Party apparatus, which "represented the Party members to the leaders, the leaders to the Communists, and the Party to the masses."

Evidence that blue-collar workers did not perceive the CPSU as representing their interests is furnished by the amount of energy the Party traditionally had to put into what was clearly the difficult job of recruiting workers as members. At the beginning of 1990 manual workers made up only 27.6 per cent of the membership, while employees made up 40.5 per cent. When, later that year, Party membership began to drop, the evidence indicated that blue-collar workers were the first to quit.

"The workers have rejected the CPSU," ran an article in the newspaper *Rabochaya tribuna* on 9 October 1991; "will they [now] turn to the trade unions?" The author, Igor Zaramensky, a former official of the CPSU Central Committee, was not hopeful. The Communist Party, he wrote, had turned its back on the workers by permitting their "alienation from power." Since the Party was aided and abetted in this by the official trade unions, many workers had turned against the unions too, Zaramensky concluded. As Zaramensky acknowledged, the very trade unions to which Soviet blue-collar workers belonged were firmly controlled by the Party-state apparatus. Indeed the official unions—the only labour unions permitted to exist in the USSR until the Gorbachev era—were (and remain) so tightly tied to the state that they are perhaps best described as part of it. Charged with the quasi-governmental function of administering social security payments, the unions received (and still receive) financial allocations directly from the USSR state budget. Just like Supreme Soviet deputies, union officials were appointed on the say-so of the Communist Party. Therefore they looked up to the apparatus for their instructions, not down to their worker-members. Organizers of strikes and unofficial trade unions, on the other hand, were harshly repressed by the authorities.

While they were estranged from political and economic power, Soviet workers did have a high level of job security, though at a low level of real income. In addition the Soviet economy for many years provided its workers with full, even over-full, employment; moreover, low levels of workplace discipline were routinely tolerated. Whether this came about by accident or design has for some time been the subject of dispute among Western scholars. Philip Hanson has suggested that full employment and job security were unplanned and ultimately dysfunctional side-effects of centrally-planned economies in which enterprises operate with soft budget constraints. Others, including Peter Hauslohner and the late David Granick, have postulated the existence of an implicit "social contact," under the terms of which blue-collar workers were fostered by the Soviet authorities as a source of political support for the regime.

If there was such a thing as a Soviet "social contract," the workers' side of the bargain would require them to remain politically passive. The state in return would guarantee them job security, full employment, and lax labour discipline; it would implement an active incomes policy aimed at minimizing wage disparities between blue-collar workers; and it would ensure, in contrast to the situation in the developed capitalist countries, that blue-collar workers were relatively better paid than white-collar ones.

At first sight this explanation is persuasive—pay for certain skilled and professional personnel, such as teachers and doctors, was notoriously low for example—but it soon runs up against the problem that plagues all attempts to evaluate real wage levels in the USSR. The difficulty is that, while income disparities were generally smaller in the USSR than in the West, Soviet citizens had widely varying degrees of access to consumer goods. Such goods were in short supply throughout the country, and this encouraged the creation of all sorts of distribution networks that ensured that state officials and workers in prestigious plants had privileged access to special outlets. A member of the *nomenklatura* would have the right to order luxuries from a closed store; a worker in a factory producing high-priority goods could eat in a specially stocked canteen. Moreover, it was a major source of real-income advantage to possess a Moscow residence permit, or merely to have time to spend standing in line, which of course had nothing to do with performance at work. This element of access played a real but unquantifiable role in creating significant differentials between different groups of Soviet citizens. . . .

The working population was assigned a central role in Gorbachev's early reform efforts, the initial aim of which was to revitalize the flagging Soviet economy. The first period of *perestroika* (1985–6) was characterized by initiative from above; during this first period Gorbachev used a combination of carrot and stick to try to prod the population into working harder and more conscientiously. There was much talk at this time about widening wage differentials, increasing worker participation and even, perhaps, using the threat of unemployment as a way of spurring the workforce to greater effort. One of Gorbachev's main ideas in this first phase of *perestroika* was that increased responsibility and participation in decision making on the part of rank-and-file workers would release a surge of productivity. "Activating the human factor" was therefore an integral feature of Gorbachev's early policies of "intensification" and "acceleration"; that is, achieving enhanced economic growth by more efficient use of inputs (manpower in particular) and the application of modern technology in the workplace.

The early years of Gorbachev's leadership also saw growing acknowledgment of the existence of conflicting group interests, both of workers as a whole and of different groups of workers, and more scope was allowed for articulation of these interests (though not at that stage for their organized expression). Gorbachev envisaged a modernized Soviet Union as a society in which the public could and should be given more information and responsibility and in general be trusted by the rulers more than before. In a major speech delivered in Krasnodar, in September 1986, Gorbachev for the first time described the "democratization" of Soviet society as his main priority. He said that, when he was talking to crowds on the city streets earlier in the day, "I thought of how much our people have grown up, of what intellectual potential they possess, creative potential, and of how, in resolving issues in the country, we still do not make use of this potential, relying on administrative injunction, giving orders and issuing commands. We must," Gorbachev went on, "include the people in the process of restructuring via the democratization of society. Our people," he stated the following day, "have matured to the extent that they must be trusted to administer themselves."

The other side of the coin was that Gorbachev expected the population to work harder and with less economic security than before. This aspect of his programme did not meet with widespread public approval. Indeed Gorbachev's initial efforts to revive the economy by exhortation and tinkering changes failed to arouse popular support. The reason for the population's failure to respond was that, for all Gorbachev's efforts to increase participation and openness, what he was engaged upon was a within-system reform. The overarching dominance of the CPSU and the central planning apparatus remained undiminished, and powerful institutional interest groups retained the ability to block reforms. As a result, ordinary people were mistrustful since they feared that, as had happened in the past, change could be easily reversed. In 1987, therefore, the Soviet leader turned to deeper political reforms. During the next phase of *perestroika* (1987–9), much greater political openness was permitted and the formation of unofficial trade unions and ad hoc strike committees was tolerated.

In particular the USSR Law on the State Enterprise of 1987 sought to involve workers in the management of their factories and plants by offering them the power to elect their managers and, through the institutionalization of councils of the work collective, to enforce the rights of codetermination that workers had been promised—but had been unable to exercise—under the 1977 USSR constitution. In the vast majority of cases, however, the 1987 law ran up against fierce resistance from the branch ministries and the official trade unions, neither of which was eager to share its powers with the elected representatives of the workforce, and the law failed to operate in the way it had been intended. It was eventually superseded by the 1990 USSR Law on Enterprises which stripped the work collective of the right to participate in enterprise decision making in anything other than a purely advisory capacity. . . .

If the first phase of Gorbachev's *perestroika* was greeted with apathy on the part of the workforce, the second phase saw the population begin to respond to the increased opportunities his reforms offered, though not always in the way Gorbachev had hoped. As a result, his leadership found itself increasingly obliged to react to events, rather than directing them. For example, the formation of the first unofficial trade unions and strike committees took place against an escalation of industrial action, much of it sparked by ethnic and national grievances. In general, strike activity by Soviet workers proved in this period far more likely to be sparked by ethnic conflicts than by the kind of bread-and-butter demands normally viewed as typical workers' issues. In response the official Soviet trade unions began to agitate for the legalization of the right to strike: since workers' protests were becoming commonplace, the unions sought (unsuccessfully) to secure the exclusive right to organize them.

The miners' strike of July 1989, which made nearly half a million workers idle, was a major turning point in the relationship between workers and the state. Strikers ignored their official union representatives and spontaneously organized their own strike committees. Even more significant, the miners resolved to keep these strike committees in existence after the strike was over in order to monitor the government's compliance with the agreements on the basis of which the miners returned to work. The experience spurred the Gorbachev leadership into introducing a bill legalizing strikes—though the new law contained so many restrictions that it was clear that its aim was to make it harder rather than easier for workers to organize their protests.

The miners' strike of July 1989 prompted the official trade unions—long a bastion of conservatism—to undertake a fundamental policy review. At the Sixth Plenum of the All-Union Central Council of Trade Unions (AUCCTU) in September 1989 the unions announced that they were formally abandoning the role, which they had played since the days of Lenin, of "transmission belts" of Communist Party policy to the masses. From now on, the unions declared, they would operate in complete independence from the CPSU. The unions, which had rarely been known to defend any interests other than those of the Party-state apparatus, retained their anomalous, quasi-governmental function of distributing state social welfare benefits, but asserted that, henceforth, the protection of working people would be their prime task.

There were several reasons for this change. The communist-dominated official unions had been badly frightened by the hostility to them shown by the miners during the 1989 strike, and resolved in the future to court the workers with promises to defend them against the hardships (which the unions stressed at every available opportunity) of the switch to a market economy. In addition the official unions saw the writing on the wall a good deal sooner than the Communist Party did. Evidently aware of how unpopular the CPSU and its doctrines were among working people, the unions anticipated the move to a multi-party system. They sought to distance themselves from the Party in the public eye and proclaimed their readiness to work with any political party approved by the population.

Perestroika moved into its third phase (1990–1991) as Gorbachev and the central government lost the initiative to newly self-assertive governments in the republics which, in a number of cases, were responding to and being driven by popular pressure. Economic chaos, not economic reform, was the result of the collapse of central authority and the "war of laws" that ensued. Working people were alarmed by the fall in their living standards and by threats of unemployment and dislocation. The urge for national self-determination grew stronger in an ever-increasing number of regions. Again the trade unions seemed to grasp earlier than the Communist Party the fact that, once the CPSU lost its monopoly on power, the Marxist–Leninist ideology that glued the USSR together would also dissolve. In October 1990, in anticipation of such an event, a congress of the official unions decentralized the union structure and turned the AUCCTU into a loose confederation, renamed the General Confederation of Trade Unions of the USSR (VKP). From then on, as power flowed to republican bodies, the All-Union trade union centre began to look more and more like a dying organization.

Particularly significant was the establishment, early in 1990, of the Russian Federation of Independent Trade Unions (FNPR). Despite the word "independent" in its title, this organization sprang from the official trade union structure and continued to maintain close links with the state. Even more conservative than its All-Union parent, indeed, the FNPR lost no time in expressing its opposition even to the timid proposals for "a regulated market economy" advanced by the then Soviet prime minister Nikolai Ryzhkov in autumn 1990. After the election of Boris Yeltsin as head of state of the Russian Republic in the spring of that year, the FNPR sought to present itself as the Russian government's natural negotiating partner on economic and social issues.

Trade union federations in other republics acted in a similar way as did, on the All-Union level, the VKP which, under its then leader Gennadii Yanaev, offered to sign an annual "collective agreement" with the government on behalf of the workforce. The VKP proposed that, as long as the government kept its side of the bargain, it would dissuade its members from embarking on strike action. But, the union hinted darkly, should the government fail to keep its side of the bargain, then it would call its members out on strike.

Even as they courted the workers with promises of support, therefore, the unions projected themselves in a corporatist role as guarantors of industrial peace; in return they demanded an assured place in whatever configuration of political forces took shape in the USSR. Observers expressed doubts, however, as to whether the USSR's VKP or the official trade union federations in the various Soviet republics really enjoyed enough influence among Soviet workers to be able to control the behaviour of the workforce in such a way.

Similarly, in abandoning the role of "transmission belt" and moving into an explicitly adversarial role *vis-à-vis* the government, the official unions seemed to be taking a leaf out of the book of Poland's OPZZ (National Alliance of Trade Unions). From its inception, the OPZZ disavowed the role of "transmission belt"; instead, it deliberately adopted an attitude of confrontation, first towards Poland's communist government—in order to attract workers into its ranks and to defuse their anger through the protests it organized—and later towards the Solidarity-led government. Overall the official Soviet unions have shown every sign of learning from the experience of Eastern Europe, where the unions have displayed an ability almost unique among formerly communist-dominated organizations to retain their property and much of their membership in the post-communist world. . . .

By August 1991 the average levels of material welfare of the Soviet population had declined sharply. At the same time, income differentiation had probably increased: certainly traditional patterns of differentiation had been drastically changed. These changes could not be reliably measured, however. Neither inflation rates nor real levels of supply could be tracked through 1991, though it seemed probable that, in the first three quarters of 1991, per capita real consumption in the USSR fell by a little less than 12 per cent. Real wages were falling. Those who worked in cooperatives and joint ventures (around three million people) were receiving very high incomes by Soviet standards—typically, some two to four times the state-sector average. But every member of the population was subject to the impact of rapid inflation, possibly approaching 400 per cent a year in August 1991. The State Statistics Committee (Goskomstat) no longer provided an average state wage figure, but the closely equivalent "enterprise consumption fund per worker" was 400 rubles a month in January–September 1991, and the average income per household member of worker (*rabochie*) families was reported as 274 rubles per month.

Estimates of the "poverty level" proliferated and varied widely—between 166 rubles a month and 500 rubles a month in autumn 1991. Certainly, on many of the definitions that were circulating in the USSR, the *average* member of a worker household, on 274 rubles a month, would have been below the "minimum income level" (*prozhitochnyi minumum*), while the average pensioner, on 182 rubles a month, would have been well below most definitions. On 28 October 1991, indeed, Boris Yeltsin told the RSFSR parliament that 55 per cent of families in the Russian Federation were living below the poverty line.

Meanwhile workers began to brace themselves for the widespread cyclical and structural unemployment that threatened to accompany the Soviet Union's long-awaited move to a market economy. In January 1991 the USSR adopted a framework law on employment that called for the creation of a Union-wide State Employment Service that would, for the first time since the 1920s, register the jobless, maintain a bank of job vacancies, administer training programmes and coordinate the payment of unemployment benefits. The service was to be financed through mandatory contributions (equivalent to one per cent of payroll) by state-run and private enterprises, factories, cooperatives and joint ventures. . . .

Meanwhile a plethora of independent unions and worker-oriented organizations began to compete for the worker constituency. As 1991 neared its end, the Independent Miners' Union (created in 1990) was debating whether it was strong enough to set up a confederation of independent trade unions to rival the VKP. On the Stalinist "right," the arch-conservative United Workers' Front (founded in 1989) was trying to organize worker opposition to the market. In October 1991 members of the Socialist Party, the Anarcho-Syndicalist group and the CPSU's former Marxist Platform joined forces to form a Party of Labour. Modelled on the British Labour Party of the 1920s, the new party would be aimed specifically at workers, who would mobilize in support of the (official) trade union movement. Also in October, the Interrepublican Union of Work Collectives met in Moscow to hammer out policy on worker ownership and self-management; with strong support in defence industry enterprises, the union made it its aim to save the jobs of skilled workers in the military-industrial complex. On the liberal "left," the independent union "Sotsprof" was trying to build a grassroots base by helping workers to defend their rights through the courts. New organizations aimed at workers were also springing up in other parts of the former USSR.

However, officials in the new independent organizations complained about the difficulty of mobilizing the workers, the majority of whom, the activists alleged, were "lumpenized" and as yet uninterested in collective action. Their complaints underscored the conclusions reached in this [essay], that is, that the traditional Soviet view, according to which blue-collar workers formed a self-conscious, homogeneous "working class," is of little value as a tool for analysis in today's conditions. As Peter Rutland exclaimed in November 1991, "There's no organized workers' movement in the Soviet Union today because there's no working class."

It has been argued above that, despite the changes wrought during the Gorbachev era, the interests of workers are still rather poorly represented in the Soviet political system. A case might be made that the existence of strong workers' organizations, prepared to fight in defence of workers' interests, could derail efforts to institute a market reform and that the absence of such bodies in the USSR today therefore bodes well for the reform's success. An equally good case might also be made that the absence of strong defence mechanisms threatens to leave Soviet workers with so little protection that they may have little choice but to resort to strikes and even violent protests to express their grievances. The leaders of the former Soviet Union will tread a knife-edge in the coming months as they try to balance the interests of the working population against the imperatives of the reform process.

Prospects for Democracy

Will Russia's transition end in democracy or authoritarianism? In the fall of 1991, the newly established Foundation for Socio-Economic and Political Science Research (better known as the Gorbachev Foundation) sponsored a roundtable discussion of this key question, with the participation of leading Russian social scientists. Their remarks were published in the journal of the Institute of World Economy and International Relations in Moscow. An updated version of the discussion was subsequently translated into English in the collection *MEMO*.

From "Authoritarianism or Democracy?" Roundtable of the Soviet Foundation for Social and Political Studies, in *MEMO* 3, pp. 43–46, 50–53, 55–58, 60–64, 66, 75–77. BNA Books. Copyright © 1992 by BNA Books. Reprinted by permission of the publisher.

A. Galkin:[1] . . . It must be said that our society is split politically and psychologically and this split can be seen even on the most basic level of values.

Various terms can be used for the groups into which society is divided. I prefer to use terms that are not judgmental, and hence emotional, in nature. The first group I would call reformers in the broad sense of the word. These are supporters of profound changes and a renewed value system. This group, like the second, which I would roughly characterize as fundamentalists, is, in turn, internally differentiated. The third group consists of what one might call an aggregate of embittered pragmatists. . . . I would venture to say that most of the population belongs to the category of embittered pragmatists. This is particularly true of Russia.

It follows that the political alignment in the near future will be largely determined by the evolution of the last group—by either its growth, or its movement toward support of one of the other two groups.

The second objective factor that must be taken into account is that nationality problems have assumed a life of their own. Obviously, nationality problems have always existed in the public consciousness, regardless of how things appeared on the surface. So what has occurred over the past six years? Removal of administrative pressure has opened the channels of national self-expression. An exacerbation of nationality problems was not inevitable after this opening, but combined with the country's economic deterioration, it has created the potential for such an exacerbation.

Hence the close connection between nationality problems and economic and social problems at the first stage of develop-

---

[1] . . . This is a condensed transcript of the discussion, the participants in which are Prof. Yu. A. Krasin, doctor of philosophy and director of the Center of Social Programs of the foundation; Prof. A. A. Galkin, doctor of history and deputy general director of the foundation; Prof. H. H. Diligensky, doctor of history and editor in chief of MEMO; E. V. Klopov, doctor of history and deputy director of the Institute for Problems of Employment; A. M. Salmin, doctor of history and department head at the Institute for Problems of the Workers' Movement and Comparative Political Science; Prof. G. G. Vodolazov, doctor of philosophy and project director at the Institute of Political Forecasting; Prof. V. T. Loginov, doctor of history and department head at the foundation; and B. G. Kapustin, doctor of philosophy and project director at the Institute of Political Forecasting.

ment after 1985. What we at the time called a rise of nationalism primarily reflected nationalities' desire to isolate and thereby save themselves. As the economic situation worsened, that desire grew. Can this characterization be fully applied to the present situation? I think not. Now the nationality problem, having received an initial impetus, has begun to assume a life of its own.

I think that this conclusion is important. It contradicts the naive notion that the imperatives of maintaining a common market and a single economic space, as well as general economic difficulties, will inevitably revive the urge for cohesion and unity, and that, consequently, centrifugal tendencies will be replaced by centripetal impulses. If that is possible at all, it is possible only for some of the less important regions. . . .

Turning to the subjective factors, we are dealing now with a disintegrating political-party structure (or, in essence, one that has never been integrated). One wing has been thoroughly destroyed, and I see no prospects for its restoration anytime soon. In the other wing, the democratic bloc is breaking up. This is not just a matter of conflicting personal ambitions or misunderstandings; an inevitable differentiation is occurring. In Eastern Europe the collapse of the blocs that had been based on a negative consensus, on enmity rather than a positive program, took a year or so. In our country this has taken less than a month. The underlying conflicts that the negative consensus kept a lid on have not simply come to the surface but have intensified with unprecedented speed.

It is no less important that our present political parties are actually quasi-parties. They have no social base. This is not just because they are unable to find one, although that is sometimes the case, but primarily because social groups have not really been formed and have not yet recognized their own real interests. In this situation, a political party cannot rely on a specific social base by presenting a specific social program. Hence, it is doomed to remain a small group of intellectuals that includes many brilliant individuals with often original, but usually abstract ideas. Without interaction between political activists and an appropriate social base, political parties' chances will be extremely small. If any such chances exist now, they are for mass movements, which will coalesce around popular individuals, rather than programs.

I think that, in the near future, political life in the country will be defined by the formation of such movements. These new movements will most likely reject all the old leaders, regardless of their current orientation. They will start to unite around new figures with whom we are not yet acquainted. And herein lies a great danger, because movements, especially if they are oriented toward an individual rather than a program, may easily assume a right-wing populist or left-wing populist identity. . . .

A. Salmin: . . . First, for the first time in Russian history, a revolution has been carried out in defense of the law rather than against it. This is only the foundation of a state based on the rule of law, but it is nonetheless a foundation. And that is something new.

Second, continuity with the past has been restored, and in this sense the return to the tricolor flag is symbolic.

Third, the knot of a sizable number of nationality conflicts has been cut—cut painfully, but cut. The insoluble conflicts we encountered in drafting the Union Treaty—namely, the problem of the autonomy of the union republics, and the problem of the makeup of the Union. This whole knot has now been not untied, but cut. . . .

And fourth, the problem of the CPSU has been solved. The extreme ambiguity of that organization lay in the fact that, on the one hand, it really was an accumulator of the elite and of people who really were far from the worst in society, people who for decades had joined it because it was the only avenue for those who sought to be active in the state; and on the other hand, it had turned into an absolutely stagnant organization, an obstacle in the path of development. It was probably impossible to resolve this contradiction painlessly. . . .

Now a word about the longer-term forces, the cultural forces. I see four cultural strata or types here: national culture and nationalistic ideas; the religious type; the modernizing group; and the traditional stratum of society. This is a rough division, of course; there are also other groups and subgroups.

Since August there has been a resurgence of what was once a weak Russian national idea. The social, political, ideological, and even geopolitical preconditions make this possible. The social preconditions are the prospect of economic difficulties and marginalization. The political preconditions include weak political structures, but also the existence of certain nationalistic political organizations. The ideological preconditions are a rich reserve of right-wing national ideas existing not just in today's Russian culture, but to an even greater extent in 19th- and early 20th-century culture, as well as an untapped reserve of such ideas built up among emigrés. I have in mind the idea of Russian fascism. And finally, the geopolitical factor. A certain pattern is already apparent in electoral geography. Makashov and Zhirinovskiy together got a fairly large vote—up to one fourth of the electorate—in clearly defined zones along the borders, from the border with China to the border with Estonia, and areas that had been under occupation during the war.[2]

But I would still not overestimate the danger of the national idea's turning into a nationalistic idea or a national-socialist idea. In my view, for the near future it will lack the social base that created that cultural type in Germany, Italy, and other European countries.

Second, we are seeing a certain religious upswing, which I would not exaggerate, either. I have fairly good empirical data on this subject, and I can say that, in political terms, the religious upswing works for integration in certain contexts and for disintegration in others. . . .

Third, the modernization segment. This includes the political elite, our emerging business elite, and the economic elite. The general attitude of the economic elite inspires no hope: it is grab and run, and has no future. Its concern is making money, not creating business. This is a short-term, passing phenomenon, but it is also inevitable. We presently have a unique situation in which the economy and business are separate, politics is separate, administration is separate from both of them, law is separate from all three, and if they mesh at all, they do so chaotically. But all this will pass, and the integration of these elements will inevitably occur fairly soon—it may be good, and it may be bad, but it

[2] The reference is to the Russian presidential election won by Yeltsin in June 1991. General Albert Makashov ran as a candidate of a conservative Communist Party faction, and Vladimir Zhirinovskiy as a candidate of his own Russian-nationalist Liberal Democratic Party. Zhirinovskiy won 8 percent of the vote, coming in third place, after former Soviet premier Nikolay Ryzhkov.—Trans.

will be some sort of integration. How this will occur is another question. There is the well-known Western path, and there is the Eastern path, whereby a bureaucratic economy operates in a political and administrative system, partly following its own laws, partly following the laws of that system. Perhaps we will take some third path. But in any case, a new elite will emerge that will integrate what may be the best and what may be the worst of what we have.

Fourth and finally, there is the traditional stratum, the provinces, which have been affected only slightly by recent events. Political processes occur there, but they have been derived from the center rather than emanating from the provinces, or at the very least, the conflicts that exist there do not mirror conflicts occurring in the center. That is my first thesis.

My second thesis is that the particularly large outlying areas generally remain fairly passive. We lack the conditions for the sort of activation that occurred in 1917—an unresolved agrarian problem, plus an army sent to the provinces. Conflicts in the outlying areas will be local, and they will probably never come together in such a way that the whole provincial area explodes simultaneously. . . .

H. Diligensky: . . . There is a question here as to what will happen to the regime and the state. That question is very closely tied to the problems of social and economic forecasting, with the question of what sort of social and economic structure we are moving toward. If we abandon the stereotypes of capitalism, convergence, and so forth, which have already been undermined by the actual course of events, I think that two scenarios are possible. One scenario, which might very loosely be called the Latin American scenario, presupposes the kind of development of a market economy in which economic activity continues to rely on the preservation of ties with state structures. In this case, both the power of the state sector and the customary orientation of our management, which, naturally, would continue to draw its new personnel from among state sector managers, would be influential. Such a system would reflect the formula of state-monopoly, bureaucratic capitalism to a far greater extent than present-day Western economy. Yesterday's state economy managers would strongly resist attempts to break up monopolies. The implementation of this scenario would impede movement to a free market and damage all economic development.

The second scenario is a free, pluralistic market. It presupposes, in part, the extensive development of new small and medium-sized business (private, cooperative, and so forth) capable of both competing and cooperating with the large successors to state-sector enterprises. The implementation of this scenario depends largely on the extent to which governmental institutions are democratic and are able to take into account the interests of the most diverse types of economic activity. But the tendency that we see toward a strengthening of authoritarian executive power will most likely "work" for the state-monopoly scenario, as well as for a strengthening of corrupt ties between governmental agencies and certain business groups.

The central problem of economic development today, I think, is the problem of a strong state economic policy. In all likelihood, in our situation the lack of intelligent state regulation of market processes in the interests of society as a whole would result in the abnormally large growth of nonproductive, profiteering business that thrived parasitically off shortages, and in the merger of that business with government in the republics. This would be especially true if government was authoritarian and executive bodies operated without checks by elective bodies. All this would result in a prolonged domination, for many years to come, by mafia groups, some operating on the national level, others on the local, regional and republic levels; that part of the party nomenklatura that has gotten into business and is oriented toward profiteering would readily become integrated into those groups.

A scenario oriented toward genuinely free competition presupposes a balance between the executive and legislative branches and, at the same time, a carefully considered, multilevel, state regulation of market processes. Some essential elements of such regulation would require first, dismantling the existing centralized monopolistic structures, no matter what nameplates they may be hiding behind (ministries, state concerns, and so forth); second, utmost encouragement of the development of small and medium-sized enterprises that offer alternatives to those structures; third, the use of economic levers to encourage investment, including foreign investment, to promote the priority development of the industries that are most important for saturating the consumer market.

I am not entertaining any illusions regarding democratic political personnel; they really are very weak today. This is evidently an inevitable stage in the development of democracy, and to get through this stage, we must strengthen, not weaken, democratic institutions. The more active they can become, the faster competent and honest people will be chosen, and the sooner they will acquire the necessary skills and sophistication.

A strong economic policy should clearly define priorities and guidelines: what to develop, what to encourage. Let us take, for example, the most difficult of all socioeconomic problems: developing private farming and, in general, straightening out the agricultural situation. So far we have merely talked about the fact that private farmers are necessary and good, and have kept passing one new law after another that is not implemented at the local level. We could most likely take an entirely different approach—the targeted development of private farming in certain regions where it would be easiest to develop, such as the Russian Non-Black-Earth Zone,[3] especially in animal husbandry, where the collective farms have been a total fiasco. . . .

The inevitable emergence of group interests during transition to a market economy will probably exert growing influence on political developments in the near future. A differentiation among these interests—for example, among those of workers, various groups of entrepreneurs, peasants, and so forth—will take the place of the pre-August confrontation between the nomenklatura and the amorphous populist democratic camp, and that differentiation will lead to the emergence of parties, groups, and platforms that express these interests. And real policy—the policy, which we are presently lacking, of deeds rather than words—will most likely be developed in the course of struggle and compromise among various interests. . . .

G. *Vodolazov:* . . . I would characterize the situation after the coup as the collapse of the old totalitarian world without the birth of a new democratic one. The barracks-socialism, planned-economy system, the system of noneconomic coercion to work,

---

[3] Northern Russia, where farming is poor.—Ed.

is being replaced (so far, only as a trend) by a system of economic terrorism, economic coercion, and mafia money wealth.

The second conflict, in the political realm, is between the neototalitarian forces that rely on that mafia-controlled, shadow economy, which today is coming together and merging with the former, nomenklatura-bureaucratic economy, and the genuinely democratic forces.

In social relations there are also new conflicts between the forces of nationalism and chauvinism (which, joining with the old forces of bureaucratic totalitarianism, are giving rise to a bureaucratic-nationalistic totalitarianism) and the democratic forces (both national democratic and federal democratic).

As for the alignment of political forces, I see three main forces: the new totalitarianism, the popular, democratic forces, and in between, an alliance of liberal and new authoritarian-bureaucratic forces.

The totalitarian forces include the remaining vestiges of the old totalitarianism, although the latter play a subordinate role today. These are the remnants of the reactionary conservative part of the CPSU, the spiritual kin of the State Committee for the State of Emergency. They include the Marxist Platform, headed by Prigarin, the newly created "parties of communists," and Nina Andreyeva's "party." And there are forces of the new totalitarianism. So far these exist not in the form of political parties (a form they are hardly likely to take), but as lobbying groups. Some are in the White House, and some are also in many of the democratic parties and groups.[4]

On the other side are the democratic forces, those that want to rely on a civilized market economy. They include the civilized entrepreneur, the modern manager from the intelligentsia, and the modern worker. For all the internal differences among them, they stand in opposition to the forces of the mafia-bureaucratic economy.

Today the position of genuine democrats should evidently be to express the aggregate interests of these three social groups, and to bring about a democratic reconciliation of their interests.

---

[4] The Russian "White House" is the building that houses the Russian parliament and government.—Trans.

In other words, we are talking about activities of a leftist-socialist, social-democratic type, to use the Western terminology. The results of a survey were cited here, and the ratio of 2:3 was given, that is, two parts of the population favor new, market, entrepreneurial relations, while three parts favor state and public regulation. I think that this indicates that the general ambiance is psychologically close to social-democratic values, which combine support for market-oriented, entrepreneurial activity with the protection or regulation of the market economy, and the influencing of market relations by the civil society and state agencies. That is, the predominant desire is to create a society where every citizen will have the opportunity to take part in economic decisions in a situation in which private ownership exists.

And between these two forces are the new authoritarian-bureaucratic forces. Their representatives believe that the establishment of a strong executive authority and executive structures will provide a counterweight to both the mafia-dominated economy and the nonfunctioning democracy. I think that these middle of the road, authoritarian-bureaucratic organizations, lacking a clear social base, either will become hostages of the neototalitarian forces (which to some extent is already happening), or will be bought off and blocked by them. Or, in another alternative that is more favorable for the Russian people, they may ally themselves with democracy, but a functioning democracy, which does not exist today. There is no democracy today because there are no civilized market or real political parties, but merely embryonic parties and political lobbying groups. For all practical purposes, there is no representative democracy, that is, no legislators elected on a multiparty basis, and no developed ideological and political culture in society.

It is among these three political forces and in relation to the problems I have mentioned that the next political struggle will unfold.

B. Kapustin: . . . The CPSU has been removed; it has been abolished. But the problem of it has not been solved. In my opinion, the putsch itself and the fact that the CPSU has been eliminated attest primarily to the defeat of democrats within the CPSU. They, together with all other democrats, were unable to bring about the sort of real solution to the problem of the CPSU that would have allowed political forces to arise in its place and would have enabled the millions of ex-Communists holding various political views to take part in politics. What has happened now is that those former Communists have been disorganized and depoliticized. That is dangerous for democracy of any type.

Incidentally, this sort of abolition of the CPSU will result—already is resulting—in great difficulties for the democrats: in the breakup of their movement into opposing populist and liberal groups and in their "peripheralization" and relegation to the back of the political stage as a whole. All this is blocking development toward the emergence of a civil society. A democracy has triumphed whose foundation is provided by a demoralized, destructured society that has little chance—at least in the foreseeable future—of evolving in the direction of a civil society. And there is even less chance that intermediate structures will emerge between the regime and the people that, from the standpoint of classic political theory, are an essential condition for the functioning of democratic institutions. This, in my view, is the sense in which the consequences of the coup substantially worsened chances.

The problem is the same with the transition to a market economy. We are in many respects continuing to reason in the spirit of Hayek liberalism,[5] believing that there is and can be only one market, or a Market with a capital *M*. If that is the case, everything boils down to the question of how fast we are moving toward a market. But the problem is that theoretically you can have markets of absolutely different types. Right now the concern should be not simply the pace of reforms, but what type of market they are creating. And which social interests are being served in the process, and which type of market do they favor? When I spoke of the determinism of the era we have entered, I meant that what is happening is the formation of a definite type of market, and that definite interests are working in that direction. At present these interests are the most politically influential interests in our society. . . .

. . . The forces that were able to exert influence and were able to stand out amid the negative consensus that became most

[5] Reference to Friedrich von Hayek's free-market economic theory.—Ed.

apparent during the days the coup was suppressed are the new business entities, the directors of state enterprises, the liberal intelligentsia, and the new "democratic" bureaucracy. The alignment of these forces and relations among them developed after the August events in favor of the formation of an oligarchical type of market.

On the other hand, the large state commercial structures that were calling, in pure Gorbachev style, for consolidation were perfectly content. As a result of their nature and symbiosis of state authority and commerce, they have a stake in the exercise of a monopolistic-type of control over the economy, and in the formation of a Third-World type of market. I think that Volsky's fairly prominent role[6] in forming the new bloc of our post-coup elite is by no means accidental.

I would like to make another point. I do not think that anyone can seriously object to the contention that our legislative branch has become degraded, and that at present there is not and cannot be any balance among the three branches. . . .

The legislative branch's loss of an independent role and its reduction to a camouflage for the new authoritarianism are the natural consequence of the factors and circumstances I have discussed.

I think that we must speak not simply of a strengthening of the executive branch, but of the emergence—although incomplete—of an authoritarian regime. . . .

. . . I would define the present stage of development, at least if we remain in the context of Russia, as the stage of a new Bonapartism. This is Bonapartism more in the spirit of the Second Empire than the First, a Bonapartism not in the sense of some sort of far-reaching structural, institutional, or other analogy with classic models, but in the sense of the regime's high degree of freedom in an unstructured and amorphous society whose evolution toward forming intermediate structures between state authority and the people has been severely retarded. . . .

G. *Vodolazov:* . . . Here is the type of society that will prevail if the neototalitarian forces dominate and do not meet sufficient

[6] Arkadiy Volsky, president of the Union of Producers and Entrepreneurs.—Trans.

resistance. The neototalitarian forces are the forces of the monopolistic market, profiteering capital, and mafia and shadow-economy structures, linked with the international mafia-controlled and profiteering economy. Whereas totalitarianism used to exist politically in the form of so-called "proletarian democracy," the "dictatorship of the proletariat," and the "state of the whole people," present-day totalitarianism is striving to establish itself politically behind the front of ostensibly representative democracy. It needs a nonworking, prattling parliament, a powerless state, and an absolutely "independent" private press that can be bought, rather than a press that includes, along with independent publications, party publications that might be controlled by parties and political organizations. Behind this pseudodemocratic facade, the new totalitarians are striving to establish a real shadow regime. They need an ostensibly free market that, in reality, is free of competitors and the influence of civil society, a market without democracy, a market that is *not* free of their own monopolistic domination. They need a society without real political parties; they "consent" only to pro forma political parties behind whose facades lobbying groups operate.

This, of course, is so far just a tendency, but it is already apparent today. And if these forces gain the upper hand and dominate, it will mean not a solution of economic problems, but what has been mentioned here: grab and run, finish robbing what has not yet been robbed. It will lead to rebellions and social clashes, and consequently, to a much greater likelihood of a dictatorship based on totalitarian power structures like the State Committee for the State of Emergency, or even a fascist-type regime. That is, of course, if this tendency is not offset by opposite, democratic tendencies. When I reflect on the neodemocratic tendency, its programs, and its social base, I conclude that the new democracy is also striving for a market economy, but striving to reach it through real, working democracy. What do I mean by working democracy? I mean a working parliament elected on a multiparty basis, a parliament or democratic representative bodies that exercise real control over a strong executive branch.

I think the type of society we have, its economic and political identity, will be determined in the clash or confrontation between these two forces—the neototalitarian force and the neodemocratic force. I do not think either tendency will gain the upper hand in the near future. It seems the struggle between the two, more or less evenly balanced poles, will result in the establishment of authoritarian-bureaucratic rule, with some preservation of democratic potential. The extent to which that democratic potential is preserved will depend on how well organized the democratic forces are.

I think that the most likely form for our society in the near future is an authoritarian regime that incorporates some degree of democratic political and economic principles. At the same time, I do not rule out the possibility that the democratic forces will prove sufficiently well organized that the authoritarian regime will be less authoritarian and more democratic. Such a possibility does exist.

I also think that an authoritarian regime with a greater or lesser degree of democracy (headed by such leaders as Yeltsin, Popov, and the like) will probably end up in the situation that Gorbachev found himself in during the pre-August period, that is, caught in the middle between opposite, warring poles.

James H. Billington

A New Time of Troubles?

Concluding his account of the crisis of 1991, the eminent historian of Russia and present Librarian of Congress, James Billington, likens the upheaval to Russia's "Time of Troubles" of the early seventeenth century. He weighs the possible outcomes—pluralistic democracy or nationalistic authoritarianism—but concludes mainly with the hope that moral force will prevail.

Abridged and reprinted with the permission of author and the Free Press, Macmillan Publishing Co. From *Russia Transformed: Breakthrough to Hope* by James H. Billington, pp. 151–154, 156–160, 164–165, 171–173. Copyright © 1992 by James H. Billington.

A historian of Russia could not avoid thinking about the more purely Russian and inherently gloomy analogy that Russians themselves used in thinking about the crisis they were going through.

This was for most Russians another *smutnoe vremia:* a Time of Troubles. In its original "Address to the Soviet People" the junta had appealed "to all true patriots, people of good will to put an end to our present time of troubles." After the coup had failed, I asked the greatest living scholar of Old Russia, Dmitry Likhachev, what was the most important single, simple thing currently needed in Russian culture. He suggested a reproduction of the history of Russia by Sergei Platonov, whose specialty was this original *smutnoe vremia:* the period of tumultuous interregnum between Boris Godunov and the first Romanov Tsar. Platanov, the semiofficial historian of the Romanov dynasty, had lived through another time of troubles, the interregnum between tsars and commissars, and died in Stalin's gulag in 1933. His classical analysis of Russia's original Time of Troubles from 1605 to 1613 seemed relevant to Russia's situation in early 1992.

The disintegration at the beginning of the seventeenth century of the absolutist empire put together by Ivan III and Ivan IV (the Terrible) resembled the disintegration at the end of the twentieth of the totalitarian empire put together by Lenin and Stalin and centered on the same Moscow Kremlin that the Ivans had built. In both cases stagnation induced by terror combined with the breakdown of a traditional line of authoritarian succession to open the way for a new type of leader to initiate Westward-looking reforms (Boris Godunov/Gorbachev) legitimized by proto-parliamentary bodies (*zemsky sobors*/revitalized Supreme Soviets).

In Platnov's view, the first or "dynastic" stage of the original Time of Troubles occurred within the imperial leadership of Muscovy, preparing the way inadvertently for a second, "social" stage of the crisis in which central authority broke down amid growing violence from below. To many in Moscow, such a process seemed to be happening as inexorably after the fall of Gorbachev late in 1991 as it had after the death of Boris Godunov early in 1605. Partisans of an authoritarian, xenophobic identity for Russia could take heart from the fact that the social breakdown of stage two was eventually overcome by a broader uprising that ushered

in a third, "national" stage. In this stage of reconsolidation, imperial and social unity was reestablished around a new Tsar (Michael, the first Romanov), who installed a new and more stable
dynasty that restored most of the old governmental system. More
moderate conservatives could use the analogy to argue that the
new Tsar was a more limited and constitutional monarch than
his predecessors, chosen by a nationwide "council of all the land"
(*zemsky sobor*) and watched over by a church in many ways more
powerful than the state (with the new title of Patriarch conferred
on Tsar Michael's father, Filaret).

But it seemed to me that the analogy of a new Time of
Troubles was losing validity just as it was gaining popularity. . . .

In Russia of early 1992 there seemed to be neither a credible
alternative leader nor a legitimate pretext for an authoritarian
nationalist uprising. Lenin had provided the one, and the degradation of World War I the other, for an authoritarian resolution of
Russia's last Time of Troubles, the revolutions of 1917 and the
subsequent civil war. But the fact that the current crisis was
different did not provide any reassurance that the outcome would
be positive.

With the resignation of Gorbachev and the formal dissolution
of the USSR at the end of 1991, both the alleged victim of the
putsch and the government that was preparing to prosecute the
putschists simply vanished. In its final reports, the all-union parliamentary commission investigating the August coup observed
wryly that it was difficult legally to distinguish between the unsuccessful move against Gorbachev in August and his successful
removal in December. As the state prosecutor of the Russian
Republic, Valentin Stepankov, took over the criminal investigation from the defunct Soviet government, Russian deputies asked
him if all charges would be dropped, since the Soviet Union no
longer existed. He was constrained by a vote in the Russian
parliament from arresting even someone the commission had
implicated in working out specific plans to seize the White House,
the former Deputy Minister of Defense Vladislav Achalov. A
slackening of interest in punishing the putschists seemed implicit
in the commission's finding that only seven of the thirty-two high-
ranking KGB officers implicated in the coup had been dismissed
(one had even been promoted), while a number of the new repub-

lic leaders were shown to have been at least for a time willing to work with the junta (Leonid Kravchuk in Ukraine, Nursultan Nazarbaev in Kazakhstan, and, most strongly, Ayaz Mutalibov in Azerbaijan and Zviad Gamsakhurdia in Georgia).

Whatever the legal judgment might be on those involved in the coup, a political judgment was already possible by the beginning of 1992. The coup was the last in a series of three improvised and increasingly desperate attempts by the Communist political and security machine during 1991 to repress the forces seeking democracy within and independence beyond the Russian Republic. Unlike the attempt to have Yeltsin removed as Russian President in March, 1991, and the attempt to have All-Union Prime Minister Pavlov take over most of Gorbachev's authority as All-Union President in June, the August coup attempt by the Committee on the Extraordinary Situation was not merely rebuffed. It was answered by a counter-coup from the resurgent democratic forces around Yeltsin.

The new Yeltsin government rapidly brought to an end the legal existence of the previously ruling Communist Party and the political-economic dominance of the military-industrial complex. These actions were justified on the basis of evidence that rapidly came to light of structural involvement in the coup by both of those overlapping forces. Although many documents of the central figures in Moscow were destroyed, the takeover of the Central Committee files revealed secret telegrams of August 19 from local Party secretaries that expressed support for the putsch and urged even stronger measures. . . .

. . . By the end of 1991 Yeltsin seemed to have repudiated an imperial identity for a democratic one, as he joined with the heads of the other republics in crafting a loose new Commonwealth of Independent States in place of a disintegrating Union of Soviet Socialist Republics.

But, as Yeltsin began implementing his program of economic austerity, Russian democracy seemed to be entering as cold a world as that which the babies placed in outdoor crêches must have felt during Russia's first public Christmas pageants since 1916. Yeltsin's decision to bite the bullet of radical economic reform that Gorbachev had merely nibbled at for six years required him to postpone the implementation of a new and genu-

Nostalgia never dies: an elderly Communist with poster of Lenin. (AP/ Wide World Photos)

inely democratic and decentralizing constitution that had been prepared by a commission under Oleg Rumiantsev. The partisans of radical reform who sought to increase Yeltsin's executive powers during the Sixth Congress of People's Deputies in April 1992 were frustrated by the partisans of increased legislative control. But some measure of increased central authority seemed increasingly desirable to many Russians concerned with preventing violence and sustaining basic social services. Once reconsolidation began and new legitimacy developed for strong central authority, would not this create a dynamic leading to dictatorship?

Even before the coup attempt, some had suggested that the three right-wing candidates who polled 35 percent of the votes for President of Russia (against Yeltsin's 57 percent) might prove to be stalking horses for an ostensibly more reasonable military dictator who would "become our Soviet Pinochet."[1] Many looked to Yeltsin's increasingly autocratic Vice President Rutskoi to fulfill this function. Others either feared or hoped that Yeltsin himself might assume such a role. The reduction in size and prestige of the army and claims to parts of it by the newly independent republics led to fears that, as the ultranationalist Aleksandr Prokhanov had prophesied already in 1990, "the army is not a blind function of power. Today it is finding political will."

But the real discovery of political will during these last two turbulent years has been among the younger generation of ordinary Russians, the generation that has grown up since Khrushchev without ever sharing Gorbachev's illusion of that era that Communism could be reformed. The events of August inspired this new generation in particular to believe that Russia could be reformed only by getting rid of Communism. Young soldiers no less than students, priests no less than entrepreneurs felt the exhilaration of living by hope rather than fear, whether or not they had been on the barricades.

They felt pride as Russians that they were now not just more open and free than the Communist nomenklatura, but better people for having defied them. Of all the words spoken from the [Russian] White House balcony during the crisis, none has

---

[1] The reference is to Augusto Pinochet, the right-wing military dictator of Chile, 1973–1989.—Ed.

lingered in mind more clearly than Elena Bonner's[2] simple words of affirmation to the crowd and defiance to the junta: "We are higher, we are cleaner." Even in the cold and hungry winter that followed, there was a feeling that Russians had rediscovered a common consciousness along with their individual consciences.

But how democratic was this awakened national consciousness, and what were the long-run prospects for democracy in Russia? Despite the historic lack of a democratic tradition in Russia, there had been a rapid development of democratic groups and activities in the four short years leading up to August 1991. . . .

The democratic forces came together to create four important new political parties in 1990 after the Communist Party gave up its exclusive "leading role" in February. Superficially they seemed to be replicating both the standard European two-party system (with Christian Democratic and Social Democratic parties) and the American version (with Democratic and Republican Parties). But the real news was their common action, together with a bewildering variety of grassroots organizations from the emerging civil society in the two great election campaigns of 1991 in the Russian Republic: the March campaign that garnered a 70 percent mandate for conducting an unprecedented popular election of a Russian President, and the June campaign that elected Yeltsin.

This mass activity occurred under the leadership of a loose coalition called Democratic Russia, which amounted to a kind of democratic popular front. Elections had created the alternate source of legitimacy to both the Communist Party and the Soviet government that proved so essential in resisting the coup in August. But it was the giant demonstration of March 28 in Moscow against the attempted overthrow of Yeltsin that anticipated and inspired the resistance from below and turned the disparate democratic forces into something that became—quite literally—a movement.

Denied by military force the chance to meet near the traditional sites of power in the center of Moscow, the democratic forces marched instead in a festive way to another location, gathering numbers and solidarity as they moved. The epic of endless

---

[2] Elena Bonner: widow of Andrei Sakharov.—Ed.

Communist success was being challenged by a carnival in the streets, a festivity from below that in August drew a circle around a White House through which the high priests of the old rituals did not dare to pass. But the nagging question grew during this Time of Trouble about whether the carnival spirit of August was the prelude to democracy rooted in law or only to chaos leading to dictatorship.

I had first heard the word "carnival" used to describe Russian reality in August 1990, in a boat on Lake Baikal in the company of the conservative writer Valentin Rasputin. He described the parliament of the USSR in which he was then sitting as a "madhouse," and his friends added the words "circus" and "carnival" in a far less respectful sense than the word had been used by Bakhtin. In the aftermath of the putsch, Rasputin seemed to have concluded that all of Russia had succumbed to such indiscipline and that the only hope for Russia was "the preservation of its governing power, the revival of its former glory and honor." Certainly, many Russians who had resisted the Committee on the Extraordinary Situation in 1991 seemed to be looking for something like such a committee to take over in 1992. . . .

. . . Could Russia in search of a post-Communist identity harmonize its strivings toward liberal, pluralistic democracy with its search to recover conservative, religious authority? Many of the participants in the defense of the White House, such as Viktor Aksiuchits in Moscow and Ilya Konstantinov in St. Petersburg, became appalled at the seeming loss of central authority in Russia under democratic leadership. They sought to lead a new "center-right" opposition to the Yeltsin government, apparently believing that they could control their new ultranationalist and crypto-fascist allies rather than be controlled by them.

The sense that Russia was being humiliated under democratic leadership was shared even by many who stayed with Yeltsin. The relatively liberal Metropolitan Cyril of Smolensk received a warm ovation from a congress of army officers in the Kremlin Palace of Congresses on January 17 with his suggestion that the political separation of Russia from Ukraine and Belorus shattered "the commonalities of a thousand years" Although he defended the wisdom of "voluntary self-limitations on governmental power," he denounced the "politics of radical sovereignty," which "separates children from parents, creates boundaries between man and wife." Atheistic Marxist professors publicly implored the Patriarch to rally the forces of central authority against the social disintegration that democracy was bringing. . . .

The August events were a breakthrough more to hope than to faith. The young took the lead and did not seem likely to forget—the grandson of Semion Budenny, Stalin's special friend and organizer of the original Red Army cavalry; the son of Aleksandr Yakovlev, the former Politburo member; and two daughters of Stepan Volk from the Marx-Engels-Lenin Institute, both of them converts to Catholicism. There were also more than a few hooligans, as the junta had claimed. But all were treated as equals, behaved in an orderly way, and were willing to follow orders.

The lines that symbolized the inefficiency of everyday life and the helplessness of the individual in Soviet society did not go away with the collapse of Communism. But the memory of the magic circle they had formed in August sustained the hope that a new beginning was really possible. In February, many of those who had defended the White House came back together and named themselves "the living ring."

There was some solid basis for hope, because Russians in August had discovered not only freedom but responsibility. They were forced to accept the responsibility for moral choices that had always been avoided in the Communist era. When Likhachev was later asked if he knew the putsch would fail when he spoke out against it on August 20, he replied that he knew only "on whose side is the truth": "If I had spoken out because I was certain that the government would prevail over the putchists, it would have had no moral meaning." Inspired by people like Likhachev, Russians were recovering a moral sense, reinventing a moral vocabulary, and—in increasing numbers—accepting responsibility to a God that Marxism had tried to stamp out.

Many Russians thought of the August days as a "heroic deed" of the kind traditionally performed by saints no less than warriors, but for many if not most of the participants it was just their ordinary response to a truly extraordinary situation. The state committee that the Leninist machine had created to deal with that situation had simply been overtaken by a "spontaneously beginning transformation . . . issuing forth from the depths within people . . . with the aim of creating democratic space." In place of the Soviet claim that utopia could be created by those who normalized heroism, Russians now listened to the ironic disclaimer of Echo Moscow [the underground radio] against "the heroization of normality": accepting excessive praise for simply doing "what should have been done."

But how could such a simple moral impulse prevail against the largest organized armed force in the history of the world? The proceedings of the parliamentary investigation of the attempted putsch make it clear that a far greater amount of that strength than was realized at the time was in fact mobilized and deployed around Moscow in August 1991. The junta clearly believed that a massive military procession would have the same intimidating effects as Soviet armored parades in Red Square. . . .

The democratic uprising of August 1991 broke Russia away from this attitude, which Nicholas Berdiaev later described as the "eternally womanish" aspect of the Russian character. But much of the strength to resist the military forces of the coup came . . . precisely from those long-suffering, often invisible "eternal women" of ordinary Russian life: the babushkas who talked with the soldiers. As these women acted like "men," the men in the tanks began to feel something of Rozanov's "womanish" desire simply to "be around" people who were very much like their mothers.

Force has always required some higher legitimacy in Russia. The heroes of Russian folk tales always consulted with older people and independent sources of moral authority before entering battle, "thus sharing with them a responsibility for the results." In the world of legend where many Russians are still at home, moral force prevails over material forces—and the retelling of a heroic tale becomes in itself a moral force for the community of listeners. Russia was at last listening to its women. But the events of August were not the work of any particular category of people or of any individual person bigger than life. . . . Russia's horizons seemed somehow to be widening even as its borders contracted. Russians had been released in August from the fear of power to discover the power of hope.

Suggestions for Additional Reading

There is already a plethora of books and articles in many languages on the era of *perestroika*, not to mention the Soviet system that preceded it, and the total is being added to daily. The problem in learning more about such a challenging and compelling subject as the reform and collapse of communism in the Soviet Union is not finding information but selecting among the multitude of sources that are now available. This list will be confined to books that have appeared in English.

For a first cut there is nothing better than to take the original works from which the selections in this book have been extracted. There is no need to repeat them in the listing that follows.

There are many good overviews of the history of the USSR and the background of the Gorbachev years. Two short and clear surveys are M. Kamil Dziewanowski, *A History of Soviet Russia*, 4th ed., Englewood Cliffs, NJ, Prentice-Hall, 1993, and Mary McAuley, *Soviet Politics, 1917–1991*, Oxford and NY, Oxford University Press, 1992. Robert V. Daniels, *Russia—the Roots of Confrontation*, Cambridge, MA, Harvard University Press, 1985, includes the tsarist background and emphasizes foreign relations. A sharply critical view by two Russian émigré historians is Mikhail Heller and Alexander Nekrich, *Utopia in Power: The History of the Soviet Union from 1917 to the Present*, NY, Summit Books, 1986. Particular interpretations of interest are Cyril E. Black, *Understanding Soviet Politics: The Perspective of Russian History*, Boulder, CO, Westview Press, 1986; Robert Conquest, *Stalin: Breaker of Nations*, NY, Viking Press, 1991; Dmitrii S. Likhachev, *Reflections on Russia*, Boulder, CO, Westview Press, 1989 (by a venerable Russian cultural historian); Roy A. Medvedev, *Let History Judge: The Origins and Consequences of Stalinism*, rev. and expanded ed., Columbia University Press, 1989 (by a leading Marxist dissident); Zhores A. Medvedev, *Gorbachev*, NY, Norton, 1986; T. Harry Rigby, *The Changing Soviet System: Mono-organizational Socialism from its Origins to Gorbachev's Restructuring*, Brookfield, VT, Elgar, 1990. For primary sources consult Robert V. Daniels, *A Documentary History of Communism in*

I

Russia, 3rd ed., Hanover, NH, University Press of New England, 1993.

General books on the time of *perestroika* are mostly multi-author collections: Seweryn Bialer, ed., *Politics, Society and Nationality inside Gorbachev's Russia*, Boulder, CO, Westview Press, 1989; Walter Joyce, Hillel Ticktin, and Stephen White, eds., *Gorbachev and Gorbachevism*, London and Totowa, NJ, Frank Cass, 1989; Vitaly Korotich, ed., *The Best of "Ogonyok": The New Journalism of Glasnost*, London, Heinemann, 1990; Martin McCauley, ed., *Gorbachev and Perestroika*, NY, St. Martin's Press, 1990; Andrei Melville and Gail W. Lapidus, *The Glasnost' Papers: Voices on Reform from Moscow* (exerpts from Soviet articles), Boulder, CO, Westview Press, 1989. Individual analyses include Valery Boldin, *Ten Years that Shook the World: The Gorbachev Era as Witnessed by his Chief of Staff*, NY, Basic Books, 1994; Robert V. Daniels, *The End of the Communist Revolution*, London and NY, Routledge, 1993; Geoffrey Hosking, *The Awakening of the Soviet Union*, 2nd ed., Cambridge, MA, Harvard University Press, 1991; Eugene Huskey, *Executive Power and Soviet Politics: The Rise and Decline of the Soviet State*, Armonk, NY, M. E. Sharpe, 1992; Boris Kagarlitsky, *The Dialectic of Change*, London and NY, Verso, 1990 (view of a Russian democratic socialist); John W. Parker, *Kremlin in Transition*, 2 vols., Boston, Unwin Hyman, 1991; Marilyn Vogt-Downey, *The USSR 1987–1991: Marxist Perspectives*, Atlantic Highlands, NJ, Humanities Press, 1993; Martin Walker, *The Waking Giant: Gorbachev's Russia*, NY, Pantheon Books, 1986; Tatiana Zaslavskaya, *The Second Socialist Revolution: An Alternative Soviet Strategy*, Bloomington, IN, Indiana University Press, 1990. For documents, *see* J. L. Black, ed., *USSR Documents Annual*, Gulf Breeze, FL, Academic International Press, 1987 and succeeding years. A detailed chronology is Joseph P. Mastro, *USSR Calendar of Events, 1987–1991*, 5 vols., Gulf Breeze, FL, Academic International Press, 1987–91.

For the immediate background of *perestroika*, *see* Seweryn Bialer, *The Soviet Paradox: External Expansion, Internal Decline*, NY, Knopf, 1986; Robert F. Byrnes, ed., *After Brezhnev: Sources of Soviet Conduct in the 1980s*, Bloomington, IN, Indiana University Press, 1983; Dusko Doder, *Shadows and Whispers: Power Politics inside the Kremlin from Brezhnev to Gorbachev*, NY, Random

House, 1986; Jerry Hough, *Soviet Leadership in Transition*, Washington, Brookings Institution, 1980; Marshall I. Goldman, *USSR in Crisis: The Failure of an Economic System*, NY, Norton, 1983; Alec Nove, *Stalinism and After: The Road to Gorbachev*, 3rd ed., London and Boston, Unwin Hyman, 1989; James R. Millar, ed., *Cracks in the Monolith: Party Power in the Brezhnev Era*, Armonk, NY, M. E. Sharpe, 1992; Richard Owen, *Comrade Chairman: Soviet Succession and the Rise of Gorbachev*, NY, Arbor House, 1987; Theresa Rakowska-Harmstone, ed., *Perspectives for Change in Communist Societies*, Boulder, CO, Westview Press, 1979; Andrei Sakharov, *Memoirs*, NY, Knopf, 1990; Alexander Simirenko, *The Professionalization of Soviet Society*, New Brunswick, NJ, Transaction Books, 1982; Jonathan Steele, *Andropov in Power: From Komsomol to Kremlin*, Garden City, NY, Anchor Press/ Doubleday, 1984; Ilya Zemtsov, *Chernenko—the Last Bolshevik: The Soviet Union on the Eve of Perestroika*, New Brunswick, NJ, Transaction Books, 1989.

The successive steps and problems in political reform under Gorbachev are detailed in Donald D. Barry, ed., *Toward the Rule of Law in Russia? Political and Legal Reform in the Transition Period*, Armonk, NY, M. E. Sharpe, 1992; Archie Brown, ed., *New Thinking in Soviet Politics*, London, Macmillan, 1992; Timothy Colton, *The Dilemma of Reform in the Soviet Union*, rev. ed., NY, Council on Foreign Relations, 1986; Dusko Doder and Louise Branson, *Gorbachev: Heretic in the Kremlin*, NY, Viking, 1990; Barukh A. Hazen, *Gorbachev's Gamble: The 19th All-Union Party Conference*, Boulder, CO, Westview Press, 1990; Geoffrey A. Hosking, Jonathan Aves, and Peter J. S. Duncan, *The Road to Post-Communism: Independent Political Movements in the Soviet Union, 1985–1991*, London, Pinter, 1992; Robert T. Huber and Donald R. Kelley, eds., *Perestroika-Era Politics: The New Soviet Legislature and Gorbachev's Political Reforms*, Armonk, NY, M. E. Sharpe, 1991; Robert G. Kaiser, *Why Gorbachev Happened: His Triumphs and his Failures*, NY, Simon & Schuster, 1991; Brendan Kiernan, *The End of Soviet Politics: Elections, Legislatures, and the Demise of the Communist Party*, Boulder, CO, Westview Press, 1993; Walter Laqueur, *Black Hundred: The Rise of the Extreme Right in Russia*, NY, HarperCollins, 1993; Roy A. Medvedev and Giulietto Chiesa, *Time of Change: An Insider's*

View of Russia's Transformation, NY, Pantheon Books, 1989; E. A. Rees, ed., *The Soviet Communist Party in Disarray: The XXVIII Congress of the Communist Party of the Soviet Union*, NY, St. Martin's, and London, Macmillan, 1992; Alfred J. Rieber and Alvin Z. Rubinstein, eds., *Perestroika at the Crossroads*, Armonk, NY, M. E. Sharpe, 1991; Andrei Sakharov, *Moscow and Beyond, 1986 to 1989*, NY, Knopf, 1991; Eduard A. Shevardnadze, *The Future Belongs to Freedom*, NY, The Free Press, 1991; Anatoly Sobchak, *For a New Russia: The Mayor of St. Petersburg's Own Struggle for Justice and Democracy*, NY, The Free Press, 1992.

Glasnost and its manifestation in the writing of history are represented by R. W. Davies, *Soviet History in the Gorbachev Revolution*, Bloomington, IN, Indiana University Press, 1989; Walter Laqueur, *Stalin: The Glasnost Revelations*, NY, Scribner's, 1990; and Donald J. Raleigh, ed., *Soviet Historians and Perestroika—the First Phase*, Armonk, NY, M. E. Sharpe, 1989 (selections by Soviet historians).

Some good works on the terminal crisis of *perestroika*, including the August coup, are Marshall I. Goldman, *What Went Wrong with Perestroika*, NY, Norton, 1991; Mikhail Gorbachev, *The August Coup: The Truth and the Lessons*, NY, HarperCollins, 1991; Stuart H. Loory and Ann Imse, *Seven Days that Shook the World*, Atlanta, Turner Publications, 1991; Michael McFaul and Sergei Markov, *The Troubled Birth of Russian Democracy: Parties, Personalities, and Programs*, Stanford, CA, Hoover Institution Press, 1993; Vladimir Pozner, *Eyewitness: A Personal Account of the Unraveling of the Soviet Union*, NY, Random House, 1992; Vladimir Pribylovskii, *Dictionary of Political Parties and Organizations in Russia*, Boulder, CO, Westview Press, 1992; David Remnick, *Lenin's Tomb: The Last Days of the Soviet Empire*, NY, Random House, 1993; Angus Roxburgh, *The Second Russian Revolution: The Struggle for Power in the Kremlin*, London, BBC Books, 1991, and NY, Pharos Books, 1992; Russian Information Agency, *Putsch—the Diary: Three Days that Collapsed the Empire*, Stevenage, Eng., SPA, 1992.

For the impact of *perestroika* on Soviet society and ordinary life, see Christopher Cerf and Marina Albee, eds., *Small Fries: Letters from the Soviet People to Ogonyok Magazine, 1987–1990*,

NY, Summit Books, 1990; Walter D. Connor, *The Accidental Proletariat: Workers, Politics, and Crisis in Gorbachev's Russia,* Princeton, NJ, Princeton University Press, 1991; Maurice Friedberg and Heyward Isham, eds., *Soviet Society Under Gorbachev: Current Trends and the Prospects for Reform,* Armonk, NY, M. E. Sharpe, 1987; T. Anthony Jones, *Perestroika: Gorbachev's Social Revolution,* Boulder, CO, Westview Press, 1989; David S. Lane, *Soviet Society under Perestroika,* Boston, Unwin Hyman, 1990; Mervyn Matthews, *Patterns of Deprivation in the Soviet Union Under Brezhnev and Gorbachev,* Stanford, CA, Hoover Institution Press, 1989; Zbigniew Rau, ed., *The Reemergence of Civil Society in Eastern Europe and the Soviet Union,* Boulder, CO, Westview Press, 1991; Vladimir Shlapentokh, *Public and Private Life of the Soviet People: Changing Values in Post-Stalin Russia,* NY, Random House, 1990. For statistics, see Michael Ryan, *Social Trends in Contemporary Russia: A statistical Sourcebook,* NY, St. Martin's, 1993.

The economics of *perestroika* and its collapse have attracted an especially large volume of writings. Among the most important are Anders Åslund and P. R. G. Layard, eds., *Changing the Economic System,* NY, St. Martin's, and London, Pinter, 1993; Abram Bergson, *Planning and Performance in Socialist Economies: The USSR and Eastern Europe,* Boston and London, Unwin Hyman, 1989; Robert W. Campbell, *The Failure of Soviet Economic Planning: System, Performance, Reform,* Bloomington, IN, Indiana University Press, 1992; Padma Desai, *Perestroika in Perspective: The Design and Dilemmas of Soviet Reform,* updated ed., Princeton, NJ, Princeton University Press, 1990; Philip Hanson, *From Stagnation to Catastroika,* NY, Praeger, 1992; Ed A. Hewitt and Victor H. Winston, eds., *Milestones in Glasnost and Perestroyka: The Economy,* Washington, Brookings Institution, 1991; Vladimir Kontorovich and Michael Ellman, eds., *The Disintegration of the Soviet Economic System,* London and NY, Routledge, 1992; James R. Millar, *The Soviet Economic Experiment,* Urbana, IL, University of Illinois Press, 1990; William Moskoff, *Hard Times: Impoverishment and Protest in the Perestroika Years,* Armonk, NY, M. E. Sharpe, 1993; Nikolai Shmelyov and Vladimir Popov, *The Turning Point: Revitalizing the Soviet Economy,* NY, Doubleday, 1989.

A variety of works address the national minority question or individual nationalities. See John A. Armstrong, *Ukrainian Nationalism*, 3rd ed., Englewood, CO, Ukrainian Academic Press, 1990; John Dunlop, *The Rise of Russia and the Fall of the Soviet Empire*, Princeton, NJ, Princeton University Press, 1993; Gregory Gleason, *Federalism and Nationalism: The Struggle for Republican Rights in the USSR*, Boulder, CO, Westview Press, 1990; Gail Lapidus and Victor Zaslavsky, eds., *From Union to Commonwealth: Nationalism and Separation in the Soviet Republics*, Cambridge, Eng., and NY, Cambridge University Press, 1992; Alexander Motyl, ed., *The Post-Soviet Nations—Perspectives on the Demise of the USSR*, NY, Columbia University Press, 1992; Bohdan Nahaylo and Victor Swoboda, *Soviet Disunion: A History of the Nationalities Problem in the USSR*, NY, The Free Press, 1990; Alfred Senn, *Lithuania Awakening*, Berkeley, CA, University of California Press, 1990; Jan A. Trapans, ed., *Toward Independence: The Baltic Popular Movements*, Boulder, CO, Westview Press, 1991.

A few of the many works on parallel developments in Eastern Europe are: Timothy Garton Ash, *The Magic Lantern: The Revolution of '89 Witnessed in Warsaw, Budapest, Berlin, and Prague*, NY, Random House, 1990; Ronald Asmus *et al.*, *Soviet Foreign Policy and the Revolution of 1989 in Eastern Europe*, Santa Monica, CA, Rand Corporation, 1991; Ivo Banac, ed., *Eastern Europe in Revolution*, Ithaca, NY, Cornell University Press, 1992; Karen Dawisha, *Eastern Europe, Gorbachev, and Reform: The Great Challenge*, 2nd ed., Cambridge, Eng., and NY, Cambridge University Press, 1990; Charles Gati, *The Bloc that Failed: Soviet-East European Relations in Transition*, Bloomington, IN, Indiana University Press, 1990; Jeffrey Gedmin, *The Hidden Hand: Gorbachev and the Collapse of East Germany*, Washington, AEI Press, 1991; Jan Kubik, *The Power of Symbols against the Symbols of Power: The Rise of Solidarity and the Fall of State Socialism in Poland*, University Park, PA, Penn State Press, 1993; Bernard Wheaton and Zdenek Kavan, *The Velvet Revolution: Czechoslovakia, 1988–1991*, Boulder, CO, Westview Press, 1992.

Some of the principle works on Soviet relations with the non-communist world during *perestroika* are: Bogdan Denitch, *The End of the Cold War: European Unity, Socialism, and the Shift in Global Power*, Minneapolis, University of Minnesota Press, 1990; W. Raymond Duncan and Caroly M. Ekedahl, *Moscow and the Third World under Gorbachev*, Boulder, CO, Westview Press, 1990; Jerry Hough, *Russia and the West: Gorbachev and the Politics of Reform*, NY, Simon & Schuster, 1988; Allen Lynch, *Gorbachev's International Outlook: Intellectual Origins and Political Consequences*, Boulder, CO, Westview Press, 1989; Don Oberdorfer, *The Turn—from the Cold War to a New Era: The United States and the Soviet Union, 1983–1990*, NY, Poseidon Press, 1991; Strobe Talbott and Michael Mandelbaum, *Reagan and Gorbachev*, NY, Vintage Books, 1987.

Some interesting reflections in the aftermath of *perestroika* and the breakup of the Soviet Union include Susan Gross Solomon, ed., *Beyond Sovietology: Essays in Politics and History*, Armonk, NY, M. E. Sharpe, 1993; Peter J. Boettle, *Why Perestroika Failed*, London and NY, Routledge, 1993; Timothy Colton and Robert Legvold, eds., *After the Soviet Union: From Empire to Nations*, NY, Norton, 1992; Daniel Yergin and Thane Gustavson, *Russia 2010—And What It Means for the West*, NY, Random House, 1993; Vladislav Krasnov, *Russia Beyond Communism: A Chronicle of National Rebirth*, Boulder, CO, Westview Press, 1991; Bertram Silverman, Robert Vogt, and Murray Yanowitch, eds., *Labor and Democracy in the Transition to a Market System: A U.S.–Post-Soviet Dialogue*, Armonk, NY, M. E. Sharpe, 1992; Alexander Solzhenitsyn, *Rebuilding Russia; Refections and Tentative Proposals*, NY, Farrar, Straus & Giroux, 1991; Alexander S. Tsipko, *Is Stalinism Really Dead?* NY, HarperCollins, 1990; Stephen White, Graeme Gill, and Darrell Slider, eds., *The Politics of Transition: Shaping a Post-Soviet Future*, Cambridge, Eng., and NY, Cambridge University Press, 1993; Alexander N. Yakovlev, *The Fate of Marxism in Russia*, New Haven, Yale University Press, 1993.